RECUEIL DES COURS

433 (2023)

L'Académie de droit international de La Haye

honorée du prix Wateler de la Paix (1936, 1950), du prix Félix Houphouët-Boigny pour la recherche de la paix (1992), de l'ordre du Rio Branco, Brésil (1999), et de la médaille de l'Institut royal d'études européennes, Espagne (2000)

The Hague Academy of International Law

awarded the Wateler Peace Prize (1936, 1950), the Félix Houphouët-Boigny Peace Prize (1992), the Order of Rio Branco, Brazil (1999), and the Medal of the Royal Institute of European Studies, Spain (2000)

© Académie de droit international de La Haye, 2023
The Hague Academy of International Law, 2023

Tous droits réservés   All rights reserved

ISBN 978-90-04-54469-7

Printed by/Imprimé par Triangle Bleu, 59600 Maubeuge, France

ACADÉMIE DE DROIT INTERNATIONAL
FONDÉE EN 1923 AVEC LE CONCOURS DE LA
DOTATION CARNEGIE POUR LA PAIX INTERNATIONALE

RECUEIL DES COURS

COLLECTED COURSES OF THE HAGUE
ACADEMY OF INTERNATIONAL LAW

2023

Tome 433 de la collection

BRILL | NIJHOFF

Leiden/Boston

COMPOSITION DU CURATORIUM
DE L'ACADÉMIE DE DROIT INTERNATIONAL DE LA HAYE

PRÉSIDENT

Y. DAUDET, professeur émérite de l'Université Paris I (Panthéon-Sorbonne)

MEMBRES

M. BENNOUNA, juge à la Cour internationale de Justice

K. BOELE-WOELKI, doyenne de la faculté de droit de Bucerius, Hambourg; présidente de l'Académie internationale de droit comparé

H. BUXBAUM, professeure à l'Université de l'Indiana

H. CHARLESWORTH, *Laureate Professor* à l'école de droit de l'Université de Melbourne; professeure à l'université nationale australienne

G. CORDERO-MOSS, professeure à l'Université d'Oslo

D. P. FERNANDEZ ARROYO, professeur à l'école de droit de Sciences Po, Paris

M. T. INFANTE CAFFI, juge au Tribunal international du droit de la mer

B. B. JIA, professeur à l'Université de Tsinghua, Pékin

M. KAMTO, professeur à l'Université de Yaoundé II

M. M. MBENGUE, professeur à l'Université de Genève

D. MOMTAZ, professeur à l'Université de Téhéran

Y. NISHITANI, professeure à l'Université de Kyoto

N. J. SCHRIJVER, professeur émérite de l'Université de Leiden; Conseiller d'Etat au Conseil d'Etat des Pays-Bas

L.-A. SICILIANOS, doyen de la faculté de droit de l'Université d'Athènes; ancien président de la Cour européennne des droits de l'homme

P. TOMKA, juge et ancien président de la Cour internationale de Justice

T. TREVES, professeur émérite de l'Université de Milan; ancien juge au Tribunal international du droit de la mer

SECRÉTAIRE GÉNÉRAL
DE L'ACADÉMIE DE DROIT INTERNATIONAL DE LA HAYE

J.-M. THOUVENIN, professeur à l'Université Paris-Nanterre

COMPOSITION OF THE CURATORIUM OF THE HAGUE ACADEMY OF INTERNATIONAL LAW

PRESIDENT

Y. DAUDET, Emeritus Professor at Paris I University (Panthéon-Sorbonne)

MEMBERS

M. BENNOUNA, Judge at the International Court of Justice

K. BOELE-WOELKI, Dean of Bucerius Law School, Hamburg; President of the International Academy of Comparative Law

H. BUXBAUM, Professor at Indiana University

H. CHARLESWORTH, Laureate Professor at Melbourne Law School; Professor at the Australian National University

G. CORDERO-MOSS, Professor at the University of Oslo

D. P. FERNANDEZ ARROYO, Professor at the Sciences Po Law School, Paris

M. T. INFANTE CAFFI, Judge at the International Tribunal for the Law of the Sea

B. B. JIA, Professor at Tsinghua University, Beijing

M. KAMTO, Professor at the University of Yaoundé II

M. M. MBENGUE, Professor at the University of Geneva

D. MOMTAZ, Professor at the University of Tehran

Y. NISHITANI, Professor at Kyoto University

N. J. SCHRIJVER, Emeritus Professor at Leiden University; State Councillor at the Netherlands Council of State

L.-A. SICILIANOS, Dean of the Law Faculty of the University of Athens; former President of the European Court of Human Rights

P. TOMKA, Judge and former President of the International Court of Justice

T. TREVES, Emeritus Professor at the University of Milan; former Judge at the International Tribunal for the Law of the Sea

SECRETARY-GENERAL OF THE HAGUE ACADEMY OF INTERNATIONAL LAW

J.-M. THOUVENIN, Professor at the University Paris-Nanterre

ACADÉMIE DE DROIT INTERNATIONAL DE LA HAYE
— FONDÉE EN 1923 AVEC LE CONCOURS DE LA DOTATION CARNEGIE —
HONORÉE DU PRIX WATELER DE LA PAIX (1936, 1950), DU PRIX FÉLIX HOUPHOUËT-BOIGNY POUR LA RECHERCHE DE LA PAIX (1992), DE L'ORDRE DU RIO BRANCO, BRÉSIL (1999), ET DE LA MÉDAILLE DE L'INSTITUT ROYAL D'ÉTUDES EUROPÉENNES, ESPAGNE (2000)

L'Académie constitue un centre d'études et d'enseignement du droit international public et privé, et des sciences connexes. Son but est de faciliter l'examen approfondi et impartial des problèmes se rattachant aux rapports juridiques internationaux.

L'enseignement de l'Académie est principalement donné au Palais de la Paix, à La Haye, par des personnalités de différents États. Il porte sur le droit international, sous ses aspects théoriques et pratiques, et sur la jurisprudence internationale. La durée de ses deux principales sessions est en été de six semaines s'étendant sur les mois de juillet et d'août, et partagée en deux périodes, consacrées l'une au droit international public, l'autre aux relations privées internationales, et, en hiver, de trois semaines, consacrée en janvier au droit international. L'enseignement est dispensé en français ou en anglais, avec traduction simultanée dans l'autre langue. Les sessions de l'Académie se déroulent sous l'autorité du Secrétaire général.

L'enseignement de l'Académie est conçu dans un esprit à la fois pratique et hautement scientifique. Nettement différencié des enseignements similaires des universités et écoles nationales, il s'adresse à tous ceux qui possèdent déjà des notions de droit international et ont, par intérêt professionnel ou curiosité d'esprit, le désir de se perfectionner dans cette science.

Il n'existe pas de cadre permanent de professeurs à l'Académie. Le Curatorium, qui est le corps chargé de la direction scientifique de l'institution, et qui se compose de dix-huit membres appartenant statutairement à des nationalités différentes, adresse chaque année, en toute liberté, ses invitations aux personnes qu'il estime qualifiées pour donner un cours ou une conférence à l'Académie. Les personnes ayant donné des cours à l'Académie ne sont donc aucunement fondées à s'intituler professeur de ou à l'Académie de droit international de La Haye.

L'Académie décerne un diplôme à ceux des auditeurs qui, réunissant les qualifications spéciales exigées par le règlement en vigueur, auront subi avec succès des épreuves d'examen devant le jury de la session à laquelle ils se sont inscrits. Elle délivre en outre aux auditeurs un certificat attestant l'assiduité aux cours de l'Académie à la fin de la session suivie.

Toute personne désirant suivre l'enseignement de l'Académie doit faire parvenir par voie électronique au secrétariat de l'Académie, au Palais de la Paix, à La Haye, un formulaire d'inscription dûment rempli. L'Académie perçoit des droits d'inscription fixés par le Conseil d'administration de l'Académie.

Un programme de bourses d'études permettant d'assister aux cours d'été ou d'hiver est institué auprès de l'Académie. Le mode d'attribution de ces bourses fait l'objet d'un règlement disponible sur le site Internet de l'Académie.

Tous les cours professés à l'Académie durant les sessions d'été et d'hiver font, en principe, l'objet d'une publication dans le *Recueil des cours de l'Académie de droit international de La Haye*, ainsi que sur une plateforme Internet, dans la langue dans laquelle ils ont été professés. Certains cours sont également publiés ou réédités dans des collections spéciales.

THE HAGUE ACADEMY OF INTERNATIONAL LAW
— FOUNDED IN 1923 WITH THE SUPPORT OF THE CARNEGIE ENDOWMENT —
AWARDED THE WATELER PEACE PRIZE (1936, 1950), THE FÉLIX HOUPHOUËT-BOIGNY PEACE PRIZE (1992), THE ORDER OF RIO BRANCO, BRAZIL (1999), AND THE MEDAL OF THE ROYAL INSTITUTE OF EUROPEAN STUDIES, SPAIN (2000)

The Academy is an institution devoted to the study and teaching of Public and Private International Law and related fields. Its mission is to further the thorough and impartial examination of issues arising from international legal relations.

The courses of the Academy are dispensed principally at the Peace Palace in The Hague by personalities from different States. They deal with the theoretical and practical aspects of international law, including international jurisprudence. The duration of its two main sessions is, in Summer, of six weeks in July and August, divided into two periods of three weeks each, one devoted to Public International Law and the other to Private International Law, and, in Winter, of three weeks, in January, devoted to international law. They are taught in either English or in French, with simultaneous interpretation into the other language. The Secretary-General is responsible for managing the sessions of the Academy.

The education offered by the Academy is designed to be both practical and highly academically advanced. Clearly distinct from the teachings provided in national universities and law schools, it is intended for those who already possess some notion of international law and who, out of professional interest or intellectual curiosity, desire to deepen their knowledge in this field.

There is no permanent teaching staff at the Academy. The Curatorium, which is the body entrusted with the scientific management of the institution, and which consists of eighteen members of different nationalities, invites each year, in its unfettered discretion, whomsoever it deems best qualified to dispense a course or give a lecture at the Academy. It follows that no one who has lectured at the Academy is entitled to style himself or herself Professor of or at The Hague Academy of International Law.

The Academy awards a Diploma to those attendees who possess special qualifications as set out in the regulations, after having successfully passed examinations before the Jury of the session in which they are registered. It also delivers a certificate of attendance to registered attendees at the end of the session.

Anyone wishing to attend the courses at the Academy must send a completed electronic registration form to the Secretariat of the Academy at the Peace Palace in The Hague. The registration fee for each session of courses is fixed by the Administrative Board of the Academy.

The Academy manages a programme of scholarships to allocate at its discretion to attendees at the Summer and Winter Courses. The regulations governing scholarships are published on the website of the Academy.

All courses taught at the Academy during the Summer and Winter Courses are, in principle, published in the *Collected Courses of The Hague Academy of International Law*, which also exist in electronic format, in the language in which they were delivered. Some courses are also published or reissued in special collections.

GENERAL TABLE OF CONTENTS

The Hague Academy at 100: Its Rationale, Role and Record, by A. EYFFINGER, Doctor of Classical Philology, Law Historian   9-97

The Protection of Small and Medium-Sized Enterprises in Private International Law, by K. THORN, Professor at Bucerius Law School. . . .   99-205

Parallel Proceedings in International Arbitration. Theoretical Analysis and the Search for Practical Solutions, by S. MOOLLAN, King's Counsel   207-303

THE HAGUE ACADEMY AT 100:
ITS RATIONALE, ROLE AND RECORD

by

ARTHUR EYFFINGER

A. EYFFINGER

TABLE OF CONTENTS

The Hague Academy at 100: Its Rationale, Role and Record	19
Chapter 1. The Concept and its Implementation	21
1.1. The highest pedigree	21
1.2. The genesis of the idea	23
1.3. The implementation	25
Chapter 2. The Two Pillars of the Law	32
2.1. The public domain: "The closed circuit"	32
2.2. The private domain: Le travail de longue haleine	34
Chapter 3. The History of the Academy in Three Stages	40
3.1. The first stage (1923-1939)	40
3.2. The second stage (1947-1989)	43
3.3. The third stage (1990-2023)	50
Chapter 4. The Subject Matter: Three Categories of Courses.	55
4.1. The first category: The core mission	55
4.1.1. The appraisal of the World Court	59
4.1.2. The rising phoenix of the Hague Conference	61
4.2. The second category: Consistent concerns	63
4.3. The third category: The handmaiden of science	67
Chapter 5. An Assessment	70
Selected Bibliography	76
Annex I. Curatorium Members: Country and Membership Period	78
Annex II. Curatorium Members: Membership of IDI, ILC, World Court and Published Courses	82
Annex III. The "Grand Slam" of the Academy: Auditor, Curatorium and Published Courses	88
Annex IV. World Court Judges: Years on The Curatorium and PCIJ/ICJ .	89
Annex V. World Court Judges: Years on the Curatorium, IDI, PCIJ/ICJ and Published Courses	90
Annex VI. Involvement of Agents/Counsel Parties (1922-1939)	93
Annex VII. World Court Judges: Years on the ILC and PCIJ/ICJ	96

BIOGRAPHICAL NOTE

Arthur, Clément, Guillaume, Marie Eyffinger, born 10 October 1947 in The Hague, Dutch nationality.
Classical Philology, Latin and Greek at Leiden University (1967-1974). Postdoctoral Humanist Studies and Neo-Latinism at University of Amsterdam (1976-1981). PhD in Classical Philology at University of Amsterdam (1981). Researcher at Grotius Institute, Royal Netherlands Academy of Arts and Sciences (1970-1985). Co-editor of The Poetry of Hugo Grotius series (1975-1980, 1981-1985). Co-founder of Grotiana Foundation, The Hague, and Secretary-General of the Board (1978-2000); Executive Editor of *Grotiana NS* journal (1980-200). Semester at Cambridge University (Clare Hall) in the capacity of editor of The Poetry of Hugo Grotius (1984). Deputy-Director of Peace Palace Library, The Hague (1986-1988). Secretary-General of Dutch Library Association (NVB) (1987-1996). Head Librarian at International Court of Justice; Curator of the Nuremberg Files (1988-2003). Chairman of Netherlands 17th C. Society (1989-1994). Founder/Director of Research Centre at Judicap (2003-2023). General Editor of *Hebraic Political Studies* (Jerusalem) with G. Schochet (Washington, DC) (2005-2010).

PRINCIPAL PUBLICATIONS IN ENGLISH

Classical Philology/Grotian Studies
Text editions

Hugo Grotius, *Christus Patiens* [1608], Assen, Van Gorcum, 1978. [Co-editor with B. L. Meulenbroek].
Hugo Grotius, *De Republica Emendanda* [c. 1598-1602] and "The Emendation of the Dutch Polity" [commentary], *Grotiana NS*, Vol. 5 (1984).
Hugo Grotius, *The Poetry of Hugo Grotius: Original Poetry, 1602-1603* (The Poetry of Hugo Grotius), Assen, Van Gorcum, 1988.
Hugo Grotius, *Denken over Oorlog en Vrede*, abridged edition of Grotius's *On the Laws of War and Peace* [1625], Baarn, Ambo, 1991.
Hugo Grotius, *Sophompaneas* [1635] (The Poetry of Hugo Grotius), Assen, Van Gorcum, 1992.
Hugo Grotius, *De Vrije Zee*, critical edition/Dutch translation of Grotius's *Mare Liberum* [1609], The Hague, Jongbloed Juridische Boekhandel, 2009.
"On Good Faith and Bad Faith: Introductory Note [to Grotius's *De Fide et Perfidia* (1625)]", *Grotiana NS*, Vol. 36 (2015), pp. 79-171.
Hugo Grotius, *Een Lijdensdrama door Hugo de Groot*, poetical rendering in Dutch of Grotius's *Christus Patiens* [1608], The Hague, Boomjuridisch, 2023.

Monographs

Grotius Poeta: Aspecten van Hugo, The Hague, Gravenhage, 1981 [based on doctoral thesis completed at Amsterdam University].
Inventory of the Poetry of Hugo Grotius, Assen, Van Gorcum, 1982.
The Grotius Collection at the Peace Palace: A Concise Catalogue, Assen, Van Gorcum, 1983.
Inventory of Manuscripts by Hugo Grotius, Place, Publisher, 1984.

Articles and contributions

"In Quest of Synthesis: An Attempted Synopsis of Grotius' Works according to their Genesis and Objective", *Grotiana NS*, Vol. 4 (1983), pp. 76-88.
"Hugo Grotius, Poet and Man of Letters", in *The World of Hugo Grotius (1583-1645): Proceedings of the International Colloquium Organized by the Grotius Committee of the Royal Netherlands Academy of Arts and Sciences, Rotterdam 6-9 April 1983*, Amsterdam, Holland University Press, 1984, pp. 83-95.
"Hugo de Groot', in *The World of Hugo Grotius (1583-1645)*, pp. 1-11.
"*Exemplum Pietatis*: Patriotism in Grotius' Early Verse", *Grotiana NS*, Vol. 8 (1987), pp. 99-119, 1984.
"'La Plus Belle des Histoires': Grotius' Drama on Joseph in Egypt", *Grotiana NS*, Vol. 8 (1987), pp. 80-90.
"Justus Lipsius and Hugo Grotius", in K. A. E. Enekel and C. L. Heesakkers (eds.), *Lipsius in Leiden: Studies in the Life and Works of a Great Humanist on the Occasion of His 450th Anniversary*, Bloemendal/Florivallis, Voorthuizen, 1997, pp. 163-177.
"'Amoena gravitate morum spectabilis': *Justus Lipsius* and Hugo Grotius", *Bulletin of the Belgisch Historisch Instituut te Rome*, Vol. 68 (1998), pp. 297-327.
"'The Fourth Man': Stoic Tradition in Grotian Drama", in H. W. Blom and L. C. Winkel, *Grotius and the Stoa*, Assen, Van Gorcum, 2004, pp. 117-156. Originally published in *Grotiana NS*, Vol. 22/23 (2001).
"Introduction", in Petrus Cunaeus, *The Hebrew Republic*, ed. P. Wyetzner, Jerusalem/New York, Shalem Press, 2006, pp. ix-lxxx.
"Authority v. Authenticity: The Leiden Debate on Bible and Hebrew (1575-1650)", in

I. Zinguer, A. Melamed and Z. Shalev (eds.), *Hebraic Aspects of the Renaissance: Sources and Encounter* (Brill Jewish Studies 45), Leiden, Brill, 2009, pp. 128-148.

"'The Unacknowledged Legislators of Mankind'; Greek Playwrights as Moral Guidance to Hugo Grotius's Social Philosophy", in P. Ford and A. Taylor (eds.), *The Early Modern Cultures of Neo-Latin Drama*, Leuven, Leuven University Press, 2013, pp. 203-217.

"Literary Writings", in R. Lesaffer and J. E. Nijman (eds.), *The Cambridge Companion to Hugo Grotius*, Cambridge, Cambridge University Press, 2021, pp. 293-314.

"Natural Law and National Polity: The Leiden Discourse on State and Church (1575-1625)", in H. W. Blom (eds.), *Sacred Policies, Natural Law and the Law of Nations in the 16th-17th Centuries*, Leiden, Brill, 2022, pp. 29-55.

"Grotius on Natural Law: An Inventory of Propositions" in *Sacred Policies*, pp. 173-199.

History of international law/International law at The Hague

Monographs and edited volumes

The Peace Palace: Residence for Justice, Domicile of Learning, The Hague, Carnegie Foundation, 1988. Reprinted several times from 1988 to 2013.

Het Vredespaleis, Amsterdam, Sithoff, 1988. Reprinted several times from 1988 to 2013.

Compendium Volkenrechtsgeschiedenis, Deventer, Kluwer, 1989. New edition published in 1991.

Cornelis van Vollenhoven (1874-1933), The Hague, T.M.C. Asser Instituut, 1992.

The International Court of Justice, 1946-1996, The Hague, Kluwer Law International, 1996.

La Cour internationale de Justice, The Hague, Kluwer Law International, 1999.

The 1899 First Hague Peace Conference: "The Parliament of Man, the Federation of the World", The Hague, Kluwer Law International, 1999.

The Hague, International Centre of Justice and Peace, 2nd ed., The Hague, Jongbloed Law, 2005. 1st edition published in 2003.

The Trusteeship of an Ideal: The Carnegie Foundation, Vignettes of a Century 1904-2004, Amsterdam/The Hague, Enschedé/Carnegie Foundation, 2004.

The 1907 Hague Peace Conference: The Conscience of the Civilised World, The Hague, JudiCap, 2007.

Self-Defence as a Fundamental Principle (Hague Colloquium on Fundamental Principles of Law Series), The Hague, Hague Academic Press, 2009. [Co-editor with A. Stephens and S. Muller].

Guide to International Organizations in The Hague, The Hague, City of The Hague, 2009. New editions published in 2011 and 2013.

T.M.C. Asser (1838-1913), Founder of The Hague Tradition: Dreaming the Ideal, Living the Attainable, The Hague, T.M.C. Asser Press, 2011.

The Stars of Eternal Truth and Right: Bertha Von Suttner's Campaigning for Peace, Social Justice, and Womanhood, Oisterwijk, Wolf Legal Publishers, 2013.

T.M.C. Asser (1838-1913): "In Quest of Liberty, Justice, and Peace" (Studies in the History of International Law 30/13), 2 vols, Leiden, Brill, 2019.

The Institut de droit international: Cradle and Creed of the City of Justice and Peace, 2nd ed., Oisterwijk, Wolf Legal Publishers, 2020. 1st edition published in 2019.

The World Court, Vol. 1: *The Constitution (1870-1920)*, Vol. 2: *The PCIJ (1921-1946)*, The Hague, Boom Juridisch, 2023.

Catalogues/exhibitions

The Future of War, St Petersburg, Hermitage Museum, 1998.

The Hague, City of Peace and Justice, Centennial First Hague Peace Conference, 1999.

Museum of the International Court of Justice, The Hague, 1999.

European Peace Museum, Burg Schlaining, Austria, 2000.

Internationalism and Peace Studies, exhibitions in Geneva and Lucerne, 2002.

International Centre of Justice and Peace, Exhibition The Hague, 2003.
Commission Netherlands Ministry Foreign Affairs occasioned by Chairmanship OSC, 2003-2004.
Exhibitions on the international institutions at The Hague on display in Vienna (Hofburg), 2003; Vienna (UN International Centre), Geneva (Palais des Nations), Sofia (Municipal Art Gallery), St Petersburg (Law Faculty, *Dom Juridika*), Moscow, 2004; Exhibition in Atrium, The Hague City Centre, 2006; Exhibitions in Perth (Australia) and Colombo (Sri Lanka).
The Carnegie Foundation (1904-2004), Museum Mesdag, The Hague, 2004.
Bertha von Suttner, Public Library, The Hague, 2005.
Feodor Martens and The Hague, Exhibition in Tallinn, Estonia, 2007.
Centre for Internationalism, Atrium, The Hague City Centre, The Hague, 2008.
A Grotian Moment, New Church, Delft, 2012.
Women for Peace, Atrium, The Hague City Centre, The Hague, 2013.

Articles and contributions

"Europe in the Balance: An Appraisal of the Westphalian System", *Netherlands International Law Review*, Vol. 45 (1998), pp. 161-187.
"The Morality of Necessity: Dutch Foreign Policy and the International Legal Order", in Editor, *The Foreign Ministry 200 Years*, Place, Publisher, 1998, pp. 145-163.
"The Beginning, Not the End! An Appraisal of the 1899 Hague Peace Conference", speech transcript in Fr. Kalshoven (ed.), *The Centennial of the First International Peace Conference: Reports and Conclusions*, Leiden Brill, 2000, Annex Speeches: speech13.pdf.
"In the Midst of the Throng and Crush: The Dutch Policy at the First Hague Peace Conference", in Fr. Kalshoven (ed.), *Centennial of the First International Peace Conference: Reports and Conclusions*, Leiden, Brill, 2000; Historical Contributions, pp. 1-26 (1899nl.pdf).
"Frieden durch Recht, Symbole des Friedens. Eine Sprache ohne Grenzen?", in W. Vogt (ed.), *Zur Kultus des Friedens*, Katalog der Burgenländischen Landesausstellung, Bürgenländischen Landesregierung, Eisenstadt 2000, pp. 182-191.
"*A Place in Valhalla!* A Portrait of Elie Ducommun Retraced in The Hague", *Elie Ducommun 1833-1906 / Association "Genève – un lieu pour la paix"* (2002), pp. 51-92.
"The Hague, International Centre of Peace and Justice", *The Low Countries*, Vol. 12 (2004), pp. 214-223.
"Living Up to a Tradition", in P. J. van Krieken and D. McKay (eds.), *The Hague: Legal Capital of the World*, The Hague, T.M.C. Asser Press, 2005, pp. 29-45.
"Vreedzame geschillenbeslechting", in N. Hornbach, R. Lefeber and O. Ribbelink (eds.), *Handboek Internationaal Recht*, The Hague, T.M.C. Asser Press, 2007, pp. 347-384. [Co-author with P. Kooijmans].
"Self-Defence, or the Meanderings of a Protean Principle", in A. Eyffinger, A. Stephens and S. Muller (eds.), *Self-Defence as a Fundamental Principle* (Hague Colloquium on Fundamental Principles of Law Series), The Hague, Hague Academic Press, 2009, pp. 103-138.
"A Caravan Passes By: The Centenary of the Netherlands Society of International Law", *Netherlands International Law Review*, Vol. 57 (2010), pp. 143-168.
"Diplomacy", in B. Fassbender and A. Peters (eds.), *The Oxford Handbook of the History of International* Law, Oxford, Oxford University Press, 2012, pp. 814-839.
"Tobias Asser's Legacy: The Pertinence of the Institut de droit international to The Hague", *Netherlands International Law Review*, Vol. 66, No. 2 (2019), pp. 313-351.
"The World Court at One Hundred: Some Cursory Remarks at a Centenary", *Jus Gentium: Journal of International Legal History*, Vol. 7. No. 2 (2022), pp. 239-330.
"The Dutch Branch – Koninklijke Nederlandsche Vereeniging voor Internationaal Recht", in C. Kessedjian, O. Descamps and T. Fabrizi (eds.), *Au service du droit international. Les 150 ans de l'Association de droit international / To the Benefit of international Law. 150 years of the International Law Association*, Paris, Editions Panthéon-Assas, 2023, pp. [329]-340.

THE HAGUE ACADEMY AT 100:
ITS RATIONALE, ROLE AND RECORD

Our discipline has historically lacked recognition on a global scale [1]. The relevance of law in international affairs has consistently been met with conceptual doubt, even though politicians intuitively understand when to emphasise its rules and regulations. Unfortunately, history shows that major advancements in our field occur in the aftermath rather than the eve of political upheaval, driven more by regret or the search for forgiveness than wisdom [2]. It requires great perseverance to maintain faith in humanity's inherent goodness and advocate for lofty ideals such as the rule of law, social justice and peace.

The Hague Academy embodies this unwavering perspective from a scientific standpoint. It relentlessly pursues progress through critical inquiry, relying on intellectual acumen and independent thinking. The Academy does not promote a specific doctrine, school or unified approach [3]. Instead, it embraces *le choc des opinions* and fosters challenging dialogues among cultures and generations. Its primary ambition is to pass on wisdom, expertise and confidence from generation to generation, symbolising the solidarity within our discipline. The *Recueil des Cours* or *Collected Courses* offered by the Academy serve as a relay race of excellence, showcasing its commitment to intellectual development [4].

Despite its intellectual focus, the Hague Academy recognises the practical demands of life. It does not confine itself to empty speculation or isolated study. It actively engages in in-depth research while maintaining social openness, never shying away from critical encounters. However, the Academy's position in this discourse remains

---

1. This manuscript is an edited version of the inaugural lecture delivered during the Hague Academy's Winter Courses programme in January 2023. The author acknowledges his debt to H. E. Judge Peter Tomka, Prof. Nico Schrijver and Dr Johan Joor for their kind review of an earlier draft of this text and their instructive information.
2. For example, the Napoleonic Wars triggered the Peace Movement, the Crimean War (1853-1856) led to humanitarian intervention, and the Franco-Prussian War (1870-1871) played a role in the establishment of the IDI and the ILA. The First World War resulted in calls to establish a World Organisation and World Court.
3. See Skubiszewski in Bardonnet 1998, pp. 21-62, at p. 31. Works that are cited regularly appear in author-date format. See the selected bibliography for full details.
4. For more on the *Recueil des Cours*, see https://www.hagueacademy.nl/about-the-publications/. The full catalogue of editions to date can be found at https://brill.com/display/serial/RADI.

unwavering. Through over four hundred *Collected Courses* [5], it echoes the call of the human conscience and emphasises the importance of moral principles. These volumes contain the answers formulated by advocates of the rule of law from around the world, addressing the challenges posed by a century of ideological conflicts, social unrest, remarkable technological progress and disheartening moral stagnation. They serve as a testament to the champions of normativity in human affairs.

Our journey has been an uphill battle throughout history, and you, the upcoming generation, must recognise that you, too, will face the arduous task of soul-searching. When the Academy opened its doors in 1923, millions of refugees were traversing Europe, searching for new homes, nationalities and identities. Given the current state of the world, the approaching centenary of the Academy demands not only congratulations but also an unwavering determination to keep going with its mission to embody the human moral conscience and help create a better world through the application of law to international society.

---

5. To be precise, 427 volumes up to 2023.

CHAPTER 1

THE CONCEPT AND ITS IMPLEMENTATION

1.1. The highest pedigree

Noblesse oblige! In its conceptual ambition to ensure an open-minded discourse *sans parti pris* between the generations on the relevance of the law to international society, the Hague Academy embodies one of humankind's loftiest aspirations. While our esteemed institution embarks upon its second century, the concept boasts a track record of two and a half millennia and claims the highest intellectual pedigree. Plato first invited like-minded individuals and pupils to an olive grove named after the mythical hero, Academos [6] – similar to how Christ imparted his Gospel to his disciples in the Garden of Olives [7]. Aristotle eagerly joined this informal debate, giving rise to some of the most thought-provoking and captivating dialogues in world literature [8].

However, Plato's Academy began to slide into scepticism two centuries later. It came under the leadership of Carneades, the Machiavelli of his time, whom Hugo Grotius selected as his fictive opponent when presenting his advocacy of the law in 1625 [9]. A century later, Cicero in Athens received the first inklings of natural law [10] and absorbed the Stoic philosophy of *oikeiosis* that Emperor Marcus Aurelius sought to implement [11]. Nine centuries after its establishment, the Academy was suspended by the edict of Emperor Justinian – an emperor revered by lawyers for other reasons [12].

---

6. Plato (427-347 BC) founded the Academy in 387 BC. The myth of Academos is found in Plutarch's *Life of Theseus*.
7. Mark 13:3 *et seq.*; Matthew 26:36 *et seq.*
8. Aristotle (384-322 BC) was involved with the Academy from 367 to 347 BC. Upon Plato's death, he founded the Lyceum.
9. Carneades (215-129 BC) headed the Third or New Academy from 155 BC onwards. Grotius (1583-1645) refers to him in the "Prolegomena" (*Prol.* paras. 5, 6, 16-18) of his *De jure belli ac pacis* (1625) as the epitome of the *raison d'état* in denial of natural law as the outcome of right reason. To avoid polemics, Grotius preferred referring to a classical model rather than to contemporaries. Thomas Hobbes (1588-1679), the author of *Leviathan* (1651), would be a case in point.
10. Marcus Tullius Cicero (106-43 BC) studied in Athens in 79-78 BC.
11. Marcus Aurelius was Roman emperor between 161 and 180 and the author of *Meditations*.
12. Justinian I (482-565) was Byzantine emperor from 527 to 565. He codified Roman law in his *Corpus Iuris Civilis* (529-534). The Academy was reputedly discontinued by an edict of Justinian in 529.

Yet, as an emblem of the intellectual Renaissance in Europe, the concept was reignited in the New Athens of Medici Florence during the days of Ficino and Pico. Raphael's magnificent mural immortalised the School of Athens [13], solidifying the concept's conquest of Europe. Colbert and Richelieu established the Académies Royales in Paris [14], Newton and Locke flourished at their equivalent institutions in London [15] and Leibniz played a pivotal role in founding academies in Berlin and St Petersburg [16]. In 1872, Johann Caspar Bluntschli (1808-1881) drafted statutes for an Akademie des Völkerrechts – a respected *compagnie des savants* that launched in September the following year with an alternative name, the Institut de droit international or Institute of International Law ("IDI") [17]. Herein lies the cornerstone of our institution. Over the past century, this research body, where members and associates engage in free discourse, has inspired the vision and shaped the policies of the Hague Academy. The first Curatorium of the Academy consisted of former Presidents of the IDI. Study programmes were developed based on its guiding principles and standards, and lecturers were carefully selected [18]. And this brings us to the very essence of the Hague Academy.

---

13. In 1462, Marsilio Ficino (1433-1499), a Neo-Platonic scholar and the editor of Plato's works, under the patronage of Cosimo de Medici (1389-1464), opened an "Academy" in a villa near Florence. Here Pico de Mirandola (1463-1494) famously discussed the "dignity of man". To suggest the link with Plato's Academy, Raphael (1483-1520) produced his stunning mural, the *School of Athens*, in 1510, which in 1897 inspired Henri-Camille Danger (1857-1939) to create a counterpart featuring the advocates of arbitration, *Les artisans de l'arbitrage*.

14. In 1635, Cardinal Richelieu (1585-1642) launched the Académie française, a literary *côterie*. The Académie royale des sciences was established in 1666 by Jean-Baptiste Colbert (1619-1683), State and finance minister.

15. In London, scholars and scientists gathered in the Royal Society, founded in 1660. John Locke (1632-1704) became a member in 1668, and Isaac Newton (1642-1726) presided over the Society from 1707 to 1727. In 1768, a Royal Academy was founded, primarily dedicated to the fine arts and architecture.

16. The Academy of Sciences in St Petersburg, established in 1725, was the brainchild of Tsar Peter the Great (1672-1725) and German Gottfried Wilhelm von Leibniz (1646-1716). In 1700, Leibniz had initiated the Prussian Academy of Sciences in Berlin.

17. An academy exclusively focused on legal or social sciences was likely never considered before. On the genesis of the Institut de droit international, see Dietrich Schindler in IDI, *ll engl enllLivre du Centenaire*, Basel, Karger, 1973, pp. 45-60; M. Koskenniemi, *From Apology to Utopia*, The Structure of International Legal Argument, Cambridge, CUP,, 2005, pp. 42-43; Eyffinger 2019, Vol. 1, pp. 542-564.

18. The membership of the Curatorium was gradually expanded from seven to the current eighteen. Long dominated by IDI members, the Curatorium appoints the Secretary-General, who is, by statute, a native French scholar.

1.2. The genesis of the idea

The Hague Academy was not conceived in isolation, and its location was not a matter of chance [19]. From the beginning, the institution was envisioned as an integral part of the *Oeuvre de La Haye*, serving as the intellectual counterpart to the Peace Conferences and a balancing force to the International Courts [20]. The idea for the Academy emerged around 1900 to create "a watchdog of learning" that would critically evaluate arbitral awards and the Hague Conventions based on principles of justice and the law. Let us briefly examine the origins of this idea [21].

In 1899, when the Civilised Powers regrettably rejected the concept of compulsory arbitration at the First Hague Peace Conference, German scholar Ludwig von Bar proposed an alternative path [22]. He suggested the establishment of an international academy comprised of independent scholars of impeccable moral standing who could help resolve disputes and prevent armed conflicts by providing advisory opinions to the Powers [23]. However, this idea faced the same resistance that the Optional Clause encountered two decades later [24] as it was seen as a step backwards out of despair at the ideal of mandatory adjudication. This assessment was fair, and the idea was put on hold.

---

19. In this section, I frequently refer to jubilee volumes produced by the Academy. The first volume, edited by René-Jean Dupuy in 1973, is referred to as "Dupuy 1973", and its sequel, edited by Daniel Bardonnet in 1998 to commemorate the seventy-fifth anniversary, is referred to as "Bardonnet 1998". See the bibliography for full details.
20. For the role of the Netherlands in the project, refer to J. H. van Royen's contribution in *Recueil des Cours*, Vol. 138 (1973). Hereafter, citations to the *Collected Courses* will take the abbreviated form: *RdC* 138. Years may or may not follow in parenthesis, depending on the context.
21. The genesis of the idea is thoroughly reviewed by Stefan von Verosta in his comprehensive survey of the history of the first half-century of the Academy, as detailed in Dupuy 1973, pp. 7-64.
22. Carl Ludwig von Bar (1836-1916), hailing from Hannover, was an expert in criminal law and a pupil of Von Savigny. He was elected as a member of the IDI in 1875 and presided over its 1891 Session in Hamburg. Von Bar became a member of the PCA in 1900.
23. Von Bar did not himself advocate for obligatory arbitration and instead sought to establish an alternative avenue based on conciliation. He introduced this concept in 1898 through a paper published in the German journal *Die Nation*, No. 15 (1898) and elaborated on the idea in 1900 in his treatise titled *Der Burenkrieg, die Russifizierung Finnlands, die Haager Friedenskonferenz und die Errichtung einer internationalen Academie zur Ausgleichung von Streitigkeiten der Staaten*. See Von Verosta in Dupuy 1973, p. 15; Eyffinger 1988, p. 165, Joor 2023, p. ???.
24. The concept of an Optional Clause was first suggested in 1907 by Swiss scholar Max Huber (1874-1960). It was further developed in 1920 by Brazilian diplomat Raul Fernandes (1877-1968) during the discourse on the Statute of the PCIJ. For more details on the discourse and the position of the Powers in the First Assembly of the League in December 1920, refer to Eyffinger 2023, Vol. 1, chap. 26.

In 1907, the concept was revived during the Second Hague Peace Conference amid intense discussions surrounding international courts [25]. German-Swiss scholar Otfried Nippold [26] advocated for a research institute and a "nursery" for students to be situated on the premises of the future Peace Palace [27]. Envisioned as a State organ sponsored by the Powers, it would critically evaluate awards and conventions, contribute to the development and codification of international law, and promote global understanding through education. The project was lauded by Alexander de Nelidov, the President of the Second Hague Peace Conference, who likened it to Hippocrates's Asklepion in Kos [28], and received significant interest from Dimitru Sturdza, the Romanian First Delegate [29]. Sturdza welcomed the idea of bridging diplomacy and science and submitted draft statutes to establish a body consisting of ten scholars to be selected by nations [30].

---

25. Despite a promising start, the Second Hague Peace Conference ended in significant (short-term) disappointment. Its reputation suffered due to the inability to agree on the composition of the bench for the envisioned Permanent Court of Arbitral Justice (PCAJ) and International Prize Court. Such a verdict is unduly harsh. The discourse during the conference represented the most profound exchange of views on arbitration and adjudication in the pre-war era, addressing the complex concept of the equality of sovereign States before the law. This debate laid the groundwork for the ACJ of 1920 and served as a shortcut to the establishment of the World Court.

26. Otfried Nippold (1864-1938) from Bern was an attorney at law. In 1924, he was elected as a member of the IDI and delivered a lecture at the Hague Academy on the history of international law in the same year; see *RdC* 2 (1924). His views on the "Haager Friedenskonferenzen und Völkerrechtshochschule im Haag" were first published in a series of submissions to the *Deutsche Revue* in April 1907, December 1907 and December 1908. Nippold dismissed Von Bar's earlier proposition, suggesting that the PCA could fulfil a similar role. Nippold's text was forwarded to Russian Count De Nelidov, the President of the Peace Conference, by Richard Fleischer, the editor of the *Revue*, who presented the Peace Conference, the PCA and the Academy as a coherent triad. See Von Verosta in Dupuy 1973, p.16; Skubiszewski in Bardonnet 1998, p. 26.

27. The foundation stone for the Peace Palace was laid during a ceremony held midway through the Peace Conference of 1907. The Palace was officially opened in 1913.

28. President Alexander de Nelidov (1838-1910) presented the idea to the Plenary of the Conference in an address dated 20 July 1907, as documented in *Actes et Documents* 1907, 3 Vols, The Hague, Imprimerie Nationale 1907, Vol. 1, pp. 65.

29. Dimitru Sturdza (1833-1914), a Romanian statesman and nationalist publicist, served as prime minister four times, including his last term in 1907, during which he had to contend with a peasants' revolt.

30. Sturdza provided commentary on Nippold's project in a letter to President De Nelidov dated 3 August 2007. He included Draft Statutes comprising seven articles, as documented in *Actes et Documents* 1907, 3 Vols., The Hague, Imprimerie Nationale, 1907, Vol. 1, pp. 124-125, 130-131. Sturdza proposed that from May-July 1908, young diplomats, lawyers, government officials and military men should be invited to attend high-standard courses in English, French, German and Italian to help develop a consolidated doctrine. The Powers were expected to bear the costs, including housing for the Academy, which the PCA's Administrative Council would manage.

President De Nelidov, however, favoured an independent think-tank [31] and proposed seeking private sponsorship in the tradition of Carnegie, suggesting the formation of a preparatory committee comprising university professors. This latter idea was met with reservation from the Powers. Nevertheless, it resonated strongly with the Dutch advocates of a project to transform The Hague Region into the "World Capital of Internationalism" [32]. Under Nippold's guidance, an ambitious plan was devised to establish an academic centre of excellence offering two-year courses in legal and political sciences [33]. Widely criticised for being financially unrealistic, the project also faced resistance from established university centres, leading to protracted legal battles [34]. It required a highly pragmatic mind to breathe life into the idea and set it in motion.

1.3. The implementation

In September 1862, a young professor of private law from Amsterdam, Tobias Asser [35], delivered a remarkable presentation [36] that astounded the inaugural congress of Auguste Couvreur's Association of Social Studies in Brussels [37]. On that occasion, the Jewish Tobias

---

31. As mentioned in an address to the Plenary on 7 September (*Actes et Documents* 1907, Vol. 1, p. 124), William Stead commented on the idea in his *Courrier de la Conférence* on 13 September.
32. This ambitious project was advanced by Dutch physician Pieter Eykman and his assistant Paul Horrix. See Eyffinger 2004, pp. 53-65, for further details. Eykman's brochure for an Academy of Legal and Political Sciences reignited Nippold's interest in 1910. Additional insights can be found in W. Roosegaarde Bisschop's article in *Jahrbuch des Völkerrechts*, Vol. 1 (1913), pp. 363 *et seq*.
33. Scholars such as Von Bar, Huber, Pasquale Fiore (1837-1914) and Theodor Niemeyer (1857-1939) provided favourable comments on the project. Elihu Root (1845-1937) emphasised the importance of academic autonomy, and Léon Bourgeois (1851-1925) suggested submitting the idea to the IDI. In 1910 (London) and 1911 (Paris), the ILA passed resolutions of support.
34. For further details, see Robbers in Eyffinger 2004, pp. 177-182. The plan for the World Capital, with the Peace Palace at its core, was designed by architect K. P. C. de Bazel (1869-1923) following the octagonal concept of the *città ideale* (1905). This concept was also incorporated in the unrealised extension plans for The Hague (1908) by H. P. Berlage (1856-1934). As a form of poetic justice, the present headquarters of the ICC now stand on the spot that was once reserved for the World Capital.
35. Tobias (T.M.C.) Asser (1838-1913) served as the first Amsterdam professor of the law of commerce and headed a family law firm specialising in maritime law. For more information, see Eyffinger 2019, Vol. 1, chaps. 13-16.
36. Asser delivered lectures on the emerging phenomenon of *sociétés anonymes* and discussed the execution of foreign judgments in his discourse, which he further elaborated on in Ghent in 1863. He maintained close involvement with the project and organised a follow-up Congress at the Royal Palace in Amsterdam in 1864.
37. The pioneering Association internationale pour le progress des sciences sociales (1862-1865) was founded by Belgian Auguste Couvreur (1827-1894) as a counterpart

Asser formed a lifelong friendship with the Roman Catholic Gustave Rolin-Jaequemyns (1835-1902) from Ghent and the High Church John Westlake (1828-1913) from Cambridge. When Couvreur's Association and its yearbook [38] succumbed to tensions between France and Prussia in 1868, the young triumvirate founded the *Revue de droit international et de législation comparée*, the first-ever journal of international law [39]. Four years later, prominent internationalists such as Friedrich Carl von Savigny (1779-1861), Gustave Moynier (1826-1910) and Caspar Bluntschli relied on the dedication and determination of these "angry young men" to establish the IDI following the Franco-Prussian War (1870-1871) and the *Alabama* arbitration of September 1872 [40].

Twenty years later, Asser, who had become an authority on private international law at the IDI [41], initiated the first series of Conférences de La Haye or Hague Conferences on Private International Law ("HCCH"), from 1893 to 1904, marking the beginning of the international era in The Hague [42]. In August 1898, Asser chaired the Silver Jubilee Session of the IDI at The Hague, which adjourned on the same day the Russian tsar proclaimed his famous Rescript urgently calling for a moratorium in the escalating arms [43].

In the following months, Feodor F. Martens (1845-1909), the tsar's State Council, transformed Nicholas II's peace propositions into a comprehensive Conference Programme based on the research projects of the IDI [44]. In a shrewd *quid pro quo*, Martens offered Asser, his close associate at the IDI, the position of sole arbitrator in the *Whaling and Sealing Claims* dispute between Russia and the United States, which

---

to the British National Association for the Promotion of Social Science (established in 1857) that emerged from Gladstonian liberalism. In 1865, Francis Lieber (1798-1872) and Samuel Elliot (1821-1898) established an American counterpart in Boston. For an overview, see Eyffinger 2019, Vol. 1, pp. 332-357.

38. The *Annales de L'association Internationale Pour Le Progrès Des Sciences Sociales* (1862-1865).

39. Legend has it that Asser and Rolin-Jaequemyns conceived the journal while strolling through the Harlem woods; see Eyffinger 2019, Vol. 1, pp. 517-538. The first issue of the *Revue* was published in early 1869. The journal remained prominent until the outbreak of the First World War.

40. Eyffinger, 2019, Vol. 1, pp. 539-564.

41. During the project that resulted in the Hague Conferences (founded in 1893), Asser faced intense opposition from Pasquale Mancini (1817-1888).

42. Eyffinger 2019, Vol. 1, pp. 742-769.

43. Eyffinger 2019, Vol. 2, pp. 1146-1157. The IDI convened from 17-24 August 1898. During the session, Asser delivered a lecture on arbitration's legal and political aspects. On 24 August, the tsar issued his Rescript.

44. Asser maintained a close relationship with Martens. For the latter's involvement, see Eyffinger 2019, Vol. 2, pp. 1167-1177.

earned Asser the lasting gratitude from Washington[45]. In return, he sought Asser's assistance and network in hosting the Peace Conference in the Netherlands, which Asser readily[46].

In 1907, Asser played a role in helping his dear friend Louis Renault (1843-1918) receive the Nobel Peace Prize; three years later, Renault and Charles Lyon-Caen (1843-1935) reciprocated the gesture, with Asser winning the same prize in 1911[47]. Asser, an inspired university don, dedicated half of his prize money to breathe life into the stranded Academy project, his "Last Dream"[48]. He secured additional funding, assembled an impressive national think-tank[49], and reached out to Elihu Root and James Brown Scott, who headed the new Carnegie Endowment for Peace (founded in 1910)[50].

---

45. Martens approached Asser with the idea in February 1899. The *Whaling and Sealing Claims* case (1901-1902) between the USA and Russia proceeded on the first premises of the PCA at The Hague (1900-1913, along Prinsegracht), although not yet under its auspices. See Eyffinger 2019, Vol. 2, pp. 1257-1266.
46. Regarding Asser's connections with Washington, see Eyffinger 2019, Vol. 2, pp. 1265-1266. Asser's reputation with the State Department and close ties with James Brown Scott (1866-1943) at the Second Hague Peace Conference significantly contributed to his relations with the Carnegie Endowment from 1911 onwards.
47. In 1901, Asser and others had sought to support Rolin-Jaequemyns for the prize. In 1904, the IDI itself received the prize, and in 1907, Renault was awarded. Finally, Asser received the prize in 1911, recommended by Renault and Lyon-Caen. Asser was considered Renault's counterpart in the private realm of law, explaining why their statues are positioned on either side of the entrance doors to the Japanese Room in the Peace Palace.
48. Eyffinger 2019, Vol. 2, pp. 1733-1744. Asser contributed 30,000 florins, matched by the Hague-based industrialist Adriaan Goekoop (1854-1914). See Lysen 1934; *Bibliotheca Visseriana*, Vol. 11, p. 146. In his last will in 1913, Asser pledged an additional sum.
49. In 1910, Asser formed an impressive national "Provisional Committee" consisting of statesmen and scholars. On 2 December 1910, Jhr. A. P. C. van Karnebeek (1836-1925) recommended the idea in Parliament. In 1912, Asser himself delivered a remarkable address at the Royal Academy of Arts and Sciences in Amsterdam. See *Versl. Meded. KNAW*, Afd. Lett. Vol. 11 (1912), pp. 282 *et seq*. Additionally, former Foreign Minister De Beaufort's supportive address can be found in *Versl. Meded. KNAW*, Vol. 12 (1913), pp. 423-428. Expert opinions in response to the Dutch "Provisional Committee's" request from 1912 can be found in Walther Schücking, "Eine internationale Hochschule für Völkerrecht", *Berliner Tageblatt*, 9 August 1912 and Karl Strupp, "Die Zukunft der Haager Völkerrechtsakademie", *Vrede door Recht*, 28 September 1913. Schücking was involved in the project from its early stages and delivered a lecture in 1927, see *RdC* 20. He served on the Curatorium from 1923 until his passing in 1935 and was a member of the PCIJ from 1931 to 1935.
50. Asser first contacted the Carnegie Endowment in January 1911, and negotiations, mainly with Scott, continued for two years. For details on these contacts, refer to the volumes of the *Year Book of the Carnegie Endowment for International Peace* (1911-1914); Lysen 1934, pp. 144-148; Von Verosta in Dupuy 1973, pp. 24-28; Eyffinger 2019, Vol. 2, pp. 1618-1636 (Nobel Peace Prize) and *ibid.*, pp. 1733-1744 (Academy). For recent overviews, see Joor 2023, pp. ???, Nico Schrijver, "Four International Law Sisters (IDI, ILA, Hague Academy and ILC): Similarities, Differences, and Interactions", in Jubilee Book Institut de droit international (forthcoming 2023), pp. 179-202.

Root, former Secretary of State (1905-1909) and Scott, founder of the American Society of International Law (ASIL) and the American Journal of International Law (AJIL). Root was not an international lawyer. This is why JB Scott was added to him in 1920 at the ACJ. Scott was many things, but not a thorough-bred diplomat., drew a hard bargain [51], and Asser won the day by sheer pragmatism. By replacing the university model with a more modest format of Summer Courses, Asser significantly reduced the budget and overcame opposition from established academic institutions, securing professors to deliver the courses in the summer breaks [52]. Moreover, to meet Scott's demand for high academic standards, Asser had the IDI draft the Statutes and recruit its former Presidents to serve on the Academy's governing board, the Curatorium [53]. The Carnegie Endowment generously sponsored the project until 1945. The Statutes were passed in January 1914 [54], with the inauguration scheduled for October 1914 [55]. The first courses were

---

51. Root, a former US Secretary of State (1905-1909), and Scott, who founded the American Society of International Law (established in 1906) and its *American Journal of International Law* (established in 1907), played significant roles during the negotiations. At the time of their meeting with Asser, Root served as the head of the Endowment while Scott chaired its Legal Division. Both emphasised the importance of strict organisation and high academic standards.

52. On 11 October 1911, Asser presented his less ambitious project, which greatly appealed to Scott. For more information, see *Year Book Carnegie Endowment* 1911, p. 111, and Scott's review in *Year Book* 1913-1914, p. 102.

53. The IDI addressed the Academy project for the first time during its session in Oslo in 1912. It established an Advisory Committee, which still included Asser and Renault, and this committee convened in 1913 during the next session in Oxford. On 9 August 1913, the IDI passed a Resolution of Recommendation. In early 1914, after Asser's passing in July 1913, the Committee in The Hague discussed the Draft Statutes and examined a comprehensive Report prepared by Scott in a joint session with the Dutch Committee, presided over by Albéric Rolin. The Curatorium was to be composed of (former) Presidents of the IDI, while the Administrative Council of the Academy was to be formed by the Dutch Carnegie Foundation. The lectures were scheduled to take place between July and October, during the summer break of universities, and were to be presented exclusively in French. The Statutes were approved on 12 January 1914. For further details on the IDI deliberations, refer to *Annuaire de l'Institut de droit international* (hereafter *Annuaire IDI*), Vol. 25 (1912), pp. 135 *et seq.*, and *Annuaire IDI*, Vol. 26 (1913), pp. 76 *et seq.*, *Documents*, pp. 20-27. Scott's Report can be found in *Year Book Carnegie Endowment* 1913/1914, Washington, Carnegie Endowment, Document Section, pp. 29-296. To emphasise its connection with the IDI, the Hague Academy adopted the same motto, "Justitia et Pace."

54. The formal establishment of the Hague Academy took place on 27 January 1914, and the Statutes are reproduced in *Grotius Annuaire* (1914), pp. 81 *et seq.* as well as in *ibid.* (1919-1920), pp. 337 *et seq.* (cf. *American Journal of International Law*, Vol. 8 (1914), pp. 357 *et seq.*). The annual contribution of the Endowment amounted to US$ 40,000.

55. During the first meeting of the Curatorium, held from 31 January to 2 February 1914 at the Ecole libre des sciences politiques in Paris, Louis Renault was elected President.

planned to coincide with the Third Hague Peace Conference in July 1915 [56].

Another private initiative was necessary to revive "La belle au bois dormant", as Van Kleffens called the Academy [57]. In June-July 1920, during their attendance at the meetings of the Advisory Committee of Jurists ("ACJ") that drafted the Statute of the Permanent Court of International Justice ("PCIJ") at the Peace Palace, Root and Scott initiated a Recommendation to the Council of the League of Nations to expedite the Academy project [58]. In 1921, the IDI recruited a new Curatorium [59], which in early 1923 scheduled the ceremonial inauguration for 14 July that year, the French national holiday [60]. Two days later, the Academy welcomed 353 attendees from thirty-one countries, including notable figures like Philip Jessup (1897-1986) and Frede Castberg (1893-1977). Among the participants, one in every ten students was a female, and they all eagerly attended the first series of courses delivered by twenty-eight lecturers from all over the globe [61]. The formula's success,

---

56. On 14 August 1914, the Dutch Foreign Minister, Jhr. J. Loudon (1913-1918), announced the postponement of the inauguration, which also affected the Third Hague Peace Conference scheduled for the summer of 1915. As a result, the conference never took place.
57. Van Kleffens in *Grotius Annuaire International* (1924), pp. 17-42, at p. 34. The IDI provisionally discussed the project in Paris in 1919 (cf. *Annuaire IDI*, Vol. 27 (1919), p. 65).
58. The ACJ met at The Hague from 16 June to 24 July 1920. It was no coincidence that Root and Scott, the latter attending as private secretary to Root, insisted on the project's revival. For the proceedings of the ACJ in 1920, refer to Eyffinger 2023, Vol. 1, Part 2. Further information on the vicissitudes of the Academy project can be found in the same source, in chaps. 16.2, 20.4 and 26.8.
59. During its Twenty-Eighth Session in Rome in September 1921, the IDI adopted Root's Recommendation and filled the vacant seats in the Curatorium. Charles Lyon-Caen was elected President, and Albéric Rolin became the Secretary-General (*Annuaire IDI*, Vol. 28, p. 217 *et seq.*). The following year, in Grenoble, the IDI finalised the preparations. It drafted a brochure in six languages for global distribution, in which it developed the unique character of the Academy, its rationale and its ambition for unbiased research.
60. For a comprehensive review of the meeting held in the Great Hall of Justice, see Eyffinger 1988, p. 169 and as well as to Eyffinger's book *The Trusteeship of an Ideal: The Carnegie Foundation, Vignettes of a Century 1904-2004*, Amsterdam/The Hague, Enschedé/Carnegie Foundation, 2004, pp. 109-118. For the favourable global response, see Von Verosta in Dupuy 1973, p. 42, n. 52.
61. The great majority of Academy auditors (i.e. attendees of courses) were professionals, with one-third being attorneys-at-law. The courses were quite experimental and spanned a mere three weeks (Dupuy 1973, pp. 42-46). Ten speakers represented the American continent, and nearly fifty students participated in both sessions. For statistics, consult Van Leeuwen Boomkamp in Dupuy 1973, pp. 197-227, and refer to Bardonnet 1998, p. 23, and Joor 2023, pp. ???. Thirty-one courses were planned, but some, such as those by Adatci, Anzilotti and Schücking, had to be cancelled. Eleven out of the twenty-eight courses delivered were included in the first volume of the *Recueil des Cours*. The remaining seventeen courses were published in volumes 2 and 3 of the

combining high-standard research with postgraduate education, was immediate and enduring [62].

Within weeks, James Brown Scott headed an Amicale, an association facilitating student camaraderie and organisation. The Amicale soon gained formal recognition as the Association des auditeurs et anciens auditeurs ("AAA") [63]. Over the following decades, the AAA expanded into an impressive global network of National Affiliations and Professional Groups [64], which organised congresses and published

---

Bibliotheca Visseriana. Eminent scholars, many of whom were former members of the ACJ or current judges on the World Court, taught the courses. During the session on the public domain, held between 16 July and 3 August, courses were given by Politis (ten lectures on international arbitration), Scott (six on conventional law, custom and comity), De Lapradelle (five on the freedom of the seas), Van Eysinga (five on international rivers and canals), Alvarez (three on the Pan-American Union), Loder (one on arbitration and international justice), De Bustamante (one on the PCIJ) and Butler (one on the development of the international spirit). In the session on the private domain, held 13 to 30 August, courses were given by Le Fur (ten lectures on the general theory of State), Basdevant (ten on the general theory of treaties), Cavaglieri (five on the effects of change of sovereignty), Hammarskjöld (six on neutrality), Niemeyer (five on international unions), Stowell (five on the attributions of consuls), Borchard (three on the protection of nationals abroad), Rolin (three on extradition) and Garner (two on the international regulation of air navigation). The decision to publish the lectures in a series *(Recueil des Cours)* was a fortuitous afterthought. Sales records were impressive from the beginning and served as a valuable source of income for the Academy.

62. In the 1920 and 1930s, an average of 350-400 students from numerous countries worldwide attended the courses.

63. The AAA was initiated by auditors and established on 26 July 1923. It represented half of the attending students and was governed by a five-member Committee. James Brown Scott, serving as Honorary President, was a prominent figurehead of the Association. Early contributors included Frede Castberg (1893-1977) and Alfred von Overbeck (1925-2016). The AAA received support from the Curatorium and was provided with an office (Room 13). It facilitated affordable accommodations for students, such as at the Oranje Hotel in Scheveningen, organised gatherings at De Witte and the Golf Country Club and supplied foreign journals and weeklies. By the mid-1930s, the AAA had evolved into a type of pressure group as students sought to have a say in course programming. To ensure cohesion and continuity, the AAA introduced a *Bulletin* and a journal titled *Echos de La Haye*. In 1951, the *Bulletin* was taken over by the Curatorium, and the AAA launched an *Annuaire*, which was transformed by Boutros-Ghali in 1955 into a scholarly journal serving as a platform for young scholars from developing countries. The publication also welcomed submissions from postgraduates at the Centre for Studies and Research. Prominent board members during the AAA's heyday from the 1930s to the 1980s included Martinus Willem Mouton, André Gardot and Frits W. Hondius. For a comprehensive overview, refer to the reviews by Nonnenmacher and Hondius in Dupuy 1973, pp. 243-277.

64. National affiliations, including a Hispano-American Group, were soon established throughout Europe to disseminate "L'Esprit de La Haye". These initiatives fostered regional and professional collaborations involving attorneys (from 1952) and university professors. The Association remained relatively successful until the end of the twentieth century. However, the AAA was officially dissolved in 2017 due to the revolutionising impact of internet facilities and modern communication devices. Its responsibilities were transferred to an Alumni Office within the Academy's Secretariat. Nevertheless, some National Groups persist today, including one in Germany. See Joor 1923, pp. ???. See above.

yearbooks worldwide [65]. As an example of its reach, in the 1950s, the French group founded the Annuaire français de droit international ("AFDI") during the days of Susanne Bastid and Daniel Vignes [66].

However, the Academy's success also brought challenges. The overwhelming response to the institution coincided with an unforeseen heavy caseload for the World Court. This combination resulted in acute logistical problems within the Peace Palace, whose dimensions had been criticised as far too ambitious back in 1913 [67]. Years of intense competition for space with the PCIJ, the Permanent Court of Arbitration ("PCA") and the Peace Palace Library, as well as numerous reconstructions, finally came to a resolution in 1931 when the Academy found new accommodations in the newly erected Academy Hall within the grounds. The hall had a rather austere appearance and its acoustics were dramatically poor, but it served the institution until it was replaced by the present luxury lodgings in 2004 [68].

---

65. The idea of holding annual international meetings and congresses on topical themes spanning three continents emerged during the silver jubilee meeting in Brussels in January 1949. Subsequently, from 1950 onwards, these meetings were organised with the assistance of governmental subsidies. Reports from congresses and papers commissioned for the Centre were regularly published in the *Annuaire*. In subsequent years, notable congress themes included "Humanity" in Oslo in 1968, "Communications" in Montreal in 1970 and "Environmental Issues" in Rabat in 1971.

66. In 1958, the French affiliation, led by Susanne Bastid (1906-1995), Gilbert Gidel (1880-1958), Georges Scelle (1878-1961) and Daniel Vignes (1924-2011), initiated the impressive AFDI. All four French scholars were closely involved with the Academy and the World Court in various capacities. See Annexes I and II.

67. The Academy's first President, Lyon-Caen, had already addressed similar issues in his inaugural address at the opening ceremony of the Academy.

68. For further references, see Lysen 1934, pp. 144-148; Eyffinger 1988, pp. 165-173; Joor 2013, pp. 101-106; Joor 2023, pp. 22-23; Eyffinger 2023, Vol. 2, chap. 5. Van Kleffens, in his lively review (Dupuy 1973, p. 76), recalls his journey to England in search of a fireplace to enliven the cold atmosphere of the lounge referred to as the "cigar box".

CHAPTER 2

THE TWO PILLARS OF THE LAW

2.1. The public domain: "The closed circuit"

The enduring success of the Hague Academy as an institution was far from accidental. It was the result of a carefully crafted formula that may be called the "closed circuit". This formula relied on high professional standards, overseen by a Curatorium then comprised of recruits from the IDI, the leading think-tank in the discipline [69]. This ensured that the Academy had a global network to draw upon for recruiting lecturers and attracting students as auditors [70]. Additionally, being members and associates of the IDI made these individuals prime candidates for positions in the PCA and World Court or as national judges, agents or counsel in court proceedings. Their close proximity to the Academy facilitated their involvement with the courses and added to the allure of maintaining an "international spirit".

Statistical data provides robust evidence of these institutional connections. Ninety out of one hundred scholars who served on the Curatorium were members of the IDI [71]. Throughout the past century, over 350 members of the IDI gave 630 of the 1,400 courses offered at the Academy [72]. Furthermore, more than 400 IDI members actively

---

69. Although the formal prerequisite of an "institutional" link was dropped in subsequent decades, statistics indicate that the relationship between the two research bodies remained close throughout.

70. The predominance of the IDI naturally may have led to some bias. While notable scholars returned on multiple occasions, there were also notable absentees. Struycken, in his review of the private domain in 1998, highlighted the absence of Ernst Rabel (1874-1955), Jan Kosters (1874-1951), Jan Offerhaus, Alain Pellet (b. 1947), and others, contrasting it with the frequent appearances of Hans Lewald (1883-1963), Jean Paulin Niboyet (1886-1952), B. A. Wortley (1907-1989) and others who delivered four lectures each. Refer to Struycken in Bardonnet 1998, pp. 63-104, particularly pp. 67-68. Generally, lecturers are invited based on their overall status and expertise, and they have relative freedom in selecting their themes. Over the years, various issues have been addressed. Still, there have also been deliberate omissions, either due to myopia or policy, which we will discuss later.

71. For a chronological list of Curatorium members, their country of origin and membership period, see Annex I. For their involvement with the Academy as auditors and lecturers, as well as with the IDI, ILC and World Court, see Annex II.

72. Over the past century, the Academy has presented some 1,400 courses. Some 750 scholars delivered a single lecture, while 650 returned to lecture one or more times. Among these lecturers, 165 scholars delivered two lectures, fifty delivered

participated in Hague-based institutions, with some 150 members serving on panels of the PCA and more than eighty as members of the World Court [73]. Likewise, the reverse is true. Fifty out of the (as of spring 1923) 111 judges of the International Court of Justice ("ICJ") delivered lectures at the Hague Academy, with some of them doing so up to five times.[74] Twenty-seven World Court judges served on the Curatorium [75], amassing over four hundred years of jurisprudence. In addition, sixty-six judges *ad hoc* provided 122 courses [76], and numerous agents and counsel also lectured, showcasing an impressive level of expertise [77]. Many scholars seamlessly combined their positions at the IDI, the Curatorium and the World Court for extensive periods [78]. Some individuals even achieved the "Grand Slam" of the Academy – attending as an auditor, delivering and publishing a course as a lecturer, and becoming a member of the Curatorium – demonstrating the Academy to be an *estafette d'excellence*, a courier of excel-

---

three, twenty-five delivered four and ten delivered five. Notably, Hans Wehberg lectured six times between 1925 and 1951, while the record for the most lectures is held by Maurice Bourquin, who delivered seven lectures between 1924 and 1953.

73. The *Collective Courses* effectively demonstrates the wisdom of Article 38, para. 1*d* of the Statute of the Court, which recognises the relevance of academia as a "subsidiary means" to aid in defining the rules to be applied by the international judiciary. The concept was a significant topic of discussion within the ACJ in 1920. For more information, refer to Eyffinger 2023, Vol. 1, chapter 15.5. Regarding the implementation of this source by the World Court, often implicitly, consult Skubiszewski in Bardonnet 1998, pp. 58-60.

74. In total, judges have contributed to eighty-eight courses. Among them, Charles de Visscher (five), Mohammed Bedjaoui (five), Manfred Lachs (four), and Sir Hersch Lauterpacht (four) were the most prolific lecturers.

75. Please refer to Annex IV for a comprehensive list. Among these judges, Charles de Visscher served on the Curatorium for forty-one years, Alvarez for thirty-six years, Ago for thirty-three years, Lachs for twenty-five years and Jiménez de Aréchaga for twenty-three years. Judges Crawford, Ranjeva and Cançado Trindade each served on the Curatorium for nineteen years. Currently, the cumulative years that judges have spent on the Curatorium amount to 411 years. The Curatorium has consistently included at least two to three judges. In recent years, the terms of Curatorium membership have been shortened. Please see Section 3.3 below for further details.

76. For a comprehensive overview, please refer to Annex V. Out of the sixty-six judges *ad hoc*, seventeen later became regular members of the Court. Among them, eleven also delivered lectures as regular members, accounting for sixteen of the aforementioned 122 lectures. This count includes six judges *ad hoc* from the PCIJ, who collectively presented twelve courses. Notably, Charles de Visscher lectured both before and after the war.

77. Additional information can be found in Annex VI. It appears that some judges in the early years had reservations or believed that public lectures were incompatible with their position on the bench.

78. Refer to Annex V for details. These judges, collectively, accounted for nearly one-third (55) of all lectures (140) delivered by members of the Curatorium.

lence [79]. Some even went beyond the "Grand Slam". For example, in 1923, a student from Yale University named Philip Jessup attended the courses at the Academy. He returned in 1929 as a lecturer, was elected a member of the IDI in 1948, joined the Curatorium in 1957, and finally assumed a position on the ICJ in 1961. Jessup lectured at the Academy four times [80]. One of his students in 1929 was Roberto Ago, who later delivered five lectures between 1936 and 1983. Ago became a member of the IDI in 1952, served on the Curatorium from 1963 to 1995, and was a member of the ICJ from 1979 to 1995 [81]. The same pattern, minus the position of student auditor, applies to twenty-two other World Court judges [82]. And then, in 1954, a certain Egyptian student from Columbia University attended by the name of Boutros Boutros-Ghali. Thus, each year, the Secretariat unknowingly registered future celebrities [83], and surely, they must have enrolled another such "mystery guest" this jubilee year. At all events, so far all of you are on the right track.

2.2. The private domain: Le travail de longue haleine

One might object that the involvement of the World Court only pertains to one half of the Academy's domain. After all, the Summer

---

79. Please see Annex III for a list of individuals who have achieved the "Grand Slam" of the Academy.

80. Philip Jessup served the Curatorium from 1957 to 1968 and the ICJ from 1961 to 1970. He lectured at the Academy in 1929 (*RdC* 29), 1956 (*RdC* 89), 1960 (*RdC* 99) and 1970 (*RdC* 129).

81. Roberto Ago (1907-1995) delivered lectures in 1936 (*RdC* 58), 1939 (*RdC* 68), 1956 (*RdC* 90), 1971 (*RdC* 134) and 1983 (*RdC* 182).

82. For a comprehensive overview, please refer to Annex V. These distinguished scholars served on both the World Court and the Curatorium, delivered lectures at the Academy and were members of the IDI. In addition to Judges Jessup, Ago and Ranjeva, this applies to the following judges (in alphabetical order): Alvarez, Anzilotti, Badawi, Bennouna, Cançado Trindade, Charlesworth, Crawford, Ch. De Visscher, Elias, Fitzmaurice, Huber, Hurst, Jiménez de Aréchaga, Lachs, Mbaye, McNair, Mosler, Oda, Ruda, Schücking, Tomka, Waldock and Xue Hanqin.

83. To provide a sampling (although the selection is not exhaustive), here are some notable international lawyers who "matriculated" at the Academy during its first stage between 1923 and 1939: Jessup and Castberg in 1923; Verzijl, Wenger and Offerhaus in 1924; Politis and Schindler in 1925; Briggs and Guggenheim in 1926; Morelli, Cavaré and Spiropoulos in 1927; Ago, Scerni, Wengler and Ziegler in 1929; Batiffol and Dumbauld in 1930; Gross in 1931; Von Verosta in 1934; Monaco, Quadri and Reuter in 1935; Lewald, Kopelmanas and Morelli in 1936; and Bierzanek, Grewe and Van Hecke in 1938.

The post-war decades also witnessed an impressive roster of participants: Bourquin, Lalive and Wortley in 1947; Seidl-Hohenfeldern and Vignes in 1948; Capotorti, Kiss and Skubiszewski in 1949; Ehrenzweig, Nonnenmacher and Rigaux in 1950; Baxter, Bowett, Malintoppi, McWhinney, Oda and Schwebel in 1951; Boutros-Ghali, Memon, Salmon, Singh and Zemanek in 1954; Reisman and Ziegler in 1955; Bernhardt, Von Overbeck and Watts in 1956; Bockstiegel and Condorelli in 1961; Pellet, Ranjeva and Treves in 1967; Delbrück, Rezek and Vukas in 1968; and Cançado Trindade in 1973.

Courses are divided into two Sessions, each (currently) lasting three weeks, one focusing on public international law and one on private international law [84]. Thus, there is equal emphasis on the public and private domains. However, this balance between the two domains has only been the case for the past seventy years. Before the early 1950s, the public domain overwhelmingly dominated the Academy's focus. This is particularly interesting, considering that the institution's founder, Tobias Asser, was a great champion of the private domain [85]. It was in the realm of private international law that the Dutch "Elegant School" had made its mark, with legal scholars like the Voetii and Cornelius van Bynkershoek first formulating the concept of comity [86]. In fact, the very roots of the *Oeuvre de La Haye* of the early 1890s can be found in this discipline. In 1913, Asser personally selected Albéric Rolin, professor of private international law at Ghent University, to lead the Peace Palace Library. Rolin went on to serve as the Academy's first Secretary-General for fifteen years [87].

There were several social, academic and pragmatic grounds for this shift in emphasis. Starting in 1905, increasing political tensions and economic conflicts began to undermine the international and comparative approach of Asser's Conference System, which had always faced some degree of contestation [88]. Rising nationalism led to changing paradigms of legal doctrine [89], and interest in the Conference

---

84. For more on the Summer Courses, see https://www.hagueacademy.nl/programmes/the-summer-courses/.
85. Asser held the first chair of private international law in the Netherlands from 1877 to 1893 (Eyffinger 2019, Vol. 1, pp. 650-693).
86. As the legend goes, "Les Hollandais ont frayé la route" (Eyffinger 2019, Vol. 1, pp. 622-632). See Briggs in *RdC* 354 (2012) for a recent review of the concept. Paulus Voetius (1619-1667), Johannes Voetius (1647-1713), Ulric Huber (1636-1694) and Cornelis van Bynkershoek (1673-1743) were prominent members of the Dutch School.
87. Albéric Rolin (1843-1937) was the younger brother of Gustave, Asser's close friend. In 1913, despite his advanced age, Asser pushed Albéric, who held the chair of private international law in Ghent, to become the director of the Peace Palace Library ("Poudreux est le flacon, mais vive est la liqueur"; Eyffinger 2019, Vol. 2, pp. 1723-1733). His years at the Library (1913-1920) were not particularly happy for Rolin, as he tragically lost three sons in the First World War, which deeply affected him. In 1922, he was appointed Secretary-General of the Academy. Unfortunately, his role in later years, as remarked on with some regret by his successor Van Kleffens in 1937, became primarily honorary.
88. The divergence of views between Asser and Renault in 1893 regarding the concept of General Principles and the overall perspective of the Conference is legendary. See Van Loon "Quelques réflexions", in J. Erauw and F. Laurent (eds.), *Liber Memorialis François Laurent (1810-1887)*, Brussels, E. Story-scientia, 1989, pp. 1133-1141; Eyffinger 2019, Vol. 2, chap. 24.
89. The competing national perspectives are exemplified by Franz Kahn's *Gesetzskollisionen* (1891) and Theodor Neumeyer's *Positives internationales Privatrecht* (1894). In 1897, Etienne Bartin expressed despair over the concept of universality

System waned [90]. Attempts by Bernard Loder to reignite enthusiasm in the mid-1920s proved short-lived [91]. The crisis was reflected in the courses at the Academy, which showcased the disagreements over General Rules and methodologies [92], as well as the stark differences between civil law and common law traditions [93]. Lecturers grappled with the perplexing challenges from the days of Pasquale Mancini, Asser and Edouard Clunet (1845-1922), such as issues of domicile and nationality [94], the complexities of *renvoi* [95] and the enforcement of foreign judgments [96]. Clashes between proponents and opponents of

---

in the *Journal Clunet*. In England, Albert Dicey, the author *of Conflict of Laws* (1897), countered Westlake's "Theoretical Method" and Asser's search for "General Principles" with his "Positivist Method". In 1908, Jan Kosters, in his inaugural address at Groningen, was the first to challenge Asser's authority at home (Eyffinger 2019, Vol. 1, pp. 821-831). Within the body of the ACJ in 1920, the juxtaposition of the two domains was also questioned.

90. Therefore, attempts to establish an international court for private matters, which had gained momentum from 1910 onwards (such as in the ILA's Dutch affiliate, the Royal Netherlands Society of International Law) consistently failed.

91. Under Bernard Loder's guidance, two new Conferences were initiated in 1925 and 1928, but their success was limited (Eyffinger 2019, Vol. 1, pp. 831-834).

92. These topics were prominent in the courses at the Academy. In 1928 (*RdC* 21), Arminjon discussed the object and method of the discipline. In 1930 (*RdC* 33), Frankenstein explored new tendencies, while in 1933 (*RdC* 44), Arminjon addressed *droits acquis*. Straznicky discussed the legacy of Asser's Conferences in 1933 (*RdC* 44), and Nolde touched on the codification process in 1936 (*RdC* 55). The theory of the discipline was covered by Szaszy in 1934 (*RdC* 47), and Balogh lectured on comparative law in 1936 (*RdC* 57). The General Rules of the discipline were addressed relatively late, successively by Maury in 1936 (*RdC* 57), Ago in 1936 (*RdC* 58), Davies in 1937 (*RdC* 62) and Lewald in 1939 (*RdC* 69).

93. For an overview of the first stage of the Academy's history in the interwar period, refer to Struycken in Bardonnet 1998, pp. 63-104, particularly pages 73-74 and 80-81. Struycken explicitly distinguishes between the Continental, British and American (Federal) traditions. In 1924 (*RdC* 2), Pillet addressed the Continental school, while Bellot (*RdC* 3) discussed the Anglo-Saxon tradition. Meijers discussed the European tradition in 1933 (*RdC* 57). After the Second World War, American interest waned, and its prominent representatives, apart from Reese, were German and Austrian scholars in exile, such as Ehrenzweig, Juenger and Von Mehren. In 1960 (*RdC* 99), Graveson compared the English and American schools.

94. The persistent issue of domicile and nationality continued to intrigue lecturers over the decades. It was raised sixteen times: by Isay in 1924 (*RdC* 5), Barbosa de Magelhaes in 1928 (*RdC* 23), Kunz in 1930 (*RdC* 31), Niboyet in 1930 (*RdC* 31), Cassin in 1930 (*RdC* 34), Rebslob in 1931, *RdC* 37), Bentwich in 1934 (*RdC* 49), Bartin in 1935 (*RdC* 52); Makarov in 1937 (*RdC* 60), Louis-Lucas in 1938 (*RdC* 64), Makarov in 1949 (*RdC* 74), Bentwich in 1955 (*RdC* 87), Castro in 1961 (*RdC* 102), Valladao in 1962 (*RdC* 105), Winter in 1969 (*RdC* 128), Rezek in 1986 (*RdC* 198), Vera in 1996 (*RdC* 261), Verwilghen in 1999 (*RdC* 277) and Nascimbene in 2013 (*RdC* 367).

95. The theme of *renvoi* was raised three times: by Lewald in 1929 (*RdC* 29), by Davi in 2010 (*RdC* 352) and by Kassir in 2015 (*RdC* 377).

96. The enforcement of foreign judgments has always been a pillar of the law in the English and American traditions. In Academy courses, it has been raised fifteen times: by De Cock in 1925 (*RdC* 10), Sperl in 1931 (*RdC* 36), Gutteridge in 1933 (*RdC* 44),

legal autonomy (autonomists v. anti-autonomists) further complicated matters [97]. Comparative studies were undertaken in an uphill battle to overcome national particularism and enhance the effectiveness of the discipline [98].

Still, there was something else. The Academy serves the double purpose of education and research. The first aspect, education, focused on the courses provided for the benefit of students, while the second aspect manifested in the scholarly publications of the *Collected Courses* series. Private international law has always been known as "the brain's rack", the realm of intricate and highly technical concepts, if not outright abstruse [99]. As the members of the Curatorium soon discovered, it was one thing for scholars to publish a course in the *Collected Courses*, but

---

Lalive in 1953 (*RdC* 84), Fragistas in 1961 (*RdC* 104), Mann in 1964 (*RdC* 111) and 1984 (*RdC* 186), Abdallah in 1973 (*RdC* 138, on the Arab League), Gónzalez Campos in 1977 (*RdC* 156), Von Mehren in 1980 (*RdC* 167), Trooboff in 1986 (*RdC* 200), Lagarde in 1986 (*RdC* 196), Loewenfeld in 1994 (*RdC* 245), Brand in 2011 (*RdC* 358) and Cuniberti in 2017 (*RdC* 394). See Struycken in Bardonnet 1998, pp. 63-104, at pp. 84-85.

97. Refer to Struycken in Bardonnet 1998, pp. 63-104, specifically pages 99-104, which discusses the explicit anti-autonomism of Joseph Beale in the USA, Niboyet in France and Meijers in the Netherlands (in contrast to Kosters). Struycken examines the prevailing sentiments at the Conference of 1955, Batiffol's intermediate position and Lagarde's thesis of *proximité* as expressed at the Academy in 1986 (*RdC* 196). For a comprehensive overview, see Von Overbeck in 1992 (*RdC* 233).

98. In Bardonnet 1998, Struycken addresses Bartin's "particularism" in 1931 (*RdC* 31) on page 70 and Batiffol's response in 1959 (*RdC* 97) on pages 71 and 77. Throughout the interwar period at the Academy, the emphasis was undoubtedly on national traditions. Simons discussed the German tradition in 1926 (*RdC* 15), Diena explored the Italian tradition in 1927 (*RdC* 17), Streit delved into the Greek tradition in 1927 (*RdC* 20), Kuhn examined the American tradition in 1928 (*RdC* 21), Péritch addressed the Yugoslavian tradition in 1929 (*RdC* 28), Yepes covered the Latin American school in 1930 (*RdC* 32), Trias de Bes discussed the Spanish tradition in 1930 (*RdC* 31), Daneff explored the Bulgarian line of thought in 1930 (*RdC* 33), Makarof focused on the Russian school in 1931 (*RdC* 35), while Colombos in 1931 (*RdC* 36) and Foster in 1938 (*RdC* 65) discussed the British tradition. Pontes de Miranda explored the Brazilian line in 1932 (*RdC* 39), Sulkowski covered the Polish tradition in 1932 (*RdC* 41), Fabre-Surveyer discussed the Canadian line in 1935 (*RdC* 53) and, finally, Cardahi examined the Islamic line of thought in 1937 (*RdC* 60). Non-Western traditions gained increasing focus in the 1960s with Mahmassani's courses in 1966 (*RdC* 117) on Islam, Sastry's courses in 1966 (*RdC* 117) on the Hindu tradition and Jayatilleke's courses in 1967 (*RdC* 120) on the Buddhist line of thought. For a recent review of the global horizon of the discipline, refer to Van Loon in 2015 (*RdC* 380).

99. Commentators have frequently argued that the complexities of the private international law discipline are less suitable for compelling oral presentations in public courses aimed at broader audiences. Even Asser, an inspired and talented teacher, struggled to generate wider interest among his students in Amsterdam; Eyffinger 2019, Vol. 1, pp. 656-657, and cf. Struycken in Bardonnet 1998, pp. 63-104, at pp. 89-90 ("au prix de recherches approfondies et d'efforts intellectuels extrêmes"). When budget constraints at the Academy led to cutbacks in 1945, courses on the subject were temporarily discontinued, only to be fully resumed in 1949; see Oppetit in 1992 (*RdC* 234) for more details.

presenting a series of lectures in an engaging format for students was an entirely different challenge [100].

The breakthrough came in 1945 when Swiss scholar Max Gutzwiller advocated for the revival of the Hague Conferences [101] but from a different perspective. He suggested moving away from the former dominance of Roman law and the universalist ambitions of the natural law tradition. Gutzwiller's initiative was transformative [102], setting the stage for a new era. In 1951, under the leadership of Dutch jurist Jan Offerhaus, the first post-war Conference was held in a "modern style" [103], signalling a departure from traditional approaches. The adoption of a new Statute in 1955 marked a significant milestone [104], establishing a Permanent Bureau [105] and providing a secure foundation for the *travail de longue haleine* of Tobias Asser [106]. The interaction between the HCCH and the Academy has proven highly beneficial. The ties between what Struycken referred to as "les soeurs jumelles" (the

---

100. Refer to the interesting observations by Von Overbeck in Dupuy 1973, p. 134, where he discusses the Hague Academy's "triptych" approach of oral presentations for students, scholarly publications for colleagues and the intergenerational exchange of ideas on-site.

101. Regarding Asser's close friendship with Swiss scholar Friedrich Meili (1848-1914), see Eyffinger 2019, Vol. 1, chaps. 24-25. Swiss scholar Max Gutzwiller (1889-1989) from Freiburg was greatly encouraged in his aspirations by C. De Visscher, Basdevant and Meijers. In 1929 (*RdC* 29), Gutzwiller first examined the historical development of private international law at the Academy, marking the beginning of an impressive series of comprehensive reviews, mostly presented as General Courses, that delved into the evolution of methodology and changing paradigms. Notable contributions include Lalive in 1975 (*RdC* 155), Droz in 1980 (*RdC* 168) and 1989 (*RdC* 229), Von Overbeck in 1982 (*RdC* 176), Parra-Aranguren in 1988 (*RdC* 210), Rigaux in 1989 (*RdC* 213), North in 1990 (*RdC* 220), McClean in 2000 (*RdC* 282), Von Mehren in 2002 (*RdC* 295), Struycken in 2004 (*RdC* 311), Bucher in 2010 (*RdC* 341), Van Loon in 2015 (*RdC* 380), Symeonides in 2015 (*RdC* 384) and, more recently, Lequette (*RdC* 387) and Muir Watt (*RdC* 389) in 2017.

102. With Wortley's first General Course in 1947 (*RdC* 71), the discipline achieved equal footing. Wortley provided insights into the General Principles of the discipline from the English perspective.

103. Dutchman Jan Offerhaus (1892-1966) earned the nickname "Asser Reborn" due to his visionary thinking, tact, resourcefulness and determination. He presided over the Seventh to Tenth Conferences (1951, 1956, 1960 and 1964). For further details, refer to Eyffinger 2019, Vol. 1, chap. 26.7.2.

104. The Statute came into effect on 15 July 1955.

105. The Permanent Bureau was overseen by the Dutch Staatscommissie.

106. Today, the HCCH has around forty conventions and is a prominent global player and the leading permanent intergovernmental organisation dedicated to harmonising private and commercial law. Within the Academy, the progressive codification process has been addressed on eight occasions. These include contributions by Maridakis in 1954 (*RdC* 85, Greece), the long-standing Secretary of the HCCH, Van Hoogstraten, in 1967 (*RdC* 122, Hague Conference), Stricky in 1968 (*RdC* 123, Czechia), Ferrer-Correia in 1975 (*RdC* 145), Von Overbeck in 1982 (*RdC* 176), Jayme in 1982 (*RdC* 177), Kessesdjian in 2002 (*RdC* 300) and Weizuo in 2012 (*RdC* 359, China).

twin sisters) have become almost institutional. Secretaries-General, Delegates, Rapporteurs and lecturers collaborate closely, working in harmony to advance the field [107]. The synergy between these entities has greatly benefited Preparatory Committees ("PrepComs") for Conventions, legislators and judges in their pursuit of global parameters and legal standards. Lecturers at the Academy have made substantial contributions to disseminating interest in the Hague Conferences and promoting harmonised thought through their assessment of the codification process and critical comparative research. Their work has significantly influenced the field and facilitated the harmonisation of legal principles. In recognition of the rapid expansion and growing importance of the HCCH, the need for a new Academy Hall became evident. This led to the opening of the new facility in 2007, providing a modern and well-equipped space to accommodate the Academy's activities. The establishment of this hall reaffirmed the commitment to fostering collaboration and intellectual growth within the field of international law.

---

107. The significant roles played by successive Secretaries-General Van Hoogstraten, Droz, Van Loon and Lagarde testify to the organisation's progress. Prominent members of the Curatorium in this field included Kosters (1932-1939), Ruegger (1948-1985), Batiffol (1962-1984), Ago (1963-1995), Yasseen (1967-1981), Reese (1975-1990), Riphagen (1977-1994), Boutros-Ghali (1982-2016), Dupuy (1985-1997), Skubiszewski (1994-2010), Struycken (1995-2016), Conforti (1998-2010) and Bastid-Burdeau (2005-2017). For further details, refer to Struycken in Bardonnet 1988, pp. 63-104, at pp. 88-90.

CHAPTER 3

THE HISTORY OF THE ACADEMY IN THREE STAGES

3.1. The first stage (1923-1939)

One can discern three distinct stages in the history of the Academy, each characterised by its own specific features. The first period encompassed the interwar period, from the Academy's founding in 1923 to the outbreak of the Second World War in 1939. In retrospect, this era appears particularly tumultuous, marked by the tragic collapse of all too ambitious ideals. In response to the devastation of the First World War, the Treaty of Versailles sought to establish a world organisation and usher in an era of the rule of law [108]. The League of Nations, the concept of collective security and the World Court were bold experiments challenging the unrestrained sovereignty of nations [109].

International lawyers enthusiastically embraced these new paradigms with zeal. They believed that with the World Court, the discipline had finally found its rightful place, liberated from the constraints of diplomacy. However, their unchecked optimism led them astray. They placed undue faith in the law as not just another tool but the panacea for the defence of peace *without* acknowledging that peace and social justice were prerequisites for the effective implementation of the law. This optimism was exemplified by the Locarno Treaties (1925), the Briand-Kellogg Pact (1928) [110] and the persistent call for the Hague

---

108. Typically, at the Academy, historians treated the period leading up to the First World War as a closed book and, on the cusp of a new era, evaluated the achievements of their predecessors. A total of twenty-nine courses delved into the history of the discipline. Notably, Barcia Trelles (*RdC* 17, 32, 43, 67), De Taube (*RdC* 11, 32, 42, 53, 67) and C. Dupuis (*RdC* 2, 32, 60) emerged as prominent representatives of that era. In addition, several courses explored the historical influence of religion on the discipline, including the works of Hobza in 1924 (*RdC* 5), Goyau in 1925 (*RdC* 6), Boegner in 1925 (*RdC* 6) and again in 1929 (*RdC* 29), as well as Muller-Azúa in 1930 (*RdC* 31).

109. The Academy's exploration of the boundaries of State sovereignty began with Politis (*RdC* 6) and Gidel (*RdC* 10) in 1925, followed by Andrassy in 1937 (*RdC* 61). The discourse on this topic continued to be an integral part of the Courses programme, with contributions from Van Kleffens in 1953 (*RdC* 82), Korowicz in 1961 (*RdC* 102), Arangio-Ruiz in 1972 (*RdC* 137), Flory in 1974 (*RdC* 141), Dunbar in 1971 (*RdC* 132), Sperduti in 1976 (*RdC* 153), Sinclair in 1980 (*RdC* 167), Anand in 1986 (*RdC* 197, focusing on sovereign equality), Achour in 1994 (*RdC* 245) and Carillo-Salcedo in 1996 (*RdC* 257).

110. The Covenant of the League was examined in various aspects, including the works of Mandelstam in 1926 (*RdC* 14), Schücking in 1927 (*RdC* 20), Rutgers in 1931 (*RdC* 38) and Kunz in 1932 (*RdC* 39).

Codification Conference (1930). Their downfall was their naiveté in relying on the efficacy of paper treaties to shape national policies [111].

The same held for the Academy. As Eelco van Kleffens noted in 1973, the institution was an unprecedented experiment [112]. The Statute provided only minimal guidance for its policies [113]. While the institution's "unique physiognomy" was widely acclaimed, it proved as cumbersome as it was daring [114]. The Academy operated in a constant state of flux, with an annual turnover of both lecturers and students. The discipline's lofty aspirations were reflected in the courses, where lecturers emphasised the relevance of the law to society [115]. They dismissed the traditional distinction between the laws of peace and the laws of war as outdated, proclaiming war as a thing of the past [116]. Neutrality was deemed obsolete in light of the collective security system [117]. In 1929, the Academy introduced its General Courses programme, which soon became the cornerstone of the institution. These courses focused on the General Rules of the law of peace [118], extolled the virtues of the League and the Court [119] and championed the law of international organisations

---

111. Article 1 of the 1928 Pact built upon the provisions of the 1919 Covenant, which allowed for self-defence and the auxiliary defence of third parties.

112. Van Kleffens in Dupuy 1973, pp. 65-81, at p. 67.

113. In navigating unchartered waters and with little help from the ageing Albéric Rolin in appeasing the "shock of opinions", Van Kleffens relied on the legal genius of Gilbert Gidel, who incidentally was a skilled yachtsman.

114. Skubiszewski in Bardonnet 1998, pp. 21-62, at p. 30. The first Curatorium noted the institution's entirely different "physiognomy"; see *RdC* 1 (1923), pp. v-vi.

115. As seen in Hersch Lauterpacht's renowned course from 1930 (*RdC* 34) on justiciable and non-justiciable disputes.

116. The outlawing of war was addressed by Wehberg in 1928 (*RdC* 24) and Descamps in 1930 (*RdC* 31). War prevention was discussed by Brouckère in 1934 (*RdC* 50) and Efremoff in 1937 (*RdC* 59). Various aspects of modern warfare were explored by Higgins in 1926 (*RdC* 11), Van Eysinga in 1927 (*RdC* 16), Werner in 1928 (*RdC* 21), McNair in 1937 (*RdC* 59), Smith in 1938 (*RdC* 63), Baldoni in 1938 (*RdC* 65) and Sandiford in 1939 (*RdC* 68). Cf. footnote 248.

117. The thirteen Neutral Powers in the First World War all reconsidered their position. At the Academy, the concept of neutrality was reviewed in light of the collective security system by Whitton in 1927 (*RdC* 18), Boye in 1938 (*RdC* 64) and Dollot in 1939 (*RdC* 67). It was subsequently reconsidered after the Second World War by Komarnicki in 1952 (*RdC* 80), Chaumont in 1956 (*RdC* 89), Schindler in 1967 (*RdC* 121) and, nearly fifty years later, Corten in 2014 (*RdC* 374).

118. These series of sixteen lectures were formally titled "Courses on General Rules of the Law of Peace". The series commenced with Cavaglieri's brilliant course on State recognition *de jure* and *de facto* in 1929 (*RdC* 26).

119. During the interwar period, the role of the PCIJ was examined by Hudson (*RdC* 8), Salvioli (*RdC* 12), C. De Visscher (*RdC* 26), Caloyanni (*RdC* 38), Beckett (*RdC* 39 and *RdC* 50), Rundstein (*RdC* 43), Ripert (*RdC* 44), Negulesco (*RdC* 57), Feinberg (*RdC* 59), Bruns (*RdC* 62) and Scerni (*RdC* 65). No post-war courses on the PCIJ are documented, as research into this period was effectively abandoned. For courses covering the ICJ, see below, footnote 229. The League was discussed in twenty-eight courses. Aspects of the Covenant were addressed by Mandelstam in 1926 (*RdC* 14),

as the new guiding principle. The multitude of multilateral treaties concluded under the auspices of the League was hailed as a significant source of new law [120].

The collapse of Wall Street in the autumn of 1929 triggered the Great Depression, casting a shadow over the world. Lecturers now addressed the financial crash, national debts and the downward spiral of reparations. Previously, they had welcomed the Dawes Plan in 1924, which aimed to remove politics from the equation. They now turned their attention to its revision in the Young Plan (1929) and President Hoover's debt moratorium (1931), focusing on the protection of investments [121]. In the following years, ideological strife and civil wars from Brazil to China to Spain served as wake-up calls, signalling the path toward an impending abyss [122]. The Courses programme of 1939 was held under the dark clouds of imminent war, with judges, scholars and students eager to return to their homelands [123]. This period marked the conclusion of fifteen years, during which 6,000 postgraduate students from seventy nationalities had attended 400 courses, all compiled in seventy *Collected Courses* green volumes [124]. While the statistics were impressive, none of this prevented the outbreak of war. An era had ended, and the Second World War marked a significant turning point in all aspects

---

Schücking in 1927 (*RdC* 20), Rutgers in 1931 (*RdC* 38) and Kunz in 1932 (*RdC* 39). By comparison, forty-three courses delved into international law's theory, status and development.

120. By 1946, the number of treaties registered with the *League of Nations Treaty Series* had reached an impressive 4,834, filling 205 volumes. This extensive collection far surpassed any pre-war collections.

121. The Academy extensively discussed economic and financial challenges, including the Dawes Plan (1924) and the Young Plan (1929). Courses on international finance problems were delivered by Andréades in 1924 (*RdC* 5), Strupp in 1925 (*RdC* 8), Milhaud in 1926 (*RdC* 15), Sulkowski in 1929 (*RdC* 29), Fischer Williams in 1930 (*RdC* 34), Aftalion in 1932 (*RdC* 39) and Griziotti in 1934 (*RdC* 49). After the Second World War, reparations claims were abandoned to avoid a repetition of the trauma experienced in the 1920s. Instead, the massive relief provided by the Marshall Plan (1948-1952) was implemented. However, the issue of national debts resurfaced in 1989 with the collapse of communism, prompting courses by MacLean (*RdC* 214) and Gianviti (*RdC* 215) in the same year. Skubiszewski, in Bardonnet 1998, addresses the legal implications of political and social destabilisation, such as mass migrations, on pages 49-50.

122. Civil war was addressed by Wehberg in 1938 (*RdC* 63). Subsequent reviews on this topic only emerged in 1979, with Nahlik (*RdC* 164) and Abi-Saab (*RdC* 165).

123. For an in-depth exploration of the World Court and the Academy during the years 1939-1945, refer to Eyffinger 2023, Vol. 2, chap. 14.

124. Volumes 1-69 of the *Recueil des Cours* were complemented by volumes 2 and 3 of the *Bibliotheca Visseriana*, which reproduced most of the lectures from 1923.

of life [125]. Few pre-war Academy courses (or court judgments) would retain their relevance and value.

3.2. The second stage (1947-1989)

On 25 April 1945, fifty nations gathered in San Francisco to draft the charter of a new world security organisation, which led to the creation of the United Nations on 24 October that same year. San Francisco thus witnessed a resurgence of civilisation and international law, but they were again mired in crisis [126]. New global priorities overshadowed memories of the interwar period, the League of Nations and the PCIJ [127]. It recalled the situation in Versailles and Geneva twenty years earlier, where references to the *Oeuvre de La Haye* and the PCA were deemed unpalatable or unwelcome [128]. Preserving human dignity emerged as a paramount concern, and when the Hague Academy was revived in 1947 after a six-year hiatus, it reflected these pressing issues. Courses on the International Bill of Human Rights [129], the Universal Declaration of Human Rights [130], the UN Human Rights Commission and its regional counterparts [131], the Geneva

---

125. These events had personal repercussions as well. For example, prominent German and Austrian lawyers such as Schücking, Lewald, Nussbaum, Strupp, Frankenstein, Raape and Kaufmann were discredited and forced into exile by the Nazi regime.
126. Refer to Kunz's course in 1955 (*RdC* 88) for an examination of the crisis of law and its transformation.
127. Rappard's lecture at the Academy in 1947 (*RdC* 71) was a notable exception.
128. At the time, this phenomenon intrigued and concerned many commentators. The refusal at League headquarters to accept the PCA as part of the World Organisation led advocates of the *Oeuvre de La Haye*, as in the case of the ACJ in 1920, to choose the policy of integrating the PCA in the nomination/election procedure of the PCIJ. For more information, see Eyffinger 2023, Vol. 1, chaps. 11-13.
129. This includes the two Covenants from 1946 on Civil and Political Rights and Economic, Social and Cultural Rights. From the interwar period, there were only two courses on human rights issues, presented by Mandelstam in 1931 (*RdC* 38) and Dumas in 1937 (*RdC* 59), which may have been among the first to explore the concept of human rights. The post-war discourse began in 1947 with Hersch Lauterpacht's pioneering classic on human rights (*RdC* 70), followed by the courses of René Cassin (*RdC* 79 and *140*). In the following years, numerous specific aspects were addressed by Hamburger (*RdC* 97), Golsong (*RdC* 110), Ermacora (*RdC* 124), Migliazza (*RdC* 137), Vasak (*RdC* 140), Gros Espiell (*RdC* 145 and *RdC* 218), Schreiber (*RdC* 145), Uribe Vargas (*RdC* 184), Cançado Trindade (*RdC* 202), Pastor Ridruejo (*RdC* 228), Rchid (*RdC* 268), Kinsch (*RdC* 318), Meron (*RdC* 301), Mazzeschi (*RdC* 333), Reisman (*RdC* 351), Ahlf (*RdC* 369), Najurieta (*RdC* 376), Marrella (*RdC* 385), Chinkin (*RdC* 395) and Shany (*RdC* 409).
130. See GA Res 217A (III), dated 10 December 1948.
131. For example, refer to Pastor Ridruejo's lecture in 1991 (*RdC* 228). The Centre first addressed human rights issues in 1967. In subsequent years, the European

Conventions [132] and international criminal law [133] addressed the acute predicaments of the time.

The Academy itself underwent significant changes during its relaunch. It adapted to the shifting times by introducing courses in English alongside French [134], which expanded the pool of scholars available for teaching and attracted a broader range of students. The Registration Office saw a substantial surge in subscriptions as a result [135]. At the academic level, the IDI and Curatorium faced a major challenge with the establishment of a competing research body in 1947, the International Law Commission ("ILC") [136], under UN auspices. The ILC shared the same mission as the IDI and International Law Association ("ILA") did in 1873: the development and progressive codification of international law [137]. However, the ILC represented a new phase and operated with a different perspective. The IDI and ILA had marked the transition from individual inquiry to collective research bodies in 1873, while the Second Hague Peace Conference in 1907 had introduced

---

Commission on Human Rights was discussed by Gros Espiell in 1989 (*RdC* 218), Rideau in 1997 (*RdC* 265), Matscher in 1997 (*RdC* 270) and Beaumont (*RdC* 335). The Inter-American Commission on Human Rights was covered by Novak (*RdC* 392), and the African Charter of Human Rights by Bello (*RdC* 194). At the Academy, these concerns culminated in the creation of Special Courses on Human Rights in 1991.

132. Borel had initially addressed these issues in 1923 (*RdC* 1). Regarding the 1949 Conventions, refer to Pictet's lecture in 1950 (*RdC* 76), Ruegger in 1953 (*RdC* 82) and Draper in 1965 (*RdC* 114). Comments on the 1977 Protocols were made by Schindler in 1979 (*RdC* 163), Draper in 1979 (*RdC* 164), Nahlik in 1979 (*RdC* 164) and Abi-Saab in 1979 (*RdC* 165).

133. In 1920, Baron Descamps, the President of the ACJ, had suggested the creation of an international criminal court. For contemporary comments, see Saldaña in 1925 (*RdC* 10) and Donnedieu de Vabres in 1929 (*RdC* 26). The Nuremberg Trials led to courses by Donnedieu de Vabres in 1947 (*RdC* 70), Graven in 1950 (*RdC* 76) and Glaser in 1960 (*RdC* 99). For the genesis and role of the ICC, see Jorda in 2004 (*RdC* 307) and David in 2005 (*RdC* 313).

134. Although the exclusivity of the French language had never been absolute, incidental courses in English and German were presented in 1933 and 1934, respectively. However, the policy change in 1947 had significant consequences, considerably increasing the number of qualified scholars and students. As Jessup recalled in 1973 (Dupuy 1973, pp. 61-64, at p. 62), many students in the interwar period actually had a better understanding of courses delivered in French by non-native French speakers, such as Scott's lectures in 1929. Major improvements were made later with the introduction of interpreter booths in 1954 and consistent simultaneous interpretations in 1966.

135. In 1947, nearly 600 students attended. Indeed, based on attendance numbers, the first post-war decade marked the peak of the Academy's popularity. See Van Leeuwen Boomkamp in Dupuy 1973, pp. 202-209.

136. To understand the genesis, Statute, and subsequent expansion of the ILC, consult Article 13(1) of the UN Charter, UNGA Resolution 174 (II) dated 21 November 1947, and the subsequent amendments to the Statute in UNGA Resolutions 485 (V) dated 12 December 1950, 984 (X) dated 3 December 1955, and 985 (X) dated 3 December 1955, as well as UNGA Resolution 36/39 dated 18 November 1981.

137. Refer to Article 15 of the ILC Statute for further details.

Governmental PrepComs, public think-tanks, alongside private research bodies [138]. The aim was to combine theory and practice, science and politics, under one umbrella. This line of thought was further explored in the interwar period through the so-called Committee of Seventeen [139]. In 1947, these endeavours culminated in the establishment of a public representative body under the UN General Assembly's auspices.

Despite its focus on the public sphere [140], the ILC's research overlapped considerably with that of the IDI, both *ratione personae* [141] and in the research projects tackled [142], benefiting the discipline as a whole. Over the past seventy-five years, more than a third of the ILC's 230 members also held membership in the IDI, meaning they operated from both academic and governmental or regional perspectives [143]. This

---

138. The better to prepare for its sequel in 1915. It was widely believed that the 1907 Conference had failed due to inadequate preparation by the Russian Organising Committee. Therefore, numerous National Committees were established in anticipation of an International PrepCom scheduled for 1913. However, this planned initiative never materialised.

139. During the interwar period, there was a gradual enhancement of this concept. The role of the pre-war National PrepComs was initially assumed by the ACJ, tasked by the Council of the League of Nations to create rules for the establishment of a permanent World Court in 1920. The ACJ drafted a statute that was then reviewed by the Council and passed to the Third (Legal) Committee of the Assembly of the League, similar to how the current ILC closely collaborates with the Sixth (Legal) Committee of the UN General Assembly. The next step was the establishment in 1924, in close consultation with the IDI, of the Committee of Seventeen experts on codification issues. This Committee was created through a League Assembly resolution and operated as a standing organ. For further information on these matters, see Schrijver 2023, p. 2. This initiative, in turn, prompted additional research by the IDI from 1925 to 1927. The outcome was the Codification Declaration of 1928, which preceded the Codification Conference in The Hague in 1930. The Conference and the body itself emphasised a commitment to purely scientific research in line with their overall policy. By then, a second ACJ had also revised the PCIJ Statute in 1929 at Geneva.

140. Alongside its research on the law of the seas, one of the remarkable early achievements and ongoing sources of pride for the ILC was its contribution to developing the Vienna Convention on the Law of Treaties (1969).

141. It is worth noting that the IDI is a much larger research body, with approximately four times the number of members compared to the ILC, and encompasses a dozen commissions. Following a regional distribution formula, the ILC's membership gradually increased from fifteen in 1949 to thirty-four in 1982. It holds two sessions per year, each lasting approximately five weeks, at the UN headquarters in Geneva, typically in late spring and early summer.

142. The IDI initiated its work on codification at its first session of the post-war period in Lausanne in 1947, with Alejandro Alvarez serving as its Rapporteur.

143. The coexistence of academic and political perspectives, inherent to the discipline of international law and often the subject of discussion, prompted the publication of Charles de Visscher's seminal work, *Théories et réalités en droit international* (1953). Back in 1920, one of the major challenges faced by the ACJ, for example, was the ambiguous position of its members. It remained uncertain whether they considered themselves appointed based on personal merit or as representatives of their respective governments.

cross-fertilisation of outlooks and interests proved advantageous for the discipline and the Academy [144]. A total of seventy-seven ILC members delivered 130 courses at the Hague Academy [145]. While simultaneous membership in the politicised ILC and a position on the ICJ was considered incompatible, thirty-three ILC veterans served on the World Court, with most of them relinquishing ILC membership upon their election to the bench [146].

At the Academy, early concerns focused on the UN Charter [147] and the ICJ [148] soon gave way to the ideological deadlock of the Cold War [149], which hindered global aspirations and led to a reliance on regional structures such as the European Communities [150], the Arab League [151] and the Organization of American States [152]. Lecturers, starting in 1949, began discussing the extensive range of multilateral Codification Conferences initiated under UN auspices. These conferences aimed to address issues of humanitarian law, the law of the sea (1958-

---

144. Given the overlapping nature of research projects, it was natural for scholars to serve as Rapporteur for the IDI and as Special Rapporteur for the ILC. Hersch Lauterpacht embodies this duality. The initial programme of the ILC was outlined in the influential document known as the Lauterpacht Memorandum (1949). Lauterpacht, a British scholar, was elected as a member of the IDI in 1947 and subsequently served on the ICJ from 1955 to 1960.

145. Only seventeen of these seventy-seven ILC members did not concurrently hold membership in the IDI.

146. This pattern remained consistent throughout the nearly seventy-five-year period. Notably, in the other direction, only three judges joined the ILC after their tenure on the bench (Ferrari Bravo, Hudson and Krylov). For a complete record, refer to Annex VII.

147. See Kaeckenbeeck in 1947 (*RdC* 70) and Preuss in 1949 (*RdC* 74) for further information.

148. The ICJ was addressed by Hambro in 1950 (*RdC* 76, jurisdiction), Kerno in 1951 (*RdC* 78, UN and ICJ), Bastid in 1951 (*RdC* 68, case law) and Briggs in 1958 (*RdC* 93, compulsory jurisdiction). For the full listing of couirses on the ICJ see below, footnote 229.

149. This deadlock was symbolised by the construction (in 1948) and demolition (in 1989) of the Berlin Wall.

150. Over the past seventy-five years, numerous courses have explored the progressive development of European integration, including lectures by Kohnstamm in 1956 (*RdC* 90), Rieben in 1956 (*RdC* 90), Soto in 1956 (*RdC* 90), Robertson in 1957 (*RdC* 91), Pescatore in 1961 (*RdC* 103), Hahn in 1963 (*RdC* 108), Laubadère in 1964 (*RdC* 111), Donner in 1965 (*RdC* 115), Vignes in 1970 (*RdC* 130), Teitgen in 1971 (*RdC* 134), Luchaire in 1975 (*RdC* 144), Ganshof van der Meersch in 1975 (*RdC* 148), Boulouis in 1978 (*RdC* 160), Badiali in 1985 (*RdC* 191), Vignes in 1988 (*RdC* 210), Simmonds in 1989 (*RdC* 218), Boulouis in 1992 (*RdC* 235), Struycken in 1992 (*RdC* 236), Piontek in 1992 (*RdC* 236), Vera in 1996 (*RdC* 261), Bermann in 1997 (*RdC* 263), Oreja Aguirre in 1997 (*RdC* 267) and Maresceau in 2004 (*RdC* 309).

151. Refer to Boutros-Ghali in 1972 (*RdC* 137), Abdallah in 1973 (*RdC* 138) and Farajallah in 1991 (*RdC* 228).

152. See Jiménez de Aréchaga in 1964 (*RdC* 111), Selpulveda in 1972 (*RdC* 137) and Caminos in 1998 (*RdC* 273).

1959)[153], diplomacy and consular law (1961, 1963)[154] and, the jewel in the crown, the law of treaties (1969)[155].

In 1947, the Academy faced a critical concern regarding its financial position due to a change in policies at the Carnegie Endowment, its main sponsor[156]. As a result, courses had to be downgraded, and the share / contribution of the private domain was temporarily diminished. It took the Curatorium several years to adapt, but the financial challenges inspired a comprehensive policy overhaul and the elevation of standards. In 1949, the pre-war *certificate d'attendance*, which lacked significance, was supplemented and later replaced in 1956 by an optional diploma awarded after rigorous exams[157]. Embracing modernity, the traditional concept of formal lectures was alternated with seminars, dialogue and interactive Q&A sessions.

In 1957, at Jessup's initiative, in-depth research underwent significant enhancement with the establishment of the Centre d'Etudes or Centre for Studies and Research, strictly reserved for PhD-level scholars and Academy diploma holders[158]. Divided into French and English-

---

153. The Law of the Sea Conferences of 1958-1959 were primarily driven by economic interests facilitated by advancements in modern technology. However, the discourse on this topic did not cease with the conclusion of the UNCLOS Convention at Montego Bay in 1982. It has continued to evolve and undergo reassessments in various Academy courses, as noted below (see footnote 252).

154. For an exploration of diplomatic practice during the interwar period, refer to the courses delivered by Vaughn Williams in 1924 (*RdC* 4), Hurst in 1926 (*RdC* 12), Basdevant in 1926 (*RdC* 15), Stuart in 1934 (*RdC* 48), Niboyet in 1935 (*RdC* 52) and Wolfgast in 1937 (*RdC* 60). Regarding modern practice, valuable insights are provided in the courses by Dillard in 1957 (*RdC* 91), Giuliano in 1960 (*RdC* 100), P. de Visscher in 1961 (*RdC* 102), Bartos in 1963 (*RdC* 108) and Nahlik in 1990 (*RdC* 222).

155. Regarding the Vienna Convention of 1969, consult Ago in 1971 (*RdC* 134), Yasseen in 1976 (*RdC* 151), Gaja in 1981 (*RdC* 172) and Villiger in 2011 (*RdC* 344). The Treaty stands out as a remarkable achievement resulting from the fruitful collaboration between the political and academic spheres, benefiting significantly from forty years of jurisprudence at the World Court.

156. The loss of the Carnegie Endowment as sponsor necessitated the amendment of the Academy's Statutes in 1957; see Joor 2023, p. ??.

157. To illustrate the high standards upheld by the Academy, it is worth noting that in 1950, forty-four candidates applied, nineteen were accepted, ten passed the exams and three graduated *cum laude*. Throughout its history, the Academy has maintained a commitment to excellence. The diploma ceremony is an integral part of the course.

158. The establishment of the Centre was a response to dissatisfaction with the overall quality of students obtaining the diploma. Georges Scelle, who had been involved with the Academy since 1933, notably expressed his discontent. As Boutros-Ghali recalls (in Dupuy 1973, pp. 137-157, at p. 139), J.P.A. (Jean) François (1889-1978) at the PCA and Bartholomeus (Bart) Landheer (1904-1989) at the Library actively supported the idea. In light of this, Gilbert Gidel, then President of the Curatorium, and Van Kleffens reached out to the Rockefeller Foundation. In 1957, the Centre d'Etudes was inaugurated, providing an informal platform for a dozen postgraduate scholars to engage in three weeks of intensive debates and in-depth analyses of topics covered in that year's General Courses. The Peace Palace Library contributed bibliographies,

speaking sections, each section supervised by a Director of Studies, the Centre conducted highly specialised and thematically focused research projects lasting six weeks, immediately following the regular Courses programme. The Centre quickly developed into a renowned "Laboratory of the Law". Its remarkable achievements represent a synopsis of the cumulative challenges the discipline has faced over the past sixty-five years [159]. The subsequent restructuring of the regular Courses programme took place in 1958, strictly demarcating and finally equalising the public and private sectors into successive three-week Sessions.

In 1966, the Academy introduced another innovative addition with the launch of Special Seminars. Subsequently, from 1968 onwards, Workshops addressed contemporary and "trendy" issues such as the environment, economic integration and the role of the UN in dispute settlement [160]. These developments reflect the Curatorium's dedication to staying in touch with the pulse of society. However, the body seemed to share a common blind spot with many Western law students regarding the paramount dynamics of the period. This blind spot pertained to the unprecedented expansion of the international community resulting from the decolonisation process and the intricate issues of State succession it entailed.

---

and Wolfgang Friedmann was pivotal in establishing a specialised book collection. The early years highlighted linguistic challenges and significant discrepancies in participants' training and expertise. For further details on the Centre, refer to Bardonnet in Bardonnet 1998, pp. 9-19, particularly p. 16. Additional information on the Centre can be found at the Academy website: https://www.hagueacademy.nl/programmes/centre-for-studies-and-research/.

159. Over the past forty years, the Centre has focused on various topics, including environmental issues in 1985, 2001, 2002, 2005 and 2011; trade, transport and communications in 1990, 1997, 1998 and 1999; humanitarian issues in 1986, 1989, 2010 and 2015; terrorism in 1988 and 2008; nuclear energy in 1993; national finances and investments in 1995 and 2007 respectively; State succession in 2000; international crimes and their jurisdiction in 2002 and 2014; economic sanctions in 2004, food issues in 2006; cultural issues in 2008 and 2013; women's rights in 2016; and citizenship in 2018. Until 1985, the publication of the discourse under the auspices of the Academy was not foreseen, with most participants' papers scattered across various academic journals, with the *Yearbooks* of the AAA being particularly prominent. However, in 2000, the *Centre for Studies and Research in International Law and International Relations* series was launched to address this gap. For a list of publications, see https://brill.com/display/serial/CERS.

160. Workshops on various topics were held in 1973, 1982 and 1984, addressing environmental issues and natural resources; in 1968, 1971 and 1980, focusing on economic issues; in 1978, exploring human rights; in 1983, examining the multicultural world; and in 1985, 1990 and 1992, delving into the UN System. Papers from these Workshops have been collected with other Academy publications in the *Colloques / Workshops – Law Books of the Academy* series. Publications in this series can be viewed at https://brill.com/display/serial/RADC (see below, footnote 162).

The controversial *South West Africa* judgment of the ICJ in 1966 likely opened the eyes of the Curatorium to this crucial aspect. In 1967, under the leadership of Wolfgang Friedmann, a Study Group was established, which resolved to initiate an External Programme and bring the Academy Courses programme to the Third World [161]. This successful endeavour aimed to reinforce the Academy's aspiration for universality while preserving the vulnerable unity of the discipline [162]. A similar initiative was undertaken during the Summer Courses programme, leading to a remarkable range of lectures on non-Western legal cultures [163],

---

161. The need for renewal was closely connected to the impact of the ICJ judgment in the *South West Africa* case of 18 July 1966. Third World countries harboured significant resentment towards the Western-centric nature of the Hague institutions. The call to actively engage with the non-Western legal world emerged from a meeting held in April 1967 in Bellagio, Italy, organised by a Study Group led by Wolfgang Friedmann. Participants included Boutros-Ghali, Dupuy, Jennings, Oda, Van Panhuys and representatives from the Carnegie Endowment, invited by Jessup. Hambro's Dag Hammarskjöld Seminars for young diplomats from so-called developing countries also served a similar purpose. Initially organised in The Hague from 1963 to 1966, the seminars later relocated to Uppsala. On 20 January 1968, a recently expanded Curatorium (increased from nine to fifteen members) passed the Constitution for the External Programme of the Academy. The first executives of the programme included Battifol, Boutros-Ghali, Castberg, Elias, Lachs, Ruda, Schachter, C. De Visscher and Yasseen. In collaboration with UNITAR, the United Nations Institute for Training and Research (established in 1963), programmes were implemented in Latin America, Asia, the Near East and Africa. For further information on the External Programme, visit see https://www.hagueacademy.nl/programmes/the-external-programme/.

162. The External Programme has significantly expanded beyond its original scope and has established itself as a global institutional exchange. In 2009, the Programme took place in China, followed by India in 2013 and Singapore in 2018. Another initiative launched by the Study Group in 1967, involving a series of Colloquia on topical issues, met with only moderate success. The series, which began in 1968 with a focus on international trade and continued with an emphasis on economic integration in 1971, saw fifteen subsequent editions until 2007 but experienced a decline after 1995. Publications in this series have since been folded in with other Academy publications, notably Workshops papers, into a single series (see above, footnote 160).

163. The Islamic law tradition was the subject of two courses during the first stage of the Academy's history, delivered by Cardahi and Rechid in 1937 (*RdC* 60). Milliot continued the discussion in 1949 (*RdC* 75), followed by Mahmassani in 1966 (*RdC* 117). Chacko addressed the Indian legal tradition in 1958 (*RdC* 93), while Sastry focused on the Hindu tradition in 1966 (*RdC* 117). In the same year, Jayatilleke discussed Buddhism (*RdC* 120), and Iriye covered Confucianism (*RdC* 120). Two decades later, in 1990, Wang Tieya (*RdC* 221) and Haopei Li (*RdC* 224) comprehensively reviewed the Chinese legal and cultural tradition. Xu (*RdC* 270) and Chen Weizuo (*RdC* 359) extensively explored the domain of Chinese private law in 1997 and 2012, respectively. Xu also revisited both domains in 2012 (*RdC* 355). The African tradition was initially addressed by Francescakis in 1964 (*RdC* 112), followed by Alexandrowicz in 1968 (*RdC* 123), Szaszy in 1973 (*RdC* 138), Uche in 1991 (*RdC* 228) and Boye in 1993 (*RdC* 238). The Latin American tradition was discussed by Valladao in 1952 (*RdC* 81), Vieira in 1970 (*RdC* 130), Parra-Aranguren in 1979 (*RdC* 164) and De Maekelt in 1982 (*RdC* 177).

and the world's main religions [164] and the issue of State succession [165].

During the Silver Jubilee in 1973, esteemed figures such as Frede Castberg, Philip Jessup, Eelco van Kleffens and Stefan von Verosta lovingly reminisced about the early decades of the Academy [166]. Alfred Von Verdross, Robert Y. Jennings and Alfred von Overbeck proudly reviewed the impressive collection of 140 volumes of *Collected Courses* published up to that point [167]. These reflections underscored the Academy's enduring commitment to excellence and its significant contributions to the field of international law.

3.3. The third stage (1990-2023)

The third stage in the Academy's history commenced with the conclusion of the Cold War era and the establishment of the Organization for Security and Co-operation in Europe ("OSCE"), aimed at revitalising the Helsinki Agreements of 1975. This momentous event marked a significant turning point in international affairs, opening up new horizons for the legal discipline. In 1989, in response to the era of

---

164. In 1925 (*RdC* 6), Goyau addressed the Catholic Church, and Boegner discussed Protestantism. In 1929, both returned to examine the missionary zeal of their creeds (*RdC* 26 and *RdC* 29, respectively). In 1976, Riedmatten reviewed the influence of Catholicism on the development of international law (*RdC* 151), while Kooijmans focused on Protestantism (*RdC* 152). Weil addressed Judaism in the same year (*RdC* 151).

165. The discourse on State succession began with courses of historical orientation by Paradisi in 1951 (*RdC* 78) and Von Verosta in 1964 (*RdC* 113). This was followed by courses by O'Connell and Bejaoui in 1970 (*RdC* 130).

166. As witnesses to their times (cf. Dupuy 1973, pp. 7-81), Castberg lectured three times at the Academy, in 1931 (*RdC* 35), 1933 (*RdC* 43) and 1973 (*RdC* 138); Jessup delivered four lectures in 1929 (*RdC* 29), 1956 (*RdC* 89), 1960 (*RdC* 99) and 1970 (*RdC* 129); Van Kleffens spoke in 1953 (*RdC* 82), and Von Verosta in 1964 (*RdC* 113). Van Kleffens served as Secretary-General from 1937 to 1939 and was a member of the Curatorium from 1947 to 1968. Jessup was on the Curatorium from 1957 to 1968. In the jubilee volume, edited by R.J. Dupuy in 1973, Boutros-Ghali reviewed the Centre for Studies and Research (pp. 137-157), and Secretary-General Dupuy discussed the External Programme (pp. 159-173). Boutros-Ghali served on the Curatorium from 1982 to 2016, while Dupuy was the Secretary-General from 1967 to 1984 and a member of the Curatorium from 1985 to 1997.

167. Von Verdross addressed legal theory in the early years of the Academy (Dupuy 1973, pp. 83-96). Jennings and Von Overbeck reviewed fifty years of public law (*ibid.*, pp. 99-115) and private law (*ibid.*, pp. 117-135), respectively. Von Verdross was a member of the Curatorium from 1931 to 1938 and from 1961 to 1976. He delivered five lectures: in 1927 (*RdC* 16), 1929 (*RdC* 30), 1931 (*RdC* 37), 1935 (*RdC* 52) and 1953 (*RdC* 83). Jennings lectured in 1949 (*RdC* 75) and 1967 (*RdC* 121), while Von Overbeck delivered lectures in 1961 (*RdC* 104), 1971 (*RdC* 132), and returned in 1992 (*RdC* 233). By the end of the period, in 1989, the *Recueil des Cours* covered approximately 220 volumes.

détente and the heightened activities at the ICJ, the PCA only came in gear with SG Jonkman in the late 1990s. The General Assembly declared the period 1990 to 1999 as the UN Decade of International Law [168]. At the Academy, this period will forever be associated with an esteemed alumnus, a former lecturer and by then a long-standing member of its Curatorium, who served as the Secretary-General of the UN from 1992 to 1997 [169]. Boutros Boutros-Ghali, the Egyptian diplomat, launched his Agenda for Peace upon his election in New York [170].

In 1993, as a response to the humanitarian crisis in the Balkans, Boutros-Ghali selected The Hague as the seat for the International Criminal Tribunal for the Former Yugoslavia ("ITCY"), citing the city's designation as the "Judicial Capital of the World". This landmark decision not only greatly enhanced The Hague's international prestige but also had a profound impact on its infrastructure. The city became home to numerous international courts, tribunals, governing bodies and research institutes. The influx of expats transformed the town, leading to a boom in international schools and establishing a multicultural community that set new social paradigms. The new *élan* also revitalised the PCA, which expanded its scope to include commercial arbitration [171]. The cross-fertilisation of disciplines greatly benefited research, exemplified by advancements in areas such as criminal law, with the establishment of the International Criminal Court ("ICC") [172], and chemical warfare, with the founding of the Organisation for the Prohibition of Chemical Weapons ("OPCW") [173]. Regional institutional bodies like Europol, Eurojust and the European Patent Office further enriched the discourse [174].

---

168. UN GA Res. 44/23, dated 17 November 1989.

169. Boutros-Ghali holds a prominent position in the annals of the Academy. He first came to The Hague as an auditor in 1954 and delivered lectures in 1960 (*RdC* 100), 1972 (*RdC* 137) and 2000 (*RdC* 286). He was elected member of the IDI in 1973 and served on the ILC from 1979 to 1991.

170. Boutros-Ghali's influential "Agenda for Peace" report, requested by the UN Security Council in January 1992 and presented in July that year, focused on preventive diplomacy, peace-making and peacekeeping. See https://digitallibrary.un.org/record/145749?ln=en.

171. This expansion into commercial arbitration (arbitration in *lex mercatoria*) was reflected in the courses offered by the Academy. Please refer to footnote 269 for more details.

172. The Rome Statute was adopted on 17 July 1998 and entered into force on 1 July 2002. The hearings of the ICC in The Hague were first launched in 2006.

173. The OPCW was established in The Hague in 1997 as the executive organ of the Chemical Weapons Convention (1992) when the Convention entered into force.

174. Europol, created as a result of the Treaty of Maastricht, has been operational in The Hague since July 1999. Its counterpart EU agency, Eurojust, has been operational in The Hague since 2003. The European Patent Office was founded in 1977 under

With the support of the Dutch Foreign Ministry and the Carnegie Foundation, spearheaded by Max van der Stoel and Peter Kooijmans, substantial investments were made in the Peace Palace's infrastructure. Structural repairs and extension projects, including the launch of the new Academy and Library Building [175], embodied this commitment. As a result, over the past twenty-five years, the Academy has provided its students, now totalling 650 annually, with a completely transformed learning environment and endless opportunities to explore their careers through critical engagement with a diverse community of like-minded colleagues.

In response to these developments, the Curatorium also embraced change and launched a series of new initiatives, earning widespread recognition for its efforts [176]. The surge of innovation began in the early 1990s with the introduction of courses on human rights [177]. In 2003, Geneviève Bastid-Burdeau (*née* Burdeau) or Bastid née Burdeau?, the first female Secretary-General (1999-2004), introduced a Seminar for Advanced Studies focused on topical key issues for legal professionals. In 2008, her successor, Yves Daudet (2005-2016), initiated the publication of a series of affordable French and English *Livres de Poche* or *Pocketbooks* to disseminate the knowledge gained from the Courses programme to a broader audience, a highly successful endeavour [178].

In 2015, the Curatorium introduced tailormade professional training courses as the Programmes on Demand [179]. The following year, crash

---

the auspices of the European Patent Organisation (established in 1977). While its headquarters are in Munich, it has a branch in The Hague (Rijswijk) and various sub-offices.

175. The construction of the new Academy and Library building was a response to the urgent request of the HCCH, the city's oldest institution, which experienced substantial growth in its membership. The building, designed by architects Michael Wilford and Manuel Schupp, was opened on 18 January 2007. It also houses the library stacks, which currently hold over a million volumes.

176. In its early years, the Academy received prestigious accolades such as the [Carnegie] Wateler Peace Prize in 1936 and 1950. In 1992, it was honoured with the renowned UNESCO Félix Houphouët-Boigny Peace Prize. Subsequently, the Brazilian Government (1999), Spanish Government (2000) and French Government (2001) bestowed further tokens of public recognition.

177. Despite a promising start, the courses on human rights gradually diminished due to financial constraints.

178. At the time of writing, the *Pocketbooks* series comprises approximately thirty-five volumes available in French and English. For more information on the *Pocketbooks*, please visit https://www.hagueacademy.nl/about-the-publications/. A list of volumes published to date can be found at https://brill.com/display/serial/HAPB.

179. In response to the Mexican Government's request in 2015, the Academy initiated training courses on human rights. Similarly, in 2019, the Academy addressed Thailand's request by launching courses on human trafficking and collaborated with the HCCH to organise courses for Californian judges. For further details about the

courses on European and comparative law were implemented. To crown the series of innovations and aspirations, in 2019, the Board, under the leadership of current Secretary-General Jean-Marc Thouvenin (since 2017), introduced the Winter Courses programme spanning three weeks [180], the "Day of Crisis" Competition [181] and the "Case of the Day" Lecture [182]. Adapting to Covid-19 restrictions, the Academy explored the use of Zoom conferences and the global broadcasting of the Courses programmes. Afternoon Lectures and Embassy Programmes were also introduced, and in collaboration with the ICC, a French Moot Court Competition on international criminal law was established [183].

The Curatorium also took significant steps to modernise itself, implementing restrictions on terms of office and introducing a maximum entrance age for membership [184]. This reflects yet another tangible sign of social progress: the gender ratio at the Academy. While women constituted only 10 per cent of the auditorium in 1923, female attendees now outnumber their male counterparts. Although the first course given by a woman, the American political scientist Sarah Wambough, took place as early as 1927 [185], the number of female lecturers remained relatively modest for a long time. Notable pioneers in the 1950s

---

Programmes on Demand, please refer to https://www.hagueacademy.nl/programmes-on-demand/.

180. On average, the Winter Courses attract approximately 350 students on-site and through global video attendance. To learn more about the Winter Courses, please visit https://www.hagueacademy.nl/programmes/the-winter-courses/.

181. The Day of Crisis Competition was initially established by Thouvenin at Paris Nanterre University in 2012. Since 2022, the competition has been organised at the Academy's premises. For additional information, please refer to https://www.hagueacademy.nl/day-of-crisis/.

182. The objective is to allow specialists to share their day-to-day experiences of case law with a broader audience. The first lecture presented as a "Case of the Day" was delivered by Mr Philippe Cavalieros in January 2019. For more details, please see https://www.hagueacademy.nl/2019/01/case-of-the-day-lecture-during-the-academys-first-winter-courses/.

183. "Le procès simulé devant la Cour pénale internationale" was a joint initiative of the French Embassy and the ICC, which received an immediate and positive response. In addition to the national (Dutch) Telders Moot Competition (established in 1977) and the internationally renowned Jessup Moot Competition (established in 1960), this initiative serves as a valuable addition to the specific domain of criminal law. For further information on the Moot Court Competition, please visit https://www.hagueacademy.nl/moot-court-competition/.

184. For more details on the process, refer to Von Verosta in Dupuy 1973, pp. 7-56 (specifically p. 51); Joor, 2013, p. 174; Joor, 2023, pp. 34-35. In 1995, membership in the Curatorium was reduced to three terms of six years; in 2018, it was further reduced to two terms. The maximum age limit was set at seventy. The term of office for the Secretary-General was also reduced to six years.

185. In 1927 (*RdC* 18), the American political scientist Sarah Wambough (1882-1955) delivered a lecture on "La pratique des plébiscites internationaux".

included Susanne Bastid and Denise Bindschedler in the 1960s[186]. Even in subsequent decades, female lecturers like Isabella Diederiks-Verschoor[187], Dame Rosalyn Higgins[188] and Geneviève Bastid-Burdeau[189] were the rare exception.. However, female lecturers are abundant today, and the Curatorium includes five women, including a World Court judge[190].

As such, the Hague Academy is exceptionally well-positioned in terms of infrastructure, transparency and dynamics to confidently embrace the new century. You, the students, have never had it so good! However, we should pose a question. Do the intellectual achievements of the past century justify all the investments made, and, more importantly, does the Academy's legacy warrant optimism? Having examined the Academy's history, let us now evaluate its intellectual substance and content in light of the original vision of its founding fathers.

---

186. Susanne Bastid is widely recognised as the first female judge *ad hoc* at the ICJ. In 1982, she represented Tunisia in the *Application for Revision and Interpretation of the judgment of 1982 in the Case concerning the Continental Shelf (Tunisia v. Libyan Arab Jamahiriya)*. Bastid delivered lectures at the Academy in 1951 (*RdC* 78), 1957 (*RdC* 92) and 1962 (*RdC* 107). Denise Bindschedler (1920-2008), a Swiss international lawyer, gave a lecture in 1968 (*RdC* 124).

187. Isabella Diederiks-Verschhor (1915-2017), an expert in air and space law, presented a lecture in 1981 (*RdC* 172).

188. Rosalyn Higgins delivered lectures in 1982 (*RdC* 176) and 1991 (*RdC* 230) before serving as a Judge (1995-2009) and President (2006-2009) of the ICJ. She will deliver the inaugural address at the official centenary ceremony of the Academy in the summer of 2023.

189. Geneviève Bastid-Burdeau lectured in 1988 (*RdC* 212) and later served as the Secretary-General of the Academy from 1994 to 1999. She was then invited to join the Curatorium.

190. Xue Hanqin, the Chinese ICJ Judge (2010-) and former Vice-President (2018-2021), served on the Curatorium from 2010 to 2016. She delivered a lecture in 2011 (*RdC* 355). Currently, Hilary Charlesworth, the Australian judge on the ICJ (2021-), is a member of the Curatorium.

CHAPTER 4

THE SUBJECT MATTER: THREE CATEGORIES OF COURSES

4.1. The first category: The core mission

The courses offered by the Academy can be categorised into three main areas. The first and most essential category revolves around the core mission of the discipline of international law itself. This includes examining its history [191] and sources [192], upholding its axioms and General Principles [193], defining its overarching theory and

---

191. Around twenty courses had a predominantly historical or retrospective focus, with most of them exploring matters related to the public sphere. Notable figures who lectured in these courses include Nippold (*RdC* 2), Boegner (*RdC* 4), Van der Vlugt (*RdC* 7), De Taube (*RdC* 11 and 67), Lange (*RdC* 13), Mirkine-Guetzévitch (*RdC* 22), Yepes (*RdC* 32), Barcia Trelles (*RdC* 32), Le Fur (*RdC* 41), Potter (*RdC* 64), Moreau-Reibel (*RdC* 77), Boissier (*RdC* 88), Oliver (*RdC* 88), Matine-Daftari (*RdC* 102), Dupuy (*RdC* 138), Fitzmaurice (*RdC* 138), Weil (Judaism, *RdC* 151), Riedmatten (Catholicism, *RdC* 151), Kooijmans (Protestantism, *RdC* 152), Skubiszewski (*RdC* 271) and Jia (*RdC* 382). In the private sphere, six courses had a historical or retrospective orientation, featuring lectures by Gutzwiller (*RdC* 29), Viera (*RdC* 130), Von Overbeck (*RdC* 233), McClean (*RdC* 233), Boggiano (*RdC* 233) and Struycken (*RdC* 271).
192. The sources of international law was a highly topical issue in these early years and reflected in the polemics on (the hierarchy of) sources within the ACJ in 1920. The theme continued to feature in courses right up into the twenty-first century. Scholars such as Heilborn in 1926 (*RdC* 11), Von Verdross in 1927 (*RdC* 16), Finch in 1935 (*RdC* 53) and Guggenheim in 1958 (*RdC* 94) addressed the history and interpretation of sources. In the same volume (*RdC* 94), Tammes proposed accepting the decisions of international organs as an additional source of law. The role of custom in comparison to conventional law was examined by Baxter in 1970 (*RdC* 129), Ferrari Bravo in 1985 (*RdC* 192), Bernhardt in 1987 (*RdC* 205), Mendelson in 1998 (*RdC* 272) and Dinstein in 2006 (*RdC* 322). It was at the Academy that Roberto Ago first presented his theory of "spontaneous" law in 1956 (*RdC* 90).
193. No less than fifty courses addressed matters of principle. Within the public domain, noteworthy courses during the first fifty years included Scott in 1932 (*RdC* 42), Kelsen in 1932 (*RdC* 42), Winiarski in 1933 (*RdC* 45), Von Verdross in 1935 (*RdC* 52), Rolin in 1950 (*RdC* 77), Guggenheim in 1952 (*RdC* 80), C. De Visscher in 1954 (*RdC* 86), Schwarzenberger in 1955 (*RdC* 87) and 1966 (*RdC* 117), Fitzmaurice in 1957 (*RdC* 92), Rousseau in 1958 (*RdC* 93), Sørensen in 1960 (*RdC* 101), Reuter in 1961 (*RdC* 103), Jennings in 1967 (*RdC* 121) and Virally in 1967 (*RdC* 122). Notable contributions in the private domain were made by Meijers in 1934 (*RdC* 49), Wortley in 1947 (*RdC* 71) and 1958 (*RdC* 94), Batiffol in 1959 (*RdC* 97), Graveson in 1960 (*RdC* 99) and 1963 (*RdC* 109), Yasseen in 1965 (*RdC* 116), Ehrenzweig in 1968 (*RdC* 124), Van Hecke in 1969 (*RdC* 126) and Lipstein in 1972 (*RdC* 135).

methodology [194] and, crucially, pursuing its reform [195], development and streamlining the codification process [196]. The Academy's remarkable legacy over the past century is particularly evident in its exceptional dedication to fulfilling these core assignments, aligning closely with the ambitions of the ILA and the IDI.

Indeed, as Jennings aptly noted in 1973, early luminaries of international law still "painted with a rather large brush" [197]. They felt obligated to solidify their position in society and reconcile the traditional divide between natural law and positivism. The introduction of the Academy's General Courses programme in 1929 marked a significant turning point, allowing for a more comprehensive and in-depth exploration of the discipline [198]. These courses, known as "Lighthouses of the Law", are unparalleled in their depth and serve as a reliable source for tracing the gradual shift in paradigms [199]. Across approximately sixty General Courses, the most influential issues that have shaped the discipline over the past century have been meticulously analysed and calibrated by some of the greatest luminaries it has produced [200]. Exploring these

---

194. To demonstrate the continuity of these endeavours, notable contributions include Triepel in 1923 (*RdC* 1), Cohn in 1939 (*RdC* 68), McDougal (*RdC* 82) and Kelsen (*RdC* 84) in 1953, Truyol y Serra in 1981 (*RdC* 173) and Schachter in 1982 (*RdC* 178).

195. For instance, Kunz in 1955 (*RdC* 88) explored the post-war crisis of the law, while Wright in 1959 (*RdC* 98) discussed strengthening the discipline.

196. The process of codification in public international law was examined by C. De Visscher in 1925 (*RdC* 6), Urrutia in 1928 (*RdC* 22), Liang in 1948 (*RdC* 73), Briggs in 1969 (*RdC* 126), Såhovic in 1972 (*RdC* 137), Treves in 1990 (*RdC* 223) and Daudet in 2003 (*RdC* 303).

197. Jennings in Dupuy 1973, pp. 99-115, at p. 102.

198. During the first decade of the Academy, courses generally consisted of a series of five lectures. However, the General Courses series, which began during the Hague Codification Conference (1930), initially comprised ten lectures and expanded to fifteen lectures from 1958 onwards. The first General Course in the public domain of law was delivered by Italian Arrigo Cavaglieri in 1929 (*RdC* 26). For a comprehensive overview, refer to Robert Kolb's work, *Les cours généraux de droit international de l'Académie de la Haye*, Brussels, Bruylant, 2003.

199. As Jennings concluded fifty years ago (Dupuy 1973, pp. 99-115, at p. 112), the continual reassessment of fundamental issues by successive generations of scholars and the divergent responses to identical questions and challenges have established the *Recueil des Cours* as a significant resource for verifying and potentially influencing the development of international law. The Academy's contribution to the field of law was examined by Lachs in 1976 (*RdC* 151) and by Struycken and Skubiszewski in 1998 (*RdC* 271).

200. Contemporary and prospective developments in the public domain were addressed by Schücking (*RdC* 20), Garner (*RdC* 35), Fischer Williams (*RdC* 44), Hostie (*RdC* 69), Liang (*RdC* 73), Lachs (*RdC* 92 and 169), Zourek (*RdC* 93), Ehrlich (*RdC* 105), Bereszkowski (*RdC* 128), Lauterpacht (*RdC* 152), Zhukov (*RdC* 161), Sinclair (*RdC* 167), Gotlieb (*RdC* 170), Higgins (*RdC* 176), Bowett (*RdC* 180), Nahlik (*RdC* 222), McRae (*RdC* 260), Boutros-Ghali (*RdC* 286) and Cançado Trindade (*RdC* 376). In the private sphere, see Yepes (*RdC* 32), Bentwich (*RdC* 49), Valladao

courses is akin to visiting a gallery of legal heroes, and every law student can assemble their own "Dream Team" and personal canon from these illustrious names [201].

These core issues were of utmost concern during the Academy's early years. Despite fifty years of in-depth research by the IDI and ILA and the experience gained from two Peace Conferences, the discipline was unprepared for the challenges posed by the League of Nations era. As a wealth of Academy courses demonstrates, it was an uphill battle to serve "two masters" and maintain a delicate balance between the expanding World Organisation and the conflicting interests of the major Powers. The discipline grappled with compelling nations to comply with the limitations and partial delegation of their once-sacrosanct sovereignty [202], as well as neutralising the deep-seated suspicions between the Great Powers and Small Powers in the Council and Assembly [203].

(*RdC* 133), Parra-Arranguren (*RdC* 164), Carbone (*RdC* 166), North (*RdC* 166), Gold (*RdC* 174), Lalive (*RdC* 181), Struycken (*RdC* 232) and Pfund (*RdC* 249).

201. On the public domain, such leading lights during the first stage of the Academy's history between the wars included Kelsen (*RdC* 14, 42 and 84), Brierly (*RdC* 23 and 58), Castberg (*RdC* 35, 43 and 138), Scelle (*RdC* 46 and 55), Von Verdross (*RdC* 16, 30, 37 and 52). In the second stage, between the Second World War and the fall of the Berlin Wall, equivalent stars of the field included Guggenheim (*RdC* 40, 74, 80 and 94), Morelli (*RdC* 61 and 89), Rousseau (*RdC* 73 and 93), Schwarzenberger (*RdC* 87 and 117) and C. De Visscher (*RdC* 6, 26, 52, 86 and 138.) Von Verdross served on the Curatorium from 1931 to 1938 and again from 1963 to 1976; C. De Visscher did the same from 1933 to 1972. Luminaries lecturing on the private domain in the interwar period included Ago (*RdC* 58 and 68), Arminjon (*RdC* 21, 44 and 74), Lewald (*RdC* 9, 29, 57 and 69) and Baron Nolde (*RdC* 3, 27, 39 and 55). In the next quarter-century, leading voices in this domain were Batiffol (*RdC* 72, 97, 120 and 139), Von Overbeck (*RdC* 104, 132, 176 and 233), Sperduti (*RdC* 90, 122 and 153), Graveson (*RdC* 99, 109 and 141), Yasseen (*RdC* 106, 116 and 151), Wengler (*RdC* 104 and 158), Van Hecke (*RdC* 106 and 126) and De Nova (*RdC* 104 and 118). Of these scholars, three served on the Curatorium: Ago (1963-1995), Batiffol (1962-1984) and Yasseen (1967-1981).

202. A standout moment was Nicolas Politis's remarkable course in 1925 (*RdC* 6) on the limitations of sovereignty. Known for his eloquence, as demonstrated through his frequent appearances as an agent before the PCIJ, Politis delivered intricate lectures and presented an innovative thesis effortlessly. In the same year, Gilbert Gidel (*RdC* 10) discussed the rights and duties of sovereign States. Andrassy addressed sovereignty and the League in 1937 (*RdC* 61). Following the Second World War, Reuter reignited the discussion in 1952 (*RdC* 81) with his course on the 1950 Schuman Plan, followed by Van Kleffens in 1953 (*RdC* 82), Korowicz in 1961 (*RdC* 102), Flory in 1974 (*RdC* 141), Sperduti in 1976 (*RdC* 153), Ben Achour in 1994 (*RdC* 245) and Carillo-Salcedo in 1996 (*RdC* 257). Reuter also explored the delegation of powers to the emerging European Communities in 1952 (*RdC* 81).

203. It should be noted that due to the persistent pessimism of the ACJ on the matter, the Commission decided to involve the National Groups of the PCA in the nomination (election) process of the judges of the PCIJ.

In confronting the far-reaching implications of the New World Order, lecturers at the Academy skilfully navigated the need to "serve two masters" and keep both perspectives in their sights. By focusing on the paramount players, they examined the theory of State, the rights and duties of the Powers [204], the protection of citizens and minorities [205], and the interaction between the private and public spheres [206], as well as the domestic and international realms of law [207]. They also delved into the League of Nations in at least two dozen courses [208], exploring topics such as the covenant [209] and collective security [210], and shedding light on the mandate system [211] – a precursor to the challenging process of trusteeship [212] and decolonisation. Another dozen courses were dedicated to the PCIJ [213], further highlighting the major issues of that period.

---

204. This topic was first addressed by Gidel in 1925 (*RdC* 10).

205. See Mandelstamm in 1923 (*RdC* 1).

206. It seems that the interwar generation of lawyers and legal scholars did not prioritise the interaction between the private and public domains. However, in a significant course in 1954 (*RdC* 85), Wortley first addressed this issue in the context of his time. For further exploration of various aspects, refer to later courses by Riphagen in 1961 (*RdC* 102), Kowalski in 2001 (*RdC* 288), Reed in 2003 (*RdC* 306), Beaumont in 2010 (*RdC* 340) and Hess in 2018 (*RdC* 388).

207. This theme was first addressed by Triepel in 1923 (*RdC* 1), and it has remained relevant to both the public and private domains. See Mestre in 1931 (*RdC* 38), Walz in 1937 (*RdC* 61), Scheuner in 1939 (*RdC* 68), P. de Visscher in 1952 (*RdC* 80), Mosler in 1957 (*RdC* 91), Van Panhuys in 1964 (*RdC* 112), Donner in 1965 (*RdC* 115), Sperduti in 1976 (*RdC* 153), Cassese in 1985 (*RdC* 192), Arangio-Ruiz in 1990 (*RdC* 225), Roucounas in 2002 (*RdC* 299), Lagrange in 2012 (*RdC* 356) and Cataldi in 2017 (*RdC* 386). Struycken observed (in Bardonnet 1998, pp. 63-104, at p. 66) that the interaction remains sub-optimal. Consequently, one would rarely find references to the Academy's courses in the decisions of national supreme courts.

208. See e.g. Wolfgast (*RdC* 60), Potter (*RdC* 64), Van Kan (*RdC* 66), Eagleton (*RdC* 76), Jenks (*RdC* 77), Kerno (*RdC* 78), Von Verdross (*RdC* 83), Lalive (*RdC* 84) and Dupuy (*RdC* 100). In the early years, significant topics covered the Red Cross Organization, with contributions from Borel (*RdC* 1), Pictet (*RdC* 76) and Ruegger (*RdC* 82). The International Labor Organization (ILO) was explored by Mahaim (*RdC* 4), Janouloff (*RdC* 51) and see also Wolf (*RdC* 121) and Valticos (*RdC* 123). Courses addressing issues of transport and communications include Dupuis (*RdC* 2), Hostie (*RdC* 40 and 78) and De Leener (*RdC* 55).

209. Like, for example, Schücking in 1927 (*Recueil des cours*, Vol. *RdC* 20), Rutgers in 1931 (*Recueil des cours*, Vol. *RdC* 38), and Kunz in 1932 (*Recueil des cours*, Vol. *RdC* 39).

210. See Bourquin in 1934 (*RdC* 49), Heilperin in 1939 (*RdC* 68) and, later, Jimenez de Arechaga (*RdC* 111) and Gross (*RdC* 138).

211. See the case of the *Nationality Decrees in Tunis and Morocco* (1923) and cf. Diena in 1924 (*RdC* 5), Rolin in 1927 (*RdC* 19), Bentwich in 1929 (*RdC* 29), Cardahi in 1933 (*RdC* 43) and Feinberg in 1937 (*RdC* 59).

212. See Vedovato in 1950 (*RdC* 76).

213. For courses covering the PCIJ, see above, footnote 119.

4.1.1. The appraisal of the World Court

By 1920, the discipline of international law was far from speaking with one voice. This was evident in the heated debates within the ACJ, which often led to personal conflicts regardless of the topic being discussed. However, nowhere was discord more apparent than when it came to the Rules of Law that the PCIJ was authorised to apply as sources [214]. The challenge of reconciling the conflicting perspectives of civil law and common law traditions, along with the *mésalliance* of judges from national courts and international law experts, proved to be an ongoing conundrum. The lack of a shared perspective undermined the *esprit de corps* and resulted in judgments and opinions significantly qualified by numerous dissenting opinions [215]. Additionally, throughout the League era, the legitimacy of the World Court's second mandate – to provide advisory opinions to the Council and Assembly – was consistently questioned [216].

Again, the League era was primarily focused on Europe, and the World Court exemplified this regional emphasis. Despite the ACJ's insistence on global composition and the inclusion of diverse cultural and legal traditions, the caseload of the PCIJ was largely determined by the aftermath of war and the repercussions of the contentious Paris Peace Treaties, which had redrawn the European map. As Van Kleffens concluded in 1973, the Curatorium was also trapped in this Eurocentrism, never transcending its limitations [217]. The Academy failed to initiate innovative thinking or consider non-Western legal sources, only changing its approach under external pressure and the traumatic experience of the decolonisation process in the 1960s.

Another notable challenge arose when the PCIJ was unexpectedly confronted with cases outside its traditional scope of public law. The Court's verdicts on the governance of international water-

---

214. See Eyffinger 2023, Vol. 1, chap. 15.5.
215. The Court's first ever judgment, in the *Wimbledon* dispute (1923), being a case in point; see Eyffinger 2023, Vol. 2, Part 2, Judges.
216. The idea of compulsory jurisdiction, introduced by the PrepCom of the League in 1919, was initially met with scepticism by members of the ACJ. However, its application before the PCIJ underwent substantial changes within a matter of years. For more information on the development of the idea, refer to the courses given by Hudson in 1925 (*RdC* 8), Salvioli in 1926 (*RdC* 12), C. De Visscher in 1929 (*RdC* 26) and Negulesco in 1936 (*RdC* 57).
217. For a slightly different assessment of the issue, refer to Skubiszewski in Bardonnet 1998, pp. 21-62, specifically page 31, where Dupuy's 1973 course (*RdC* 138) is cited.

courses [218], boundary disputes [219] and the interpretation of the Versailles Treaties [220] and their sequels all came within its "natural territory". But unanticipated issues such as mass migration, minority rights, discrimination, contested nationality [221], property confiscation and financial misconduct [222] pushed the Court well beyond its comfort zone. Despite stretching the concept of diplomatic protection to its limits [223], the Court often found itself powerless to address systemic social injustices [224]. To avoid denial of justice due to deficient international law [225], the Court resorted to interpreting national legislation and comparative law [226]. This predicament reignited the discourse on monism or dualism within the Academy, with prominent figures such as Heinrich Triepel, Hans Kelsen, Dionisio Anzilotti and Georges Scelle engaging in the debate [227].

---

218. The PCIJ dealt with four cases related to this area of law: *Wimbledon* (1923), *Jurisdiction of the European Commission of the Danube* (1927), *Jurisdiction of the Oder Commission* (1929) and *Diversion of Water from the Meuse* (1937).

219. Boundary disputes brought before the PCIJ involved conflicts between Poland and Czechoslovakia (1923), Albania and Serbia (1924), Turkey and Iraq (1925), Lithuania and Poland (1931, 1932), Norway and Denmark (1932, 1933) and Turkey and Italy (1933).

220. In numerous cases, the PCIJ addressed various aspects of treaty law, including the status of treaties, their interpretation, the performance of parties and the obligations they imposed on third parties. For a comprehensive list, see Eyffinger 2023, Vol. 2, Documents, chap. 20.

221. The PCIJ handled twenty-one cases covering a wide range of issues in a troubled Europe. Pertinent lectures at the Academy include Mandelstam in 1923 (*RdC* 1) and 1931 (*RdC* 38), Dumas in 1937 (*RdC* 59) and Feinberg in 1937 (*RdC* 59). The post-war era opened with Hersch Lauterpacht's famous course in 1947 (*RdC* 70). See above, footnote 129.

222. These were significant issues after the war and featured in no less than fifteen PCIJ cases.

223. Likewise, diplomatic protection and its limits featured in no less than fifteen PCIJ cases between 1924 and 1939.

224. For example, see the embarrassing observations made by Registrar Hammarskjøld in the *Yearbooks* of the PCIJ. For an assessment, see Eyffinger 2023, Vol. 2, Documents, chap. 7.

225. This dilemma had already been anticipated by Descamps in 1920. In his critique of the counterproductive *Quellenpurismus* advocated by extreme positivists, he proposed a hierarchy of sources and suggested "General Principles" such as *bona fides* or *res judicata*, along with jurisprudence and the consensus of prominent scholars, as subsidiary sources for the Court.

226. Within a few years, the Peace Palace Library, renowned as the world's leading collection of international law materials, proved inadequate in meeting the Court's needs for national legislation and comparative jurisprudence. This embarrassment resulted in an anomaly: in the 1930s, the PCIJ established a second library exclusively for the Court's use on its premises.

227. While Anzilotti advocated for a strict separation of spheres, Kelsen asserted the primacy of international law as a reflection of the "conscience juridique universelle" even in municipal law. In contrast, George Scelle argued for a distinct "domaine reserve". Triepel first addressed this issue at the Academy in 1923 (*RdC* 1), followed

In 1920, case law played a relatively marginal role. However, by 1940, the jurisprudence of the PCIJ encompassed approximately sixty cases and had become a significant source of analysis at the Academy. This brings us to a critical observation of broader significance. It appears that the Curatorium has always handled the World Court delicately, seldom acknowledging its low points or moments of acute crisis in Academy lectures [228]. This was true for cases like the German-Austrian *Zollverein* (1931) and *South West Africa* (1966), which led entire continents to shun The Hague for decades. Similarly, the opportunities presented by the Court's opinions in the *Nuclear Weapons* cases in the 1990s were perhaps not fully explored [229]. In 1973, Jennings suggested a similar "ostrich attitude" regarding the legal equality of States [230]. This reluctance may reflect a consistent policy, first established in Ghent in 1873, to keep politics at bay.

4.1.2. The rising phoenix of the Hague Conference

In a parallel world, the realm of private international law faced significant challenges, both externally and in terms of substance [231]. As we have observed, the first stage of the Academy's history between 1923 and 1939 was far from a harmonious era for the discipline. Private international law struggled due to the absence of a universally shared perspective, as exemplified by the prominence of national traditions. The discipline was burdened by the deep-seated divergence between

---

by Kelsen in 1926 (*RdC* 14) and 1932 (*RdC* 42), and Scelle in 1933 (*RdC* 46). Various aspects of the controversy were discussed by Mestre in 1931 (*RdC* 38), Walz in 1937 (*RdC* 61) and Scheuner in 1939 (*RdC* 68); see also Baker in 1927 (*RdC* 19). For a review, see Von Verdross in Dupuy 1973, pp. 83-96. In the UN era, Mosler in 1957 (*RdC* 91), Ténékidès in 1963 (*RdC* 110), Donner in 1965 (*RdC* 115), Miele in 1970 (*RdC* 131), Von Overbeck in 1971 (*RdC* 132), Ouchakov in 1974 (*RdC* 141) and Sperduti in 1976 (*RdC* 153) revived the discussion. In 1990, Arangio-Ruiz delivered a General Course on the "domaine réservé" (*RdC* 225).

228. The ICJ's role and record were the subjects of thirteen courses, which may not be considered a particularly impressive collection. These courses primarily focused on the Court's role within the UN System, jurisdictional matters and procedural issues. Notable courses include those by Bastid in 1951 (*RdC* 78) and 1962 (*RdC* 107), Kerno in 1951 (*RdC* 78), Briggs in 1958 (*RdC* 93), Gross in 1967 (*RdC* 120), Thierry in 1980 (*RdC* 167), Mbaye in 1988 (*RdC* 209), Oda in 1993 (*RdC* 244, a personal review), Torres Bernardes in 1995 (*RdC* 256), Bedjaoui in 1996 (*RdC* 257), Reisman in 1996 (*RdC* 258) and Abou-el-Wafa in 2009 (*RdC* 343). See footnotes 148 and 214.

229. Arangio-Ruiz initially addressed this issue in 1962 (*RdC* 107), and it was subsequently discussed at the Centre in 1993. Non-proliferation was examined by Goldblat in 1995 (*RdC* 256) and Shaker in 2006 (*RdC* 321).

230. Jennings in Dupuy 1973, p. 114.

231. See Von Overbeck in Dupuy 1973, pp. 117-135.

the theoretical and empirical-inductive methods of civil law and common law traditions. The lukewarm reception of the revived Hague Conferences in 1925 and 1928 reflected this ideological crisis [232]. The unresolved quandaries from the days of Asser and Mancini continued to persist [233]. However, in 1930, the discipline took a critical turn when René Cassin advocated for domicile rather than nationality as the key criterion [234]. The discipline deserves credit for engaging in vigorous debates that led to remarkable courses, such as Pierre Arminjon's critique of Antoine Pillet's 1925 thesis on acquired rights in 1933 [235] or Jacques Maury's attack on Roberto Ago's "extremist" theories in 1936 [236].

Everything changed in the early 1950s with the resurgence of the Conference System, the establishment of a Permanent Bureau in The Hague and the rapid expansion of codification efforts [237]. Lecturers recruited from among the Hague Conference delegations increasingly included practitioners and courses in English facilitated a focus on the Anglo-Saxon tradition. In 1947, private international law was elevated to a position more or less on par with public international law. A General Course on Private International Law was implemented, and the number of lectures expanded from ten to fifteen. The series commenced in 1958 with B. A. Wortley's magisterial course on codification [238], marking the beginning of an unprecedented period of creative thinking that spawned a plethora of conflicting theories on fundamental principles. Across four remarkable General Courses between 1948 and 1973, Henri Batiffol,

---

232. Cf. Nolde's comments from 1936 (*RdC* 55).
233. As illustrated by the positions taken by Isay in 1924 (*RdC* 5), Barbosa de Magelhaes in 1928 (*RdC* 23), Kunz in 1930 (*RdC* 31), Cassin in 1930 (*RdC* 34), Redslob in 1931 (*RdC* 37), Bentwich in 1934 (*RdC* 49) and 1955 (*RdC* 87), Louis-Lucas in 1938 (*RdC* 64) and Makarov in 1937 (*RdC* 60) and 1949 (*RdC* 74).
234. See Cassin in 1930 (*RdC* 34) and cf. Bentwich in 1934 (*RdC* 49).
235. Cf. Pillet in 1925 (*RdC* 8), Arminjon in 1933 (*RdC* 44) and the comment made by Von Overbeck in Dupuy 1973, pp. 117-135, at p. 122.
236. The discourse on monism and dualism also captured the attention of scholars in the private sphere. A notable exchange took place in 1936 between Ago (*RdC* 58), who proposed an extreme dualism, and Maury (*RdC* 57), who raised questions about it. For further analysis, refer to Von Overbeck in Dupuy 1973, pp. 117-135, at p. 124.
237. As mentioned in Chapter 2, the Seventh Session of the Hague Conference in 1951 introduced a new "modern style". The revised Statute adopted during this session came into force on 15 July 1955. Presently, the HCCH has ninety Member States and the EU, and since 1961, it has enacted forty conventions and instruments. See above, footnotes 104 to 106.
238. Wortley's General Course in 1958 (*RdC* 94) made a significant contribution. Moreover, his impressive involvement with the Academy included addressing the topic of expropriation in 1939 (*RdC* 67) and presenting an overview of the English position in 1947 (*RdC* 71).

in his pursuit of harmony through a comparative approach, addressed all aspects of methodology, including the interaction between public and private, international and municipal domains, engaging in an exceptionally stimulating exchange with Willem Riphagen, Ronald H. Graveson and George van Hecke [239]. Giuseppe Sperduti challenged Ago's pre-war monist theories [240], while Albert A. Ehrenzweig and Willis L. M. Reese engaged in polemics with Gerhard Kegel and Giorgio De Nova on choice of law [241].

4.2. The second category: Consistent concerns

Certain areas of law have consistently troubled the discipline and preoccupied lecturers at the Academy due to their profound impact on enduring human concerns. One of the most poignant among these is human rights, a topic that can be traced back to the Valladolid debate in 1550 [242]. As we have witnessed, the PCIJ grappled with disputes and questions related to minorities and refugees throughout its existence [243]. The violation of basic rights during the Second World War and deliberate acts of genocide prompted the establishment of global research bodies, treaties and documents, which subsequently inspired regional conventions, commissions and courts [244]. The Academy was actively engaged

---

239. Batiffol's presence was remarkable. He served as an auditor in 1930 and delivered lectures in 1948 (*RdC* 72), 1959 (*RdC* 97), 1967 (*RdC* 120) and 1973 (*RdC* 139). Additionally, he served on the Curatorium from 1962 to 1984. Riphagen proved to be a worthy counterpart, delivering lectures in 1961 (*RdC* 102) and returning on three subsequent occasions: 1970 (*RdC* 131), 1983 (*RdC* 182) and 1994 (*RdC* 246). He also served on the Curatorium from 1972 to 1994. Graveson lectured in 1960 (*RdC* 99), 1963 (*RdC* 109) and 1974 (*RdC* 141), while Van Hecke delivered lectures in 1962 (*RdC* 106) and 1969 (*RdC* 126).
240. Sperduti provided a comprehensive review of the general theory of the discipline. He re-evaluated Ago's previous positions in 1956 (*RdC* 90), 1967 (*RdC* 122) and notably in 1976 (*RdC* 153).
241. Ehrenzweig delivered a lecture in 1968 (*RdC* 124), while Reese presented lectures in 1964 (*RdC* 111) and 1976 (*RdC* 150). Reese served on the Curatorium from 1975 to 1990. Kegel lectured in 1964 (*RdC* 111), and De Nova delivered lectures in 1961 (*RdC* 104) and 1966 (*RdC* 118).
242. In the famous polemic between the Dominicans Bartolomé De Las Casas (1484-1566) and Juan Ginés de Sepúlveda (1490-1573) on the treatment of the native peoples of Latin America.
243. The Academy's keen interest in the issue is demonstrated by the courses of Mandelstam (*RdC* 1 and *RdC* 38), Vichniac (*RdC* 43), François (*RdC* 53), Dumas (*RdC* 59) and Feinberg (*RdC* 59). After the Second World War, the debate was rekindled by Ermacora (*RdC* 182), Vukas (*RdC* 231), Achour (*RdC* 245) and Van der Stoel (*RdC* 296). The PCIJ dealt with no less than twenty-one cases addressing minorities and resulting discrimination, covering Europe from the Baltic to the Balkans.
244. On the introduction of post-war instruments and how Academy courses covered them, see above, footnotes 129-133.

in analysing and discussing these developments [245]. The same holds for humanitarian issues and international criminal law [246].

Perhaps in no other field of study did lawyers of the early twentieth century experience such stern chastisement of their optimism and brutal shattering of their confidence as when they prematurely abandoned the laws of war [247] and renounced aggression [248]. The hubris regarding the disciplinary reach and the influence of a mere paper ban on State policies was epitomised in the Kellogg-Briand Pact of 1928. Even after a second cataclysm, the theme was only reluctantly revisited in 1945, as lamented by Eelco van Kleffens (1973) and Krzysztof Skubiszewski (1998) in their commemorative reviews [249]. In recent decades, the challenges posed by the exclusive use of force by the Powers, issues of civil war, tribal conflicts and terrorism have only broadened the spectrum of aggressive acts and complicated the discourse.

---

245. Approximately thirty-three courses highlight the enduring relevance of these issues, including Lauterpacht (*RdC* 70), Balogh (*RdC* 75), Cassin (*RdC* 79 and *RdC* 140), Van Heuven Goedhart (*RdC* 82), Mirkine (*RdC* 83), Hamburger (*RdC* 97), Golsong (*RdC* 110), Schnyder (*RdC* 114), Ermacora (*RdC* 124), Migliazza (*RdC* 137), Vasak (*RdC* 140), Schreiber (*RdC* 145), Gros Espiell (*RdC* 145 and *RdC* 218), Arangio-Ruiz (*RdC* 157), Uribe Vargas (*RdC* 184), Cançado Trindade (*RdC* 202), Pastor Ridruejo (*RdC* 228), Rideau (*RdC* 265), Moulay Rchid (*RdC* 268), Matscher (*RdC* 270), Meron (*RdC* 301), Kinsch (*RdC* 318), Carlier (*RdC* 332), Pisillo Mazzeschi (*RdC* 333), Beaumont (*RdC* 335), Ortiz Ahlf (*RdC* 369), Najurieta (*RdC* 376), Marrella (*RdC* 385), Novak (*RdC* 392), Chinkin (*RdC* 395) and Shany (*RdC* 409).

246. The call for an international criminal court was first raised in 1920 by ACJ President Descamps (see above, footnote 133). However, it was cursorily dismissed by the Council and the Assembly of the League, mainly for the lack of a proper code of law: *nulla poena sine lege*. See Eyffinger 2023, Vol. 1, chap. 19.2.

247. An issue explicitly addressed only twelve times in the interwar period by Higgins (*RdC* 11), Van Eysinga (*RdC* 16), Werner (*RdC* 21), Wehberg (*RdC* 24 and *RdC* 63), Descamps (*RdC* 31), Brouckère (*RdC* 50), McNair (*RdC* 59), Efremoff (*RdC* 59), Smith (*RdC* 63), Baldoni (*RdC* 65) and Sandiford (*RdC* 68). Cf. footnote 116.

248. Only one course explicitly addressed the concept of aggression during the first stage of the Academy's history: Fischer Williams in 1930 (*RdC* 34). However, in the post-war era, it appears in Komarnicki (*RdC* 75), Zourek (*RdC* 92), Schwebel (*RdC* 136) and Broms (*RdC* 154).

249. As previously mentioned, former Dutch Foreign Minister Van Kleffens had been involved with the League and the Academy since its inception. In 1973, he regretted this lack of interest (in Dupuy 1973, pp. 65-80, at p. 80). However, it is worth noting the courses by Gardot (*RdC* 72), Marina Luna (*RdC* 92), Jessup (*RdC* 99), Röling (*RdC* 100), Pinto (*RdC* 114), Fischer Williams (*RdC* 133), Bogdanov (*RdC* 133), Migliazza (*RdC* 137), Klafkowski (*RdC* 149), Draper (*RdC* 164), Nahlik (*RdC* 164), Abi-Saab (*RdC* 165) and Ronzitti (*RdC* 242). In 1998, Skubiszewski (Bardonnet 1998, pp. 21-62, at 56-57) made similar observations regarding the ambiguity surrounding internal conflicts with external implications, referring to Wehberg's course on civil war from 1938 (*RdC* 63).

Another classical domain of study, with roots tracing back to the origins of modern international law [250], revolves around the law of the seas [251]. The discourse gained momentum in the 1950s when the legal complexities of modern technology became apparent. Conundrums encompassed the territorial sea [252], the Continental Shelf [253], the exclusive economic zones [254], islands [255], fisheries [256], the seabed [257], and the quest for natural resources and minerals [258]. The pursuit of the Arctic, Antarctic and polar regions followed suit [259]. It is no coincidence that these quandaries were among the first addressed by the ILC. Decades of research and diplomacy culminated in the United Nations Convention on the Law of the Sea ("UNCLOS"), which was concluded in Montego Bay in 1982 [260]. Throughout this period, maritime boundary disputes continued to occupy the World Court [261], leading to the establishment of the International Tribunal for the Law of the Sea (ITLOS) in Hamburg in 1982 [262].

Yet another domain that has consistently captured interest is reflected in the frequency of courses offered at the Academy. The search for progressive economic integration as a recognised instrument to foster peace and harmony has spearheaded nineteenth-century legal thought [263].

---

250. The debate between Grotius (*Mare Liberum*, 1609) and Selden (*Mare Clausum*, 1635) on the freedom of the seas during the early period of British-Dutch economic and colonial rivalry led to bilateral conferences in London (1613) and The Hague (1615).
251. The discourse on this matter at the Hague Academy spanned from Jessup in 1929 (*RdC* 29) to Oda in 1969 (*RdC* 127), Treves in 1990 (*RdC* 223) and Scovazzi in 2000 (*RdC* 286).
252. See Wilson in 1923 (*RdC* 1) and Gidel in 1934 (*RdC* 48).
253. See Mouton in 1954 (*RdC* 85) and Marotta Rangel in 1985 (*RdC* 194).
254. Discussed by Orrego Vicuna in 1986 (*RdC* 199).
255. Reviewed by Murphy in 2016 (*RdC* 386).
256. As illustrated by the courses by Gros in 1959 (*RdC* 97) and Fleischer in 1988 (*RdC* 209).
257. Cf. the course by Paolillo in 1984 (*RdC* 188).
258. Successively addressed by Gros (*RdC* 97), Oda (*RdC* 127), Elian (*RdC* 149), Brownlie (*RdC* 162), Francioni (*RdC* 260) and Bothe (*RdC* 318).
259. These highly contested but vulnerable regions were discussed by Mouton (*RdC* 107), Guyer (*RdC* 139), Pharand (*RdC* 163) and Francioni (*RdC* 260).
260. The UNCLOS Convention was examined by Marrotta Rangel in 1985 (*RdC* 194), Evensen in 1986 (*RdC* 199), Caminos in 1987 (*RdC* 205), Symonides in 1988 (*RdC* 208) and Simmonds in 1989 (*RdC* 218).
261. For example, the disputes concerning the Continental Shelf between Greece and Turkey (submitted in 1976), the Tunisia-Libya dispute (1979), and the Canada-USA dispute concerning delimitation in the Gulf of Maine (1982).
262. The decision to establish the ITLOS Tribunal was made during the Third UNCLOS Conference. The Tribunal was officially formed on 19 December 1982, in accordance with the Montego Bay Convention, which came into effect on 16 November 1994.
263. This idea traces its roots back to the British and Belgian associations of the 1860s (see above, footnote 37) and was formally adopted by the ILA in 1873. Courses

Around thirty-five lecturers have addressed international commerce [264], while many more have delved into finance, investments [265] and monetary issues [266]. After the celebrated *Island of Palmas* case (1928) the PCA became virtually obsolete and State arbitration lost its appeal [267]. Still, commercial arbitration was a significant asset at the Academy from first to last. Its entrance into this field of arbitration in the 1990s occasioned the revitalisation of the PCA [268].

The topics mentioned above, of course, represent only a partial overview. Third World issues and underdevelopment have persistently captivated legal minds at the Academy over the past six decades [269]. Related to these concerns are emerging challenges that are bound

---

covering this theme span all three stages of the Acasdemy's history: Kaufmann (*RdC* 3), Milhaud (*RdC* 15), Da Veiga Simões (*RdC* 35), Patterson (*RdC* 37), Aftalion (*RdC* 39), Rappard (*RdC* 61), Heilperin (*RdC* 68), Röpke (*RdC* 86), Sereni (*RdC* 96), Hyde (*RdC* 105), Spofford (*RdC* 113), Schwarzenberger (*RdC* 117), Feliciano (*RdC* 118), Ustor (*RdC* 134), Jenks (*RdC* 138), Aramburú (*RdC* 150), Seidl-Hohenfeldern (*RdC* 163, *RdC* 198), Kalénsky (*RdC* 208), Piontek (*RdC* 236), Murase (*RdC* 253), Fallon (*RdC* 253), Smits (*RdC* 300), Kessedjian (*RdC* 300), Nennouma (*RdC* 300), Muir Watt (*RdC* 307), Buxbaum (*RdC* 399), and Wouters (*RdC* 407).

264. A selection of which includes: Nolde (*RdC* 3), Niemeyer (*RdC* 4), Kuhn (*RdC* 8), Fedozzi (*RdC* 10), Higgins (*RdC* 30), Travers (*RdC* 32), De Balás (*RdC* 51), Skapsi (*RdC* 136), Elian (*RdC* 149), Rasjski (*RdC* 174), Long (*RdC* 182), Chemaly (*RdC* 209), Strenger (*RdC* 227), Kessedjian (*RdC* 300), Draetta (*RdC* 314), Kronke (*RdC* 369), Bonell (*RdC* 388) and Gama (*RdC* 406).

265. On (the protection of) investments, see Shawcross (*RdC* 102), Broches (*RdC* 136), Nwogugu (*RdC* 153), Adede (*RdC* 180), Shihata (*RdC* 203), El Chiati (*RdC* 204), Juillard (*RdC* 250), Sacerdoti (*RdC* 269), Leben (*RdC* 302), Alvarez (*RdC* 344), Lamm (*RdC* 354) and Parra (*RdC* 374).

266. Monetary issues first entered the debate with Sulkowski in 1929 (*RdC* 29) and Griziotti in 1934 (*RdC* 49). Later reviews include Malaurie in 1978 (*RdC* 160), Gold in 1982 (*RdC* 174), Bastid-Burdeau in 1988 (*RdC* 212), Gianvilli in 1989 (*RdC* 215), Carreau in 1998 (*RdC* 274), Smits in 2002 (*RdC* 300) and Sorel in 2020 (*RdC* 404).

267. The gamut of courses on this theme is meagre: Schindler in 1928 (*RdC* 25), Makowski in 1931 (*RdC* 36), De Taube in 1932 (*RdC* 42) and Carabiber in 1950 (*RdC* 76). In later decades, two PCA Secretaries-General addressed their institution: François in 1955 (*RdC* 87) and Jonkman (*RdC* 279); the latter was a major player in the institution's revival.

268. Some fifteen courses assessed arbitration within the *lex mercatoria*: Carabiber (*RdC* 99), Lalive (*RdC* 120), Sanders (*RdC* 145), Luzzato (*RdC* 157), Lebedev (*RdC* 158), Hascher (*RdC* 279), Grigera Naón (*RdC* 289), Fernandez Rosas (*RdC* 290), Radicati (*RdC* 315), Cordero Moss (*RdC* 372), Boele-Woelki (*RdC* 379), Costin (*RdC* 394), Jacquet (*RdC* 396), Chedly (*RdC* 400) and Dasser (*RdC* 402). See also Struycken in Bardonnet 1998, pp. 63-104, at p. 85.

269. However, the patent needs of developing countries have received relatively less attention in comparison. The discussions at the Academy commenced with Zemanek's courses in 1965 on State succession in the context of the decolonisation process (*RdC* 116). For various perspectives on this issue, refer to Adede in 1982 (*RdC* 180), Mahiou in 1993 (*RdC* 241) and the exploration of related topics in the Centre for Studies and External Programmes.

to endure. These include the pursuit of a balance between ecology and economy within the concept of sustainable development [270], as well as concerns for the global environment and climate change [271]. The demands of modern society and the repercussions of high-tech trade and industry have put all four elements in jeopardy. The scarcity of drinking water has turned it into a precious commodity, while pollution has made clean air increasingly scarce. The earth is burdened by the ever-increasing needs of our global population, which now stands at eight billion. Moreover, the unrestrained use of fossil energy is igniting the fire of climate change, steadily heating our planet.

4.3. The third category: The handmaiden of science

If the subject matter of Academy courses in the first category undoubtedly resides within the comfort zone of legal scholarship, in the second category, lawyers and scholars can to some extent rely on the foundation laid by their predecessors. However, the third and final category delves into mostly unfamiliar enquiries and unchartered territory, compelling lawyers to venture far beyond their established boundaries. These areas revolve around the legal oversight of technological advancements, which inherently require international monitoring. The trajectory of social progress is unpredictable and challenging to navigate. It necessitates continuous mental adaptation and innovative applications of the law. From a purely technical standpoint, the role of law in this domain is somewhat limited. Our discipline primarily serves as an auxiliary, a handmaiden to science, aiming to channel the turbulent currents of change [272]. However, the normative role of international lawyers becomes especially relevant as they seek to establish an ethical framework for the moral dilemmas arising from scientific endeavours and their occasional aberrations.

---

270. See notably Schrijver in 2007 (*RdC* 329).
271. Successive courses by Bilder (*RdC* 144), Yturriaga (*RdC* 162), Barboza (*RdC* 247), Murase (*RdC* 253), Von Bar (*RdC* 268), Wolfrum (*RdC* 272), Fitzmaurice (*RdC* 293), Bothe (*RdC* 318), Schrijver (*RdC* 329), Rajamani (*RdC* 404), Brunnée (*RdC* 405) and Maljean-Dubois (*RdC* 407) have explored this issue.
272. The interplay between science and law was first examined in principle by Bourquin in 1947 (*RdC* 70) and later by Mouton in 1966 (*RdC* 119). The development of international law as a scientific discipline was addressed by Ago in 1956 (*RdC* 90) and Ehrlich in 1962 (*RdC* 105).

The journey began in the 1920s with the emergence of labour law [273], air law and, subsequently, outer space law and celestial bodies [274]. As discussed earlier, the law of the sea presented a myriad of technical challenges in the 1950s. Over time, other issues arose, such as atomic energy [275], nuclear arms [276] and nuclear proliferation [277]. In recent decades, a rapid succession of novel enquiries necessitated legal intervention, including terrorism [278], the protection of cultural heritage in conflict zones [279], environmental concerns [280], sustainable development [281], women's rights [282], biodiversity [283], climate change and pandemics [284]. At The Hague, the proliferation of the international judiciary posed challenges due to the lack of clear demarcation of competencies, leading to forum shopping by parties. Future quandaries are likely to revolve around artificial intelligence and the energy crisis.

One disconcerting aspect is the ever-changing nature of these challenges. Some emerge naturally as a consequence of growth, such

---

273. From its early days, the PCIJ faced a barrage of requests for advisory opinions from the ILO. In total, the Court dealt with five cases involving labour law between 1922 and 1932.
274. Notable contributions in this field of study include the courses by F. De Visscher (*RdC* 48), Sandiford (*RdC* 68), Pépin (*RdC* 71), Goedhuis (*RdC* 81), Lachs (*RdC* 113), Bentivoglio (*RdC* 119), Berezowski (*RdC* 128), Matte (*RdC* 166), Zhukov (*RdC* 161), Marcoff (*RdC* 168), Diederiks-Verschoor (*RdC* 172), Gorove (*RdC* 181) and Cachard (*RdC* 373).
275. Explored by Charlier in 1957 (*RdC* 91), Arangio-Ruiz in 1962 (*RdC* 107) and further discussed by the Centre in 1993.
276. Examined by Arangio-Ruiz in 1962 (*RdC* 107) and Garcia Robles in 1971 (*RdC* 133).
277. Noteworthy contributions include Goldblat in 1995 (*RdC* 256) and Shaker in 2006 (*RdC* 321). For a review, see Skubiszewski in Bardonnet 1998, pp. 21-62, at pp. 55-56. It is worth noting that the ICJ's inability in 1996 to reach a consensus on an absolute ban on the use of nuclear weapons attracted significant criticism.
278. See Sottille in 1938 (*RdC* 65), Guillaume in 1989 (*RdC* 215) and Klein in 2006 (*RdC* 321).
279. See Nahlik in 1967 (*RdC* 120), Prott in 1989 (*RdC* 217), Frigo in 2014 (*RdC* 375) and the Centre in 2008 and 2013.
280. See Struycken in Bardonnet 1998, pp. 63-104, at p. 87 and cf. the successive courses by Bilder (*RdC* 144), Yturriaga (*RdC* 162), Galenskaya (*RdC* 198), Prott (*RdC* 217), Siehr (*RdC* 243), Barboza (*RdC* 247), Murase (*RdC* 253), Bar (*RdC* 268), Wolfrum (*RdC* 272), Fitzmaurice (*RdC* 293), Bothe (*RdC* 318) and Brunnée (*RdC* 405). Keen interest in this area is also evidenced by the publications of the Centre in 1985, 2001, 2002, 2005, 2006 and 2011, as noted in footnote 159.
281. An issue also triggered by the *Gabčikova-Nagymaros* case before the ICJ in 1997. See Murase in 1995 (*RdC* 253), Wolfrum in 1998 (*RdC* 272), Bothe in 2005 (*RdC* 318) and Schrijver in 2007 (*RdC* 329). See also the *Pocketbook* by N. Schijver, titled *The Evolution of Sustainable Development in International Law: Inception, Meaning and Status* (2008).
282. First addressed by the Centre in 2016.
283. See Maljean in 2020 (*RdC* 407).
284. See Rajamani in 2020 (*RdC* 404).

as the establishment of international and regional organisations. Others stem from technological innovations, like the legal implications surrounding the Continental Shelf and the exclusive economic zone. Some challenges manifest dramatically, as seen with the emergence of human rights and genocide issues following the Holocaust. Others gradually capture our attention as they expose the blind spots created by outdated ideologies. Environmental concerns, climate change, fossil fuel dependency and water resource management exemplify this phenomenon. Furthermore, some challenges are self-inflicted due to our obstinate resistance to change, as seen in the decolonisation process and gender issues.

While certain challenges can be effectively addressed, others, like the nuclear threat, prove difficult to define or contain within legal parameters. Some quandaries, in retrospect, prove to be ephemeral or transitional, becoming dated or obsolete as scientific progress marches forward. Nevertheless, their immediate impact at the time might have been significant [285]. Conversely, some challenges continue to grow in scale and encompass broader issues, such as data protection and privacy concerns. In such instances, intuition and timing are crucial. As the old-age adage goes, "Life precedes the law." [286] However, one cannot impede the arrival of spring. The law must remain vigilant, adaptable and open-minded. And this principle holds particularly true for a renowned institution like the Hague Academy, whose independent status allows it to operate on the cutting edge of existing and evolving laws, leveraging its global prestige to make a meaningful impact through its findings.

---

285. An illustrative example is the discussion at The Hague in 1899 regarding war balloons and the so-called dumdum bullets.
286. The adage is attributed to Benjamin Cardozo (1870-1938) and can be found in his work *The Growth of the Law* (1924).

CHAPTER 5

AN ASSESSMENT

So, how should we conclude? After one hundred years, what have been the strengths and weaknesses of The Academy of International Law? Without a doubt, the founding fathers of the Academy established an excellent and sustainable formula in terms of organisation and infrastructure, which has consistently proven its enduring value over the past century. The Curatorium, with its shared purpose and close ties to research bodies like the IDI, ILA and ILC [287], and its reliance on the recruitment of distinguished individuals from the ICJ and HCCH, has ensured that the scientific board of the Academy has always been composed of the best minds in both the public and private law. The Academy's prestige and global network have attracted the most eminent scholars and inspired gifted students to gravitate towards The Hague, creating an unmatched connection between generations. As we have seen, several inspired auditors have returned to the Academy at various stages of their careers to deliver lectures and in turn inspire new students. The references to earlier courses by lecturers further reinforce this sense of continuity. Van Kleffens and Struycken called the passing of the inextinguishable torch of knowledge from one generation to the next the perfect symbol of the institution [288].

The Academy is driven by two key aspirations: education and research. The Courses programme serves as a means of achieving the first objective, while the publication of the *Collected Courses* fulfils the second. However, it is worth considering a suggestion in this context. One of the greatest assets of the Courses programme is the invaluable personal contacts and exchange of ideas between generations and cultures made in the Academy's fully equipped conference hall on the grounds of the Peace Palace, shared with many judicial organs and legal institutions. But the world is constantly evolving. A century ago, war led to an overhaul of all social parameters and labour conditions, most notably for women [289]. In today's world, the Covid-19 pandemic

---

287. Nico Schrijver, a current member of the Curatorium, recently referred to the "Four Sisters" of the Academy, the IDI, ILA and ILC. See Schrijver 2023.

288. To paraphrase Van Kleffens in Dupuy 1973, pp. 65-81, at p. 75 and cf. Struycken in Bardonnet 1998, pp. 63-104, at p. 69.

289. Various cases presented by the ILO to the PCIJ, including those concerning the working conditions of women, vividly highlighted these dilemmas, as mentioned above in footnote 274.

has had irreversible consequences of comparable scale on social interactions, ushering in a period of forced isolation from which we are only now emerging at different speeds and in different ways across the world. Amid restrictions on movement, advancements in technology provided a silver lining by enabling the inclusion of students from around the globe through Zoom conferences. In many areas of life, such digital solutions have persisted, either complementing or replacing in-person communication. Back in 1967, the Academy established a Study Group to launch the External Programme and bring its work to the world's underdeveloped nations [290]. One proposal worth exploring is to establish a similar study group or taskforce that can assess all options and optimise the global impact of the Academy's precious tradition, by finding a balance between the traditional in-person format and the benefits of digital connectivity.

Now, let us assess the scholarly pursuits undertaken by the Academy and the substantive content of its Courses programme. We have already provided ample evidence of their profound relevance. However, can we claim that these four hundred courses comprehensively cover the breadth of legal knowledge? Perhaps not entirely. Nevertheless, it is arguable that the Curatorium has consistently displayed a forward-thinking vision in anticipating future demands [291]. It has repeatedly demonstrated its capacity to transcend doctrinal, political and even ideological barriers [292] to pursue collaborative partnerships [293]. The courses, widely regarded as a reliable barometer of the field's social consciousness, have time and again served as catalysts for opening new

---

290. See Section 3.2 above.
291. Cf. Skubiszewski in Bardonnet 1998, pp. 21-62, at pp. 35-36. In 1973 (*RdC* 138), Dupuy distinguished the elements of "révélation" and "anticipation".
292. For example, during the years Walter Schücking struggled against Nazi opposition at the ICJ (1931-1935), the Nazi regime was represented in Court cases by lawyers Gleispach and Grimm. Similarly, at the Academy, National Socialist lawyer Baron Axel Freytagh-Loringhoven delivered lectures in 1936 (*RdC* 56) alongside individuals marginalised by the Nazi regime, such as Kaufmann (*RdC* 54), Lewald (*RdC* 9, 29, 57 and 69), Nussbaum (*RdC* 43) and Strupp (*RdC* 8, 33 and 47). In the immediate post-war years, the Curatorium invited Soviet scholars to present their views. Throughout the Cold War era, communist ideology was strongly represented by Judge Krylov, a committed Stalinist, and explored in successive lectures by Tunkin and Lebedev. Krylov first discussed the Soviet Doctrine in 1947 (*RdC* 70). Tunkin delivered lectures in 1958 (*RdC* 95) and, following the implementation of the Brezhnev Doctrine (named after the Soviet General-Secretary, 1964-1982), returned in 1966 (*RdC* 119), 1975 (*RdC* 147) and 1989 (*RdC* 219). Tunkin served on the Curatorium from 1969 to 1993. Lebedev lectured in 1977 (*RdC* 158). In 1990, Orlov (*RdC* 221) and Carpenter (*RdC* 222) compared the communist and capitalist perspectives on joint enterprises. For more on these issues, refer to Skubiszewski in Bardonnet 1998, pp. 21-62, at pp. 32-33, 42-43.
293. See the courses given by Såhovic and Arangio-Ruiz in 1972 (*RdC* 137).

pathways and highlighting emerging trends, thanks to the pivotal role played by lecturers. But lawyers, like anyone else, are children of their times. Even the Curatorium itself may exhibit certain inclinations or biases. As Struycken noted during the jubilee celebrations in 1998 [294], alongside prominent scholars who frequently delivered lectures, there were also noticeable absences [295]. The same holds in terms of subject matter. At the PCIJ, a clear Eurocentric perspective led to waning interest from non-European judges, resulting in their frequent absence [296]. It remains unclear whether this predicament ever concerned the Curatorium, and the issue was never raised in the courses.

How should we evaluate the fulfilment of the Academy's original purpose and core mission, which is the promotion of the rule of law in global society and the development and codification of the discipline of international law? In our earlier discussions, we highlighted the Academy's role in complementing and evaluating the practices of courts and diplomatic circles through theoretical norms and standards [297]. It is crucial to distinguish between public and private law in this regard. The private sphere, which aims to reconcile conflicting legal traditions and has been central to The Hague's tradition since the 1890s, has experienced mixed results. During the first stage of the Academy's history (1923-1939), the courses predominantly acknowledged conceptual dilemmas and national variations rather than challenging them. At that time, proactive approaches or pre-emptive measures were not the Curatorium's defining characteristics. It was only in the mid-1950s, with Max Gutzwiller's external initiative, that the field truly regained its momentum. From that point onwards, however, the Curatorium and the HCCH engaged in a highly stimulating exchange of ideas that

---

294. On 9 November 1998, a special session took place in the Great Court Hall of the Peace Palace. In addition to speeches by Judge N. Valticos, the President of the Curatorium, and Mr S. Royer, the President of the Carnegie Stichting and the Administrative Council of the Academy, Prof. K. Skubiszewski, the then President of the Iran-USA Claims Tribunal, and Prof. A. V. M. Struycken from Nymegen University, reviewed the public and private domains from 1923 to 1998.
295. Regarding the private sphere, Struycken highlighted certain patterns of attendance and absence, as mentioned earlier (see footnote 70). Similarly, the representation of judges on the ICJ appears somewhat imbalanced.
296. A few statistics illustrate this point. Judge Altamira was absent from seven successive sessions between 1931 and 1935. Judge De Bustamante missed twenty-four of the thirty-five Court sessions before his departure in 1935. Judge Pessôa attended only six of the sixteen sessions until 1931. Judge Moore was absent from six of the fourteen sessions, while Judge Kellogg attended just three of the sixteen sessions during his term.
297. See above, footnote 20.

fulfilled the Academy's purpose of connecting theory with practice and enriching legal life with doctrinal wisdom.

This leads us to the observation that the realm of law, despite the steadfast aspirations of the IDI, can never wholly extricate itself from politics. Thinking it can, is precisely the delusion that has been the Academy's Achilles heel. Its ambitious objective was to implement the rule of law and establish peace and social justice under a unified framework [298]. This was what initially prompted lawyers to intervene in the social process in the 1870s and serves as the shared motto of both the Institut de droit international and the Academy: "Justitia et Pace." However, the unpredictable forces of geopolitics pose a formidable obstacle to rational scholarship. This ambition had its pitfalls, as evidenced by the events of 1920 and 1929 when successive Advisory Committees of Jurists, despite their extensive knowledge, found themselves outmanoeuvred by astute politicians. In 1928, there was a fleeting moment of hubris when lawyers genuinely believed they were making significant progress. At the time, the Curatorium, bolstered by confidence in the collective security system, deemed the laws of war and neutrality beyond its purview. Unfortunately, this turned out to be a fallacy. Nevertheless, by faithfully documenting the ebb and flow of the discipline, its aspirations and setbacks, and its visionary ideas alongside its myopic moments, the *Collected Courses* stand as a remarkably dependable treasure trove for retracing how legal scholars have interpreted the world and assessing the influence of law over the past century.

One intriguing aspect of the Curatorium's policy that catches the attention of modern observers is the founding fathers' vision for the Academy. They intended it to go beyond serving the law and actively engage in other domains. The Academy's Statute states its objective as teaching international law "and annexed sciences" [299]. This is why nations were encouraged to send not only their law students to The Hague but also their government officials, diplomats and military personnel [300]. The rationale behind this approach, established in 1914, was that the delegations participating in the Hague Peace Conferences and the National Groups at the PCA comprised the same amalgam of

---

298. For an overview, see Von Verdross in Dupuy 1973, pp. 83-96, at pp. 89 *et seq.*
299. Article 2.
300. In its inaugural year (1923), the Courses programme attracted not only twelve law professors, fifty-five law graduates, eleven judges and 122 attorneys but also an impressive number of attendees from other fields. Among them were sixty-seven diplomats and consuls, twenty-seven military personnel and thirty financial experts.

lawyers and judges, diplomats and politicians, political scientists and military men. To some extent, the same was true for the PCIJ. But it is worth noting that, as its President Max Huber once lamented, most members of the First Bench lacked even a rudimentary understanding of international law. Another President, Dionisio Anzilotti expressed concern that for most of them, their sojourn at the Court was merely an *intermezzo* in their political careers [301]. Fortunately, practice has proven these concerns unfounded.

In principle, the original ambition still holds to this day. The Centre for Studies and Research, too, explicitly seeks to extend its reach to the field of international relations in its programme. The Curatorium itself consists of lawyers, judges and diplomats. However, the promise of inclusivity was never quite fulfilled in the practice of the Courses programme. While non-law students are warmly invited to hear "our" perspective, their voices have seldom been heard. Perhaps introducing an occasional representative from one of the "annexed sciences", possibly on a rotation basis, to present their outlook on our area of study could add a tantalising and enriching element to the courses. Such an approach could facilitate an informative and stimulating dialogue, broaden horizons and bridge gaps in understanding across the legal sciences.

Another suggestion relates to the impact of social change on the functioning of legal institutions, using the World Court as an illustrative example. The Court's jurisdiction is limited to resolving disputes exclusively between nation-States, a policy that has faced significant criticism from its inception. Bernard Loder, later the first President of the PCIJ, strongly reprimanded this exclusivity in 1920, and critical voices have never ceased. The caseload of the PCIJ further fuelled scholarly inquiries into the wisdom of this approach. Several courses at the Academy reflect this predicament [302]. While the exclusivity principle was firmly upheld in San Francisco, the world we inhabit today vastly differs from when the Charter was conceived, a world characterised by clear-cut divisions. The boundaries between the international and municipal spheres are becoming increasingly blurred, as Jennings

---

301. Eyffinger 2023, Vol. 2, chap. 15.2-4.
302. This theme has long captivated scholars, as evidenced by Struycken's exploration in Bardonnet 1998, pages 62-104, particularly pages 79-80, which refers to the courses by Wortley in 1954 (*RdC* 85), Riphagen in 1961 (*RdC* 102), Hambro in 1962 (*RdC* 105), as well as the notable interest in reciprocity aspects examined by Niboyet in 1935 (*RdC* 52) and Lagarde in 1977 (*RdC* 154).

astutely observed back in 1973[303]. An educational institution that has earned its reputation by relentlessly pursuing innovative thought, operating as a Laboratory of the Law, and inspiring future generations is ideally positioned, and indeed obliged, to proactively research and keep pace with societal developments while offering an inquisitive exploration of new avenues[304].

In my concluding observation, I address you, the "Next Generation". For nearly ninety years, attendees and alums of the Academy formed the association known as AAA. Through the fruitful exchange of ideas within their National and Professional Groups, they constituted a distinct think-tank of their own. In the 1930s, they even boldly asserted their influence over the Academy's Programme[305]. Their yearbooks and annual conferences provided a platform for sharing insights and expressing their perspectives on law and society. However, in the modern era of communication, which has discredited previous forms and modes of contact, these voices have been silenced – a sad consequence and curious paradox. It is argued here that involving the Next Generation critically in the discourse outlined above could, to the benefit of us all, diversify the answers our discipline can offer to address the numerous challenges of our time. Over the past century, international law has navigated a meandering path, encountering various challenges along the way. In turbulent conditions, the discipline has consistently adjusted its approach and charted a new course. However, these adaptations were never made due to a lack of a clear destination. From the outset, the goal was unequivocally defined, as eloquently expressed by the first President of this institution during its inauguration in August 1923: "Un jour le droit sera le souverain du monde!"[306]. Now, it is your generation that stands at the forefront, entrusted with the responsibility of turning these visionary words into reality.

***

---

303. See Jennings in Dupuy 1973, pp. 99-115, at pp. 112-113.
304. To illustrate the point, the Vienna Convention has consistently held a prominent place in the discipline since 1969. Its various aspects have been repeatedly addressed in Academy courses. However, in 2017 (*RdC* 385), Sir Franklin Berman intriguingly questioned its relevance.
305. See Nonnenmacher in Dupuy 1973, pp. 243-269, at pp. 263-265 ("le syndicat d'étudiants"). In 1934, a young Stefan von Verosta actively participated in the efforts to reform the programme and courses.
306. The words quoted by Charles Lyon-Caen are attributed to Mirabeau (1749-1791), a French revolutionary and publicist.

SELECTED BIBLIOGRAPHY

Bardonnet, D., "Présentation", in Bardonnet 1998, pp. 7-19.
Bardonnet, D. (ed.), *Soixante-quinzième anniversaire de l'Académie de droit international de La Haye / Seventy-Fifth Anniversary of The Hague Academy of International Law*, The Hague, Hague Academy of International Law, 1998. [Bardonnet 1998].
Boutros-Ghali, Boutros, "Le Centre d'étude et de recherche de droit international et de relations internationales de l'Académie de droit international de La Haye", in Dupuy 1973, pp. 137-158.
Dupuy, R. J., "Le programme extérieur", in Dupuy 1973, pp. 159-174.
Dupuy, R. J. (ed.), *Livre jubilaire / Jubilee Book: 1923-1973*, Leiden, A. W. Sijthoff, 1973. [Dupuy 1973].
Eyffinger, A., *The Peace Palace: Residence for Justice, Domicile of Learning*, The Hague, Carnegie Foundation, 1988. [Eyffinger 1988].
Eyffinger, A., *The Trusteeship of an Ideal: The Carnegie Foundation, Vignettes of a Century 1904-2004*, Amsterdam/The Hague, Enschedé/Carnegie Foundation, 2004.
Eyffinger, A., *T.M.C. Asser (1838-1913): "In Quest of Liberty, Justice, and Peace"*, Leiden, Brill, 2019. [Eyffinger 2019].
Eyffinger, A., *The Institut de droit international: Cradle and Creed of the City of Justice and Peace*, 2nd ed., Oisterwijk, Wolf Legal Publishers, 2020. [Eyffinger 2020].
Eyffinger, A., *The World Court*, Vol. 1: *The Constitution (1870-1920)*, Vol. 2: *The PCIJ (1921-1946)*, The Hague, Wolf Legal Publishers, 2023. [Eyffinger 2023].
Hondius, F., "The A. A. A.: A Meeting-Place for the New Generation in International Law", in Dupuy, 1973, pp. 271-277.
Jennings, R. Y., "Fifty Years of Hague Academy Lectures on Public International Law", in Dupuy 1973, pp. 99-116.
Jessup, P. C., "A Half-Century of The Hague Academy of International Law", in Dupuy 1973, pp. 61-64.
Joor, J., "The Way of Law Above the Way of Violence", in B. Duynstee, D. Meijer and F. Tilanus (eds.), *The Building of Peace: A Hundred Years of Work on Peace Through Law: The Peace Palace 1913-2013*, The Hague, Eleven International Publishing, 2013, pp. 15-286. [Joor 2013].
Joor, J., "The Hague Academy of International Law: One Hundred Years of a Global Centre of Learning, Treasury and Workshop for International law, 1923-2023", in Jubilee Book Hague Academy, 2023, pp. 15-94 [Joor 2023].
Lysen, A., *History of the Carnegie Foundation and of the Peace Palace at The Hague*, Leiden, Brill, 1934. [Lysen 1934].
Nonnenmacher, G., "Cinquante ans d'Association des auditeurs et anciens auditeurs de l'Académie de droit international de La Haye", in Dupuy 1973, pp. 243-270.
Schrijver, N., "The Four International Law Sisters: Similarities, Differences and Interactions", in Editor(s), *Livre jubilaire de l'Institut de droit international*, Place, Publisher, 2023, pp. 179-202. [Schrijver 2023].
Scott, J. B. (ed.), *Year Books Carnegie Endowment for International Peace*, Washington, Carnegie Endowment for International Peace, 1911-1914.
Skubiszewski, K., "The Contribution of the Academy to the Development of the Science and Practice of Public International Law", in Bardonnet 1998, pp. 21-62.
Struycken, A. V. M., "La contribution de l'Académie au développement de la science et de la pratique du droit international privé", in Bardonnet 1998, pp. 63-104.
Van Kleffens, E. N., "L'Académie de droit international en 1923 et avant", in Hugo Grotius, *Annuaire international pour 1924*, The Hague, Martinus Nijhoff, 1924, pp. 17-42.
Van Kleffens, E. N., "Recollections and Reflections", in Dupuy 1973, pp. 65-82.

Van Leeuwen Boomkamp-Oppenhuis de Jong, M., "Faits divers et données statistiques sur les activités et le développement de l'Académie de droit international de La Haye", in Dupuy, 1973, pp. [175]-232.

Von Overbeck, A. E., "L'enseignement du droit international privé à l'Académie de droit international de La Haye de 1923 à 1970", in Dupuy 1973, pp. 117-136.

Von Verosta, S., "L'histoire de l'Académie de droit international de La Haye", in Dupuy 1973, pp. 7-56.

ANNEX I

CURATORIUM MEMBERS: COUNTRY AND MEMBERSHIP PERIOD

(IN CHRONOLOGICAL ORDER)

NAME	COUNTRY	MEMBERSHIP PERIOD
ALVAREZ, Alejandro	Chile	1923-1958
CATELLANI, Enrico Levi	Italy	1923-1924
DESCAMPS, Baron Édouard Eugène François	Belgium	1923-1932
GIDEL, Gilbert Charles	France	1923-1958
HAMMARSKJÖLD, Knut Hjalmar	Sweden	1923-1939
HEEMSKERK, Theodorus	Netherlands	1923-1932
LYON-CAEN, Charles	France	1923-1935
PHILLIMORE, Lord Walter George Frank	United Kingdom	1923-1929
POLITIS, Nikolaos Sokrates	Greece	1923-1942
SCHÜCKING, Walther	Germany	1923-1935
SCOTT, James Brown	United States	1923-1938
STRISOWER, Leo	Austria	1923-1930
TAUBE, Baron Mikhail Alexandrovich	Russia/France	1923-1957
ANZILOTTI, Dionisio	Italy	1924-1939
HIGGINS, Alexander Pearce	United Kingdom	1930-1935
VON VERDROSS, Alfred	Austria	1931-1938 & 1963-1976
KOSTERS, Jan	Netherlands	1932-1939
DE VISSCHER, Charles	Belgium	1933-1973
HURST, Sir Cecil James Barrington	United Kingdom	1935-1939
SCELLE, Georges	France	1935-1937 & 1960-1961

BRUNS, Viktor	Germany	1936-1939
HUBER, Max	Switzerland	1938-1939
HYDE, James Nevins	United States	1938-1939 & 1969-1974
AGHNIDES, Theophilos	Greece	1947-1968
FINCH, George Augustus	United States	1947-1956
MASARYK, Jan Garrigue	Czech Republic	1947
McNAIR, Sir Arnold Duncan	United Kingdom	1947-1962
PILOTTI, Massimo	Italy	1947-1962
SCHINDLER, Dietrich	Switzerland	1947
UNDEN, Östen	Sweden	1947
VAN KLEFFENS, Eelco Nicolaas	Netherlands	1947-1968
CASTBERG, Frede	Norway	1948-1976
HSU MO	China	1948-1956
RUEGGER, Paul	Switzerland	1948-1985
JESSUP, Philip Caryl	United States	1957-1968
BADAWI, Abdel Hamid	Egypt	1960-1965
SCHÄTZEL, Walter	Germany	1960-1961
DE YANGUAS MESSÍA, José María	Spain	1960-1967
AGO, Roberto	Italy	1963-1995
BATIFFOL, Henri C.	France	1962-1984
FITZMAURICE, Sir Gerald Gray	United Kingdom	1963-1976
JIMÉNEZ DE ARÉCHAGA, Eduardo	Uruguay	1966-1988
VAN PANHUYS, Jhr. Haro Frederik	Netherlands	1966-1976
YASSEEN, Mustafa Kamil	Iraq	1967-1981
CORTINA MAURI, Pedro	Spain	1969-1974
LACHS, Manfred	Poland	1969-1993
TSURUOKA, Senjin	Japan	1969-1987
TUNKIN, Grigory Ivanovich	Russia	1969-1993
DE VISSCHER, Paul	Belgium	1974-1996
ELIAS, Taslim Olawale	Nigeria	1976-1991

REESE, Willis L. M.	United States	1975-1990
TRUYOL Y SERRA, Antonio	Spain	1976-2001
MOSLER, Hermann	Germany	1977-1997
RIPHAGEN, Willem	Netherlands	1977-1994
WALDOCK, Sir Humphrey	United Kingdom	1978-1981
SØRENSEN, Max	Denmark	1979-1981
BOUTROS-GHALI, Boutros	Egypt	1982-2016
VALLAT, Sir Francis	United Kingdom	1983-1998
CASTAÑEDA, Jorge	Mexico	1983-1993
PHILIP, Allan	Denmark	1984-2001
DUPUY, René-Jean	France	1985-1997
UMBRICHT, Victor H.	Switzerland	1986-1988
ODA, Shigeru	Japan	1989-2001
RUDA, José Maria	Argentina	1989-1994
SCHÜRER, Wolfgang	Germany	1990-2009
TROOBOFF, Peter D.	United States	1991-2017
MBAYE, Kéba	Senegal	1993-2003
SKUBISZEWSKI, Krzysztof	Poland	1994-2010
URIBE VARGAS, Diego	Colombia	1994-2008
STRUYCKEN, Antoon (teun) Victor Marie	Netherlands	1995-2016
VALTICOS, Nicolas	Greece	1995-2003
BARBERIS, Julio Alberto	Argentina	1996-2004
FELICIANO, Florentino P.	Philippines	1996-2015
CONFORTI, Benedetto	Italy	1998-2010
JAYME, Erik	Germany	1998-2016
BARDONNET, Daniel	France	1999-2004
CRAWFORD, James Richard	Australia	1999-2017
RANJEVA, Raymond	Madagascar	2003-2021
CANÇADO TRINDADE, Antônio Augusto	Brazil	2004-2022

CARRILLO-SALCEDO, Juan Antonio	Spain	2004-2012
MOMTAZ, Djamchid	Iran	2004-
MURASE, Shinya	Japan	2004-2016
BASTID-BURDEAU, Geneviève	France	2005-2017
JÄNTERÄ-JAREBORG, Maarit	Sweden	2005-2017
FERNÁNDEZ ARROYO, Diego P.	Argentina	2009-
SKOTNIKOV, Leonid Alexejevitsj	Russia	2009-2010
HESS, Beat W.	Switzerland	2010-
SICILIANOS, Linos-Alexander	Greece	2010-
TREVES, Tullio Rodolfo	Italy	2010-
XUE Hanqin	China	2010-2016
TOMKA, Peter	Slovakia	2013-
KAMTO, Maurice	Cameroon	2015-
BENNOUNA, Mohamed	Morocco	2016-
BOELE-WOELKI, Katharina	Germany	2016-
JIA Bing Bing	China	2016-
SCHRIJVER, Nico J.	Netherlands	2016-
CHARLESWORTH, Hilary	Australia	2017-
DAUDET, Yves	France	2017-
NISHITANI, Yuko	Japan	2017-
BUXBAUM, Hannah L.	United States	2019-
CORDERO-MOSS, Giuditta	Norway	2019-
MBENGUE, Makane Moïse	Senegal	2021-

ANNEX II

CURATORIUM MEMBERS:
MEMBERSHIP OF IDI, ILC, WORLD COURT
AND PUBLISHED COURSES

(IN ALPHABETICAL ORDER)

The Hague Academy at 100: Its Rationale, Role and Record 83

MEMBER	AUDITOR	CURATORIUM	IDI	ILC	PCIJ/ICJ	PUBLISHED COURSES
AGHNIDES		1947-1968				
AGO	1929	1963-1995	1952	1957-1978	1979-1995	58, 68, 90, 134, 182
ALVAREZ		1923-1958	1931		1946-1955	
ANZILOTTI		1924-1939	1908		1922-1945	
BADAWI		1960-1965	1948		1946-1965	
BARBERIS		1996-2004	1987			179, 235
BARDONNET	1959	1999-2004	1987			153
BASTID-BURDEAU	1973	2005-2017	1999			212
BATIFFOL	1930	1962-1984	1948			72, 97, 120, 139
BENNOUNA		2016-	1985	1987-1998	2006-	177, 300, 383
BOELE-WOELKI		2016-				
BOUTROS-GHALI	1954	1982-2016	1973	1979-1991		100, 137, 286
BRUNS		1936-1939				
BUXBAUM		2019-				
CANÇADO TRINDADE	1971	2004-2022	1997		2009-2022	202, 316, 317, 376, 391
CARRILLO-SALCEDO	1959	2004-2012	1983			160, 257
CASTAÑEDA		1983-1993	1965	1967-1986		129
CASTBERG	1923	1948-1976	1947			35, 43, 138
CATELLANI		1923-1924	1891			46
CHARLESWORTH		2017-	2011		2021-	371

CONFORTI	1954	1998-2010	1989	142, 212
CORDERO-MOSS		2019-		
CORTINA MAURI	1960	1969-1974		
CRAWFORD		1999-2017	1985	1992-2001	2015-2021	319, 365
DAUDET		2017-		
DE VISSCHER, C.		1933-1973	1921	1937-1952	6, 26, 52, 86, 138
DE VISSCHER, P.		1974-1996	1954		80, 102, 136
DE YANGUAS MESSÍA		1960-1967		
DESCAMPS		1923-1932	1892		31
DUPUY		1985-1997	1967		100, 138, 165, 214
ELIAS		1976-1991	1969	1962-1975	134
FELICIANO		1996-2015	1965		118
FERNÁNDEZ ARROYO		2009-		
FINCH		1947-1956	1950		53
FITZMAURICE		1963-1976	1948	1955-1960	73, 92, 138
GIDEL		1923-1958	1921		10, 48
HAMMARSKJÖLD		1923-1939	1906		135
HEEMSKERK		1923-1932		
HESS		2010-		
HIGGINS		1930-1935	1921		11, 30, 40
HSU MO		1948-1956		1949-1961	

HUBER	1938-1939	1921		1922-1930	
HURST	1935-1939	1922		1929-1945	12
HYDE	1938-1939 & 1969-1974				
JÄNTERÄ-JAREBORG	2005-2017				
JAYME	1998-2016	1981			177, 251, 282, 375, 381
JESSUP	1957-1968	1948		1961-1970	29, 89, 99, 129
JIA	2016-				
JIMÉNEZ DE ARÉCHAGA	1966-1988	1961	1960-1969	1970-1979	85, 111, 159
KAMTO	2015-	2005	1999-2016		310
KOSTERS	1932-1939				
LACHS	1969-1993	1963	1962-1966	1967-1993	92, 113, 151, 169
LYON-CAEN	1923-1935				
MASARYK	1947				
MBAYE	1993-2003	1983		1982-1991	209
MBENGUE	2021-				
McNAIR	1947-1962	1931		1946-1955	22, 43, 59
MOMTAZ	2004-	1999		2000-2006	292
MOSLER	1977-1997	1957		1976-1985	91, 140
MURASE	2004-	2016	2011	2009-2022	253
NISHITANI	2017-				
ODA	1989-2001	1969		1976-2003	127, 244

PHILIP	1984-2001	1977		96, 160
PHILLIMORE	1923-1929	1921		1
PILOTTI	1947-1962			
POLITIS	1923-1942	1904		6
RANJEVA	2003-2021	1995	1991-2009	270
REESE	1975-1990	1971		111, 150
RIPHAGEN	1977-1994	1977-1986		
RUDA	1989-1994	1965	1973-1991	146
RUEGGER	1948-1985	1954		82
SCELLE	1935-1937 & 1960-1961	1929	1964-1972	46, 55
SCHÄTZEL	1960-1961	1950		95
SCHINDLER	1947	1937		25, 46
SCHRIJVER	2016-	2007		329
SCHÜCKING	1923-1935	1910	1931-1935	20
SCHÜRER	1990-2009			
SCOTT	1923-1938	1908		42
SICILIANOS	2010-	2011		339
SKOTNIKOV	2009-2010		2006-2015	
SKUBISZEWSKI	1994-2010	1971		271
SØRENSEN	1979-1981	1956		81, 101
STRISOWER	1923-1930	1891		1

RANJEVA 1967
SCHINDLER 1925
SKUBISZEWSKI 1949
SCELLE 1949-1960

STRUYCKEN	1995-2016	2005		232, 271, 311, 374
TAUBE	1923-1957	1910		11, 32, 42, 53, 67
TOMKA	2013-	2011	1999-2002	
TREVES	1967	2010-	1999	2003-
TROOBOFF	1967	1991-2017		223
TRUYOL Y SERRA		1976-2001	1977	200
TSURUOKA		1969-1987		96, 116, 173, 182
TUNKIN		1969-1993	1959	1961-1981
UMBRICHT		1986-1988		1957-1966	95, 119, 147, 219
UNDEN		1947		
URIBE VARGAS		1994-2008		
VALLAT		1983-1998	1965	1973-1981	97
VALTICOS		1995-2003	1973	123, 144
VAN KLEFFENS		1947-1968		
VAN PANHUYS	1952	1966-1976	1967	112
VON VERDROSS		1931-1938 & 1963-1976	1928	1957-1966	16, 30, 37, 52, 83
WALDOCK		1978-1981	1950	1961-1972	1973-1981	81, 106
XUE		2010-2016	2005	2002-2010	2010-	355
YASSEEN		1967-1981	1961	1960-1976		106, 116, 151

ANNEX III

THE "GRAND SLAM" OF THE ACADEMY: AUDITOR, CURATORIUM AND PUBLISHED COURSES

(IN ALPHABETICAL ORDER)

NAME	AUDITOR	CURATORIUM	PUBLISHED COURSES
AGO	1929	1963-1995	58, 68, 90, 134, 182
BARDONNET	1959	1999-2004	153
BASTID-BURDEAU	1973	2005-2017	212
BATIFFOL	1930	1962-1984	72, 97, 120, 139
BOUTROS-GHALI	1954	1982-2016	100, 137, 286
CANÇADO TRINDADE	1971	2004-2022	202, 316, 317, 376, 391
CARRILLO-SALCEDO	1959	2004-2012	160, 257
CONFORTI	1954	1998-2010	142, 212
CRAWFORD	1960	1999-2017	319, 365
JAYME	1967	1998-2016	177, 251, 282, 375, 381
JESSUP	1923	1957-1968	29, 89, 99, 129
ODA	1951	1989-2001	127, 244
RANJEVA	1967	2003-2021	270
SCHINDLER	1925	1947	25, 46
SKUBISZEWSKI	1949	1994-2010	271
TREVES	1967	2010-	223
TROOBOFF	1967	1991-2017	200
VAN PANHUYS	1952	1966-1976	112

ANNEX IV

WORLD COURT JUDGES: YEARS ON THE CURATORIUM AND PCIJ/ICJ

(IN CHRONOLOGICAL ORDER)

JUDGE	CURATORIUM	YEARS	PCIJ/ICJ	YEARS
SCHÜCKING	1923-1935	13	1931-1935	5
ALVAREZ	1923-1958	36	1946-1955	10
ANZILOTTI	1924-1939	16	1922-1945	24
DE VISSCHER, C.	1933-1973	41	1937-1952	16
HURST	1935-1939	5	1929-1945	17
HUBER	1938-1939	2	1922-1930	9
McNAIR	1947-1962	16	1946-1955	10
JESSUP	1957-1968	12	1961-1970	10
BADAWI	1960-1965	6	1946-1965	20
FITZMAURICE	1963-1976	14	1960-1973	14
AGO	1963-1995	33	1979-1995	17
JIMÉNEZ DE ARÉCHAGA	1966-1988	23	1970-1979	10
LACHS	1969-1993	34	1967-1993	17
ELIAS	1976-1991	16	1976-1991	16
MOSLER	1977-1997	21	1976-1985	10
WALDOCK	1978-1981	4	1973-1981	9
RUDA	1989-1994	6	1973-1991	19
ODA	1989-2001	13	1976-2003	28
MBAYE	1993-2003	9	1982-1991	10
CRAWFORD	1999-2017	19	2015-2021	7
RANJEVA	2003-2021	19	1991-2009	19
CANÇADO TRINDADE	2004-2022	19	2009-2022	14
SKOTNIKOV	2009-2010	2	2006-2015	10
XUE	2010-2016	7	2010-	14
TOMKA	2013-	12	2003-	21
BENNOUNA	2016-	7	2006-	18
CHARLESWORTH	2017-	6	2021-	3

Arthur Eyffinger

ANNEX V

WORLD COURT JUDGES: YEARS ON THE CURATORIUM,
IDI, PCIJ/ICJ AND PUBLISHED COURSES

(IN ALPHABETICAL ORDER)

JUDGE	COUNTRY	CURATORIUM	IDI	PCIJ/ICJ	PUBLISHED COURSES
AGO	Italy	1963-1995	1952	1979-1995	58, 68, 90, 134, 182
ALVAREZ	Chile	1923-1958	1931	1946-1955	
ANZILOTTI	Italy	1924-1939	1908	1922-1945	
BADAWI	Egypt	1960-1965	1948	1946-1965	
BENNOUNA	Morocco	2016-	1985	2006-	177, 300, 383
CANÇADO TRINDADE	Brazil	2004-2022	1997	2009-2022	202, 316, 317, 376, 391
CHARLESWORTH	Australia	2017-	2011	2021-	371
CRAWFORD	Australia	1999-2017	1985	2015-2021	319, 365
DE VISSCHER, C.	Belgium	1933-1973	1921	1937-1952	6, 26, 52, 86, 138
ELIAS	Nigeria	1976-1991	1969	1976-1991	134
FITZMAURICE	United Kingdom	1963-1976	1948	1960-1973	73, 92, 138
HUBER	Switzerland	1938-1939	1921	1922-1930	
HURST	United Kingdom	1935-1939	1922	1929-1945	12
JESSUP	United States	1957-1968	1948	1961-1970	29, 89, 99, 129
JIMÉNEZ DE ARÉCHAGA	Uruguay	1966-1988	1961	1970-1979	85, 111, 159
LACHS	Poland	1969-1993	1963	1967-1993	92, 113, 151, 169
MBAYE	Senegal	1993-2003	1983	1982-1991	209
McNAIR	United Kingdom	1947-1962	1931	1946-1955	22, 43, 59

MOSLER	Germany	1977-1997	1957	1976-1985	91, 140
ODA	Japan	1989-2001	1969	1976-2003	127, 244
RANJEVA	Madagascar	2003-2021	1995	1991-2009	270
RUDA	Argentina	1989-1994	1965	1973-1991	146
SCHÜCKING	Germany	1923-1935	1910	1931-1935	20
SKOTNIKOV	Russia	2009-2010		2006-2015	
TOMKA	Slovakia	2013-	2011	2003-	
WALDOCK	United Kingdom	1978-1981	1950	1973-1981	81, 106
XUE	China	2010-2016	2005	2010-	355

ANNEX VI

INVOLVEMENT OF AGENTS/COUNSEL PARTIES (1922-1939)

(IN ALPHABETICAL ORDER)

AGENT	CASES	COUNTRY	PERIOD	PUBLISHED COURSES	IDI	CURAT/PCIJ/ICJ
BASDEVANT	13	France	1923-1937	1 (1926), 58 (1936)	1921	ICJ 1946-1964
BECKETT	1	Great Britain	1934	39 (1932), 50 (1934)	1937	
BOREL	1	International Orgainzation of Industrial Employers	1926	1 (1923), 27 (1929), 52 (1935)	1921	
BRUNS	2	Germany	1931, 1933	62 (1937)		
DE VISSCHER, C.	1	Romania	1927	6 (1925), 26 (1929), 52 (1935)	1921	
	1	Denmark	1933-1973		1932	PCIJ 1937
	3	Poland	1929-1931			
ERICH	1	Finland	1923	13 (1926), 26 (1929)	1924	PCIJ 1938
FISCHER WILLIAMS	1	Danzig	1931	1 (1923), 5 (1924), 16 (1927), 34 (1930), 44 (1933)		
GIDEL	2	Albania	1924, 1935	10 (1925), 48 (1934)	1921	1923-1958
	1	Greece	1927			
	1	Norway	1932			
	1	Bulgaria	1939			
HURST	4	Great Britain	1933-1939	12 (1926)	1922	1935-1939
JÈZE	1	Poland	1932	7 (1925), 14 (1926), 28 (1931), 53 (1935)		PCIJ 1928
KAUFMANN	7	Germany	1926-1931	54 (1935)	1931	

LIMBURG	2	Danzig	1930, 1931	
	1	Austria	1930	
	1	Netherlands	1932	30 (1929)
	2	Poland	1925, 1928	
MANDELSTAM	3	Lithuania	1931, 1938, 1939	1 (1923), 14 (1926), 38 (1931), 47 (1934)	1904
NOLDE	2	Estonia	1938-1939	3 (1924), 27 (1929), 39 (1932), 55 (1936)	1912
PILOTTI	4	Italy	1923-1932	24 (1928)	1947-1962
POLITIS	7	Greece	1924-1937	6 (1925)	1904	1923-1942
	1	Poland	1927		
ROLIN	1	Belgium	1939	19 (1927), 77 (1950)	1924
RUNDSTEIN	1	Poland	1930	23 (1928), 43 (1933)	
SPERL	1	Austria	1931	36 (1931)	1921
WINIARSKI	2	Poland	1929	45 (1933)	1929

ANNEX VII

WORLD COURT JUDGES: YEARS ON THE ILC AND PCIJ/ICJ

(IN ALPHABETICAL ORDER)

JUDGE	ILC	PCIJ/ICJ
AGO	1957-1978	1979-1995
AJIBOLA	1987-1991	1991-1994
ALFARO	1949-1953 & 1958-1959	1959-1964
AL-KHASAWNEH	1987-1999	2000-2011
BEDJAOUI	1965-1981	1982-2001
BENNOUNA	1987-1998	2006-
CÓRDOVA	1949-1954	1955-1964
CRAWFORD	1992-2001	2015-2021
EL-ERIAN	1957-1958 & 1962-1978	1979-1981
ELARABY	1994-2001	2001-2006
ELIAS	1962-1975	1976-1991
EVENSEN	1979-1984	1985-1994
FERRARI BRAVO	1995-1997	1997-1998
FITZMAURICE	1955-1960	1960-1973
GAJA	1999-2011	2012-2021
GEVORGIAN	2012-2015	2015-
GROS	1961-1963	1964-1984
HUDSON	1949-1953	1936-1942
IGNACIO-PINTO	1967-1969	1970-1979
JIMÉNEZ DE ARÉCHAGA	1960-1969	1970-1979
KORETSKY	1949-1951	1961-1970
KOROMA	1982-1993	1994-2012
KRYLOV	1954-1956	1946-1952
LACHS	1962-1966	1967-1993
LAUTERPACHT	1952-1954	1955-1960
NI ZHENGYU	1982-1984	1985-1994
PADILLA NERVO	1955-1963	1964-1973
RAU	1949-1951	1952-1953

RUDA	1964-1972	1973-1991
SCHWEBEL	1977-1980	1981-2000
SETTE CAMARA	1970-1978	1979-1988
SIMMA	1997-2002	2003-2012
SINGH	1967-1972	1973-1988
SPIROPOULOS	1949-1957	1958-1967
TOMKA	1999-2002	2003-
VERESHCHETIN	1992-1994	1995-2006
WALDOCK	1961-1972	1973-1981
XUE	2002-2010	2010-

THE PROTECTION OF SMALL AND MEDIUM-SIZED ENTERPRISES IN PRIVATE INTERNATIONAL LAW

by

KARSTEN THORN

K. THORN

TABLE OF CONTENTS

Chapter I. Introduction 111

Chapter II. The protection of structurally weaker parties: the example of consumer contracts 112

Chapter III. Conflict of laws 118
   A. Choice of law 119
      1. Starting point 119
      2. Restricted choice of law 120
      3. Cherry-picking method 123
      4. Abuse of law 126
      5. Evaluation 127
   B. Objective conflict-of-law rules 130
      1. Starting point 130
      2. B2B contracts 132
   C. Internationally mandatory rules 135
      1. Starting point 135
      2. Examples with regard to B2B contracts 139
          (a) EU: Commercial agents 139
          (b) Extension by Member States 141
          (c) Germany: Authors 145
          (d) France: Subcontractors 146
          (e) United States: Franchisees 150
   D. Evaluation 153

Chapter IV. Jurisdiction rules 157
   A. Starting point 157
   B. B2B contracts 159
      1. Protective venues/jurisdictions 159
      2. Form requirements 165
      3. Jurisdiction agreements as an abuse of law 166
      4. Evaluation 168

Chapter V. The entrepreneur as the weaker party 170
   A. Starting point 170
   B. Application to B2B relations 172

Chapter VI. Proposal for future rules to protect certain SMEs 178

Chapter VII. One step further: International commercial arbitration 181

Chapter VIII. Summary 192

Annex: List of judgments 199

Bibliography 202

BIOGRAPHICAL NOTE

Karsten Thorn, born in 1963 in Trier, Germany.
Professor Thorn holds the Chair for Civil Law, Private International and International Commercial Law, and Comparative Law at Bucerius Law School. From June 2014 through September 2015, he was also acting Dean.
He teaches and researches private international law, international commercial law and conflict of laws.
Prof Thorn studied law at the universities of Trier and Georgetown, Washington DC (US). He specialised in international private law and comparative law. He was a teaching and research assistant, postdoctoral research associate and lecturer during the Chair of Professor Dr Bernd von Hoffmann. He also taught as a guest lecturer at the universities of Orléans and Metz in France.
From 2005 through 2009, he was the German director of the programme of the Summer Law Institute in Souzhou, China, and from 2007, a lecturer within a cooperation framework of Chinese legal training, including with the China European International Business School in Shanghai and the Chinese Academy of Social Sciences in Beijing, as well as the Deutsche Gesellschaft für Internationale Zusammenarbeit (GIZ) in Berlin. In 2009 and 2010, he was a guest lecturer at the Centre for Transnational Legal Studies in London. Also in 2010, he was at The Hague Academy of International Law as Director of Studies in the Session of Private International Law for the Diploma Seminars 2010.
Among other academic or professional associations, Prof Thorn is a regional chair of the German-American Lawyers Association and a member of the German Council of International Private Law (both Commissions). In 2023, he was elected to the Board of Directors of the German Society of International Law.
In addition, he is the author and editor of numerous publications, notably a commentary on international private law within C. Grüneberg's main commentary on the German Civil Code (Bürgerliches Gesetzbuch). He is also the co-editor of the *Praxis des Internationalen Privat- und Verfahrensrechts* (IPRax), one of the most distinguished German law journals on conflict of laws.

PRINCIPAL PUBLICATIONS

A. Monographs

Der Mobiliarerwerb vom Nichtberechtigten (Arbeiten zur Rechtsvergleichung 180), Baden-Baden, Nomos, 1996.
IPRax – Abkürzungsverzeichnis deutscher und ausländischer Periodika, Bielefeld, Gieseking, 2005 [with B. von Hoffmann].
Internationales Privatrecht: einschließlich der Grundzüge des internationalen Zivilverfahrensrechts, 9th rev. ed., Munich, Beck, 2007 [with B. von Hoffmann since 8th ed. 2005].
Koordinierung von Privatrechtsordnungen durch Anwendung ausländischen Kollisionsrechts, XLVI + 520 Manuskriptseiten; angenommen zur Veröffentlichung in der Schriftenreihe "Beiträge zum ausländischen und Internationalen Privatrecht" des Hamburger Max-Planck-Instituts, unpublished.
Fälle zum Internationalen Privatrecht: mit internationalem Zivilverfahrensrecht (Schriftenreihe der Juristischen Schulung), 5th rev. ed., Munich, Beck, 2019 [with A. Fuchs and W. Hau since 1st ed. 2000].

B. Editorships

Praxis des Internationalen Privat- und Verfahrensrechts (IPRax), Bielefeld, Gieseking [co-editor since 2005 with C. Budzikiewicz, D. Henrich, B. Hess, B. von Hoffmann (†), S. Huber, E. Jayme, H. Kronke and H.-P. Mansel].
Studien zum vergleichenden und internationalen Recht / Comparative and International Law Studies, Berlin, Peter Lang [co-editor since 2007 with B. von Hoffmann (†), E. Jayme, H.-P. Mansel, C. Budzikiewicz, M. Stürner and M.-Ph. Weller].
Grenzen überwinden – Prinzipien bewahren. Festschrift für Bernd von Hoffmann zum 70. Geburtstag, Bielefeld, Gieseking, 2011 [with H. Kronke].
Festschrift für Karsten Schmidt zum 80. Geburtstag, Munich, Beck, 2019 [with K. Boele-Woelki, F. Faust, M. Jacobs, T. Kuntz, A. Röthel and B. Weitemeyer].

C. Commentaries

"Art. 39 EGBGB", in *J. von Staudingers Kommentar zum Bürgerlichen Gesetzbuch mit Einführungsgesetz und Nebengesetzen*, Berlin, Sellier / De Gruyter, 2001 [with B. von Hoffmann].
"§§ 1313-1320, 1359 BGB", in M. Herberger, M. Martinek, H. Rüssmann and S. Weth (eds.), *juris PraxisKommentar zum BGB*, Vol. 4: *Familienrecht*, 2nd ed., Saarbrücken, juris, 2005.
"Artikel 4, 5, 9, 13, 19, 21, 23 Rom I-VO", in T. Rauscher (ed.), *Europäisches Zivilprozess- und Kollisionsrecht EuZPR/EuIPR*, Band III: Rom I-VO, Rom II-VO, 5th ed., Cologne, Otto Schmidt, 2023, pp. 168-272, 385-432, 476-485, 535-544, 545-553, 556-561 [co-editor since 3rd ed. 2011].
"EGBGB Article 3-48 mit Rom I-, Rom II- und Rom III-Verordnung sowie Güterrechtsverordnungen, Haager Unterhaltsprotokoll und Erbrechtsverordnung (teilweise), Article 229, paras. 47, 48, 52", in C. Grüneberg, *Bürgerliches Gesetzbuch mit Nebengesetzen*, 82nd ed., Munich, Beck, 2023, pp. 2682-2907, 2917-2918, 2919 [co-editor since 68th ed. 2009].

D. Academic publications

"Die UN-Verjährungskonvention und ihre Geltung in Deutschland", IPRax, Vol. 13 (1993), pp. 215-216.
"Verbrauchergerichtsstand nach EuGVÜ und örtliche Zuständigkeit", IPRax, Vol. 14 (1994), pp. 426-429.
"Grenzüberschreitende Gerichtsstandsvereinbarungen in Kreditverträgen zur Finanzierung von Börsenspekulationen", IPRax, Vol. 15 (1995), pp. 294-299.

"Ausländisches Akkreditiv und inländische Zahlstelle", IPRax, Vol. 16 (1996), pp. 257-260.
"Erfolgsort bei grenzüberschreitenden Persönlichkeitsverletzungen", *Zeitschrift für das gesamte Medienrecht/Archiv für Pressrecht*, Vol. 5, No. 1 (1996), pp. 20-25 [with H. Ehmann].
"Mobiliarerwerb vom Nichtberechtigten: Neue Entwicklungen in rechtsvergleichender Perspektive", *Zeitschrift für Europäisches Privatrecht*, Vol. 5, No. 2 (1997), pp. 442-474.
"Neues Internationales Privatrecht in Italien. Eine kritische Betrachtung", *Zeitschrift für Vergleichende Rechtswissenschaft*, Vol. 96 (1997), pp. 347-385 [with Valentina Maglio].
"Termingeschäfte an Auslandsbörsen und Internationale Schiedsgerichtsbarkeit", IPRax, Vol. 17 (1997), pp. 98-106.
"Verbraucherschutz bei Verträgen im Fernabsatz", IPRax, Vol. 19 (1999), pp. 1-9. Reviewed by P. Lagarde in *Revue critique de droit international privé* (1999, No. 2), pp. 421-424.
"Länderbericht Germany", in A. von Ziegler, J. H. Rønøe, Ch. Debattista and O. Plégat-Kerrault (eds.), *Transfer of Ownership in International Trade*, The Hague, Kluwer Law International, 1999, pp. 181-200.
"Das Centros-Urteil des EuGH im Spiegel der deutschen Rechtsprechung", IPRax, Vol. 21 (2001), pp. 102-110.
"Internationale Produkthaftung des Zulieferers", IPRax, Vol. 21 (2001), pp. 561-567.
"Entwicklungen des Internationalen Privatrechts 2000-2001", IPRax, Vol. 22 (2002), pp. 349-364.
"The German Law on Same-Sex Partnerships", in K. Boele-Woelki and A. Fuchs (eds.), *Legal Recognition of Same-Sex Couples in Europe*, Antwerp, Intersentia, 2003, pp. 84-98.
"The German Conflict of Laws Rules on Registered Partnerships", in K. Boele-Woelki and A. Fuchs (eds.), *Legal Recognition of Same-Sex Couples in Europe*, Antwerp, Intersentia, 2003, pp. 159-168.
"Besondere Kollisionsnormen und allgemeine Lehren des IPR", in H.-P. Mansel, H. Kronke, R. Hausmann, C. Kohler and T. Pfeiffer (eds.), *Festschrift für Erik Jayme*, Munich, Sellier, 2004, pp. 1128-1141.
"Gerichtsstand des Erfüllungsorts und intertemporales Zivilverfahrensrecht (zu OGH 2. 9. 2003 – 1 Ob 123/03z)", IPRax, Vol. 24 (2004), pp. 354-357.
"Eingriffsnormen", in F. Ferrari and S. Leible (eds.), *Ein neues Internationales Vertragsrecht für Europa – Der Vorschlag für eine Rom I Verordnung*, Jena, Jenaer Wissenschaftliche Verlagsgesellschaft, 2007, pp. 129-149.
"Europäisches Kollisionsrecht 2008: Fundamente der Europäischen IPR-Kodifikation", IPRax, Vol. 29 (2009), pp. 1-23 [with H.-P. Mansel and R. Wagner].
"Der Unternehmer im Kollisionsrecht", in G. Bitter, M. Lutter, H.-J. Priester, W. Schönand and P. Ulmer (eds.), *Festschrift für Karsten Schmidt zum 70. Geburtstag*, Cologne, Otto Schmidt, 2009, pp. 1561-1580.
"Europäisches Kollisionsrecht 2009: Hoffnungen durch den Vertrag mit Lissabon", IPRax, Vol. 30 (2010), pp. 1-27 [with H.-P. Mansel and R. Wagner].
"Schadensersatzansprüche der Zivilbevölkerung gegen ausländische Besatzungsmächte", in A. Zimmermann (ed.), *Moderne Konfliktformen. Humanitäres Völkerrecht und privatrechtliche Folgen* (Berichte der deutschen Gesellschaft für Völkerrecht 44), Heidelberg, C. F. Müller, 2010, pp. 305-340.
"The Effect of Overriding Mandatory Rules on the Arbitration Agreement", in F. Ferrari and S. Kröll (eds.), *Conflict of Laws in International Commercial Arbitration*, Munich, Sellier, 2010, pp. 187-210 [with W. Grenz].
"Länderbericht Germany", in A. von Ziegler, J. H. Rønøe, Ch. Debattista and O. Plégat-Kerrault (eds.), *Transfer of Ownership in International Trade*, 2nd ed., Alphen aan den Rijn, Kluwer Law International, 2011, pp. 203-222.
"Europäisches Kollisionsrecht 2010: Verstärkte Zusammenarbeit als Motor der Vereinheitlichung?", IPRax, Vol. 31 (2011), pp. 1-30 [with H.-P. Mansel and R. Wagner].

"Die Flagge als Anknüpfungsmoment im Internationalen Privatrecht", in Die Fakultät der Bucerius Law School (eds.), *Begegnungen im Recht. Interdisziplinäre Ringvorlesung der Bucerius Law School zu Ehren Karsten Schmidts anlässlich seines 70. Geburtstags*, Tübingen, Mohr Siebeck, 2011, pp. 131-153.
"Internationale Zuständigkeit bei Persönlichkeitsverletzungen durch Massenmedien", in H. Kronke and K. Thorn (eds.), *Grenzen überwinden – Prinzipien bewahren. Festschrift für Bernd von Hoffmann zum 70. Geburtstag*, Bielefeld, Gieseking, 2011, pp. 746-762.
"Die Haftung für Umweltschädigungen im Gefüge der Rom II-VO", in E.-M. Kieninger and O. Remien (eds.), *Europäische Kollisionsrechtsvereinheitlichung*, Baden-Baden, Nomos, 2012, pp. 139-163.
"Europäisches Kollisionsrecht 2011: Gegenläufige Entwicklungen", IPRax, Vol. 32 (2012), pp. 1-31 [with H.-P. Mansel and R. Wagner].
"Die Haftung für Umweltschädigungen im Gefüge der Rom II-VO", in E.-M. Kieninger and O. Remien (eds.), *Europäische Kollisionsrechtsvereinheitlichung*, Baden-Baden, Nomos, 2012, pp. 139-164.
"Europäisches Kollisionsrecht 2012: Voranschreiten des Kodifikationsprozesses – Flickenteppich des Einheitsrechts", IPRax, Vol. 33 (2013), pp. 1-36 [with H.-P. Mansel and R. Wagner].
"Die Revision der Brüssel I-Verordnung und ihre Auswirkungen auf den deutsch-italienischen Rechtsverkehr", in A. Röthel, S. Frank, A. Malatesta, K. Thorn and J. von Hein (eds.), *Europäische Einflüsse auf den deutsch-italienischen Rechtsverkehr* (Jahrbuch für Italienisches Recht 25, eds. E. Jayme, H.-P. Mansel, T. Pfeiffer and M. Stürner), Heidelberg, C. F. Müller, 2013, pp. 61-86.
"Europäisches Kollisionsrecht 2013: Atempause im status quo", IPRax, Vol. 34 (2014), pp. 1-27 [with H.-P. Mansel and R. Wagner].
"Europäisches Kollisionsrecht 2014: Jahr des Umbruchs", IPRax, Vol. 35 (2015), pp. 1-32 [with H.-P. Mansel and R. Wagner].
"Palandt und IPR. Betrachtungen zur Frühgeschichte einer kollisionsrechtlichen Kommentierung", in *Festschrift zur 75. Auflage des Kurz-Kommentars Palandt, Bürgerliches Gesetzbuch*, Munich, Beck, 2016, pp. 67-78.
"Schiedsvereinbarungen in Fällen struktureller Unterlegenheit. Hinreichende Schutzmechanismen oder Regelungslücken", in J. Kleinschmidt, H. Kronke, T. Raab, G. Robbers and K. Thorn (eds.), *Strukturelle Ungleichgewichtslagen in der internationalen Streitbeilegung. Symposium in Gedenken an Bernd von Hoffmann*, Frankfurt am Main, Peter Lang, 2016, pp. 133-166.
"Europäisches Kollisionsrecht 2015: Neubesinnung", IPRax, Vol. 36 (2016), pp. 1-33 [with H.-P. Mansel and R. Wagner].
"Das Pechstein-Urteil des BGH – ein Freibrief für die Sportschiedsgerichtsbarkeit?", IPRax, Vol. 36 (2016), pp. 426-431 [with C. Lasthaus].
"Parallelverfahren nach der Brüssel Ia-VO oder 'wie man einen Torpedo entschärft'", in W. Hau and H. Schmidt (eds.), *Trierer Festschrift für Walter F. Lindacher zum 80. Geburtstag*, Munich, Beck, 2017, pp. 405-429 [with P. Paffhausen].
"Europäisches Kollisionsrecht 2016: Brexit ante portas", IPRax, Vol. 37 (2017), pp. 1-39 [with H.-P. Mansel and R. Wagner].
"Eine Ehe ist keine Ehe ist eine Ehe – Zur Qualifikation gleichgeschlechtlicher Ehen nach altem und neuem Kollisionsrecht", IPRax, Vol. 37 (2017), pp. 590-596 [with P. Paffhausen].
"Europäisches Kollisionsrecht 2017: Morgenstunde der Staatsverträge", IPRax, Vol. 38 (2018), pp. 121-154 [with H.-P. Mansel and R. Wagner].
"Der Schutz der strukturell unterlegenen Partei vor Schiedsverfahren", IPRax, Vol. 38 (2018), pp. 541-549 [with M. Nickel].
"The Effect of Overriding Mandatory Rules on the Arbitration Agreement", in F. Ferrari and S. Kröll (eds.), "Conflict of Laws in International Commercial Arbitration", special issue, *European International Arbitration Review*, Vol. 7, No. 1 (2019), pp. 43-70 [with M. Nickel].
"Europäisches Kollisionsrecht 2018: Endspurt!", IPRax, Vol. 39 (2019), pp. 85-119 [with H.-P. Mansel and R. Wagner].

"Europäisches Kollisionsrecht 2019: Konsolidierung und Multilateralisierung", IPRax, Vol. 40 (2020), pp. 97-126 [with H.-P. Mansel and R. Wagner].

"Von Pannen und Privilegien – Der Regress zwischen Kfz-Haftpflichtversicherern und die gestörte Gesamtschuld aus Sicht des Kollisionsrechts", IPRax, Vol. 40 (2020), pp. 177-185 [with M. Cremer].

"Die Qualifikation des pauschalierten Zugewinnausgleichs im Todesfall gemäß § 1371 Abs. 1 BGB nach der EuErbVO", IPRax, Vol. 40 (2020), pp. 316-322 [with K. Varón Romero].

"Der Auslandsbezug im IPR", in S. Huber and C. Benicke (eds.), *National, International, Transanational: Harmonischer Dreiklang im Recht. Festschrift für Herbert Kronke zum 70. Geburtstag*, Bielefeld, Gieseking, 2020, pp. 569-583 [with M. Thon].

"Kollisionsrecht in der Twilight Zone. Zur Reform des Internationalen Privatrechts der Fürsorgeverhältnisse", IPRax, Vol. 41 (2021), pp. 15-28 [with K. Varón Romero].

"Europäisches Kollisionsrecht 2020: EU im Krisenmodus!", IPRax, Vol. 41 (2021), pp. 105-139 [with H.-P. Mansel and R. Wagner].

"Moderne Fortpflanzungsmethoden und IPR", in C. Budzikiewicz, B. Heiderhoff, F. Klinkhammer and K. Niethammer-Jürgens (eds.), *Neue Impulse im europäischen Familienkollisionsrecht* (Dialog Internationales Familienrecht 3), Baden-Baden, Nomos, 2021, pp. 51-79.

"Europäisches Kollisionsrecht 2021: Digitalisierung als Aufgabe", IPRax, Vol. 43 (2022), pp. 97-140 [with H.-P. Mansel and R. Wagner].

"Europäisches Kollisionsrecht 2022: Bewegung im internationalen Familienrecht", IPRax, Vol. 43 (2023), pp. 109-145 [with H.-P. Mansel and R. Wagner].

ABBREVIATIONS

AAA	American Arbitration Association
App. Div.	Appellate Division
B2B	business-to-business
BeckOGK	*beck-online.GROSSKOMMENTAR*
BeckRS	beck-online – Rechtsprechung [electronic database]
BGB	Bürgerliches Gesetzbuch (German Civil Code)
BGBl.	*Bundesgesetzblatt*
BGHZ	*Sammlung der Entscheidungen des BGH in Zivilsachen*
Brussels I*bis* Regulation	Regulation 1215/2012/EU of the European Parliament and of the Council of 12 December 2012 on jurisdiction and the recognition and enforcement of judgments in civil and commercial matters, OJ 2012 L 351, p. 1
Ch. Div.	Chancery Division
CISG	United Nations Convention on Contracts for the International Sale of Goods
CMR	Convention relative au contrat de transport international de marchandises par route
COM	Commission of the European Union
EC	European Community
ECJ	European Court of Justice
EEC	European Economic Community
EGBGB	Einführungsgesetz zum Bürgerlichen Gesetzbuche (Introductory Act to the German Civil Code)
EU	European Union
EuIPR	Europäisches Internationales Privatrecht / Europäisches Kollisionsrecht (European international private law / European conflict of laws)
EuZPR	Europäisches Zivilprozessrecht (European law of civil procedure)
EuZW	*Europäische Zeitschrift für Wirtschaftsrecht*
FAA	Federal Arbitration Act
FactÜ	UNIDROIT Convention on International Factoring
FCC	German Federal Constitutional Court (Bundesverfassungsgericht)
FCJ	German Federal Court of Justice (Bundesgerichtshof)
GPR	*Zeitschrift für das Privatrecht der Europäischen Union*
GRUR	*Gewerblicher Rechtsschutz und Urheberrecht*
GWR	*Gesellschafts- und Wirtschaftsrecht*
HGB	Handelsgesetzbuch (German Commercial Code)
HRC	Higher Regional Court (Oberlandesgericht)
ICJ	International Court of Justice
IHR	*Internationales Handelsrecht*
Inc.	Incorporated
IPR	Internationales Privatrecht (international private law)
IPRax	*Praxis des Internationalen Privatrechts*

IPRspr.	*Die deutsche Rechtsprechung auf dem Gebiet des Internationalen Privatrechts*
MDR	*Monatsschrift für Deutsches Recht*
MSME	micro, small and medium-sized enterprises
NJFPA	New Jersey Food Processors Association
N.J. Stat. Ann.	*New Jersey Statutes Annotated*
NJW	*Neue Juristische Wochenschrift*
NJW-RR	*NJW Rechtsprechungs-Report*
OJ	*Official Journal of the European Union*
OJEC	*Official Journal of the European Community*
RIW	*Recht der internationalen Wirtschaft*
Rome I Regulation	Regulation (EC) No. 593/2008 of the European Parliament and of the Council of 17 June 2008 on the law applicable to contractual obligations (Rome I), OJ 2008 L 177, pp. 6 *et seq.*
Rome II Regulation	Regulation No. 864/2007/EC of the European Parliament and of the Council of 11 July 2007 on the law applicable to non-contractual obligations (Rome II), OJ 2007 L 199, pp. 40 *et seq.*
Rome III Regulation	Regulation 1259/2010/EU of 20 December 2010 implementing enhanced cooperation in the area of the law applicable to divorce and legal separation (Rome III), OJ 2010 L 343, pp. 10 *et seq.*
SMEs	small and medium-sized enterprises
TFEU	Treaty on the Functioning of the European Union
UCC	Uniform Commercial Code
UN	United Nations
UNCITRAL	New York Convention on the Recognition and Enforcement of Foreign Arbitral Awards of 1958
UNESCO	United Nations Educational, Scientific and Cultural Organization
UrhG	Urhebergesetz (German Copyright Act)
VersR	*Versicherungsrecht*
VO	Verordnung (Regulation)
ZPO	Zivilprozessordnung (German Code of Civil Procedure)

CHAPTER I

INTRODUCTION

1. When discussing the protection of structurally weaker parties in private international law, one typically refers to non-business parties like consumers or employees. In many jurisdictions worldwide, both groups are deemed in need of legal protection against the other contracting party – the entrepreneur and the employer, respectively – in light of the latter's stronger bargaining power. However, after brief reflection, one discovers that, in many cases, entrepreneurs are also protected. Well-known examples include the commercial agent under European law, the subcontractor in French law and the franchisee in many US jurisdictions.

This paper shall systematise these cases: It looks for underlying policies and develops a proposal for future private international law rules with regard to small and medium-sized enterprises (SMEs [1]). It understands private international law in the broad French sense, encompassing not only conflict of laws but also jurisdiction rules and even international commercial arbitration. The paper deals exclusively with contractual issues, although one might identify the first traces of the protection of entrepreneurs also in torts [2], where such provisions, however, follow different concepts.

---

1. Abbreviation first used in Commission Recommendation 96/280/EC of 6 May 2003 concerning the definition of small and medium-sized enterprises, OJ 1996 L 107, p. 4.
2. Regarding product liability see e.g. the producer-friendly connecting factors in Art. 5 para. 1 Regulation 864/2007/EC of the European Parliament and of the Council of 11 July 2007 on the law applicable to non-contractual obligations, OJ 2007 L 199, pp. 40 *et seq.* (hereinafter "Rome II Regulation" or "Rome II Reg."); also A. Junker, in F. J. Säcker *et al.* (eds.), *Münchener Kommentar zum Bürgerlichen Gesetzbuch*, Vol. XIII, 8th ed., Munich, Beck, 2021, Art. 5 Rome II Reg. recital 24.

CHAPTER II

THE PROTECTION OF STRUCTURALLY WEAKER PARTIES: THE EXAMPLE OF CONSUMER CONTRACTS

2. These considerations have to start with the substantive law. All known legal systems have mandatory rules to protect structurally weaker parties. Mandatory means that the parties to a contract are bound by those provisions and cannot derogate from them by agreement; thus, the contractual freedom of the parties – what is termed private autonomy – is restricted. This restriction of private autonomy is legitimised by the fact that such freedom would otherwise become perverted into the exclusive freedom of the stronger party [3]. Private autonomy in cases of economic or social imbalance between the parties always carries the risk that the stronger party will abuse it. To safeguard the self-determination of both parties, private autonomy, therefore, has to be restricted in favour of the legitimate interests of the weaker party [4]. At this point, mandatory provisions come into play as they limit the ability of the parties to determine autonomously the content of their contractual relationship. In a domestic environment, this functions properly, as can be seen in an example taken from consumer law:

B, a consumer residing in Hamburg, orders a pair of shoes by mail from the German company S. Five days after the merchandise arrives, B changes his mind and intends to cancel the whole transaction. Can he do so?

Under Article 9 of the European Consumer Rights Directive of 2011 [5], implemented into German law by Sections 312g and 355 of the

---

3. P. Mankowski, in U. Magnus and P. Mankowski (eds.), *European Commentaries on Private International Law: Rome I Regulation*, Vol. II, Cologne, Otto Schmidt, 2017, Art. 3 Rome I Reg. recital 12; M. McParland, *The Rome I Regulation on the Law Applicable to Contractual Obligations*, Oxford, Oxford University Press, 2015, recitals 9.09 *et seq.*

4. McParland, *supra* note 3, recital 9.09; E. Siesby, "Party Autonomy and the EC Draft Convention", in O. Lando, B. von Hoffmann and K. Siehr (eds.), *European Private International Law of Obligations*, Tübingen, Mohr Siebeck, 1975, pp. 206 *et seq.* at 211.

5. Directive 2011/83/EU of the European Parliament and of the Council of 25 October 2011 on consumer rights, amending Council Directive 93/13/EEC and Directive 1999/44/EC of the European Parliament and of the Council and repealing Council Directive 85/577/EEC and Directive 97/7/EC of the European Parliament and of the Council, OJ 2011 L 304, p. 64.

German Civil Code [6], a consumer is to have a period of fourteen days to withdraw from a distance or off-premises contract without giving any reason, and without incurring any costs. In accordance with Article 25 of the Directive, implemented by Section 361, paragraph 2 of the German Civil Code, this right to withdraw is mandatory; that is, the right cannot be waived by the consumer or otherwise restricted.

As a result, B can freely withdraw from the sales contract.

3. As soon as a case has ties to more than one jurisdiction, it becomes an international case, and party autonomy – that is, the freedom of the parties to choose the law applicable to their contract [7] – endangers the protection of the weaker party. Thus, the parties to the contract can simply choose a legal system that does not adopt the same level of protection as the law which would otherwise apply to the contract. In the worst case, the chosen law will not provide any protection. The following variation of the initial case will illustrate this danger.

The seller is not a German but a Californian mail-order company. Moreover, the parties choose Californian law as the law applicable to their contract. Therefore, presuming that Californian law does not provide for a mandatory right of withdrawal in cases of distance sales, the German consumer hereby might lose the protection regarded as necessary by European legislators.

4. This comparison raises several questions: How does a contract become international [8]? Indeed, it suffices if the parties to the contract reside in different countries or if the contract as a whole or parts of it have to be performed abroad. However, is it also sufficient if the parties residing within the same country just cross the border to conclude the contract abroad [9]?

---

6. Act of Transformation of the Directive on Consumer Rights and Revision of the Rules about Residental Brokerage (Gesetz zur Umsetzung der Verbraucherrechterichtlinie und zur Anderung des Gesetzes zur Regelung der Wohnvermittlung) of 20 September 2013, BGBl. I, p. 3642.
7. H. E. Yntema, "'Autonomy' in Choice of Law", *American Journal of Comparative Law*, Vol. 1, No. 4 (1952), pp. 341 *et seq.* at 343.
8. Cf. Mankowski, *supra* note 3, Art. 3 Rome I Reg. recital 383.
9. See Federal Court of Justice (Bundesgerichtshof) (hereinafter "FCJ"), judgment of 19 March 1997, VIII ZR 316/96, BGHZ 135, pp. 124 *et seq.* at 130; U. Magnus, in U. Magnus (ed.), *Einleitung zur Rom I-VO, Article 1-10 Rom I-VO* (Internationales Vertragsrecht 1) [part of the multivolume *J. von Staudingers Kommentar zum Bürgerlichen Gesetzbuch mit Einführungsgesetz und Nebengesetzen*], rev. ed., Berlin, De Gruyter, 2021, Art. 3 Rome I Reg. recital 139; P. Mankowski, "Strukturfragen des internationalen Verbrauchervertragsrechts", RIW, No. 6 (1993), pp. 453 *et seq.* at 454; J. von Hein, in T. Rauscher (ed.), *Europäisches Zivilprozess- und Kollisionsrecht EuZPR/EuIPR*, Vol. III: *Rom I-VO, Rom II-VO*, 4th ed., Cologne, Otto Schmidt, 2016, Art. 3 Rome I Reg. recital 111.

If such a step across the border fulfils the requirement for the case to have an international element, is it in accordance with the constitutional principle of equality if two cases being so close to each other are treated differently in such a manner [10]?

These fascinating issues have to be left aside in the framework of this paper, and so I will concentrate on the legal effects of the internationalisation of a case.

5. To safeguard the protection of the weaker party, the conflict-of-law rules have to be shaped so that the parties cannot opt out of the protective scheme. Consequently, Article 6, paragraph 2 of the Rome I Regulation on the law applicable to contractual obligations [11] contains a specific conflict-of-law rule for consumer contracts that

> "the parties may choose the law applicable to a [consumer] contract .... Such a choice may not, however, have the result of depriving the consumer of the protection afforded to him by provisions that cannot be derogated from by agreement by virtue of the law [of the consumer's habitual residence]".

Thus, the principle of freedom of choice under Article 3 of the Rome I Regulation also applies to consumer contracts. However, its legal effects are modified so that a choice of law can only increase but not decrease the level of mandatory consumer protection [12].

Hence, in the described variation, the Californian law chosen by the parties would only become relevant for the consumer's right of withdrawal if it is more consumer-friendly than European law, for example by granting a longer withdrawal period from the contract. However, the chosen Californian law would apply to all contractual issues not covered by mandatory German consumer protection rules.

---

10. With regard to the relevance of the principle of equality for conflict of laws, cf. E. Lorenz, *Zur Struktur des Internationalen Privatrechts*, Berlin, Duncker & Humblot, 1977, p. 60; C. von Bar and P. Mankowski, *Internationales Privatrecht*, Vol. 1, 2nd ed., Munich, C. H. Beck, 2003, § 4 recitals 37-39.
11. Regulation 593/2008/EC of the European Parliament and of the Council of 17 June 2008 on the law applicable to contractual obligations, OJ 2008 L 177, p. 6 (hereinafter "Rome I Regulation" or "Rome I Reg.").
12. C. G. J. Morse, "The EEC Convention on the Law Applicable to Contractual Obligations", *Yearbook of European Law*, Vol. 2 (1982), pp. 107 *et seq.* at 136 *et seq.*; G. Rühl, "Der Schutz des ‚Schwächeren' im europäischen Kollisionsrecht", in H. Kronke and K. Thorn (eds.), *Grenzen überwinden – Prinzipien bewahren, Festschrift für Bernd von Hoffmann zum 70. Geburtstag am 28. Dezember 2011*, Bielefeld, Gieseking, 2011, pp. 364 *et seq.* at 369; M. Wilderspin, in U. Magnus and P. Mankowski (eds.), *European Commentaries on Private International Law: Rome I Regulation*, Vol. II, Cologne, Otto Schmidt, 2017, Art. 6 Rome I Reg. recital 76.

6. This cherry-picking [13], as it might be called, is an excellent example of the increasing materialisation of conflict-of-law rules. Pursuant to the doctrine developed by von Savigny, conflict rules paid no regard to the substantive result reached in a given case [14]. During the last decades, however, the understanding has grown that, especially in cases featuring an imbalance between the parties, conflict rules can be utilised to favour a particular substantive result, such as a high level of protection for a structurally weaker party [15].

7. Nevertheless, the weaker party in an international case still faces a danger originating from the differing conflict-of-law rules. In principle, the conflict-of-law rules are not unified. They differ from one jurisdiction to the other, the Europeanisation of private international law being one of main exceptions [16]. Therefore, the forum of a lawsuit decides which conflict-of-law rules apply to a given case [17].

Let us assume that the parties in the variation have not only chosen Californian law to apply to their contract but also agreed upon a jurisdiction clause in favour of Californian courts. To determine the applicable law, the Californian court will not use the Rome I Regulation as the starting point but rather its own domestic conflict-of-law rules. This might lead to the court upholding the choice of law made by the parties without any restrictions, thereby depriving the consumer of the protection deemed necessary by European legislators.

8. To meet that danger, the law thus must provide for a venue within the European Union where the courts will apply European conflict-of-law rules to determine the *lex contractus*. This can be demonstrated by the jurisdiction provisions of the Brussels Ibis Regulation on jurisdiction and the recognition and enforcement of judgments in civil

---

13. M. Campo Comba, *The Law Applicable to Cross-border Contracts Involving Weaker Parties in EU Private International Law*, Cham, Springer, 2020, p. 114; cf. B. Heiderhoff, in T. Rauscher (ed.), *Europäisches Zivilprozess- und Kollisionsrecht EuZPR/EuIPR*, Vol. III: *Rom I-VO, Rom II-VO*, 4th ed., Cologne, Otto Schmidt, 2016, Art. 6 Rome I Reg. recital 56 ("Rosinenpicken").
14. D. Looschelders, in D. Henrich (ed.), *Internationales Privatrecht. Einleitung zum IPR* [part of the multivolume *J. von Staudingers Kommentar zum Bürgerlichen Gesetzbuch mit Einführungsgesetz und Nebengesetzen*], rev. ed., Berlin, De Gruyter, 2019, recital 56; M. Mogendorf, *Der strukturell unterlegene Unternehmer im Internationalen Privat- und Verfahrensrecht*, Tübingen, Mohr Siebeck, 2016, p. 51.
15. Rühl, *supra* note 12, p. 369; cf. G. Rühl, "Consumer Protection in Choice of Law", *Cornell International Law Journal*, Vol. 44 (2011), pp. 569 *et seq.* at 585 *et seq.*
16. The second exception are international treaties unifying conflict-of-law rules, most prominently the various Hague Conventions; see McParland, *supra* note 3, recitals 1.18 *et seq.*
17. B. von Hoffmann and K. Thorn, *Internationales Privatrecht*, 9th ed., Munich, Beck, 2007, Sec. 1, Introduction, recital 48.

and commercial matters of 2012[18]. Articles 17 to 19 of the Regulation establish a specific jurisdiction regime for consumer contracts, which aims to protect the consumer as the structurally weaker party[19]. Its core can be summarised as follows.

The consumer can sue the entrepreneur either at their own domicile or at the domicile of the entrepreneur (Art. 18, para. 1); thereby, the Regulation creates a venue at the plaintiff's domicile. In contrast, the entrepreneur can sue the consumer only at the consumer's domicile (Art. 18, para. 2). A jurisdiction agreement departing from these provisions is valid only when it is entered into after the dispute has arisen or favours the consumer in such a way that he may sue the entrepreneur in additional venues.

Thus, it is guaranteed that the consumer always has a venue within the European Union at his disposal where he can sue the entrepreneur[20]. On the one hand, such a court will apply Article 6, paragraph 2 of the Rome I Regulation to determine the applicable law, which will lead to application of the mandatory consumer protection provisions in force at the consumer's habitual residence. But, on the other hand, the entrepreneur has to sue the consumer at the domicile of the latter with the same consequences as just described.

9. Of course, the entrepreneur may still sue the consumer before Californian courts as those courts will not apply the Brussels Ibis Regulation but their own domestic jurisdiction rules to determine their jurisdiction. As a result, they might uphold the jurisdiction agreement. However, a judgment rendered by such a court would not be enforceable against the consumer within the European Union[21], thus rendering it worthless.

---

18. Regulation 1215/2012/EU of the European Parliament and of the Council of 12 December 2012 on jurisdiction and the recognition and enforcement of judgments in civil and commercial matters, OJ 2012 L 351, p. 1 (hereinafter "Brussels Ibis Regulation" or "Brussels Ibis Reg.").

19. So-called protective fora; see B. Añoveros Terradas, "Restrictions on Jurisdiction Clauses in Consumer Contracts within the European Union", *Oxford U. Comparative L. Forum* 1, 2003, https://ouclf.law.ox.ac.uk/restrictions-on-jurisdiction-clauses-in-consumer-contracts-within-the-european-union/, accessed 10 February 2022. It has to be noted that the Regulation in such cases exceptionally applies also to defendants domiciled in a non-member state; see Art. 6 para. 1 and Art. 18 para. 1 Brussels Ibis Reg.

20. Cf. P. Mankowski and P. Nielsen, in U. Magnus and P. Mankowski (eds.), *European Commentaries on Private International Law: Brussels Ibis Regulation*, Vol. I, Munich, Otto Schmidt, 2016, Art. 18 Brussels Ibis Reg. recital 2.

21. See A. Bonomi, in A. Dickinson and E. Lein (eds.), *The Brussels I Regulation Recast*, Oxford, Oxford University Press, 2015, recitals 6.90 *et seq.*; enforcement in the judgment state will in most cases be unsuccessful for lack of assets of the consumer.

10. This brief analysis has proven that effectively protecting structurally weaker parties requires a subtly coordinated interaction between the substantive law, conflict of laws and jurisdiction rules. If one part fails, the whole system collapses. We have to keep that in mind when considering the following issues.

CHAPTER III

CONFLICT OF LAWS

11. This part of the paper will appraise those existing conflict-of-law rules that intend to protect entrepreneurs as structurally weaker parties to a contract. First, it will deal with choice-of-law provisions; second, by objective conflict-of-law rules. Third, it will look at internationally mandatory rules, the *lois de police*, before evaluating the status quo.

12. But I may start with a remark on English as a legal language. When I just referred to "objective conflict-of-law rules" this might have generated some confusion, as such an expression is not found in English legal language.

This shows the difficulties when one wants to use the legal language associated with one legal culture to describe legal thoughts developed in a foreign jurisdiction. Legal thinking and legal language are closely related to each other. On the continent, private international law is regarded as an area of law highly influenced by legal dogmatics. It is well known for its elaborate vocabulary. Sometimes legal notions cross the border without being translated, like *renvoi* or *ordre public*. Thus, continental scholars have a broad common understanding regardless of whether they come from France, Italy or Germany.

In common law, pragmatism usually prevails, with the result that in many cases there does not even exist a proper translation for notions regarded as essential by continental scholars.

I would like to give two examples as anecdotal evidence.

For many years, the European Union has planned to enact a European Contract Law as a proper alternative to national codifications. The drafts have been completed in English. A colleague of mine at Bucerius Law School, one of the most prominent German scholars in contract law, became truly furious upon reviewing the 2009 Draft Common Frame of Reference (the DCFR)[22] as he counted the expression "(un-)reasonable" no less than 406 times. How can one leave those who must apply the law in such a state of ambiguity?

---

22. C. von Bar, E. Clive and H. Schulte-Nölke (eds.), *Principles, Definitions and Model Rules of European Private Law: Draft Common Frame of Reference (DCFR) – Outline Edition*, Munich, Sellier, 2009.

The Protection of Small and Medium-Sized Enterprises 119

Another colleague of mine, Professor Skouris, the former president of the European Court of Justice (ECJ), reported the following incident. During the deliberations on a judgment of the ECJ, the French and the German judge discussed for a while which notion should be used to properly describe the Court's conclusion. Their British colleague reclined in his chair and observed slyly that in English legal language, only one expression existed for what was being discussed. Thus, no choice needed to be taken.

This demonstrates how language influences the law, and the contemporary success of common law must be largely attributed to the dominance of the English language.

However, when scholars from the continent are supposed to use English as their lingua franca, they must also be permitted to develop legal English further. In this way, the law correspondingly influences language, and the future of law does not develop into a one-way street.

Now let us get back to the subject of this paper, the protection of structurally weaker parties in the conflict of laws.

A. Choice of law

1. Starting point

13. Modern conflict-of-law codifications provide for a free choice of law by the parties with regard to contractual obligations.

A famous example can be found in Article 3, paragraph 1, first sentence of the Rome I Regulation: "A contract shall be governed by the law chosen by the parties."

Recital 11 adds:

> "The parties' freedom to choose the applicable law should be one of the cornerstones of the system of conflict-of-law rules in matters of contractual obligations."

The same approach is followed, for example, by the conflict-of-law codifications of Switzerland [23], Turkey [24], China [25] and, more recently, Russia [26].

---

23. Art. 116 Federal Code on Private International Law of Switzerland of 18 December 1987, AS 1988, 1776 (hereinafter "Swiss Fed. Code PIL").
24. Art. 24 Sec. 1 Act on Private International and Procedural Law of Turkey of 27 November 2007, Act. No. 5718 (hereinafter "PIPL Turkey").
25. Art. 41 Act on the Application of Laws over Foreign-Related Civil Relationships of China of 28 October 2008 (hereinafter "FRCR China").
26. Art. 1210 Civil Code of Russia of 26 November 2001, Law 146-FZ, with the Amendment of 30 September 2013, Law 260-FZ (hereinafter "Russian Civil Code").

14. Thus, the freedom of choice is not limited by any condition requiring either a substantial relation between the contract and the law chosen or a legitimate interest of the parties to choose a non-related law. By this, such codifications differ fundamentally from the approach prevailing in the United States: Section 1-105 of the Uniform Commercial Code (UCC) in its original version from 1952 [27] requires a reasonable relation of the transaction to the chosen law [28], and Section 187, paragraph 2 of the Restatement of the Law Second – Conflict of Laws [29], either a substantial relationship of the chosen state to the parties or the transaction or another reasonable basis for the parties' choice.

15. However, in all jurisdictions granting freedom of choice in general, there are restraints for certain types of contracts to protect the legitimate interest of structurally weaker parties. One can distinguish three different methods. First, the choice of law might be restricted to a limited number of legal systems. Second, there might be a free choice of law, but the effects of such choice are modified in such a way as we have seen in our initial example on consumer protection. Third, a decision on a case-by-case basis might be taken based on abuse of law.

2. Restricted choice of law

16. Examples of a restricted choice of law in business-to-business (B2B) cases can be found in the Rome I Regulation, namely the provisions on insurance contracts (Art. 7) and passenger transport contracts (Art. 5, para. 2) [30].

17. To understand the very complex Article 7 of the Rome I Regulation, one has to recognise that it differentiates between four different types of insurance contracts: first, reinsurance contracts; second, insurance contracts covering large risks; and third and fourth, insurance

---

27. Uniform Commercial Code: Official Draft, American Law Institute, 1952.
28. An attempt to change the UCC section formally and to grant the parties autonomy to stipulate the applicable law quite independently from the transaction's version (styled Sec. 1-301) had been adopted only by the Virgin Islands by early 2008; its sponsors (the American Law Institute and the Uniform Law Commission) withdrew it. The original version thus continues in force, albeit under the new number; see American Law Institute, 85th Annual Meeting, 19-21 May 2008, pp. 10-12.
29. Restatement (Second) of Conflicts of Laws, American Law Institute, 1971.
30. Besides these examples one finds restricted choices of law mostly in the fields of international family and succession law, see e.g. Art. 5 para. 1 Regulation 1259/2010/EU of 20 December 2010 implementing enhanced cooperation in the area of the law applicable to divorce and legal separation, OJ 2010 L 343, pp. 10 *et seq.* ("Rome III Regulation").

contracts covering other-than-large risks [31] situated, respectively, inside or outside the European Union. Large risks are defined by Article 13 (27) of the European Solvency II Directive and encompass, among others, transport insurance and liability insurance for certain means of transport as well as further insurance in cases where the insured is not a small or medium-sized enterprise because of its exceeding certain threshold values [32]. We will come back to this later on.

Regarding reinsurance contracts (Art. 7, para. 1, second sentence) and insurance contracts covering large risks (Art. 7, para. 2), the insured does not need protection. In the former case, the insured is also an insurance company; in the latter case, it is a company which is likely to seek professional advice from a qualified lawyer before concluding the insurance contract [33]. Therefore, in both cases, the normal conflict rules apply. The parties can choose the applicable law without any restrictions. In the absence of choice, the contract is governed by the law of the country where the insurer, as the party required to effect the characteristic performance under the contract, has his habitual residence [34].

18. In the case of insurance contracts covering other-than-large risks outside the European Union [35], the insured might need legal protection against the insurance company, the latter being the structurally stronger party. However, European legislators showed no concern in this regard and have submitted these cases to the general conflict-of-law rules (Art. 7, para. 1, first sentence, at the end). This attitude has been heavily criticised in legal literature [36] and demonstrates once more the fixation of European conflict rules on the Internal Market. Moreover, in many cases, the legitimate interests of parties domiciled in third countries

---

31. So-called mass risks, which do not fall within the meaning of Art. 13 (27) Directive 2009/138/EC of the European Parliament and of the Council of 25 November 2009 on the taking-up and pursuit of the business of Insurance and Reinsurance, OJ 2009 L 335, p. 1 (hereinafter "Solvency II"); see H. Heiss, in U. Magnus and P. Mankowski (eds.), *European Commentaries on Private International Law: Rome I Regulation*, Vol. II, Cologne, Otto Schmidt, 2017, Art. 7 Rome I Reg. recital 29.
32. *Ibid.*
33. Cf. Heiss, *supra* note 31, Art. 7 Rome I Reg. recitals 36, 95.
34. A. Staudinger, in F. Ferrari, E.-M. Kieninger and P. Mankowski *et al.* (eds.), *Internationales Vertragsrecht. Rom I-VO, CISG, CMR, FactÜ – Kommentar*, 3rd ed., Munich, Beck, 2018, Art. 7 Rome I Reg. recital 28.
35. An example might be a French insurance company selling a life insurance police to a Serbian resident living in Belgrade; see also D. H. Wendt, in T. Rauscher (ed.), *Europäisches Zivilprozess- und Kollisionsrecht EuZPR/EuIPR*, Vol. III: *Rom I-VO, Rom II-VO*, 4th ed., Cologne, Otto Schmidt, 2016, Art. 7 Rome I Reg. recitals 15 *et seq.*
36. Staudinger, *supra* note 34, Art. 7 Rome I Reg. recital 1 with further references; Wendt, *supra* note 35, Art. 7 Rome I Reg. recital 57.

or the public interests of third countries themselves are ignored, an attitude that feeds the image of a European fortress [37].

19. The picture totally changes if the insured risk is situated inside the European Union [38]. There, the need for protection, even where the insured is a small or medium-sized enterprise, is acknowledged, resulting first of all in a restricted choice of law. Under Article 7, paragraph 3 of the Rome I Regulation, the parties to such an insurance contract can only choose between

(a) the law of any Member State where the risk is situated at the time of conclusion of the contract;

(b) the law of the country where the insured has his habitual residence;

(c) in the case of life insurance, the law of the Member State of which the insured is a national;

(d) for insurance contracts covering risks limited to events occurring in a Member State other than the Member State where the risk is situated (examples: cross-border environmental damages, product liability), the law of that Member State;

(e) where the insured is an SME, and the insurance contract covers two or more risks that relate to those activities and that are situated in different Member States, the law of any of the Member States concerned or the law of the country of habitual residence of the insured.

Thus, the chosen law needs to relate substantially to the contract; hence, the choice of a neutral law is excluded. Nevertheless, the parties can pick from this basket the legal system that offers the insured the least protection. Thus, while the risk for the structurally weaker party is limited, it persists [39].

20. The same approach has been taken by the European legislature with regard to passenger transport contracts. Again, Article 5, paragraph 2

---

37. Cf. D. Martiny, in F. J. Säcker *et al.* (eds.), *Münchener Kommentar zum Bürgerlichen Gesetzbuch*, Vol. XIII, 8th ed., Munich, Beck, 2021, Art. 7 Rome I Reg. recital 2.

38. For example, situation of risks can be the situs of immovable property, the country where the car is registered, or the habitual residence of the insured person, C. Armbrüster, in U. Magnus (ed.), *Einleitung zur Rom I-VO, Article 1-10 Rom I-VO* (Internationales Vertragsrecht 1) [part of the multivolume *J. von Staudingers Kommentar zum Bürgerlichen Gesetzbuch mit Einführungsgesetz und Nebengesetzen*], rev. ed., Berlin, De Gruyter, 2021, Prel. Rem. Art. 7 Rome I Reg. recitals 16 *et seq.*

39. Cf. Rühl, *supra* note 12, pp. 370, 373.

does not distinguish between private and business trips and protects both groups alike. We will investigate later on the underlying policy [40]. The method used by the Regulation to protect the passenger as the structurally weaker party is, again, a restricted choice of law. The parties may only choose the law of the country where:

(a) the passenger has his habitual residence; or
(b) the carrier has his habitual residence; or
(c) the carrier has his place of central administration; or
(d) the place of departure is situated; or
(e) the place of destination is situated.

Once more, a substantial relation between the contract and the law chosen is ensured, diminishing but not eliminating the risk to the weaker party.

Thus, the carrier might have located its central administration intentionally within a country well known for its liberal legislation on transportation contracts, for example a jurisdiction containing no mandatory provisions [41]. Under Article 5, paragraph 2 of the Rome I Regulation, the carrier can impose that law on the passenger, who, as a result, is not protected at all.

3. Cherry-picking method

21. A different legislative technique has already been illustrated in our initial example, one preserving the freedom of the contracting parties to choose the law applicable to their contract but limiting the effect of such choice. More precisely, the structurally weaker party keeps at least the minimum protection offered by the law determined by objective conflict rules, which in addition are also shaped in favour of the weaker party. Its mandatory provisions protecting the structurally weaker party cannot be overridden by the choice of another law offering less protection.

The chosen law prevails only when it offers a higher level of protection. This technique can even lead to a combination of the two laws [42]. Thus,

---

40. See recitals 124 *et seq.*
41. Cf. Rühl, *supra* note 12, p. 373; cf. P. Nielsen, "The Rome I Regulation and Contracts of Carriage", in F. Ferrari and S. Leible (eds.), *Rome I Regulation*, Munich, Sellier, 2009, pp. 99 *et seq.* at 107, questioning if the limitation of party autonomy in Art. 5 Rome I Reg. in reality protects the passenger.
42. G. Rühl, in B. Gsell, W. Krüger, S. Lorenz and C. Reymann (eds.), *beck-online. GROSSKOMMENTAR* (hereinafter "BeckOGK"), version 1 July 2019, Art. 6 Rome I Reg. recitals 257 *et seq.*; cf. M. Gardeñes Santiago, "La regulación conflictual del contrato de trabajo en el reglamento Roma I: una oportunidad perdida", *Anuario español de Derecho internacional privado*, No. 8 (2008), pp. 387 *et seq.* at 404 *et seq.*

one might combine the longer delay for a withdrawal under law A with the more liberal form requirements for such withdrawal under law B. The result is an kind of artificial legal order reflecting neither of the two laws involved. This cherry-picking method has been criticised to a certain extent in legal literature [43]. Still, it is a very efficient way to safeguard the protection of the structurally weaker party to a contract.

22. In the framework of the Rome I Regulation, one finds this technique used only for the protection of non-business parties.

The relevant provision for consumer contracts in Article 6, paragraph 2 has already been mentioned:

"[T]he parties may choose the law applicable to a [consumer] contract . . . in accordance with Article 3 [= freedom of choice]. Such a choice may not, however, have the result of depriving the consumer of the protection afforded to him by provisions that cannot be derogated from by agreement by virtue of the law [at the habitual residence of the consumer]."

Thus, one has to compare the mandatory consumer protection rules of the law at the consumer's habitual residence with those of the chosen law. The provision offering a higher level of protection for every single issue prevails, allowing a mosaic composed of the two different legal systems. However, with regard to non-mandatory (= optional) provisions, the chosen law applies at large [44].

23. It should also be noted that the objective conflict-of-law rule is altered in favour of the consumer. Deviating from Article 4, paragraph 2, the decisive factor is not the habitual residence of the party required to effect the characteristic performance under the contract but the habitual residence of the consumer, who most typically is the buyer or the party entitled to services.

24. A similar construction can be found with regard to individual employment contracts. Insofar, Article 8, paragraph 1 of the Rome I Regulation states:

"An individual employment contract shall be governed by the law chosen by the parties in accordance with Article 3. Such a

---

43. See e.g. S. Leible, in R. Hüßtege and H.-P. Mansel (eds.), *Bürgerliches Gesetzbuch, Rom Verordnungen*, Vol. VI, 3rd ed., Baden-Baden, Nomos, 2019, Art. 6 Rome I Reg. recital 68; G. Palao Moreno, in U. Magnus and P. Mankowski (eds.), *European Commentaries on Private International Law: Rome I Regulation*, Vol. II, Cologne, Otto Schmidt, 2017, Art. 8 Rome I Reg. recital 6.

44. Heiderhoff, *supra* note 13, Art. 6 Rome I Reg. recital 55.

choice of law may not, however, have the result of depriving the employee of the protection afforded to him by provisions that cannot be derogated from by agreement under the law [of the country in which the employee habitually carries out his work in performance of the contract]."

Again, the minimum standard is set by the mandatory provisions of a law closely related to the contract, in this case, the habitual place of work. The law chosen by the parties can only increase that standard but not diminish it.

25. While the Rome I Regulation does not apply this method to B2B contracts, a perfect example can be found in the new Código de derecho internacional privado (Code on Private International Law) of Panama of October 2015 [45].

Its Article 82 reads as follows:

"Los contratos de representación y franquicia internacional se rigen por la autonomia de las partes, pero en cuanto a la indemnización por ruptura o incumplimiento del contrato, por la ley de ejecución del contrato o la de mayor protección al concesionario o franqueado a elección de este último."

Freely translated:

"Commercial agency agreements and franchise agreements are governed by the law chosen by the parties. However, with regard to compensation for breach of contract, the commercial agent or franchisee may opt for the application of the law at the place of performance offering a higher level of protection to this party."

26. The technique is similar to the one in the two examples above. The parties have freedom of choice, but its effects are limited insofar as one has to compare a certain set of rules of the chosen law, more precisely, those dealing with potential compensation claims for breach of contract with those in force at the place of performance. The ones favouring the commercial agent or the franchisee as the structurally weaker party apply. Again, we are confronted with a cherry-picking method, albeit to a lesser degree.

---

45. Código de Derecho Internacional Privado, published in the Official Gazette No. 27885-A of 8 October 2015, replacing the version of 2014. The provisions on agency and franchise agreements were not modified in terms of content, but the numbering of the articles changed.

First, not all mandatory rules are included but only those dealing with compensation for breach of contract. It would require intensive research into the substantive Panamanian law to determine whether this encompasses, as I would suppose, compensation payments on the termination of the contractual relationship [46] – already a notorious issue under European law, as we will see [47]. Second, it is not the judge's task to establish the regime more favourable to the commercial agent or franchisee; instead, it is up to this party to opt for the law that he thinks to be more favourable to his legal position.

27. However, the most important point is that a concept developed for protecting private parties is now extended to B2B relations in which one of the entrepreneurs is regarded as the structurally weaker party.

4. Abuse of law

28. In addition to these two statute-oriented approaches, there also exists an approach which evaluates the specific choice of law on a case-by-case basis. If such a choice does not reflect the legitimate interests of both parties or goes so far as constituting an abuse of the law, it is void, and the law applicable to the contract will be determined by applying objective conflict-of-law rules.

This corresponds to the traditional US approach already described above. Both Section 1-105 of the UCC, in its original version from 1952, and Section 187, paragraph 2 of the Restatement of the Law Second – Conflict of Laws require a reasonable basis for the parties' choice of law. A substantial relationship of the chosen law to the parties, the transaction or other legitimate interests of both parties can establish such a basis. If the judge finds no such reasonable basis exists in the given case, he will disregard the choice of law and determine the applicable law by objective standards. In doing so, the judge has a considerable margin of discretion. Court rulings from the past have seen such discretion used to protect structurally weaker parties [48].

29. This method cannot be applied under the Rome I Regulation. Article 3, paragraph 1 requires a valid choice of law. Following

---

46. Concerning compensation claims by agents in German law, see Mogendorf, *supra* note 14, p. 28.
47. *Ibid.*, p. 36.
48. *Electrical and Magneto Service Co. Inc.* v. *Ambac International Corp.*, 941 F.2d 660 (8th Cir. 1991); see Mogendorf, *supra* note 14, pp. 166 *et seq.* with further references.

Article 3, paragraph 5, the existence and validity of the consent of the parties as to the choice of the applicable law is to be determined in accordance with the law chosen; only the formal validity of the choice of law and the legal capacity of the parties are subject to different conflict rules. However, this refers only to the existence and validity of the choice of law. Hence, if the choice of law has been reached by duress or fraud, it will be void under the law applicable to the contract [49].

30. On the other hand, the admissibility of a choice of law is not subject to the *lex contractus* but is conclusively determined by the Regulation itself [50]. Thus, subject to special provisions for certain types of contracts, as presented above, there are no further restraints on a free choice of law by the parties. This follows clearly from the wording, the context and the purpose of the Regulation [51]. As a result, the judge may not scrutinise a choice of law as to its legitimacy or the underlying motives of the parties.

5. Evaluation

31. To evaluate the approaches presented above, it seems advantageous to ascertain the relevant parameters based on the underlying policies.

The first parameter is the principle of free choice of law. Freedom of choice derives from party autonomy, which in many jurisdictions enjoys constitutional protection as a component of civil liberties [52]. Therefore, restrictions on party autonomy require a legitimate reason and can only go as far as necessary to reach this legitimate goal [53].

32. In addition, the choice of law enables the parties to a contract to determine the law applicable to the contract in advance, generating certainty as to the implementation of the contract [54]. Furthermore, the

---

49. von Hein, *supra* note 9, Art. 3 Rome I Reg. recital 40.
50. Cf. McParland, *supra* note 3, recitals 9.13 *et seq.*; Mankowski, *supra* note 3, Art. 3 Rome I Reg. recital 7.
51. Cf. A. L. Diamond, "Conflict of Laws in the EEC", *Current Legal Problems*, Vol. 32 (1979), pp. 155 *et seq.* at 161; McParland, *supra* note 3, recitals 9.01, 9.12.
52. E. Jayme, "Identité culturelle et intégration: le droit international privé postmoderne", *Recueil des cours* 251 (1995), pp. 1 *et seq.* at 147; Mankowski, *supra* note 3, Art. 3 Rome I Reg. recital 4; McParland, *supra* note 3, recital 9.04.
53. For the general constitutional requirements regarding restrictions, cf. H. Dreier, in H. Dreier (ed.), *Grundgesetzkommentar*, Vol. I, 3rd ed., Tübingen, Mohr Siebeck, 2013, Prel. Rem. recital 146; also cf. McParland, *supra* note 3, recitals 9.09 *et seq.*
54. Mankowski, *supra* note 3, Art. 3 Rome I Reg. recital 9; McParland, *supra* note 3, recital 9.08.

parties are generally regarded as the appropriate keepers of their own interests [55].

The efficient protection of structurally weaker parties – as the second parameter – conflicts to some extent with the freedom of choice, although it might be argued, as already mentioned, that a restriction on party autonomy serves its preservation in cases of a structural imbalance between the parties [56]. In any event, such protection is a legitimate purpose. It may therefore justify the interference with civil liberties as long as such interference still answers its original purpose and does not go beyond what is required to serve that purpose. Therefore, such limitations have to be appropriate, necessary and proportional [57].

33. Third and finally, legal certainty is the general goal of all conflict-of-law rules, as the parties should be in a position to know in advance which legal rules will govern their relationship [58].

34. The last-mentioned factor clearly argues against an approach on a case-by-case basis. If properly conducted, it certainly guarantees that each case will be decided on its own merits. In many cases, however, the parties will not know for certain before the court decision whether the choice of law will be upheld or not. Moreover, international business requires reliability in planning, an aim endangered by a case-by-case approach. Consequently, a choice of law would lose a considerable part of its advantages, and some parties might even forgo it.

35. A restricted choice of law, as the next approach evaluated here, undoubtedly creates legal certainty. It also entails a comparatively cautious interference with party autonomy. In addition, it guarantees an authentic application of one legal order [59], as under this approach the whole contract is governed by a single legal scheme rather than being the forged product of one legal order combined with another.

---

55. F. Diedrich, "Rechtswahlfreiheit und Vertragsstatut – eine Zwischenbilanz angesichts der Rom I-Verordnung", RIW, No. 6 (2009), pp. 378 *et seq.* at 379; cf. M. Whincop and M. Keyes, "Putting the 'Private' Back into Private International Law: Default Rules and the Proper Law of the Contract", *Melbourne University Law Review*, Vol. 21 (1997), pp. 515 *et seq.* at 517.
56. M. Wendland, in BeckOGK, version 1 September 2021, Art. 3 Rome I Reg. recital 31.
57. Cf. Dreier, *supra* note 53, Prel. Rem. recital 146; cf. with regard to the balance achieved by the Rome I Regulation, see Mankowski, *supra* note 3, Art. 3 Rome I Reg. recital 12.
58. U. Magnus, in U. Magnus and P. Mankowski (eds.), *European Commentaries on Private International Law: Rome I Regulation*, Vol. II, Cologne, Otto Schmidt, 2017, Introduction, recital 4.
59. Cf. with regard to the (otherwise) arising legal uncertainty of a law mix: Leible, *supra* note 43, Art. 6 Rome I Reg. recital 68.

The drawback of this solution is that it does not guarantee efficient protection of the structurally weaker party. Though the choice of law is limited to legal orders having a substantial relation to the case, this does not say anything about the level of protection each of these jurisdictions provides. Therefore, the structurally stronger party can still assert its own interests and implement a choice-of-law clause in favour of the less paternalistic law [60].

Thus, the effects of a restricted choice of law remain limited to the level of conflict of laws. Hence, it is an appropriate method to open fields of law cautiously to party autonomy, as with family law or the law of succession, but is not an appropriate means of protecting structurally weaker parties substantively.

36. By contrast, the cherry-picking approach offers very effective protection for the structurally weaker party. It keeps at least the protection offered by the mandatory rules of a law that is closely related to the contract and determined by factors mirroring the interests of the weaker party, like that party's habitual residence or the place of performance. A choice of law may only add to this and is not permitted to diminish existing protection.

Contrary to first instinct, this approach also interferes less with party autonomy than one might fear. The range of interferences depends on the existence of mandatory rules protecting the structurally weaker party in the law determined by objective standards [61]. If there exist many mandatory rules, as in the cases of consumer or labour law, the impact of the cherry-picking method is substantial. On the other hand, its impact is relatively modest in areas of law with a limited number of mandatory provisions only. It can be presumed that B2B contracts belong to the latter category, leaving a huge space for party autonomy.

In this context, it should be noted that during the negotiations on the Rome I Regulation, there had been proposals to eliminate choice of law for consumer contracts as it offers no advantages to the entrepreneur on account of the cherry-picking method [62]. Most trade associations rejected that proposal, arguing that even under the cherry-picking method, enterprises doing business in several countries can make

---

60. Rühl, *supra* note 12, p. 373; see also Mogendorf, *supra* note 14, p. 208.
61. See Magnus, *supra* note 9, Art. 6 Rome I Reg. recital 140.
62. Cf. Art. 5 of the Proposal for a Regulation of the European Parliament and the Council on the Law applicable to contractual obligations (Rome I), COM (2005) 650 final.

all their contracts subject to a single legal order by way of choice of law [63]. Even considering that such a choice of law will not cover all potential legal issues, contract management efficiency would increase considerably. This finding applies to an even greater extent to B2B contracts.

37. The only detriment of the cherry-picking approach consists of creating an artificial legal system composed of elements from two jurisdictions, resulting in a system of rules that does not properly reflect either. This might even lead to inconsistencies which have to be overcome by adjustment [64]. However, in previous decades these problems have not proved so serious as to be uncontrollable in legal practice.

38. In summary, the cherry-picking method efficiently protects the legitimate interests of structurally weaker parties without disproportionally interfering with party autonomy. Moreover, it serves legal certainty and facilitates efficient contract management in international trade.

B. Objective conflict-of-law rules

1. Starting point

39. To safeguard the protection of structurally weaker parties, objective conflict-of-law rules must complement the choice-of-law provisions. The former serves two functions: First, they have to determine the applicable law in the absence of a valid choice of law. Second, they have to identify the legal system setting the standards for the cherry-picking method: to which legal system does one compare the law chosen by the parties?

40. If such objective conflict-of-law rules are to protect the structurally weaker party, they most probably have to be based on connecting factors different from those used generally. Again, consumer protection law shall illustrate that.

---

63. J. Clausnitzer and H. Woopen, "Internationale Vertragsgestaltung – Die neue EG-Verordnung für grenzüberschreitende Verträge (Rom I-VO)", *Betriebs-Berater* (2008), pp. 1798 *et seq.* at 1801. This attitude might have been based also on the assumption that many consumers are not aware of their rights under the regulation, and therefore will not enforce them by legal action. Such illegitimate expectations in the meantime have been frustrated by the ECJ, judgment of 28 July 2016, *Verein für Konsumenteninformation* v. *Amazon*, C-191/15 ECLI:EU:C:2016:612, which obliges the entrepreneur to inform the consumer about its rights under Art. 6 para. 2 Rome I Reg. within the choice-of-law clause.

64. Leible, *supra* note 43, Art. 6 Rome I Reg. recital 68; see also Magnus, *supra* note 9, Art. 6 Rome I Reg. recitals 138, 144 *et seq.*; Rühl, *supra* note 42, Art. 6 Rome I Reg. recitals 257 *et seq.*

In nearly all modern codifications of private international law, the habitual residence of the party that renders the performance characterising the contract is the pivotal connecting factor for contractual obligations [65]. Article 4, paragraph 2 of the Rome I Regulation might serve as an example:

> "[T]he contract shall be governed by the law of the country where the party required to effect the characteristic performance of the contract has his habitual residence."

The underlying policy is that the characteristic performance is usually the one more difficult to comply with [66]. Delivering goods is more difficult than paying the purchase price; rendering services is more challenging than remunerating them. Therefore, the party obliged to effect this performance is rewarded by the application of its domestic law [67].

41. However, in the case of consumer contracts, this would normally lead to the domestic law of the entrepreneur. Therefore, the decisive connecting factor switches from the habitual residence of the party effecting the characteristic performance to the consumer's habitual residence.

Article 6, paragraph 1 of the Rome I Regulation reads:

> "[A] contract concluded by a natural person for a purpose which can be regarded as being outside his trade or profession (the consumer) with another person acting in the exercise of his trade or profession (the professional) shall be governed by the law of the country where the consumer has his habitual residence." [68]

Under Article 6, paragraph 2, this law also sets the minimum standards for the protection of the consumer as the structurally weaker party.

42. Similarly, with regard to individual employment contracts, Article 8, paragraphs 2 and 1, second sentence of Rome I Regulation points towards the country where the employee habitually carries out his work in the performance of the contract.

---

65. See Art. 117 sentence 2 Swiss Fed. Code PIL; Art. 24 Sec. 4 PIPL Turkey; Art. 41 FRCR China; Art. 1211 Sec. 2 Russian Civil Code.
66. A. Köhler, in BeckOGK, version 1 September 2021, Art. 4 Rome I Reg. recital 150.
67. Cf. *ibid.*; Magnus, *supra* note 9, Art. 4 Rome I Reg. recital 107; Martiny, *supra* note 37, Art. 4 Rome I Reg. recitals 176 *et seq.*
68. Similar provisions can be found in Art. 120 sentence 1 Swiss Fed. Code PIL; Art. 1212 Sec. 2 Russian Civil Code.

2. B2B contracts

43. With regard to B2B contracts, the picture is less conclusive. Although there are a couple of objective conflict-of-law rules based on considerations related to protecting a structurally weaker party, they are often not part of a coherent system. Instead, they are somehow statutory orphans standing alone.

The missing coherence can be illustrated by the two regimes providing for a restricted choice of law under the Rome I Regulation: insurance contracts and passenger transport contracts.

44. On the one hand, in the case of insurance contracts covering other-than-large risks situated inside the European Union, Article 7, paragraph 3, subparagraph 3 reflects the need for a protection of the insured as the structurally weaker party:

> "To the extent that the law applicable has not been chosen by the parties in accordance with this paragraph, such a contract shall be governed by the law of the Member State in which the risk is situated at the time of conclusion of the contract."

Thus, the state where the insured risk is situated replaces the habitual residence of the insurer as the decisive connecting factor, despite the insurer being the party effecting the characteristic performance. Hereby a legal order applies which is closely related to the insured as the structurally weaker party and nevertheless associated with the insurer's activities [69].

45. On the other hand, the conflict-of-law rule dealing with passenger transport contracts reveals a different picture. Article 5, paragraph 2, subparagraph 1 of the Rome 1 Regulation provides:

> "To the extent that the law applicable to a contract for the carriage of passengers has not been chosen by the parties in accordance with the second subparagraph, the law applicable shall be the law of the country where the passenger has his habitual residence, provided that either the place of departure or the place of destination is situated in that country. If these requirements are not met, the law of the country where the carrier has his habitual residence shall apply."

---

[69]. However, one should keep in mind that the availability of a restricted choice of law weakens the protective effect of these provisions considerably. See recitals 19, 35; Mogendorf, *supra* note 14, p. 88; Rühl, *supra* note 12, p. 373.

Here, the law at the habitual residence of the passenger as the structurally weaker party applies only if it is reinforced by a second connecting factor, either the place of departure or the place of destination. However, this cumulative approach fails if both the place of departure and the place of destination lie outside the passenger's home country. In that case, the Regulation returns to the general rule and calls for the application of the law where the carrier, as the party effecting the characteristic performance, has his habitual residence.

46. This immediately raises the following question: Why – in contrast to consumer contracts – does the habitual residence of the passenger alone not suffice as a connecting factor? It is no more or less associated with the activities of the carrier than with those of the entrepreneur. A possible explanation could be that the provision is not restricted to consumers [70] and thus does not require the same degree of protection [71].

Even if one agrees with this perception, there might be doubts about why one should return to the general conflict rule in this case instead of searching for a compromise. Such a compromise could be found by analogy with the conflict-of-law rules for individual employment and insurance contracts: It might consist of using the place of performance as the decisive connecting factor. However, one must admit that such a solution would have its own flaws. On the one hand, it is in the nature of international transport that performance is effected in more than one country. Thus, one would have to decide which place of performance is to prevail, the place of departure or the place of destination [72]. On the other hand, it is doubtful whether, in such a case, applying the law at the place of performance would meet the passenger's legitimate expectations as he might rely more on the domestic law of the carrier he has chosen for transport outside his own home country.

Nevertheless, the provision does not appear to have been determined with regard to the protection of passengers as the structurally weaker party to a contract.

---

70. With regard to consumers, one should be aware of Art. 6 para. 4 lit. *b* Rome I Reg., which excludes transportation contracts – with the exception of package travel contracts – from the substantive scope of application of Art. 6; see Martiny, *supra* note 37, Art. 6 Rome I Reg. recitals 29 *et seq*.
71. Cf. K. Thorn, in T. Rauscher (ed.), *Europäisches Zivilprozess- und Kollisionsrecht EuZPR/EuIPR*, Vol. III: *Rom I-VO, Rom II-VO*, 4th ed., Cologne, Otto Schmidt, 2016, Art. 5 Rome I Reg. recitals 77, 83.
72. Cf. ECJ, judgment of 9 July 2009, *Rehder v. AirBaltic*, C-204/08, ECLI:EU:C:2009:439.

47. The picture is even more clouded if one looks at further objective conflict-of-law rules that purport to protect structurally weaker parties. The rule dealing with franchise agreements is a perfect example. Such agreements contain a vast number of obligations on behalf of both contracting parties [73]. Additionally, these obligations vary from case to case. Thus, the franchisor is obliged not only to sell equipment and supplies to the franchisee but also to license trademarks and familiarise the franchisee with business concepts and know-how. On the other hand, the franchisee is obliged not only to pay a fee but also to promote the goods or services in a standardised way, displaying for example the franchisor's signs, logos and trademark in a prominent place.

Consequently, the prevailing opinion in legal literature traditionally negated the existence of a characteristic performance and determined the applicable law by having recourse to the general clause, that is, the closest relation of the given contract to a legal order [74].

48. Responding to this view, many modern codifications of private international law have introduced a specific conflict-of-law rule especially for franchise agreements.

An example can be found in Article 4, paragraph 1, lit. e Rome I Regulation:

"[A] franchise contract shall be governed by the law of the country where the franchisee has his habitual residence."

The legislative history of the rule establishes that it has been motivated by the need to protect the franchisee as the structurally weaker party [75].

This approach is shared by other codifications, like Article 1211, paragraph 6 of the Russian Civil Code in its version of 2013 [76].

---

73. F. Ferrari, in F. Ferrari, E.-M. Kieninger and P. Mankowski *et al.* (eds.), *Internationales Vertragsrecht. Rom I-VO, CISG, CMR, FactÜ – Kommentar*, 3rd ed., Munich, Beck, 2018, Art. 4 Rome I Reg. recital 44.
74. See different solutions in D. Martiny, in K. Rebmann *et al.* (eds.), *Münchener Kommentar zum Bürgerlichen Gesetzbuch*, Vol. X, 4th ed., Munich, Beck, 2006, Art. 28 EGBGB recital 230.
75. Proposal for a Regulation of the European Parliament and the Council on the law applicable to contractual obligations (Rome I Reg.), Explanatory Memorandum, COM (2005), 650, p. 6.
76. "In respect of a commercial concession contract shall apply the law of the country on whose territory it is allowed to use a set of the exclusive rights possessed by the right holder or, if the given use is concurrently allowed on the territories of several countries, the law of the country where the right holder's place of residence or the principal place of exercising activities is located shall apply", Russian Civil Code, Amendment of 30 September 2013 (Federal Law No. 260-FZ).

49. However, the purpose of protecting the franchisee is entirely frustrated by the lack of a provision limiting party autonomy in such cases [77]. Thus, the franchisor is free to insert a choice-of-law clause into the agreement that refers to a law without any mandatory rules protecting the franchisee.

This demonstrates impressively that efficient protection of structurally weaker parties can only be reached if the choice-of-law rules and objective conflict-of-law rules interlock. Otherwise, the whole system will fail miserably.

C. Internationally mandatory rules

1. Starting point

50. A tool traditionally used by many jurisdictions to protect structurally weaker parties in B2B relations is internationally mandatory rules, the so-called *lois de police* [78].

A definition of such rules can be found in Article 9, paragraph 1 of the Rome I Regulation:

> "Overriding mandatory provisions are provisions the respect for which is regarded as crucial by a country for safeguarding its public interests, such as its political, social or economic organisation, to such an extent that they are applicable to any situation falling within their scope, irrespective of the law otherwise applicable to the contract under this Regulation."

This definition is not new, and similar descriptions can be found in earlier sources of law [79].

Thus, the decision of the ECJ in *Arblade/Leloup* [80] describes "public-order legislation" as

> "national provisions compliance with which has been deemed to be so crucial for the protection of the political, social or economic order in the Member State concerned as to require compliance

---

77. See Arts. 1210-1211 Russian Civil Code.
78. Cf. Rühl, *supra* note 12, p. 368; for the term, see Martiny, *supra* note 37, Art. 9 Rome I Reg. recital 1.
79. See Art. 7 para. 1 Convention 80/934/EEC on the law applicable to contractual obligations opened for signature in Rome on 19 June 1980, OJEC 1980 L 266, p. 1 ("Rome Convention").
80. ECJ, judgment of 23 November 1999, *Arblade* v. *Leloup*, Case C-376/96, ECLI:EU:C:1999:575.

therewith by all persons present on the national territory of that Member State and all legal relationships within that State"[81].

Article 9, paragraph 1 of the Rome I Regulation is complemented by recital 37, second sentence:

"The concept of 'overriding mandatory provisions' should be distinguished from the expression 'provisions which cannot be derogated from by agreement' and should be construed more restrictively."

51. From this, one can draw the following conclusions:

(1) Overriding mandatory provisions are not subject to the regular conflict rules applicable to contractual obligations.

(2) Overriding mandatory provisions have to be distinguished from (merely) domestically/internally mandatory provisions, as described in the initial example of the right of the consumer to freely withdraw from a distance contract. Unlike those provisions, the parties cannot opt out of overriding mandatory rules by virtue of a choice of law[82].

(3) States are entitled to enact overriding mandatory provisions to safeguard their public interest, such as their political, social or economic organisation.

(4) Overriding mandatory provisions self-define their territorial scope of application; that is, they contain their own conflict-of-law rule[83].

52. With regard to the third conclusion, one might wonder whether the protection of structurally weaker parties qualifies as such a public interest[84].

Traditionally, most overriding mandatory provisions can be found in public law, such as embargos, rules prohibiting or restricting the trade with arms, drugs, pieces of art or endangered species, foreign exchange legislation or antitrust and competition law[85].

---

81. *Ibid.*, recital 30.
82. Staudinger, *supra* note 34, Art. 9 Rome I Reg. recital 6.
83. A. Bonomi, in U. Magnus and P. Mankowski (eds.), *European Commentaries on Private International Law: Rome I Regulation*, Vol. II, Cologne, Otto Schmidt, 2017, Art. 9 Rome I Reg. recitals 8 *et seq.*; F. Maultzsch, in BeckOGK, version 1 March 2022, Art. 9 Rome I Reg. recital 2.
84. Cf. F. Maultzsch, in BeckOGK, version 1 December 2021, Art. 9 Rome I Reg. recital 187.
85. Martiny, *supra* note 37, Art. 9 Rome I Reg. recital 1; cf. A. Staudinger, in R. Schulze, H. Dörner and I. Ebert *et al.* (eds.), *Bürgerliches Gesetzbuch. Handkommentar*, 11th ed., Baden-Baden, Nomos, 2022, Art. 9 Rome I Reg. recital 4.

However, for many years it has been possible to identify an additional tendency to include specific provisions of private law protecting parties regarded as in need of legal protection. It has been argued that such provisions do not exclusively serve the interest of private parties; rather, they also contribute substantially to a state's social and economic order and thereby serve the common welfare [86].

53. The ECJ followed that argument in its famous *Ingmar* decision of 2000 [87], addressing the internationally mandatory nature of compensation claims of commercial agents after the termination of a contract. It stated:

> "[I]t should be borne in mind that . . . the harmonising measures laid down by the Directive are intended, inter alia, to eliminate restrictions on the carrying-on of the activities of commercial agents, to make the conditions of competition within the Community uniform and to increase the security of commercial transactions. . .
>
> The purpose of the regime established in Articles 17 to 19 of the Directive is thus to protect, for all commercial agents, freedom of establishment and the operation of undistorted competition in the internal market. Those provisions must therefore be observed throughout the Community if those Treaty objectives are to be attained." [88]

Here the argument of undistorted competition within the Internal Market suffices as a public interest justifying the creation of an overriding mandatory provision. This sets the standard for establishing a sufficient public interest quite low.

54. With regard to the fourth conclusion mentioned above, the question arises of how one can recognise that a provision requires application, irrespective of the law otherwise applicable to the contract.

Differing from overriding mandatory provisions in the field of public law, such provisions in private law rarely use clear language to define their territorial scope of application and thereby their nature as an overriding mandatory rule [89].

---

86. Cf. Bonomi, *supra* note 83, Art. 9 Rome I Reg. recital 74; Martiny, *supra* note 37, Art. 9 Rome I Reg. recitals 15 *et seq.*
87. ECJ, judgment of 9 November 2000, *Ingmar*, C-381/98, ECLI:EU:C:2000:605.
88. *Ibid.*, recital 23.
89. Cf. A. Spickhoff, in W. Hau and R. Poseck (eds.), *Beck'scher Online-Kommentar BGB*, 61st ed., Munich, Beck, 2021, Art. 9 Rome I Reg. recital 10.

55. One of the few examples can be found in the German Copyright Act [90]. Under Section 32, paragraphs 1 and 2, an author has a right to equitable remuneration. Following Section 32a, paragraphs 1 and 2, this holds especially for situations where the proceeds and benefits from the exploitation of the work disproportionally exceed the remuneration paid to the author. Both provisions are mandatory in the sense that they cannot be derogated from by agreement (Sec. 32, para. 3, Sec. 32a, para. 3). Thus, they are, on the first level, internally mandatory rules.

Section 32b, however, elevates both provisions to overriding mandatory rules. It reads:

"§ 32b Zwingende Anwendung

Die §§ 32 und 32a finden zwingend Anwendung

1. wenn auf den Nutzungsvertrag mangels einer Rechtswahl deutsches Recht anzuwenden wäre oder

2. soweit Gegenstand des Vertrages maßgebliche Nutzungshandlungen im räumlichen Geltungsbereich dieses Gesetzes sind.

Section 32b Compulsory application

The application of Sections 32 and 32a shall be compulsory

1. if German law would be applicable to the contract of use in the absence of a choice of law, or

2. to the extent that the agreement covers significant acts of use within the territory to which this Act applies."

56. From the wording, one can draw two clear conclusions. First, the issue of the author's equitable remuneration is not exclusively governed by the law applicable to the contract, the *lex contractus*. Second, the provisions apply if either the objective conflict rules of Article 4 Rome I Regulation would lead to the application of German law or the agreement covers significant acts of exploitation within Germany [91]. A potential choice of law agreed upon by the parties has not the slightest effect insofar.

57. In most cases, however, the law remains silent on its intention to be applied regardless of the *lex contractus* and the relevant connecting factors. Subsequently, it is the task of the courts to decide on those

---

90. Copyright Act (Urheberrechtsgesetz) of 9 September 1965, BGBl. I, p. 1273, amended by Art. 1 of the Act of 20 December 2016, BGBl. I, p. 3037.

91. See e.g. FCJ, judgment of 7 December 1979, I ZR 157/77, GRUR 1980, 227, 230; A. Wiebe, in G. Spindler and F. Schuster (eds.), *Recht der elektronischen Medien*, 4th ed., Munich, Beck, 2019, Sec. 32b UrhG recitals 2 *et seq*.

issues based on the clear purpose of the law [92]. We will become familiar with some examples in just a moment.

Of course, legal uncertainty prevails until such a decision has been rendered, and even afterwards there often remain doubts about the rule's reach [93].

2. Examples with regard to B2B contracts

(a) *EU: Commercial agents*

58. The first example of overriding mandatory rules protecting business parties originates in European law, more precisely in the European Directive on the coordination of the laws of the Member States relating to self-employed commercial agents of 1986, known as the Commercial Agents Directive [94]. In Germany, for example, this instrument has been implemented in Sections 84 ss of the Commercial Code [95].

Articles 17 and 18 of the Directive specify the circumstances in which the commercial agent is, on contract termination, entitled to an indemnity or compensation for the damage he suffers due to the termination of his relations with the principal [96].

Article 17 (1) of the Directive provides:

> "Member States shall take the measures necessary to ensure that the commercial agent is, after termination of the agency contract, indemnified in accordance with paragraph 2 or compensated for damage in accordance with paragraph 3."

Article 19 of the Directive provides:

---

92. P. Hauser, *Eingriffsnormen in der Rom I-Verordnung*, Tübingen, Mohr Siebeck, 2012, p. 8, p. 13.
93. See e.g. the difficult relation to consumer protection under Art. 6 para. 2 Rome I Reg., which could lead to an overload of protective rules; Martiny, *supra* note 37, Art. 9 Rome I Reg. recitals 87 *et seq.*
94. Council Directive 86/653/EEC of 18 December 1986 on the coordination of the laws of the Member States relating to self-employed commercial agents, OJ 1986 L 382, p. 17 (hereinafter "Commercial Agents Directive").
95. Act of Transformation of the Directive on the Coordination of the Laws of the Member States Relating to Self-Employed Commercial Agents (Gesetz zur Umsetzung der EG-Richtlinie zur Koordinierung des Rechts der Handelsvertreter) of 23 October 1989, BGBl. I p. 1910.
96. For the *ratio legis*, see J. Busche, in H. Oetker (ed.), *Handelsgesetzbuch*, 7th ed., Munich, Beck, 2021, Sec. 89b HGB recitals 1 *et seq.*

"The parties may not derogate from Articles 17 and 18 to the detriment of the commercial agent before the agency contract expires."

59. Consequently, the provisions are domestically mandatory. However, the Directive remains silent regarding whether the parties to an international agency agreement can opt out of this regime by choice of law. The provisions are not explicitly declared internationally mandatory in the sense of Article 9, paragraph 1 of the Rome I Regulation.

60. This gave rise to the following case before the ECJ:

In 1989, Ingmar GB Ltd., a company established in the United Kingdom, and Eaton Leonard Technologies Inc., a company established in California, concluded a contract under which Ingmar was appointed as Eaton's commercial agent in the United Kingdom. A clause in the contract stipulated that the contract was governed by the law of the State of California.

After the termination of the agency agreement, Ingmar sued Eaton for compensation in English courts.

As Californian law chosen by the parties does not provide for such compensation, the decision depended on the legal nature of the compensation claim under the Directive, or rather, under the British implementation law.

In 2000, the ECJ [97] decided as follows:

"The purpose of Articles 17 to 19 of the Directive, in particular, is to protect the commercial agent after termination of the contract. The regime established by the Directive for that purpose is mandatory in nature. Article 17 requires Member States to put in place a mechanism for providing reparation to the commercial agent after termination of the contract. Admittedly, that article allows the Member States to choose between indemnification and compensation for damage. However, Articles 17 and 18 prescribe a precise framework within which the Member States may exercise their discretion as to the choice of methods for calculating the indemnity or compensation to be granted.

The mandatory nature of those articles is confirmed by the fact that, under Article 19 of the Directive, the parties may not

---

97. *Ingmar, supra* note 87, recital 21.

derogate from them to the detriment of the commercial agent before the contract expires."[98]

61. But what about the law's internationally mandatory character? Within the decision, it succeeds the part which has already been cited above:

> "[I]t should be borne in mind that, as is apparent from the second recital in the preamble to the Directive, the harmonising measures laid down by the Directive are intended, *inter alia*, to eliminate restrictions on the carrying-on of the activities of commercial agents, to make the conditions of competition within the Community uniform and to increase the security of commercial transactions...
>
> The purpose of the regime established in Articles 17 to 19 of the Directive is thus to protect, for all commercial agents, freedom of establishment and the operation of undistorted competition in the internal market. Those provisions must therefore be observed throughout the Community if those Treaty objectives are to be attained."[99]

Thus, the Court drew a conclusion from the purpose of the Directive, that is safeguarding undistorted competition within the Internal Market, to ascertain the law's mandatory application to all commercial agents practising their business within the Union. Hence, it found in favour of the overriding mandatory nature of the rule providing for compensation claims of the commercial agent and determined its territorial scope of application in such a way that it applies to all commercial agents engaged in a business activity within the European Union [100].

(b) *Extension by Member States*

62. Thirteen years later, this decision was confirmed and extended by the ECJ in the *Unamar* case [101]. The facts were similar to those in the *Ingmar* case, with two significant differences:

---

98. *Ibid.*, recital 22.
99. *Ibid.*, recital 24.
100. With regard to the territorial scope of application of the Directive, see also ECJ, judgment of 16 February 2017, *Agro Foreign Trade & Agency*, C-507/15, ECLI:EU:C:2017:129.
101. ECJ, judgment of 17 October 2013, *Unamar*, C-184/12, ECLI:EU:C:2013:663.

In 2005, United Antwerp Maritime Agencies (Unamar) NV, a Belgian company, as a commercial agent, and Navigation Maritime Bulgare (NMB), a company incorporated in Bulgaria, as principal, concluded a commercial agency agreement for the operation of NMB's container liner shipping service. This agreement, which was for a one-year term and was renewed annually until 31 December 2008, provided that it was to be governed by Bulgarian law and that any dispute relating to the agreement was to be determined by the arbitration chamber of the Chamber of Commerce and Industry in Sofia (Bulgaria). However, by a circular of 19 December 2008, NMB informed its agents that it was obliged, for financial reasons, to terminate their contractual relationship. Against that background, the agency contract concluded with Unamar was extended only until 31 March 2009.

Taking the view that its commercial agency contract had been terminated unlawfully, Unamar brought an action before the rechtbank van koophandel te Antwerpen (Antwerp Commercial Court) for an order that NMB had to pay various forms of compensation provided for under the law on commercial agency contracts, namely, compensation in lieu of notice, a goodwill indemnity and a supplementary compensation for dismissal of staff, amounting to nearly 900,000 euros in total.

63. Unlike the *Ingmar* case, both parties were domiciled in an EU Member State; in addition, the Commercial Agents Directive did not apply as its substantive scope of application is limited to agency contracts for the sale or purchase of goods, while in the *Unamar* case, the Court had to rule on an agency contract for the operation of a shipping service [102].

However, when implementing the Directive, the Belgian legislature had decided to apply the same treatment to both types of agency agreements, thus creating a national overriding mandatory provision for situations such as the one in *Unamar*.

64. Consequently, the ECJ had to rule on the legitimacy of such a national provision extending the substantive scope of application of an existing European overriding mandatory provision to further case groups. In doing so, it had to balance the interest of the Member States in enforcing their national public policy against the objective of the unification of conflict rules as pursued by the European Union when adopting the Rome I Regulation. The more specific conflict rules

---

102. T. von Bodungen, "EuGH: Zur Anwendbarkeit der lex fori durch das angerufene Gericht trotz fremder Rechtswahl im Handelsvertretervertrag", *Betriebs-Berater* (2014), pp. 403 *et seq.*

are enacted by the Member States, the greater the danger that the *lex contractus* established under the conflict rules of the Regulation will be perforated to such a degree that unification of law exists only in theory [103].

65. Nevertheless, the Court decided in principle in favour of the Member States and, in so doing, tried to balance the Member States' sovereign power to establish mandatory rules alongside the aim of giving full effect to the unification of private international law rules pursuant to Rome I. It stated as follows:

> "In that connection, it must be recalled that the classification of national provisions by a Member State as public order legislation applies to national provisions compliance with which has been deemed to be so crucial for the protection of the political, social or economic order in the Member State concerned as to require compliance therewith by all persons present on the national territory of that Member State and all legal relationships within that State...
>
> That interpretation is also consistent with the wording of Article 9 (1) of the Rome I Regulation . . . . According to that article, overriding mandatory provisions are provisions the respect for which is regarded as crucial by a country for safeguarding its public interests, such as its political, social or economic organisation, to such an extent that they are applicable to any situation falling within their scope, irrespective of the law otherwise applicable to the contract under this regulation.
>
> Thus, to give full effect to the principle of the freedom of contract of the parties to a contract, which is the cornerstone of . . . the Rome I Regulation, it must be ensured that the choice freely made by the parties as regards the law applicable to their contractual relationship is respected in accordance with Article 3 (1) of the [Rome I Regulation], so that the plea relating to the existence of a 'mandatory rule' within the meaning of the legislation of the Member State concerned, as referred to in (Art. 9 para. 1 of that Regulation), must be interpreted strictly.
>
> It is thus for the national court, in the course of its assessment of whether the national law which it proposes to substitute for that expressly chosen by the parties to the contract is a 'mandatory

---

103. Cf. Maultzsch, *supra* note 83, Art. 9 Rome I Reg. recital 27.

rule', to take account not only of the exact terms of that law, but also of its general structure and of all the circumstances in which that law was adopted in order to determine whether it is mandatory in nature in so far as it appears that the legislature adopted it in order to protect an interest judged to be essential by the Member State concerned. As the Commission pointed out, such a case might be one where the transposition in the Member State of the forum, by extending the scope of a directive or by choosing to make wider use of the discretion afforded by that directive, offers greater protection to commercial agents by virtue of the particular interest which the Member State pays to that category of nationals.

However, in the course of that assessment and in order not to compromise either the harmonising effect intended by (the Commercial Agents Directive) or the uniform application of the (Rome I Regulation) at European Union level, account must be taken of the fact that, unlike the contract at issue in the case giving rise to the judgment in Ingmar, in which the law which was rejected was the law of a third country, in the case in the main proceedings, the law which was to be rejected in favour of the law of the forum was that of another Member State which, according to all those intervening and in the opinion of the referring court, had correctly transposed [the Commercial Agents Directive].

Having regard to all the foregoing considerations, the answer to the question referred is that Articles 3 and (9 of the Rome I Regulation) must be interpreted as meaning that the law of a Member State of the European Union which meets the minimum protection requirements laid down by (the Commercial Agents Directive) and which has been chosen by the parties to a commercial agency contract may be rejected by the court of another Member State before which the case has been brought in favour of the law of the forum, owing to the mandatory nature, in the legal order of that Member State, of the rules governing the situation of self-employed commercial agents only if the court before which the case has been brought finds, on the basis of a detailed assessment, that, in the course of that transposition, the legislature of the State of the forum held it to be crucial, in the legal order concerned, to grant the commercial agent protection going beyond that provided for by the directive, taking account in that regard of the nature and of the objective of such mandatory provisions." [104]

66. As a result, a Member State can declare that certain mandatory rules must be applied regardless of the law applicable to the contract in order to safeguard its public interests. Moreover, if the legislature has not explicitly done so, the national courts of that Member State have a certain discretion to decide in favour of such an overriding territorial scope of application after having diligently assessed the intention of the legislature [105]. This holds even if the law applicable to the contract is the law of another Member State offering the minimum protection required by European law.

67. The opportunity created by the *Unamar* decision of the ECJ might soon be used by German courts where the protection enjoyed by commercial agents has already been extended to certain groups of authorised dealers on the level of substantive law by creating internally mandatory rules [106].

(c) *Germany: Authors*

68. Another example of an overriding mandatory rule in B2B relations is the already cited Article 32*b* of the German Act on Copyright and Related Rights (Copyright Act) [107]. The legal nature of that provision is unquestionable due to the clear-cut language of the Code.

69. However, one might wonder about the justification for such a provision. Certainly, the author is typically the structurally weaker party as against the exploiter of the rights, for example the publisher [108]. But what about the required public interests?

---

104. *Unamar, supra* note 101, recitals 47 *et seq.*
105. Cf. recent French court decisions regarding Art. L 442-6 of the French Commercial Code, which provides for civil liability in case of sudden termination of long-term distribution relationships; Cour d'appel Paris, judgment of 19 September 2018, 16/05579, *Recueil Dalloz* 2018, 2336, with further references in *Recueil Dalloz* 2019, 1963.
106. FCJ, judgment of 6 October 2010, VIII ZR 209/07, NJW 2011, 848; judgment of 13 January 2010, VIII ZR 25/08, NJW-RR 2010, 1263; judgment of 25 February 2016, VII ZR 102/15, NJW 2016, 1885; judgment of 21 July 2016, I ZR 229/15, VersR 2017, 1400; Higher Regional Court (Oberlandesgericht) (hereinafter "HRC" of Frankfurt, 9 February 2016, 11 U 136/14, GWR 2016, 339; A. Ströbl, in I. Drescher *et al.* (eds.), *Münchener Kommentar zum Handelsgesetzbuch*, Vol. I, 5th. ed., Munich, 2021, Sec. 89b HGB recital 16.
107. See recitals 55 *et seq.*
108. G. Schulze, in T. Dreier and G. Schulze (eds.), *Urheberrechtsgesetz*, 7th ed., Munich, Beck, 2022, Sec. 32a UrhG recital 2.

One probably has to go back to the general idea of copyright law. The protection of the author, which also encompasses equitable remuneration, is supposed to increase human creativity and by this promote progress and public welfare [109]. Although this theory is heavily criticised in modern legal literature [110], it should be sufficient in view of the wide discretion left to the Member States by the ECJ's *Unamar* decision, particularly as the policy decision here had already been taken by the legislature itself.

(d) *France: Subcontractors*

70. Another famous overriding mandatory provision can be found in French law, more precisely in Article 12 of the Law Relating to Subcontracting of 1975 [111].
It reads:

"Le sous-traitant a une action directe contre le maître de l'ouvrage si l'entrepreneur principal ne paie pas, un mois après en avoir été mis en demeure, les sommes qui sont dues en vertu du contrat de sous-traitance; copie de cette mise en demeure est adressée au maître de l'ouvrage.

Toute renonciation à l'action directe est réputée non écrite.

Cette action directe subsiste même si l'entrepreneur principal est en état de liquidation des biens, de règlement judiciaire ou de suspension provisoire des poursuites."

Translation:

"The subcontractor has a direct claim for payment against the customer if the main contractor does not pay to him the amount due under the subcontract within one month after the main contractor has been charged with default; a copy of the document by which the main contractor is charged with default has to be sent to the customer.

A waiver of the direct claim for payment shall be deemed not to have been written.

---

109. T. Dreier, in T. Dreier and G. Schulze (eds.), *Urheberrechtsgesetz*, 7th ed., Munich, Beck, 2022, Introduction, recital 10.

110. See G. Hansen, *Warum Urheberrecht? – Die Rechtfertigung des Urheberrechts unter besonderer Berücksichtigung des Nutzerschutzes*, Baden-Baden, Nomos, 2009, pp. 40 *et seq.*; Dreier, *supra* note 109, Introduction, recital 1.

111. Loi no. 75-1334 du 31 décembre 1975 relative à la sous-traitance, version consolidée au 14 novembre 2017.

This direct claim for payment continues even when the main contractor's assets have been subjected to insolvency proceedings, composition proceedings or a suspension of debt enforcement."

71. As in the case of the compensation claim of the commercial agent under the European Directive, the French statute declares the direct claim of the subcontractor to be mandatory in the sense that it cannot be derogated from by agreement; thus, it is domestically mandatory. However, the statute remains silent regarding whether French law prevails in an international case as against the law otherwise applicable to the contract.

72. Here, one might add the question of which contract is the relevant one, as there are two of them; first, the main contract between the customer and the main contractor, and second, the subcontract between the main contractor and the subcontractor. Both might even be subject to different laws in an international context.

In the first place, it should be up to the law applicable to the subcontract to determine whether the subcontractor has a direct payment claim against the customer [112]. However, the latter party has to be protected against the application of legal rules to which he has not consented and which might not even have been foreseeable to him. Therefore, one could argue that the law applicable to the main contract must include such a direct claim for payment or at least a functional substitute [113].

73. Going back to the legal nature of Article 12 of the French Law Relating to Subcontracting, it was again for the courts to decide on its territorial scope of application.

In 2007, the Cour de cassation as Chambre mixte [114] finally had to decide the following case:

In 1999/2000, Basell production France, a French company, contracted Salzgitter Anlagenbau GmbH (SAB), a German company, to construct an industrial site in France. The latter subcontracted the piping work to the French company Agintis; the subcontract contained a choice-of-law clause in favour of German law. After completing the work, an arbitral panel ordered SAB to pay Agintis the amounts due under the subcontract.

---

112. P. Piroddi, "International Subcontracting in EC Private International Law", *Yearbook of Private International Law* Vol. 7 (2005), pp. 289 *et seq.* at 322.

113. See Martiny, *supra* note 37, Art. 4 Rome I Reg. recital 61.

114. Cour de cassation, Chambre mixte, judgment of 30 November 2007, arrêt No. 260, 06-14.006, Bulletin 2007, Chambre mixte, No. 12.

In the meantime, however, insolvency proceedings had been instituted against SAB's assets under German law. Therefore, Agintis turned to Basell as the customer of the industrial site and requested payment of the amount due under the subcontract. Basell refused to pay because, first, both contracts were governed by German law, and second, it had not accepted Agintis as a subcontractor.

Hence, the Cour de cassation had to decide on the applicability of the French statute in a case in which the contract as such is governed by foreign law.

74. The Court found that the provisions of the French Act protecting the subcontractor as the structurally weaker party are *lois de police* (overriding mandatory provisions) in the sense of Article 9, paragraph 1 of the Rome I Regulation. They apply if the construction site is located in France, regardless of the *lex contractus* or the domicile of the parties [115].

75. The decision was confirmed by a judgment of the third chamber of the Cour de cassation in 2008 [116], when it overruled a dissenting decision of the Cour d'appel de Reims. The facts were similar to the *Agintis* case, although even more complex. The Belgian Company Unilin décor, subsequently represented by its French subsidiary, had commissioned the German company Siempelkamp Maschinen und Anlagenbau GMBH & Co KG with the planning, delivery, assembly and operational launch of machines and equipment for the production of fibreboards at an industrial site in France. The contract was made subject to Swiss law. Siempelkamp subcontracted the assembling to another German company, Hima, which for its part subcontracted parts of the assembling to a further German company, Diw. German law governed all these subcontracts. After the completion of the work, Hima went bankrupt before it could pay Diw the amounts due under their subcontract.

Although neither of the parties was domiciled in France and none of the contracts was governed by French law, the Court held that Article 12 of the French Law Relating to Subcontracting applied as an overriding mandatory provision simply because the construction site

---

115. Cour de cassation, Chambre mixte, judgment of 30 November 2007, arrêt No. 260, 06-14.006, Bulletin 2007, Chambre mixte, No. 12; cf. P. Hauser, "Das französische Subunternehmergesetz als Eingriffsnorm – Abkehr von Abwegen?", IPRax, Vol. 35 (2015), pp. 182 *et seq.* at 183; Maultzsch, *supra* note 83, Art. 9 Rome I Reg. recital 13.1.

116. Cour de cassation, Chambre civile, judgment of 30 January 2008, arrêt No. 87, 06-14.641, Bulletin 2008, III, no. 16.

was located in France [117]. Thus, it does not exclusively protect French subcontractors – which would most likely violate European law [118].

76. The Cour de cassation upheld this position in other cases [119]. Yet, in neither decision is there an explanation of the policy behind the provisions of the Act, which goes beyond the protection of the subcontractor as the structurally weaker party.

Therefore, the requirements under Article 9, paragraph 1 of the Rome I Regulation are not fulfilled literally. However, one can imagine that if further justification were needed, the French courts could hitch onto the same horse as the ECJ in *Ingmar* and justify the territorial scope of application with the need for undistorted competition.

77. In a further decision, the Cour de cassation set an important boundary regarding its jurisprudence. In 2011 [120], it had to decide on a case in which the main contract was not a construction contract but a purchase of industrial equipment.

The circumstances were as follows. Telecom Italia (an Italian company), as purchaser, had contracted with the French company CS Telecom (the "main contractor") to buy IT equipment (the "main contract"). The main contractor assigned its right of payment under the main contract to a bank. The main contractor then entered into a subcontract with another Italian company (the "subcontractor") for the manufacture of the equipment (the "subcontract"). The subcontract was governed by Swiss law.

The main contractor failed to pay the subcontractor. The main contractor was then put under administration, and the bank sought to obtain payment on the basis of the assignment. The subcontractor relied on the 1975 Law to seek a declaration that it ought to be paid directly by Telecom Italia for the amounts owed under the main contract, regardless of the assignment to the bank. Article 13-1 of the 1975 Law [121] provides:

"L'entrepreneur principal ne peut céder ou nantir les créances résultant du marché ou du contrat passé avec le maître de l'ouvrage

---

117. *Ibid.*
118. See F. Niggemann, "Eingriffsnormen auf dem Vormarsch", IPRax, Vol. 29 (2009), pp. 444 *et seq.* at 447, referring to Art. 18 TFEU.
119. Cour de cassation, Chambre civile, judgment of 8 April 2008, arrêt No. 87, 07-10.763, unpublished, Chambre Civile 3, 25 February 2009, 07-20096, Bulletin 2009, III, no. 50.
120. Cour de cassation, Chambre commerciale, judgment of 27 April 2011, arrêt No. 87, 09-13.524, Bulletin 2011, IV, no. 60.
121. See recital 70.

qu'à concurrence des sommes qui lui sont dues au titre des travaux qu'il effectue personnellement.

Il peut, toutefois, céder ou nantir l'intégralité de ces créances sous reserve d'obtenir, préalablement et par écrit, le cautionnement personnel et solidaire visé à l'article 14 de la présente loi, vis-à-vis des sous-traitants.

The main contractor may only assign or pledge claims arising from the transaction or the contract concluded with the customer up to the amount due to him for work carried out by him personally.

He shall, however, be able to assign or pledge the claims in their entirety provided that he obtains, in advance and in writing, the personal joint guarantee cited in Article 14 of this Law, with regard to the subcontractors."

78. The Cour de cassation found that the 1975 Law could not be applied as an overriding mandatory rule in this particular case given the lack of a connection of the operation with France, "having regard to the objective of the 1975 Law", meaning the protection of subcontractors [122]. The decisive factor was probably that the subcontractor did not effect its performance at a French construction site associated with the customer of the main contract but instead manufactured equipment that the main contractor then delivered to the "customer". Consequently, the subcontractor's connection to France was random [123].

(e) *United States: Franchisees*

79. The last example of overriding mandatory rules within the field of B2B contracts is taken from US law, more precisely, the law of some US states. Many of them have introduced specific legislation to protect franchisees as the structurally weaker party to a franchise contract. As of June 2013, twenty-one states and three territories had franchise relationship laws [124]. The New Jersey Franchise Practices Act [125] was one of the earliest state franchise protection statutes in the

---

122. Cour de cassation, Chambre commerciale, judgment of 27 April 2011, arrêt No. 87, 09-13.524, Bulletin 2011, IV, no. 60.
123. Cf. Hauser, *supra* note 115, p. 182, 184.
124. D. J. Kaufman, Senior Partner, Kaufmann Gildin Robbins & Oppenheim LLP, *An Overview of the Business and Law of Franchising*, Aspatore, June 2013, available at 2013 WL 3773409, at *7 (citing laws in Alaska, Arkansas, California, Connecticut, Delaware, Hawaii, Illinois, Indiana, Iowa, Michigan, Minnesota, Mississippi, Missouri, Nebraska, New Jersey, Rhode Island, South Dakota, Utah, Virginia, Washington, Wisconsin, District of Columbia, Puerto Rico and the US Virgin Islands).
125. N.J. Stat. Ann., Secs. 56:101 *et al.*

United States [126] and shall serve as an example. Although the statute's plain language appears to indicate that it is restricted to motor vehicle franchises, New Jersey courts understand that it applies to all types of franchises [127].

80. The purpose of the Act is clearly described in Section 56:10-2. I cite:

> "The Legislature finds and declares that distribution and sales through franchise arrangements in the State of New Jersey vitally affects the general economy of the State, the public interest and the public welfare. It is therefore necessary in the public interest to define the relationship and responsibilities of franchisors and franchisees in connection with franchise arrangements and to protect franchisees from unreasonable termination by franchisors that may result from a disparity of bargaining power between national and regional franchisors and small franchisees. The Legislature finds that these protections are necessary to protect not only retail businesses, but also wholesale distribution franchisees that, through their efforts, enhance the reputation and goodwill of franchisors in this State."

This purpose would fit perfectly under the definition of Article 9, paragraph 1 of the Rome I Regulation. It would fulfil its requirements even better than the German Copyright Act or the decisions of the Cour de cassation on subcontracting.

As in the ECJ *Ingmar* decision, protecting the franchisee as the structurally weaker party also serves public interests, namely the state's general economy and public welfare. The only thing missing is the reference to undistorted competition.

81. By declaring most of the provisions of the Act mandatory, the statute "level(s) the playing field for New Jersey franchisees and prevent(s) their exploitation by franchisors with superior economic resources" [128].

Section 56:10-7.3.c reads:

---

126. W. M. Garner, *Franchise & Distribution Law & Practice § 5:29*, Westlaw database, last updated December 2021.
127. *Kubis & Perszyk Associates, Inc.* v. *Sun Microsystems, Inc.*, 146 N.J. 176, 185 et seq. (NJ 1996), 680 A.2d 618; *Allen* v. *World Inspection Network Int'l, Inc.*, 389 N.J. Super 115, 120 (App. Div. 2006).
128. *Kubis, ibid.*, at 195.

"In addition to any remedy provided in the 'Franchise Practices Act', any term or condition included in a franchise . . ., in violation of this section may be revoked by the . . . franchisee by written notice to the . . . franchisor within 60 days of the . . . franchisee's receipt of the fully executed franchise . . . . This revocation shall not otherwise affect the validity, effectiveness or enforceability of the franchise."

Lit. *b* adds:

"For the purposes of this section, it shall be presumed that a . . . franchisee has been required to agree to a term or condition in violation of this section as a condition of the offer, grant or renewal of a franchise. . ., if the . . . franchisee, at the time of the offer, grant or renewal of the franchise . . . is not offered the option of an identical franchise . . . without the term or condition proscribed by this section."

82. These mandatory provisions are also enforced in interstate cases regardless of the law applicable to the contract if the performance of the franchise contemplates or requires the franchisee to establish or maintain a place of business within the State of New Jersey (Sec. 56: 10-4.*a*.).

83. Their overriding mandatory nature is complemented by jurisdiction rules supposed to guarantee the franchisee, as the structurally weaker party, a New Jersey forum where the mandatory provisions will be enforced [129].

84. Summing up, overriding mandatory provisions regarding B2B relations can be found in many jurisdictions. However, they deviate considerably from each other with regard to the specific group of entrepreneurs protected. Although an emphasis is put on distribution relationships, disagreement exists about the type of contract that should be scrutinised: Commercial agency? Dealership as in Belgian law [130] (which could have been added as a further example)? Franchising? Other cases are found specifically in one legal order or one legal family. The list could easily have been extended by including further legal orders, but time and space are limited. In the next chapter, we will

---

129. N.J. Stat. Ann. 56:10-1 *et seq.*; Mogendorf, *supra* note 14, p. 301.
130. Law of 27 July 1961 on Unilateral Termination of Exclusive Distribution Agreements of Indefinite Duration, *Moniteur belge* of 5 October 1961, p. 7518, now chapter 3 of Book X of the Code of Economic Law of Belgium; cf. Nuyts, *Revue critique de droit international privé*, Vol. 88 (1999), 31 and 244.

explore what this multiplicity means for the coherence of conflict-of-law rules.

D. Evaluation

85. From a methodological perspective, there are two ways to protect structurally weaker parties under conflict of laws. Either one develops a concise system of subjective (= choice-of-law) and objective conflict-of-law rules or one relies on overriding mandatory provisions.

86. At first sight, the latter approach has the apparent advantage of a much higher target accuracy. As they build upon mandatory provisions in substantive law, such provisions contain solutions for existing problems. Substantive law rules protecting a structurally weaker party have been proven to be of such importance to a legal order that their application must also be safeguarded in international cases if the necessary genuine link exists between the case and the law concerned. If there is no such need for protection, there will be no overriding mandatory rule.

87. However, this has a huge drawback for the system of conflict of laws.

Overriding mandatory rules are, by definition, unilateral conflict rules [131]. This means they declare only the domestic law applicable and do not care about applying foreign law. The ideal of conflict of laws, however, is multilateral rules that determine the applicable law without distinguishing between domestic and foreign law [132].

This is the condition precedent that allows for international harmony of decisions, another ideal of private international law [133]. Of course, in a perfect legal world, the outcome of a lawsuit should not depend on the forum; rather, all courts with jurisdiction should decide the case the same way. To reach that goal, one could unify either substantive law or – more likely – conflict-of-law rules. Nonetheless, if neither can be unified, one should never simply favour domestic law over foreign law. This, however, is exactly what happens by creating overriding mandatory rules.

---

131. Cf. Martiny, *supra* note 37, Art. 9 Rome I Reg. recital 107.
132. Cf. R. Freitag, in T. Heidel *et al.* (eds.), *Bürgerliches Gesetzbuch: Allgemeiner Teil/EGBGB*, Vol. I, 4th ed., Baden-Baden, Nomos, 2021, Art. 3 EGBGB recital 38; Looschelders, *supra* note 14, recital 56; J. von Hein, in F. J. Säcker *et al.* (eds.), *Münchener Kommentar zum Bürgerlichen Gesetzbuch*, Vol. XII, 8th ed., Munich, Beck, 2021, recital 4.
133. Looschelders, *supra* note 14, recital 56; von Hein, *supra* note 132, recital 7.

88. Take the following example. The overriding mandatory rule protecting commercial agents within the European Union, as determined by the ECJ in *Ingmar*, has to be applied by the courts of all Member States.

Article 9, paragraph 2 of the Rome I Regulation reads:

> "Nothing in this Regulation shall restrict the application of the overriding mandatory provisions of the law of the forum."

But are courts in third countries going to apply it as well? And are courts of EU Member States applying overriding mandatory rules of third countries which share the same values?

89. Traditionally, courts have a significant margin of discretion when it comes to taking into consideration foreign overriding mandatory rules. Article 7, paragraph 1 of the former (Rome) Convention on the law applicable to contractual obligations of 1980, the predecessor to the Rome I Regulation, serves as a perfect reference. I quote:

> "When applying under this Convention the law of a country, effect may be given to the mandatory rules of the law of another country with which the situation has a close connection, if and in so far as, under the law of the latter country, those rules must be applied whatever the law applicable to the contract. In considering whether to give effect to these mandatory rules, regard shall be had to their nature and purpose and to the consequences of their application or non-application."

Thus, under certain conditions, namely the internationally mandatory character of the foreign provision and a close connection of that law with the given case, the court may give effect to the provision. But it is in no way obliged to do so.

90. Under pressure from the United Kingdom [134], the Rome I Regulation narrowed this opening for foreign overriding mandatory rules even further. Its Article 9, paragraph 3 reads:

> "Effect may be given to the overriding mandatory provisions of the law of the country where the obligations arising out of the contract have to be or have been performed, in so far as those overriding mandatory provisions render the performance of the contract unlawful. In considering whether to give effect to those

---

134. McParland, *supra* note 3, recital 15.61.

provisions, regard shall be had to their nature and purpose and to the consequences of their application or non-application."

Thus, only the provisions in force at the place of performance which would render the performance of the contract unlawful can be taken into consideration. Other possible connecting factors establishing a close connection between the foreign rule and the contract are *a priori* excluded [135].

91. Let us take the following example, which mostly mirrors the facts of the *Ingmar* case:

A, an aeronautical engineer, and P, a company established in Germany, concluded a contract under which A was appointed as P's commercial agent in Columbia. A clause in the contract stipulated that the latter was governed by German law except for its mandatory provision in favour of commercial agents residing in Germany; in addition, any claims of A in connection with the termination of the agreement were excluded.

After the termination of the agency agreement, A sued P for compensation in the German courts.

92. The German law chosen by the parties provides for such a compensation claim (Sec. 89*b* German Commercial Code). However, concerning commercial agents performing their activity outside the European Economic Area, such a claim is not mandatory and, hence, can be waived by the parties (Sec. 92*c* German Commercial Code). This is in accordance with the European Directive, which only applies to commercial agents engaged in activity within the Internal Market. The decision, therefore, depended on the readiness of the German court to give effect to the Columbian overriding mandatory rule, which resembles its Panamanian counterpart [136].

As Columbia was the place of performance and Columbian law renders performance without compensation unlawful, even the stricter requirements of Article 9, paragraph 3 of the Rome I Regulation would have been fulfilled.

As the policy behind the Columbian law is the same as the one pronounced by the ECJ in *Ingmar*, one should have expected the German court to sympathise with the Columbian rule and apply it to the given case.

93. Yet the reverse happened. Using its discretion, the Court dismissed the complaint, presumably because applying the Columbian

---

135. Bonomi, *supra* note 83, Art. 9 Rome I Reg. recital 128.
136. See recitals 25 *et seq.*

rule would impair the competitiveness of the German principal[137].

This example perfectly illustrates the problem inherent to an overriding mandatory rule. Without a forum in the jurisdiction that has enacted it, it proves ineffective in most cases.

94. By contrast, a concise system of subjective (= choice-of-law) and objective conflict-of-law rules might overcome those impediments.

First and most importantly, such rules treat domestic and foreign provisions alike[138]. If a European conflict-of-law rule had existed concerning commercial agents consistent with the concept used for consumer contracts, the German court would have been obliged to apply the mandatory Columbian provisions protecting the commercial agent as the structurally weaker party. It would have been prevented from discriminating against foreign commercial agents.

95. But there remains the problem of forum shopping[139], as only the courts of countries that have enacted similar conflict rules would come to the same conclusion.

Such a rule in a European regulation would already safeguard its application by the courts of twenty-seven Member States. In addition, the Rome I Regulation in particular has proven to be a model law for many foreign legislators, not least in China[140], Japan[141], Russia[142] and Turkey[143]. Hence, there is reasonable cause for hope that such a system would promote international harmony of decisions.

---

137. HRC Munich, judgment of 11 January 2002, 23 U 4416/01, MDR 2002, 1385 m. Anm. P. Mankowski 1352; a similar judgment was rendered by another senate of the same court with regard to a Jamaican commercial agent – HRC Munich, judgment of 20 November 2002, 7 U 5609/01, RIW 2003, p. 302.
138. K. Thorn, in C. Grüneberg *et al.* (eds.), *Bürgerliches Gesetzbuch*, 81st ed., Munich, Beck, 2022, Introduction to Art. 3 EGBGB recital 18.
139. P. Hay, "Flexibility versus Predictability and Uniformity in Choice of Law", *Recueil des cours*, Vol. 226 (1991), pp. 281 *et seq.* at 306.
140. von Hein, *supra* note 9, Introduction, recital 35.
141. *Ibid.*
142. C. Mindach, "Weiterentwicklung des Zivilrechts und Internationalen Privatrechts in Russland", IPRax, Vol. 30 (2010), pp. 265 *et seq.* at 266.
143. Magnus, *supra* note 58, Introduction, recital 132.

CHAPTER IV

JURISDICTION RULES

A. Starting point

96. With regard to the protection of structurally weaker parties, jurisdiction rules serve two purposes. First, they might safeguard substantive public policy as they prevent forum shopping to the disadvantage of the weaker party. Second, they also promote procedural public policy.

97. As for the first purpose: As described earlier, the law applicable to the contract is determined by the conflict rules of the forum [144]. As these rules might diverge considerably, the forum may have a crucial impact on the decision on the merits: A free choice of law might be either admitted or limited in order to protect the weaker party. The general objective conflict rules might apply or, alternatively, specific ones taking into account the structural imbalance between the parties. The application of overriding mandatory rules is ensured only with regard to those of the forum but not with regard to those of foreign origin [145].

Thus, one has to preclude the structurally stronger party from using its bargaining power to obtain a forum where the least protection is offered to the weaker party. To do so, one has to restrict party autonomy regarding jurisdiction agreements and simultaneously guarantee the weaker party a venue where its interests are safeguarded [146].

98. As for the second purpose, jurisdiction rules also promote procedural public policy. Due process of law requires that each citizen has access to justice in the sense that he is offered a venue where he can pursue his legal interests [147]. Such access to courts is an element of the fundamental procedural rights protected by most, if not all

---
144. See recitals 7 *et seq.*
145. See recitals 87 *et seq.*
146. Cf. P. Gottwald, in T. Rauscher and W. Krüger (eds.), *Münchener Kommentar zur Zivilprozessordnung mit Gerichtsverfassungsgesetz und Nebengesetzen*, Vol. III, 6th ed., Munich, Beck, 2022, Art. 25 Brussels Ibis Reg. recital 69.
147. Cf. Federal Constitutional Court (Bundesverfassungsgericht) (hereinafter "FCC"), judgment of 2 December 1992, 1 BvL 1/89, NJW 1992, p. 1673 addressing national court fees.

constitutions [148]. It is endangered if the only venue offered to the weaker party is one where high transaction costs discourage that party from bringing an action before a court or defending itself against a complaint brought by the other party [149].

For example, when a distance sales contract between a Delaware company and a Dutch consumer for the purchase of a book contains a jurisdiction clause in favour of Delaware courts, the consumer is deterred from filing a complaint. From an economic point of view, it does not make sense to incur high transaction costs if the value in dispute is only in the two-digit range [150]. In addition, there are psychological barriers to commencing legal action in an unknown forum, in a foreign language and under alien rules of civil procedure [151]. Similarly, small entrepreneurs might be deterred by such an unattractive forum, as we will see later [152].

99. To respond to that problem, one has to provide the structurally weaker party with a familiar forum where it is likely to pursue its legal interests.

A fine example, as described earlier, can be found in the provisions of the Brussels Ibis Regulation dealing with consumer disputes, where Articles 17 to 19 establish a specific jurisdiction regime for consumer contracts which aims at the protection of the consumer as the structurally weaker party.

Its Article 18 reads:

"1. A consumer may bring proceedings against the other party to a contract either in the courts of the Member State in which that party is domiciled or, regardless of the domicile of the other party, in the courts for the place where the consumer is domiciled.

2. Proceedings may be brought against a consumer by the other party to the contract only in the courts of the Member State in which the consumer is domiciled."

---

148. Germany: "Justizgewährungsanspruch", derived from the rule of law in conjunction with Art. 2 para. 1 Basic Law (Grundgesetz), FCC, decision of 30 April 2003, 1 PBvU 1/02, NJW 2003, 1924; cf. M. Ultsch, "Internationale Zuständigkeit in Nachlaßsachen – Ein Beitrag zum Justizgewährungsanspruch", *Mitteilungen des Bayerischen Notarvereins, der Notarkasse und der Landesnotarkammer Bayern* (1995), pp. 6 *et seq.* at 8 *et seq.* for an international assessment; France: see Arts. 14, 15 Code Civil and Cour de Cassation, Civ. Rev. crit. 38 (1949), pp. 483 *et seq.*; EU: Art. 6 para. 1 sentence 1 European Convention on Human Rights; Art. 47 para. 2 Charter of Fundamental Rights of the European Union.
149. Mogendorf, *supra* note 14, p. 18.
150. Cf. FCC judgment 2 December 1992, *supra* note 147.
151. Mogendorf, *supra* note 14, p. 18.
152. See recital 114.

Article 19 adds with regard to prorogation clauses:

"The provisions of this Section may be departed from only by an agreement:
(1) which is entered into after the dispute has arisen;
(2) which allows the consumer to bring proceedings in courts other than those indicated in this Section."

As a result, the consumer can sue the entrepreneur either at his own domicile or at the domicile of the entrepreneur (Art. 18, para. 1); thereby, the Regulation creates a venue at the plaintiff's domicile [153]. In contrast, the entrepreneur can sue the consumer only at the consumer's domicile (Art. 18, para. 2). A jurisdiction agreement departing from those provisions is valid only when it is entered into after the dispute has arisen or favours the consumer in such way that he may sue the entrepreneur in additional venues. Thus, it is guaranteed that the consumer will always have a venue within the European Union at his disposal where he can sue the entrepreneur [154].

100. The same approach is followed with regard to individual employment contracts in Articles 20 to 23 of the Brussels I bis Regulation [155].

B. B2B contracts

1. Protective venues/jurisdictions

101. Concerning B2B contracts, the Brussels Ibis Regulation establishes a similar regime only in the case of insurance contracts.

As we have seen in the context of conflict-of-law rules [156], European law does not distinguish strictly between insurance contracts concluded by private parties and those concluded by small or medium-sized business customers. Hence, to some extent, it also protects entrepreneurs as the structurally weaker party.

---

153. Mankowski and Nielsen, *supra* note 20, Art. 18 Brussels I Reg. recitals 2 *et seq.*; Gottwald, *supra* note 146, Art. 18 Brussels Ibis Reg. recital 4; H. Schack, *Internationales Zivilverfahrensrecht*, 8th ed., Munich, Beck, 2021, recital 341.
154. Cf. A. Staudinger, in T. Rauscher (ed.), *Europäisches Zivilprozess- und Kollisionsrecht EuZPR/EuIPR*, Vol. I: *Brüssel Ia-VO*, 5th ed., Cologne, Otto Schmidt, 2022, Art. 18 Brussels Ibis Reg. recital 4.
155. Cf. J. Kropholler and J. von Hein, *Europäisches Zivilprozessrecht*, 9th ed., Frankfurt am Main, RIW Verlag, 2011, Art. 18 Brussels I Reg. recital 1.
156. See recitals 17 *et seq.*, 44.

As regards jurisdiction rules, this means that the provisions applied to consumer contracts are copied with some minor modifications:

"Article 11

1. An insurer domiciled in a Member State may be sued:

   (a) in the courts of the Member State in which he is domiciled;

   (b) in another Member State, in the case of actions brought by the policyholder, the insured or a beneficiary, in the courts for the place where the claimant is domiciled;

...

Article 12

In respect of liability insurance or insurance of immovable property, the insurer may in addition be sued in the courts for the place where the harmful event occurred...

Article 14

1. Without prejudice to Article 13 (3), an insurer may bring proceedings only in the courts of the Member State in which the defendant is domiciled, irrespective of whether he is the policyholder, the insured or a beneficiary.

...

Article 15

The provisions of this Section may be departed from only by an agreement:

(1) which is entered into after the dispute has arisen;

(2) which allows the policyholder, the insured or a beneficiary to bring proceedings in courts other than those indicated in this Section."

102. With regard to other B2B contracts, the Regulation remains silent. This might come as a surprise, especially in the case of passenger transport that are contracts subject to specific conflict rules under the Rome I Regulation. In this respect, both Regulations have not been coordinated [157].

Also not considered are those B2B contracts for which specific overriding mandatory rules exist.

---

157. Cf. A. Dickinson, in A. Dickinson and E. Lein (eds.), *The Brussels I Regulation Recast*, Oxford, Oxford University Press, 2015, recital 1.77; Martiny, *supra* note 37, Art. 5 Rome I Reg. recital 154.

The Protection of Small and Medium-Sized Enterprises 161

Thus, under the Regulation, there are no provisions to safeguard procedurally the mandatory compensation claim of a commercial agent against his principal under the European Commercial Agents Directive. As a result, the parties to such an agreement could in theory agree upon the prorogation of a forum in a third country which would ignore such mandatory compensation claims [158].

However, later on, we will see that this issue is left to the national jurisdiction rules of the Member States, where one can clearly identify tendencies to close that gap [159].

103. Two examples from other jurisdictions show a completely different attitude concerning the issue.

Earlier, we became acquainted with the conflict-of-law provision of the Panamanian Code on Private International Law of 2014 protecting commercial agents and franchisees [160]. This rule is complemented by the following jurisdiction rule:

"Artículo 83. Los tribunales panameños conocerán privativamente de las demandas derivadas de los contratos de representación y franquicia cuando dichos contratos se ejecuten dentro de la República de Panamá."

A literal translation reads:

"The Panamanian courts have exclusive jurisdiction for all complaints based upon commercial agency agreements and franchise agreements where such contracts have to be performed within the Republic of Panama."

By establishing an exclusive jurisdiction of Panamanian courts for such disputes, the prorogation of another forum by the parties becomes impermissible. Thus, the Panamanian commercial agent or franchisee always has a forum in Panama where he can enforce his compensation claims. On the other hand, although foreign courts might find themselves competent to decide upon the complaint of the principal, a judgment rendered in such a forum would not be enforceable in Panama [161].

---

158. Cf. Magnus, *supra* note 9, Art. 9 Rome I Reg. recital 191; Mogendorf, *supra* note 14, p. 233.
159. See recital 114.
160. See recitals 25 *et seq.*
161. Arts. 83, 155, 156 para. 1 nr. 1 Panamanian Code on Private International Law; see also J. Samtleben, in R. Geimer and R. Schütze, *Internationaler Rechtsverkehr in Zivil- und Handelssachen*, Vol. VI, 63rd ed., Munich, Beck, 2021, Panama Country Report, 1112, pp. 4 *et seq.* at 11 *et seq.*

104. The attentive reader will wonder about the different methods each legislature uses to deal with the problem. While the Panamanian law simply provides for the exclusive jurisdiction of Panamanian courts, the European Regulation contains a complex system of asymmetrical jurisdiction rules favouring the structurally weaker party, combined with limitations on jurisdiction agreements. This can easily be explained: While the Panamanian law as a piece of national legislation only provides for the jurisdiction of Panamanian courts, the European Regulation coordinates the jurisdiction of the courts of twenty-seven Member States, which allows for the creation of alternative fora in different Member States [162]. Thus, the insured can be given the choice to sue the insurer at the domicile of either party if both are located in a Member State.

105. The second example of protecting structurally weaker business parties by specific jurisdiction rules is taken again from US law. As we have seen earlier, many US states have enacted specific legislation to protect franchisees as the structurally weaker party to a contract [163]. Those acts have been qualified as overriding mandatory rules and are typically accompanied by specific jurisdiction rules.

Thus, Section 7-3 lit. *a* of the New Jersey Franchise Practices Act reads:

"It shall be a violation of the 'Franchise Practices Act', . . . for a . . . franchisor to require a . . . franchisee to agree to a term or condition in a franchise. . ., which:

. . .

(2) Specifies the jurisdictions, venues or tribunals in which disputes arising with respect to the franchise . . . shall or shall not be submitted for resolution or otherwise prohibits a . . . franchisee from bringing an action in a particular forum otherwise available under the law of this State."

As has already been stated, the plain language of the statute is restricted to motor vehicle franchises, but New Jersey courts have construed the provision as applying to all types of franchises [164]. In one of those decisions, namely the 1996 case of *Kubis & Perszyk*

---

162. See Dickinson, *supra* note 157, recitals 1.08 *et seq.*; Kropholler and von Hein, *supra* note 155, Introduction, recitals 13 *et seq.* for an overview on the development of international jurisdiction law in the EU.
163. See recitals 79 *et seq.*
164. See recital 79.

Associates, Inc. v. *Sun Microsystems, Inc.*[165], the New Jersey Supreme Court used the opportunity to articulate its view on the relevance of jurisdiction rules for the protection of structurally weaker parties. The case involved a franchisee-franchisor relationship created through an agreement to distribute computing products. This agreement featured a provision directing that all disputes must be governed by California law and heard in California courts. I cite the syllabus of the New Jersey Supreme Court's decision prepared by the Clerk's Office for the convenience of the reader:

"2. The Franchise Act was enacted in an attempt to remedy the effects of unequal bargaining power by prohibiting the inclusion in the contact of provisions that would relieve franchisors of liability under the Act or would unfairly prejudice the franchisee in the operation of its franchise. The Franchise Act was amended in 1989 to effectively invalidate forum-selection clauses in franchise agreements covering automobile dealerships. The legislative findings persuade the Court that the Legislature considered such clauses in general to be inimical to the rights afforded all franchisees under the Act." (pp. 11-14)

3. The prevailing approach to the enforceability of forum-selection clauses is based on *M/S Bremen* v. *Zapata Off-Shore Co.*, a US Supreme Court case. In Bremen, the Court held that a freely negotiated forum-selection clause should be enforced unless the resisting party proves that the clause is unreasonable, or enforcement would contravene the strong public policy of the forum in which suit is brought. However, some courts applying the Bremen standard have determined that forum-selection clauses need not invariably be honored." (pp. 14-23)

4. Enforcement of forum-selection clauses in contracts subject to the Franchise Act would substantially undermine the protections that the Legislature intended to afford to all New Jersey franchisees. Forum-selection clauses in such contracts are presumptively invalid because they fundamentally conflict with the basic legislative objectives of protecting franchisees from the superior bargaining power of franchisors and providing swift and effective judicial relief against franchisors that violate the Act. If unchallenged by the franchisee, a forum-selection clause can materially diminish the rights guaranteed by the Act because the

---

165. *Kubis, supra* note 127.

franchisee must assert those rights in an unfamiliar and distant forum, with out-of-state counsel, and bear the added expense of litigating in the franchisor's designated forum." (pp. 23-27)

5. Forum selection clauses in franchise agreements are presumptively invalid because the general enforcement of such clauses would frustrate the legislative purpose of leveling the playing field for franchisees and preventing their exploitation by franchisors with superior economic resources, and would substantially circumvent the public policy underlying the Franchise Act. Evidence that the forum-selection clause was included as part of the standard franchise agreement, without more, is insufficient to overcome the presumption of invalidity. Unless the franchisor provides persuasive proof that the clause was not imposed on the franchisee against its will, the clause will not be enforceable." (pp. 27-30) [166]

106. Such interdiction of an agreement in favour of the courts of a sister state was later upheld by the federal courts [167]. One of those cases was based on Section 20040.5 of the Californian Business and Professions Code [168], which recalls the New Jersey Act and reads as follows:

"A provision in a franchise agreement restricting venue to a forum outside this state is void with respect to any claim arising under or relating to a franchise agreement involving a franchise business operating within this state."

The Californian franchisee and the franchisor domiciled in Pennsylvania had agreed upon the jurisdiction of federal courts in Pennsylvania. However, when the franchisee sued the franchisor for payment of compensation before a federal court in California, the US Court of Appeal for the 9th Circuit decided in favour of the plaintiff as the trial in the contractual forum would be so gravely difficult and inconvenient that he would for all practical purposes be deprived of his day in court [169].

---

166. *Kubis, supra* note 127.
167. See e.g. *Cadapult Graphic Systems, Inc.* v. *Tektronix, Inc.*, 98 F.Supp.2d 560 (D.N.J. 2000); *Goldwell of NJ Inc.* v. *KPSS, Inc.*, 622 F.Supp.2d 168 (D.N.J. 2009); opposing decision with regard to arbitration agreements in *Doctor's Associates, Inc.* v. *Hamilton*, 150 F.3d 157 (2d Cir. 1998).
168. *Jones* v. *GNC Franchising, Inc.*, 211 F.3d 495 (9th Cir. 2000).
169. *Ibid.*, at 497 *et seq.*

107. We are still waiting for an equally distinct position from European lawmakers with regard to the subject.

2. Form requirements

108. Without specific jurisdiction rules protecting structurally weaker business parties, one might argue that existing form requirements serve the same purpose to a certain degree.

Article 25 of the Brussels Ibis regulation reads:

"1. .... The agreement conferring jurisdiction shall be either:

(a) in writing or evidenced in writing;

(b) in a form which accords with practices which the parties have established between themselves; or

(c) in international trade or commerce, in a form which accords with a usage of which the parties are or ought to have been aware and which in such trade or commerce is widely known to, and regularly observed by, parties to contracts of the type involved in the particular trade or commerce concerned.

2. Any communication by electronic means which provides a durable record of the agreement shall be equivalent to 'writing'."

109. However, form requirements only warn parties about certain provisions [170]. The parties should be prevented from rushing the conclusion of a contract. Instead, they should reflect on the contents of their declarations before they write them down (and sign them). In addition, form requirements might cure a lack of information in certain cases [171].

Form requirements, however, do not eliminate an imbalance in bargaining power and therefore are not able to protect structurally weaker parties to a sufficient extent [172]. A small franchisee desperately

---

170. A. Stadler, in H.-J. Musielak and W. Voit (eds.), *Zivilprozessordnung*, 19th ed., Munich, Vahlen, 2022, Art. 25 Brussels Ibis Reg. recital 8; cf. D. Einsele, in F. J. Säcker *et al.* (eds.), *Münchener Kommentar zum Bürgerlichen Gesetzbuch*, Vol. I, 9th ed., Munich, Beck, 2021, Sec.125 BGB recital 8.

171. U. Di Fabio, "Form und Freiheit", *Deutsche Notar-Zeitschrift* (2006), pp. 342 *et seq.* at 350; cf. for the purpose of form requirements under German law, H. Wendtland, in W. Hau and R. Poseck (eds.), *Beckscher Online-Kommentar BGB*, 61st ed., Munich, Beck, 2022, Sec. 125 BGB recital 1; J. Hecht, in BeckOGK, version 1 March 2022, Sec. 125 BGB recitals 5 *et seq.*

172. Form requirements may serve the purpose to caution weaker parties against the conclusion of certain risky or unbalanced contracts or even provide for legal advice by a third-party expert like a notary public, but they do not set mandatory substantive

needing a business opportunity does not benefit from the requirement of a written form as it does not change his bargaining position opposite the franchisor.

3. Jurisdiction agreements as an abuse of law

110. As in the case of choice-of-law clauses [173], an approach also exists that evaluates the specific jurisdiction agreement on a case-by-case basis. If such an agreement does not reflect the legitimate interests of both parties or constitutes an abuse of the law, it is void, and the venue will be determined by applying objective jurisdiction rules.

A very fine example can be found in Article 5, paragraph 2 of the Swiss Federal Code on Private International Law. It reads:

"A choice of forum has no effect if it results in abusively depriving a party from the protection granted to it by a forum provided by Swiss law."

111. This corresponds to the traditional approach of the US Supreme Court in *M/S Bremen* v. *Zapata Off-Shore Co.* [174]. There, the Court held that a freely negotiated forum-selection clause should be enforced unless the resisting party proves that the clause is unreasonable or enforcement would contravene the strong public policy of the forum in which suit has been brought [175].

112. Under the Brussels Ibis Regulation, this method cannot be applied as the case groups in which a jurisdiction agreement is not admissible are conclusively enumerated.

Article 25, paragraph 4 reads as follows:

"Agreements . . . conferring jurisdiction shall have no legal force if they are contrary to Articles 15, 19 or 23, or if the courts whose jurisdiction they purport to exclude have exclusive jurisdiction by virtue of Article 24."

---

boundaries to party autonomy. The necessity of such (additional) mandatory substantive boundaries can be exemplified by the case law of the Federal Constitutional Court of Germany, according to which contracts of guarantee are invalid despite compliance with the written form if the contract puts an unusually heavy burden on one of the two contracting parties and if it is the result of structurally unequal bargaining power. See FCC, decision 19 October 1993, 1 BvR 567/89, 1 BvR 1044/89, NJW 1994, p. 36.

173. See recitals 28 *et seq.*
174. *M/S Bremen* v. *Zapata Off-Shore Co.*, 407 US 1, 92 S.Ct. 1907, 32 L.Ed.2d 513, 1972 AMC 1407 (US 1972).
175. *M/S Bremen* v. *Zapata Off-Shore Co.*, 407 US 1, 92 S.Ct. 1907, 32 L.Ed.2d 513, 1972 AMC 1407 (US 1972), 407 US 1 at 15, 92 S.Ct. 1907 at 1916.

Although there exist dissenting opinions in legal literature [176], it is by far the prevailing view that jurisdiction agreements have full legal force in all case groups not mentioned in Article 25, paragraph 4 [177].

113. However, Article 25 of the Brussels Ibis Regulation has only a limited territorial scope of application. Essentially, it applies to jurisdiction agreements in favour of the courts of a Member State (Art. 25, para. 1, first sentence). In addition, it safeguards the protective venues established under the Regulation as well as the exclusive jurisdictions provided for by Article 24 of the Regulation from jurisdiction agreements in favour of the courts of third countries [178]. Thus, in the case of a distance sale between a Delaware company and a Dutch consumer, a jurisdiction agreement in favour of Delaware courts is regarded as null and void under European law.

On the other hand, jurisdiction agreements in favour of the courts of third countries not interfering with protective or exclusive venues under the Regulation are outside of its territorial scope of application. Hence, the national jurisdiction rules of the Member States apply [179].

114. German courts tend to evaluate jurisdiction agreements in favour of the courts of third countries under an approach similar to that of the US Supreme court in the *Bremen* case. Assuming the form requirements are fulfilled, a jurisdiction agreement will be deemed to have legal force unless it violates public policy [180].

Procedural public policy is violated if access to justice is considerably impeded such that due process of law is threatened. Substantive public

---

176. See *inter alia* O. Katholnigg, "Internationale Zuständigkeitsvereinbarungen nach neuem Recht", *Betriebs-Berater* (1974), pp. 395 *et seq.* at 396.
177. ECJ, judgment of 16 March 1999, *Trasporti Castelletti Spedizioni Internazionali*, C-159/97, ECLI:EU:C:1999:142; HRC Stuttgart, judgment of 9 November 1990, 2 U 16/90, EuZW 1991, p. 126, ECLI:DE:OLGSTUT:1990:1109.2U16.90.0A; P. Mankowski, in T. Rauscher (ed.), *Europäisches Zivilprozess und Kollisionsrecht*, Vol. I: *Brüssel Ia-VO*, 5th ed., Cologne, Otto Schmidt, 2021, Art. 25 Brussels Ibis Reg. recital 83; W. Grunsky, "EWG-Übereinkommen über die gerichtliche Zuständigkeit und die Vollstreckung gerichtlicher Entscheidungen in Zivil- und Handelssachen im deutsch-italienischen Rechtsverkehr", RIW, Vol. 23, No. 1 (1977), pp. 1 *et seq.* at 6.
178. Gottwald, *supra* note 146, Art. 25 Brussels Ibis Reg. recital 12.
179. Cf. HRC Munich, judgment of 17 May 2006, 7 U 1781/06, IPRax 2007, pp. 322 *et seq.*; G. Rühl, "Die Wirksamkeit von Gerichtsstands- und Schiedsvereinbarungen im Lichte der Ingmar-Entscheidung des EuGH", IPRax, Vol. 27 (2007), pp. 294 *et seq.* at 295 *et seq.*
180. FCJ, judgment of 30 January 1961, VII ZR 180/60, NJW 1961, 1061, 1062; Federal Labour Court, judgment of 20 July 1970, 3 AZR 417/69, NJW 1970, p. 2180; see also HRC Munich, 17 May 2006, *supra* note 179.

policy is violated if the foreign court prorogated by the parties is likely to ignore provisions of German law that are a part of its *ordre public* [181].

For example, the Higher Regional Court (court of appeal) of Munich relied upon the second of these grounds in a decision from 2006 [182]. A German and a Californian company had entered into a commercial agency relationship under which the German company was responsible for the distribution in Germany and Austria of semiconductor devices produced by the US company. The contract contained a choice of Californian law, an arbitration clause in favour of the American Arbitration Association (AAA) and a jurisdiction clause in favour of California state courts. After the termination of the contract, the German company sued its US principal for compensatory payments as mandatory under the Commercial Agents Directive. The Munich court disregarded the arbitration clause as well as the jurisdiction clause. It reasoned that the jurisdiction agreement had been concluded only to circumvent the overriding mandatory rules protecting commercial agents within the Internal Market. To prevent the loss of legal protection under the Directive, such a jurisdiction agreement is not to be enforced and must be declared null and void [183].

4. Evaluation

115. Form requirements are not appropriate to cope with the problem of structural imbalance between the parties to a contract.

116. Instead, one has to limit the admissibility of jurisdiction agreements. There are different ways to achieve this.

Whether one favours a general clause, as used by the Swiss legislature, or fully articulated provisions, as formulated by the European or Panamanian Codes, depends on the priority given to legal certainty, as precisely formulated rules allow legal practice to respond to them in advance, especially when drafting contracts [184].

Therefore, it seems preferable to establish clear rules whenever possible. Nevertheless, there might still be a need for a general clause to complement such specific rules: Not all situations where a jurisdiction

---

181. Cf. for both the procedural and substantive public policy, FCJ, decision of 22 June 2017, IX ZB 61/16, BeckRS 2017, 115833, recital 14; M. Stürner, in BeckOGK, version 1 February 2022, Art. 6 EGBGB recital 156, 158 *et seq.*
182. HRC Munich, 17 May 2006, *supra* note 179.
183. *Ibid.*, at 323.
184. Cf. Mogendorf, *supra* note 14, p. 323 *et seq.*

agreement is inconsistent with fundamental public policies – such as the right to due process – can be anticipated by the legislature [185].

117. The further question of whether one should create a complex scheme of protective venues based on the European model or just provide for exclusive venues like the Panamanian Code on Private International Law depends very much on the type of codification envisaged. In the case of an international convention or a EU regulation, the European model makes sense; otherwise, an exclusive venue offers a more modest but realistic solution.

---

185. Cf. Mogendorf, *supra* note 14, p. 324; S. Leible, in W. Heermann and J. Schlingloff (eds.), *Münchener Kommentar zum Lauterkeitsrecht*, Vol. I, 3rd ed., Munich, Beck, 2020, Part A. III. recitals 188 *et seq.*

CHAPTER V

THE ENTREPRENEUR AS THE WEAKER PARTY

A. *Starting point*

118. Up to now, this paper has recurrently referred to structurally weaker parties without clarifying under which conditions a party might be considered to be structurally weaker than his counterpart. This issue shall be addressed now based on an economic analysis.

119. The term "structurally" indicates that economic factors justify the presumption that an extensive imbalance exists between the parties [186]. This might prove wrong in particular cases, but those have to be disregarded in the light of an inevitably generalising approach [187]. Thus, a consumer is protected under the law even if he is a billionaire purchasing products in a small corner store.

Different approaches exist for establishing a structural imbalance between parties to a contract. They are partly complementary and partly overlapping.

120. The traditional approach deduces structural inferiority from the lack of economic power [188]. A party cannot assert its interests because it can easily be replaced by another one.

Take the following example: You are desperately looking for an affordable apartment in downtown Amsterdam. After visiting a flat with forty other people interested in the same apartment and somehow being the lucky one who receives an offer from the landlord, you have not the slightest chance to modify the conditions under which the tenancy agreement will be concluded. You can only turn down the offer with the consequence that the contract will be concluded with one of the remaining forty people under the very same conditions. Even worse,

---

186. H.-W. Micklitz and K. Purnhagen, in F. J. Säcker *et al.* (eds.), *Münchener Kommentar zum Bürgerlichen Gesetzbuch*, Vol. I, 7th ed., Munich, Beck, 2015, Prel. Rem. Sec. 13, 14 BGB, recitals 39 *et seq.*; see also FCC 19 October 1993, *supra* note 172, at 39 using this term.
187. Micklitz and Purnhagen, *supra* note 186, Prel. Rem. Sec. 13, 14 BGB, recital 41; F. Reichert-Facilides, "Einführung in die Thematik 'Internationales Verbraucherschutzrecht'", in K. Schnyder, H. Heiss and B. Rudisch (eds.), *Internationales Verbraucherschutzrecht*, Tübingen, Mohr Siebeck, 1995, pp. 1 *et seq.* at 2.
188. Cf. Mogendorf, *supra* note 14, p. 11; cf. FCC 19 October 1993, *supra* note 172, at 39.

the next offer you receive from another landlord might be worse than the one you just rejected. Hence, your bargaining power is close to nil.

You might have a similar experience when looking for a job in Madrid or Athens, where the unemployment rate is well above 10 per cent.

Consequently, tenants and employees are correctly regarded as structurally weaker parties who must be protected by mandatory provisions.

121. Yet the picture totally changes when we start talking about consumer contracts. In the era of the World Wide Web, the consumer typically has the choice between a large number of competing offers, at least when it comes to the sale of goods or electronic services [189]. He might still not be able to change the conditions in a given case, but he does have the power to simply accept the more favourable offer of a competitor. He might even use offers from the internet to start negotiations with a retailer on the high street. Thus, one could argue that there exists a functioning arena of free competition that puts consumers in a good bargaining position.

Unfortunately, a typical consumer is not qualified to compare the different offers properly [190]. Of course, he takes into account the quality of the goods or services he wants to acquire and the price he will pay for them. Maybe he is also attentive to the terms of financing or the modalities of performance. However, he most certainly remains ignorant with regard to the legal warranties connected to the product, especially when those are based on different legal orders. Thus, the consumer is unaware of key factors when making his decision.

122. May the consumer be blamed for such ignorance? Certainly not! Becoming fully informed would require him to invest considerable time and money. He would have to read the lengthy standard terms of which contracts typically consist and ask for legal advice. If he has to compare offers from suppliers in different countries, this effort must be multiplied by the number of legal orders involved. The transaction

---

189. Regarding the relevance of e-commerce for consumer contracts, see the statistics at https://www.nchannel.com/blog/ecommerce-stats-trends-online-shopping/, accessed 6 February 2022.
190. H.-B. Schäfer and C. Ott, *Lehrbuch der ökonomischen Analyse des Zivilrechts*, 6th ed., Berlin, Springer Gabler, 2020, p. 87; B. Scraback, "Ökonomische Analyse des Verbraucherschutzes im Internationalen Privat- und Zivilverfahrensrecht", *GPR*, No. 5 (2017), pp. 234 *et seq.*, at 235.

costs generated thereby are, in most cases, disproportionate to the regular value of such a transaction [191].

These transaction costs will be amortised only if the transaction itself has a high value, for example the purchase of a holiday home, or one undertakes a great many similar transactions to which the costs can be allocated, thus considerably reducing the cost per transaction [192]. Consumers, however, cannot take advantage of such a method to achieve cost efficiency. Therefore, their unawareness of key factors is reasonable from an economic point of view [193].

On the other hand, the business party typically conducts a large number of similar transactions to which it can allocate the transaction costs incurred for legal advice [194]. Thus, it is profitable for a business party to consult a lawyer to formulate its standard contract forms.

As a result, information asymmetries exist between the contracting parties that have to be countered by mandatory provisions protecting the consumer as the structurally weaker party [195].

B. Application to B2B relations

123. Both types of structural inferiority can also be observed with regard to B2B relations.

The phenomenon of exchangeability typically can be detected in all distribution relationships [196]. That is most obvious with franchisees. The franchisor typically offers a business model well established in the market under a well-known brand and supported by his know-how. By contrast, the franchisee solely offers his enthusiasm, readiness for action and some capital [197]. Therefore, whereas other people can easily

---

191. L. Goldman, "My Way and the Highway: The Law and Economics of Choice of Forum Clauses in Consumer Form Contracts", *Northwestern Uniform Law Review*, Vol. 86 (1992), pp. 700 *et seq.* at 716 *et seq.*; Scraback, *supra* note 190, p. 235.
192. Cf. K. Sachse, *Der Verbrauchervertrag im Internationalen Privat- und Prozeßrecht*, Tübingen, Mohr Siebeck, 2006, p. 12.
193. Goldman, *supra* note 191, pp. 716 *et seq.*; see Schäfer and Ott, *supra* note 190, p. 108 for a definition of rational behaviour.
194. This is e.g. the case when a franchisor contracts with a large number of franchisees. McDonalds, for example, contracts with more than 200 franchisees in Germany; see https://www.mcdonalds.com/de/de-de/ueber-uns/franchise-modell.html, accessed 6 February 2022.
195. Cf. Sachse, *supra* note 192, p. 12 *et seq.*; Schäfer and Ott, *supra* note 190, p. 87.
196. Cf. Mogendorf, *supra* note 14, pp. 6 *et seq.*, 13.
197. See D. Harke, in F. J. Säcker *et al.* (eds.), *Münchener Kommentar zum Bürgerlichen Gesetzbuch*, Vol. V, 8th ed., Munich, Beck, 2020, Sec. 581 BGB recital 28; cf. Mogendorf, *supra* note 14, p. 7.

replace the potential franchisee, his alternatives are normally very limited. The New Jersey legislator has also acknowledged this: "It is therefore necessary in the public interest . . . to protect franchisees from unreasonable termination by franchisors that may result from a disparity of bargaining power between national and regional franchisors and small franchisees." [198]

The situation of commercial agents and authorised dealers is pretty similar to this. Due to their specific expertise, they might initially be needed to develop a particular market. After a while, however, they become replaceable or even superfluous as the products or services sold become well established in the market [199]. This development also explains why in the case of agency agreements, the legislative focus is put on the compensation the principal must pay the commercial agent when their relationship is terminated [200].

Subcontractors are another example of the exchangeability of a business party unless they offer particular products or skills [201].

124. In other cases, there exist information asymmetries. Possible examples include insurance contracts, passenger transport contracts and persons setting up their own business [202]. As shown in the case of consumers, one has to investigate whether the unawareness on behalf of the business party seeking protection is reasonable. This depends primarily on the value of the transactions involved. For example, passenger transport contracts and insurance contracts covering other-than-large risks are typically not of such value to justify the high transaction costs of seeking legal advice [203].

125. However, the number of similar transactions entered into by the business client might shift the balance. There is a presumption that the number of similar transactions increases with the size of the business

---

198. Sec. 2 P.L.1971, c.356 (C.56:10-2).
199. B. von Hoffmann, "Uber den Schutz des Schwächeren bei Internationalen Schuldverträgen", *Rabels Zeitschrift für ausländisches und internationales Privatrecht*, Vol. 38 (1974), pp. 396 *et seq.* at 403; for the importance of commercial agents at new markets and products see https://www.marketingdonut.co.uk/sales/sales-agents-and-distributors/breaking-new-markets-with-a-commercial-sales-agent, accessed 8 January 2022.
200. See Art. 17 II lit. *a* Commercial Agents Directive or Sec. 89b German Commercial Code.
201. Cf. Mogendorf, *supra* note 14, p. 13.
202. Mogendorf, *supra* note 14, p. 13.
203. This has opened a market for start-ups such as compensation2go.com that automate the processing of consumer compensation claims for delayed and cancelled flights under the Regulation No. 261/2004 establishing common rules on compensation and assistance to passengers in the event of denied boarding and of cancellation or long delay of flights, and repealing Regulation (EEC) No. 295/91, OJ 2004 L 46, p. 1.

client involved [204]. This might explain why, in the case of insurance contracts, business clients are generally protected by European law as long as they do not exceed certain threshold values.

The key figures in the insurance arena are a balance sheet total of 6.2 million euros, net sales of 12.8 million euros and an average number of 250 persons as employees. If an enterprise exceeds two of the three threshold values, it loses protection under the Rome I and Brussels Ibis Regulations [205]. The underlying policy might be that in such a case an enterprise is big enough to bear the transaction costs incurred by comparing different offers and seeking legal information on them [206]. It might also be presumed that enterprises of such size do not conclude just one contract of that type but carry out a multitude of similar transactions in the course of their business. Thus, they do not have to allocate the transaction costs to just one transaction, instead being able to spread them out [207].

No such limitation on the personal scope of application exists concerning passenger transport contracts, although the same considerations might apply. Take, for example, a large company where employee travel is booked by special staff.

126. One might also wonder if the size of a business party affects only information asymmetries or also the exchangeability of that party within a contractual relationship. While franchisees and commercial agents are typically small enterprises, exceptional cases are known where they are large companies. Thus, a big national trading company may act as a commercial agent for a small foreign manufacturer trying to enter a market. Or a company may act as the regional or even national franchisee of a foreign fast-food chain, running not merely one but twenty establishments [208]. In these cases, it can be argued that, due to its size, the franchisee or commercial agent possesses considerable bargaining power and therefore does not need legal protection [209].

127. Finally, the threshold values, which date from 1978, might be criticised as such, given that they do not correspond properly. In particular, the average number of employees is disproportionate to the

---

204. Cf. Mogendorf, *supra* note 14, p. 332.
205. Art. 7 para. 2 Rome I Reg. and Art. 16 (5) Brussels Ibis Reg. excluding large risks as defined in Art. 13 (27) Solvency II.
206. Cf. Mogendorf, *supra* note 14, p. 11 *et seq.*
207. Mogendorf, *supra* note 14, p. 12.
208. Cf. e.g. Arcos Dorados Holdings Inc., the biggest franchisee of McDonalds Inc., or the Flynn Restaurant Group, the biggest operator of franchise-restaurants in the US.
209. Cf. Mogendorf, *supra* note 14, p. 338. Concerning the tendency of big franchisee at the market, see http://www.handelsblatt.com/adv/unternehmerboerse/franchise-wieman-ein-grosser-franchise-nehmer-wird/20058086.html, accessed 6 February 2022.

other two factors. You would expect an enterprise with 250 employees to have a larger business volume and realise higher profits [210]. In any event, the figure of 250 employees seems relatively high, reflecting the old economy more than the new one [211]. In fact, as we will see shortly, the European Union adjusted the figures in later pieces of legislation [212].

128. This leads us to the question of whether the size of a business party should serve only as an additional factor, limiting the protection based on different considerations as just described, or whether as such it might justify the protection of an entrepreneur as the structurally weaker party.

An example of a concept like this is the notion of SMEs in European law [213]. SMEs represent 99 per cent of all businesses in the European Union [214]. The definition of an SME is important for access to finance and is linked to EU support programmes [215]. SMEs are defined in EU Recommendation 2003/361 [216]. The main factors determining whether an enterprise is an SME are (1) *staff headcount* and (2) either *turnover* or the *balance sheet total*.

Company category	Staff headcount	Turnover	Balance sheet total
Medium-sized	< 250	≤ € 50 m	≤ € 43 m
Small	< 50	≤ € 10 m	≤ € 10 m
Micro	< 10	≤ € 2 m	≤ € 2 m

---

210. Mogendorf, *supra* note 14, p. 331.
211. See e.g. the fast-growing gaming industry with a small number of employees. See e.g. the distribution of companies in the Spanish video gaming industry in 2020 by number of employees, available at https://www.statista.com/statistics/434392/distribution-of-companies-in-the-video-gaming-industry-in-spain-by-employees/, accessed 6 February 2022.
212. See recital 128.
213. There does not exist a standardised international definition due to differing levels of development of national economies worldwide; cp. UNCITRAL Working Group I (MSMEs) 25th session, note by the Secretariat (A/CN.9/WG.I/WP.92), para. 11.
214. Supporting study for the evaluation of the "SME Definition", Final Evaluation Report, 30 November 2018, p. 12, https://ec.europa.eu/docsroom/documents/47114/attachments/1/translations/en/renditions/native, accessed 30 April 2022.
215. See Art. 17 para. 1 Regulation No. 651/2014 declaring certain categories of aid compatible with the internal market in application of Arts. 107 and 108 of the Treaty, OJ 2014 L 187, p. 1.
216. EU Recommendation 2003/361, OJ 2003 L 124, p. 36, http://eur-lex.europa.eu/legal-content/EN/TXT/?uri=CELEX:32003H0361, accessed 2 November 2017 (hereinafter "EU Recommendation 2003/361").

These ceilings apply to the figures for individual firms only. A firm that is part of a larger group may need to include staff headcount / turnover / balance sheet data from that group, too [217].

Apparently, the numbers have been adjusted compared to those used for insurance contracts. The number of employees on the one hand and the turnover and balance sheet total on the other hand now fit each other, and the threshold value for staff headcount has been lowered considerably. Thus, the figures much better reflect the modern economy [218].

129. However, one problem remains. The structural inferiority of a party to a contract is always the result of its interrelation with the other party [219]. A consumer is weak when facing a professional, as is an insured when confronting an insurer or a commercial agent when up against his principal. Thus, just being an SME is not in itself sufficient to justify legal protection. Rather, it is necessary that the SME faces on the other side a contracting party with superior bargaining power.

Hence, one would need at least a definition for a large enterprise as a counterpart to the SME. However, it is doubtful whether size alone should really be decisive. One only has to think of the so-called hidden champions. Such companies range slightly above the European marginal values for SMEs but are still considered medium-sized companies [220]. However, due to their specialisation and innovative capacity, they belong to the globe's market leaders, as reflected by their impressive bargaining power [221].

Again, some anecdotal evidence: On a flight to Shanghai, I entered into a conversation with my neighbouring passenger, who turned out to be the owner of a medium-sized enterprise from the greater Hamburg area. He was going to visit customers in China and Russia. To my question of how he is faring with the risks of international trade, especially the so-called exchange dilemma [222], he answered that his clients always have to pay in advance and be willing to do so as they depend on his products. Well, he was the lucky one.

---

217. Art. 3 para. 2 subpara. 5 EU Recommendation 2003/361; Mogendorf, *supra* note 14, p. 332.
218. Mogendorf, *ibid.*, p. 331 *et seq.*
219. *Ibid.*, p. 333.
220. Cf. H. Simon, *Hidden Champions – Aufbruch nach Globalia*, Frankfurt, Campus Verlag, 2012, pp. 83 *et seq.*
221. Cf. *ibid.*, pp. 297 *et seq.*
222. Cf. P. Butler and A. Harindanath, in S. Kröll *et al.* (eds.), *UN Convention on Contracts for International Sale of Goods (CISG)*, 2nd ed., Munich, Beck, 2018, Art. 58 CISG recital 1.

130. Thus, whereas size might be an indicator, bargaining power is to a much greater extent determined by market power [223]. From an economic point of view, it would therefore be preferable to choose market power as the decisive factor in establishing structural superiority, but anyone who has ever dealt with antitrust law knows how difficult it can prove to ascertain market power – especially when asked to assess not only past market power but the present situation as well [224].

Therefore, such a criterion would lead to considerable legal uncertainty [225], especially as it would have to be applied inversely to both parties to a contract; that is, the superior market power of one party would have to be reflected by the inferior market power of the other.

131. This finding leaves us with a case group-oriented approach as the only workable solution, an approach that should be supplemented by limitations based on enterprise size.

This shall be illustrated by a last example: Under German law, the protective rules of the EU Directive on Credit Agreements for Consumers [226] are also applied to persons setting up their own businesses as they are deemed to need the same level of protection as consumers. Information asymmetries are once more the reason for this. However, the protection is limited to loans of up to 75,000 euros – with loans of a higher amount, the business's founder is obviously expected to seek legal advice. The Austrian legislature takes a similar approach to the protection of business founders without relying on a numerical limit [227]. Irrespective of whether one agrees with the specific threshold value, the figure demonstrates that a larger business volume is accompanied by not more but less legal protection. The bigger the enterprise, the more one can expect the entrepreneur to take care of himself.

---

223. Mogendorf, *supra* note 14, p. 334.
224. *Ibid.*, pp. 334 *et seq.*; cf. M. Wolf, in F. J. Säcker and P. Meier-Beck (eds.), *Münchener Kommentar zum Wettbewerbsrecht*, Vol. II, 3rd ed., Munich, Beck, 2020, Sec. 18 GWB recitals 21 *et seq.*
225. Cf. Mogendorf, *supra* note 14, pp. 339 *et seq.*
226. Directive 2008/48/EG of the European Parliament and of the Council of 23 April 2008 on credit agreements for consumers and repealing Council Directive 87/102/EEC, OJ 2008 L 133, p. 66; under German law Sec. 513 BGB.
227. Sec. 1 para. 3 Law on the protection of consumers (Konsumentenschutzgesetz), Austrian BGBl. No. 140/1979.

CHAPTER VI

PROPOSAL FOR FUTURE RULES TO PROTECT CERTAIN SMES

132. Based on the conclusions reached in the previous parts, a proposal for a conflict-of-law rule as well as a jurisdiction rule shall now be made.

With regard to conflict of laws, the cherry-picking method has proven to be an efficient way to protect the legitimate interests of structurally weaker parties without interfering disproportionally with party autonomy [228]. It has to be combined with an objective conflict rule that favours the structurally weaker party by using a connecting factor closely related to that latter party.

133. But what should be the personal and/or substantive scope of application of such a rule?

The comparative research has shown that distribution relationships such as franchise agreements, authorised dealer contracts and commercial agency agreements are regarded by many different jurisdictions as being affected by a structural imbalance between the parties. The distributor is generally in a weaker position and deserves legal protection. Consequently, a broad consensus exists on the need for specific conflict rules. This paper's economic analysis has confirmed this.

With regard to other types of contracts, it was similarly possible to establish such a structural imbalance. Still, from a comparative perspective, the associated legislative responses remain isolated phenomena restricted to specific countries, such as the protection of the subcontractor under French law. Therefore, there is no need for multilateral conflict rules, and instead the issue can be left to overriding mandatory provisions [229].

134. Finally, a cap should be introduced, limiting the protection to business parties not exceeding a certain size. Taking into account key statistical data [230], the line should be drawn to include micro and small enterprises (which, as of 2015, accounted for 97 per cent of the total

---

228. See recitals 31 *et seq.*
229. See recitals 85 *et seq.*
230. SME Definition supporting study, *supra* note 214, p. 21.

number of enterprises) but exclude medium-sized enterprises, which due to their size and business volume do not require specific protection.

135. As a result, the following conflict-of-law rule is proposed:

"Article X

Distribution contracts

1. A distribution contract shall be governed by the law of the country where the distributor carries out his activities in the performance of the contract. If the distributor carries out his activities in more than one country, the contract shall be governed by the law of the country where the distributor has his habitual residence.

2. Notwithstanding paragraph 1, the parties may freely choose the law applicable to a distribution contract. Such a choice may not, however, result in depriving the distributor of the protection afforded to him by provisions that cannot be derogated from by agreement by virtue of the law, which, in the absence of choice, would have been applicable on the basis of paragraph 1.

3. The restriction as to the effects of a choice of law under paragraph 2 does not apply if the distributor employs more than fifty people and has a turnover or a balance sheet total exceeding 10 million euros."

136. Regarding jurisdiction, there are two possible solutions, depending on the type of codification envisaged.

137. In the case of an international convention or a European regulation, the following protective scheme, inspired by the provisions of the Brussels Ibis Regulation, is proposed:

"Section Y

Jurisdiction over distribution contracts

Article X1

1. In matters relating to distribution contracts, jurisdiction shall be determined by this Section, without prejudice to . . .

2. Where a distributor enters into a distribution contract with a principal who is not domiciled in a Contracting State/Member State but has a branch, agency or other establishment in one of the Contracting States/Member States, the principal shall, in disputes arising out of the operations of the branch, agency or establishment, be deemed to be domiciled in that Contracting State/Member State.

Article X2

1. A principal domiciled in a Contracting State/Member State may be sued:

- *(a)* in the courts of the Contracting State/Member State in which he is domiciled; or
- *(b)* in the courts of the Contracting State/Member State where the distributor carries out his activities in the performance of the contract

2. A principal not domiciled in a Contracting State/Member State may be sued in a court of a Contracting State/Member State in accordance with point *(b)* of paragraph 1.

Article X3

1. A principal may bring proceedings only in the courts of the Contracting State/Member State in which the distributor is domiciled.

2. The provisions of this Section shall not affect the right to bring a counterclaim in the court in which, in accordance with this Section, the original claim is pending.

Article X4

The provisions of this Section may be departed from only by an agreement:

(1) which is entered into after the dispute has arisen;
(2) which allows the distributor to bring proceedings in courts other than those indicated in this Section; or
(3) which relates to a contract with a distributor who employs more than fifty people and has a turnover or a balance sheet total exceeding 10 million euros."

138. In the case of a national codification, the following rule seems preferable:

"Article X

Exclusive jurisdiction for distribution contracts

In proceedings based upon distribution agreements, the courts of... shall have exclusive jurisdiction when the distributor carries out his activities in the performance of the contract within this country."

CHAPTER VII

ONE STEP FURTHER:
INTERNATIONAL COMMERCIAL ARBITRATION

139. Arbitration is a method of alternative dispute resolution. As such, it competes with litigation. In general, it is preferred by the international business community due to several factors [231]: first to be mentioned is its efficiency, but also of importance is the expertise of the arbitrators, the confidentiality of the proceedings and the worldwide enforceability of arbitral awards based on the New York Convention of 1958 [232].

140. Arbitration is wholly based on party autonomy. The arbitration agreement concluded by the parties has two effects. First, it constitutes a substantive contract by which the parties bind themselves to settle future disputes on a given issue by arbitration [233]. Second, procedurally it derogates from the competence of the courts to decide upon such cases. Consequently, a court which normally would have jurisdiction has to dismiss the action as inadmissible if there exists a valid arbitration agreement between the parties [234].

If arbitration is wholly based on party autonomy, one might wonder how that plays out in cases where there is a structural imbalance between the parties. Certainly, arbitration agreements involve the same risks for structurally weaker parties as jurisdiction agreements, as they might compromise substantive and procedural public policy. This shall be illustrated by two examples.

---

231. J. Black-Branch, in N. Conrad et al. (eds.), *International Commercial Arbitration*, Basel, Helbing & Lichtenhahn, 2013, p. 4, recitals 1.13 *et seq.*; G. B. Born, *International Commercial Arbitration*, 3rd ed., The Hague, Kluwer Law International, 2021, pp. 71 *et seq.*; C. Murray *et al.*, *Schmitthoff: The Law and Practice of International Trade*, 12th ed., London, Sweet & Maxwell, 2012, recital 23-005.
232. Convention on the Recognition and Enforcement of Foreign Arbitral Awards, New York, 10 June 1958, 330 UNTS, No. 4739 (hereinafter "New York Convention").
233. Born, *supra* note 231, pp. 70 *et seq.*; C. Liebscher, in R. Wolff (ed.), *New York Convention on the Recognition and Enforcement of Foreign Arbitral Awards of 10 June 1958 – Commentary*, 2nd ed., Munich, Beck, 2019, Prel. Rem. recital 2; Murray *et al.*, *supra* note 231, recital 23-016.
234. Born, *supra* note 231, pp. 74 *et seq.*; Murray *et al.*, *supra* note 231, recital 23-006.

141. The first one, which we encountered earlier, gave rise to a decision by the Higher Regional Court of Munich in 2006[235]. I briefly repeat the underlying facts, which are similar to the *Ingmar* decision[236]: A German and a Californian company had entered into a commercial agency relationship under which the German company was responsible for the distribution of semiconductor devices of the US company in Germany and Austria. The contract contained a choice of Californian law, an arbitration clause in favour of the AAA designating that arbitral proceedings be held in California and a jurisdiction clause in favour of California state courts. After the termination of the contract by the Californian principal, the German company sued the former one for payment of compensation as mandatory under the European Commercial Agents Directive and its corresponding implementation in German law.

The Munich court disregarded the arbitration clause as well as the jurisdiction agreement. It argued that the arbitration agreement, along with the jurisdiction clause, had been concluded only to circumvent the overriding mandatory rules protecting commercial agents within the Internal Market[237]. Though it is not completely certain that the arbitral tribunal would not have applied the German rules protecting the commercial agent as the structurally weaker party, there was an obvious danger that it would not have done so. This obvious danger is based on the assumption that the tribunal would have honoured the choice of Californian law made by the parties, the principal being domiciled within that State and both being merchants. Therefore, from a Californian perspective, the contract would most probably have been exclusively governed by Californian law without any commitment to the European directives or the jurisprudence of the ECJ. However, arbitration as well as jurisdiction agreements have to be held null and void in the first place if there exists an obvious danger that an arbitral tribunal will disregard substantive public policies of German law. A later decision rendered by the Austrian Supreme Court takes up the same position in a case involving a New York principal and an Austrian commercial agent where the agency agreement contained a clause referring the parties to arbitration to be conducted in New York under the rules of the Society of Maritime Arbitrators[238].

---

235. HRC Munich, 17 May 2006, *supra* note 179. See recital 114.
236. *Ingmar*, *supra* note 87, recital 60.
237. HRC Munich, 17 May 2006, *supra* note 179, at 324.
238. Austrian Supreme Court, judgment of 1 March 2017, 5 Ob 72/16y, IPRax 2018, p. 532.

The Protection of Small and Medium-Sized Enterprises 183

142. The second example is based on a series of cases and decisions by different German and Dutch courts of appeals and involves the US franchisor Subway [239]. Typical facts would read as follows. A, a German national living in Berlin, wants to establish his own business as a franchisee and contacts B, a franchisor of convenience restaurants domiciled in the State of New York. B has had tremendous international business success and maintained at that time nearly thirty-five thousand restaurants run by franchisees in ninety-eight countries. A fills out an electronic application form stating, among other details, that he possesses the necessary funds to finance the business. Hence, C, the Dutch subsidiary of B, contacts A on its own behalf and sends him its standard contract for signing. It contains in particular an arbitration clause in favour of AAA arbitration held at B's seat in upstate New York and a choice-of-law clause in favour of the law of Liechtenstein. A signs the contract and subsequently opens a convenience restaurant under B's brand in Berlin, investing 200,000 euros and engaging two employees. After two years A and C start to argue about the amount of franchise fees A has to pay. A refuses the additional payment demanded by C, whereupon C institutes proceedings in New York. Without A's participation in the proceedings, an arbitral award is rendered, which C now seeks to enforce in Germany.

The courts found the arbitration agreement null and void due to a violation of procedural public policy [240]. The agreement grossly discriminates against the franchisee. As the proceedings would take place in New York, his access to court would be impeded unacceptably. The journey to participate in the proceedings would in itself require more time and money than is reasonable. An agreement respecting the interests of both parties, the German franchisee as well as the Dutch franchisor, would likely have opted to have the hearings at the seat of either party or somewhere in between.

Especially the combination of an arbitration clause in favour of AAA with the choice of the Liechtenstein law as *lex contractus* would violate due process of law. It is inconceivable how the franchisee, a

---

239. For German court decisions see: HRC Celle, decision of 4 December 2008, 8 Sch 13/07, IPRspr. 2008 Nr. 207, p. 658; HRC Bremen, decision of 30 October 2008 – 2 Sch 2/08, IPRspr. 2008 Nr. 207, p. 649; HRC Dresden, decision of 7 December 2007, 11 Sch 8/07, IHR 2008, p. 119. For Dutch court decisions see: Amsterdam Court of Appeal, *Subway v. A Franchisee*, decision of 3 June 2014, ECLI:NL:GHAMS:2014:2270 and decision of 20 August 2013, ECLI:NL:GHAMS:2013:2580.
240. HRC Dresden 7 December 2007, at 120; HRC Bremen 30 October 2008, at 650 *et seq.*; HRC Celle 4 December 2008, at 659 *et seq.*, all *ibid.*

micro-entrepreneur who had started his business just a few years earlier, could pursue his legal interests. To do so the franchisee would need an attorney, but how should he find one – who is qualified and willing – to plead before arbitrators in upstate New York in English on Liechtenstein law. Even if the franchisee were to invest the time and money to find one, such an attorney would probably not be affordable to the founder of a small enterprise.

Moreover, there are no legitimate interests of the franchisor that could justify such a combination of an arbitration clause and the particular choice of law. The franchisor, a Dutch company, had hundreds of franchisees in Germany alone. Hence, it would have been easy for him to devise a means of asserting his rights in a way also acceptable to his contractual partners.

Thus, it could be presumed that the existing clauses aimed only at hindering the franchisee from pursuing his legal interests. They violated due process and therefore were null and void.

143. Taken such cases into account, it might come as a surprise to the reader that national legislatures normally show greater tolerance o arbitration clauses as opposed to jurisdiction clauses in favour of foreign courts.

A very fine example can be found in the United States.

We have already talked about the distrust many US states have for the courts of sister states when it comes to the protection of franchisees as the structurally weaker party to a contract [241].

Indeed, when I previously cited the relevant Section 7-3 lit. *a* of the New Jersey Franchise Practices Act, I omitted part of the provision. The full text reads as follows:

> "It shall be a violation of the 'Franchise Practices Act', . . . for a . . . franchisor to require a . . . franchisee to agree to a term or condition in a franchise, . . . which:
>
> . . .
>
> (3) Requires that disputes between the . . . franchisor and . . . franchisee be submitted to arbitration or to any other binding alternate dispute resolution procedure; provided, however, that any franchise . . . may authorize the submission of a dispute to arbitration or to binding alternate dispute resolution if the . . .

---

241. See recitals 105 *et seq.*

franchisor and . . . franchisee voluntarily agree to submit the dispute to arbitration or binding alternate dispute resolution at the time the dispute arises."

Thus, the New Jersey legislature treats jurisdiction and arbitration agreements alike, as also the latter are admissible only if entered into by the parties after the dispute has already arisen [242]. The presumptive invalidity of both forum-selection clauses and arbitration clauses in franchise agreements stems from the same legislative intent of levelling the naturally unequal bargaining power between franchisees and franchisors.

144. Unfortunately, that rule is ineffective due to the preemption of federal law, more precisely the Federal Arbitration Act. Thus, the United States Supreme Court prohibited efforts by states to regulate arbitration clauses [243], finding "that a state statute that required judicial resolution of a franchise contract, despite an arbitration clause, was inconsistent with the Federal Arbitration Act, and therefore violated the Supremacy Clause" [244].

In *Central Jersey Freightliner, Inc.* v. *Freightliner Corp.*, the District Court of New Jersey found a "clear conflict between the [Federal Arbitration Act (FAA)] and Section 56:10-7.3 *a*(3) of the NJFPA" [245]. Summarising its analysis of the nexus between the two laws, the court explained that "[b]ecause the FAA was intended to foreclose state legislative attempts to limit the enforceability of arbitration agreements, and because Section 56:10-7.3 *a*(3) of the NJFPA is just such an attempt, the Court holds that the latter violates the Supremacy Clause and is preempted by the FAA" [246]. New Jersey courts have acknowledged and affirmed this holding of federal preemption, though they have noted that

---

242. The following remarks are adopted from New Jersey Law Revision Commission, Franchise Practices Act, Draft Tentative Report, 5 January 2015, pp. 6 *et seq.*, https://static1.squarespace.com/static/596f60f4ebbd1a322db09e45/t/5cf031cc58b92b 000100d2f7/1559245260924/njfpaDTR010515r.pdf, accessed 10 February 2022; cf. Mogendorf, *supra* note 14, p. 301 (citing *Kubis*, *supra* note 127, 680 A.2d 618, 628 (Supreme Court New Jersey, 1996)).
243. *Allen*, *supra* note 127, at 126 (citing *Allied-Bruce Terminix Cos.* v. *Dobson*, 513 US 265, 268 (1995)).
244. *Alpert v. Alphagraphics Franchising, Inc.*, 731 F.Supp. 685, 688 (D.N.J. 1990) (citing *Southland Corp.* v. *Keating*, 465 US 1, 10 (1984)).
245. *Central Jersey Freightliner, Inc.* v. *Freightliner Corp.*, 987 F.Supp. 289, 300 (D.N.J. 1997).
246. *Ibid.*; see also *Doctor's Associates*, *supra* note 167, at 163 ("to the extent that *Kubis* can be read to invalidate arbitral forum selection clauses in franchise agreements, it is preempted by the FAA").

common law contract defences may still apply to invalidate arbitration provisions under certain circumstances [247].

State legislation cannot interfere with the terms featured in arbitration clauses, as "the FAA protect[s] the parties' rights' to arbitrate under the terms they had agreed upon, including . . . the choice of law applicable to the arbitration" [248]. A location-selection provision in an arbitration agreement has also been held "subject to the FAA . . . because it is part of the arbitration clause. Therefore, the clause must be analysed under general state law principles to determine whether it is unconscionable" [249]. Plaintiffs seeking to invalidate a location-selection provision in an arbitration clause may not invoke "the special burden-shifting presumption against forum selection clauses as articulated in *Kubis*, . . . because that presumption in effect discriminates against arbitration clauses" [250].

145. The awkward result of this jurisprudence is the following one: While the parties to a franchise agreement entered into by a New Jersey franchisee may not provide for the jurisdiction of the courts of a sister state, they are free to agree upon arbitration at any location despite the result of such an arbitration agreement being the same as that of a forbidden jurisdiction clause. It conflicts with the basic legislative objectives of protecting franchisees from the superior bargaining power of franchisors and providing swift and effective judicial relief against franchisors that violate the Act [251]. An arbitration clause can, just like a forum-selection clause, materially diminish the rights guaranteed by the Act because the franchisee must assert those rights in an unfamiliar and distant forum, with out-of-state counsel, and bear the added expense of litigating in the franchisor's designated forum. Moreover, the arbitrators have at least the same margin of discretion as an ordinary court when it comes to the application – or non-application – of overriding mandatory provisions like those of the New Jersey Franchise Practices Act.

---

247. See *B & S Ltd., Inc.* v. *Elephant & Castle Int'l, Inc.*, 388 N.J. Super. 160, 175 (Ch. Div. 2006) ("While the arbitral forum selection clause is not presumptively invalid under the *Kubis* decision, . . . New Jersey state contract law will be applied to analyze whether the arbitration clause and the arbitral forum selection clause are enforceable").
248. *Allen, supra* note 127, at 127 (construing *Volt Info. Sciences, Inc.* v. *Bd. of Trustees of Leland Stanford Junior Univ.*, 489 US 468 (1989)).
249. *Ibid.*, at 128-129.
250. *Ibid.*, at 129.
251. Cf. Mogendorf, *supra* note 14, pp. 316 *et seq.*

146. Does this mean that structurally weaker parties are without any protection when it comes to arbitration, or does arbitration offer its own protective schemes? The first issue which comes to mind is the threshold matter of arbitrability. Arbitrability involves the simple question of what types of issues can and cannot be submitted to arbitration [252]. In general, arbitration is possible only for disputes that the parties can settle themselves [253]. Disputes over rights about which the parties cannot contract are outside the scope of arbitration because they are not open to party autonomy, the basis of arbitration.

Thus, for example, Section 1030, paragraph 1 of the German Code of Civil Procedure [254] reads:

"Any claim involving an economic interest can be the subject of an arbitration agreement. An arbitration agreement concerning claims not involving an economic interest shall have legal effect to the extent that the parties are entitled to conclude a settlement on the issue in dispute."

However, the laws of many countries impose more specific restrictions, many of them in order to protect structurally weaker parties. For example, under German law most of the individual employment contracts and tenancy agreements are not arbitrable [255]. The same holds with regard to transactions by consumers in futures on a stock exchange [256], whereas consumer contracts in general are not excluded from arbitration [257]. Under Belgian law, exclusive distribution agreements traditionally were not arbitrable in order to protect Belgian

---

252. K. P. Berger, *Private Dispute Resolution in International Business: Negotiation, Mediation, Arbitration*, Vol. II, 3rd ed., The Hague, Kluwer Law International, 2015, recitals 16-87; N. Blackaby et al., *Redfern and Hunter on International Arbitration*, 6th ed., Oxford, Oxford University Press, 2015, recital 2.124; A. Baumann and T. V. Pfitzner, in F.-B. Weigand and A. Baumann (eds.), *Practitioner's Handbook on International Commercial Arbitration*, 3rd ed., Oxford, Oxford University Press, 2019, recitals 1.18 et seq.
253. T. Várady et al., *International Commercial Arbitration: A Transnational Perspective*, 7th ed., St. Paul, West Academic, 2019, p. 348.
254. German Code of Civil Procedure (Zivilprozessordnung) in the version of the announcement of 5 December 2005 (BGBl. I, p. 3202; 2006 I, p. 431; 2007 I, p. 1781), most recently amended by the law of 5 October 2021 (BGBl. I, p. 4607).
255. Regarding tenancy agreements: cf. Sec. 1030 para. 2 German Code of Civil Procedure. Regarding individual employment contracts: cf. Sec. 4, 101 para. 3 German Labour Court Act (Arbeitsgerichtsgesetz).
256. Cf. Sec. 37 German Securities Trading Law (Wertpapierhandelsgesetz).
257. A. J. Bělohlávek, *B2C Arbitration*, Prague, JurisNet, 2012, p. 264; W. Voit, in H.-J. Musielak and W. Voit (eds.), *Zivilprozessordnung*, 19th ed., Munich, Vahlen, 2022, Sec. 1030 ZPO recital 2.

distributors and safeguard a domestic forum where the overriding mandatory provisions of Belgian law would be applied, a court practice changed only recently [258].

147. But which law applies to the subject of arbitrability? As to this issue, different legal systems come into play depending on the procedural situation in which it arises: first, the law at the place of arbitration, as the arbitral award might be set aside there by a court due to the subject matter of the dispute not being amenable to settlement by arbitration under the law of this state [259]; second, the law of any state where the award is to be enforced, as recognition and enforcement of the award may be refused if the subject matter of the dispute is not amenable to settlement by arbitration under the law of that country [260]; and third, the law of any state where one of the parties has applied to a local court to decide on the merits notwithstanding the arbitration agreement. Thus, the issue of arbitrability is always governed by the *lex fori* of the court seised.

148. On the one hand, the concept of arbitrability proves to be very effective at protecting structurally weaker parties. On the other hand, it totally forecloses arbitration, which seems to overreach to a certain extent. This might be the reason why most legislatures shrink from deploying arbitrability as a gatekeeping mechanism, particularly because they want to present their jurisdictions as arbitration-friendly in order to promote business [261].

149. The second issue which may come to mind are form requirements with regard to the arbitration agreement.

Thus, German law has a specific form requirement for arbitration agreements entered into by consumers.

The relevant Section 1031, paragraph 5 of the German Code on Civil Procedure reads as follows:

> "Arbitration agreements to which a consumer is a party must be contained in a document which has been personally signed by the

---

258. Cf. S. Kröll, "The 'Arbitrability' of Disputes Arising from Commercial Representation", in L. A. Mistelis and S. L. Brekoulakis (eds.), *Arbitrability: International and Comparative Perspectives*, The Hague, Kluwer Law International, 2009, pp. 330 *et seq.*, recitals 16-33 *et seq.*; P. Hollander and M. Draye, in M. Ostrove *et al.* (eds.), *Choice of Venue in International Arbitration*, Oxford, Oxford University Press, 2014, pp. 15, 38, recital 1.130; H. Verbist and H. van Houtte, in F.-B. Weigand and A. Baumann (eds.), *Practitioner's Handbook on International Commercial Arbitration*, 3rd ed., Oxford, Oxford University Press, 2019, recitals 4.16, 4.69.

259. Cf. Art. 34 para. 2 lit. *b (i)* UNCITRAL Model Law, *infra* note 275; Blackaby *et al.*, *supra* note 252, recital 2.128.

260. Cf. Art. V para. 2 lit. *a* New York Convention. Blackaby *et al.*, *supra* note 252, recital 2.128.

261. Blackaby *et al.*, *supra* note 252, recital 2.127.

parties. No agreements other than those referring to the arbitral proceedings may be contained in such a document."

Yet, aside from the tricky question of which law applies with regard to the form requirements [262], it has already been shown that form requirements are not appropriate to protect parties having inferior bargaining power [263]. Form requirements should prevent parties from rushing the conclusion of a contract and partly overcome information asymmetries between the parties. But they do not influence the bargaining position of a structurally weaker party. If such party, for economic reasons, is compelled to accept the offer of the other party without any modifications, this is not changed by the mere fact that it has to be done so in writing.

150. Third and finally, one may fall back on an evaluation of the specific arbitration agreement on a case-by-case basis, as has already been proposed for a choice of law as well as for jurisdiction agreements [264]. Such a public policy control could happen at different procedural stages. Thus, an award could be set aside due to the violation of public policy [265], or the enforcement of an award could be refused for the same reason [266]. In addition, at a much earlier stage of proceedings a court applied to by one of the parties could find the arbitration agreement to be null and void due to a violation of public policy and itself decide the case on the merits [267].

In fact, such an approach on a case-by-case basis has been taken by the courts in the cases given as examples at the beginning of this section [268]. Although it proves to be efficient for protecting the legitimate interests of a structurally weaker party, it carries legal uncertainty as the discretion conceded might be exercised by different courts in different ways [269].

151. Therefore, one should look for an alternative which serves legal certainty and efficiently protects the legitimate interests of struc-

---

262. This concerns especially the potential primacy of Art. II paras. 1-2 New York Convention; cf. Born, *supra* note 231, pp. 657 *et seq.*
263. See recitals 108 *et seq.*
264. See recitals 110 *et seq.*
265. Cf. Art. 34 para. 2 lit. *b (ii)* UNCITRAL Model Law, *infra* note 275. Blackaby *et al.*, *supra* note 252, recital 10.38; Born, *supra* note 231, p. 3602.
266. Cf. Art. V para. 2 lit. *b* New York Convention. Born, *supra* note 231, p. 4000 *et seq.*; Blackaby *et al.*, *supra* note 252, recitals 11.105 *et seq.*
267. Cf. Born, *supra* note 231, pp. 962 *et seq.*
268. See recitals 141 *et seq.*
269. See Born, *supra* note 231, pp. 3611; R. Wolff, in R. Wolff (ed.), *New York Convention on the Recognition and Enforcement of Foreign Arbitral Awards of 10 June 1958 – Commentary*, 2nd ed., Munich, Beck, 2019, Art. V New York Convention recitals 494 *et seq.*

turally weaker parties without interfering disproportionally with party autonomy.

Here, the procedure for setting aside arbitral awards and with it the place of arbitration move into the spotlight.

152. Regarding their procedural treatment, arbitration law distinguishes between domestic and foreign arbitral awards. An award can be set aside only by the courts of the country in which the place of arbitration is situated[270]. Thus, for example, arbitration proceedings having their place of arbitration in Geneva are Swiss proceedings[271] and the award rendered is subject to the Swiss setting-aside procedures under Article 190 of the Swiss Code of Private International Law.

This particular distinction gains enormous importance in the recognition and enforcement of foreign awards in light of Article V, paragraph 1, lit. *e* of the New York Convention. The provision declares that recognition and enforcement of the award may be refused, if the award "... has been set aside ... by a competent authority of the country in which, or under the law of which, that award was made". Hence, an award that has been set aside in its country of origin faces a further peril on its way to being enforced in a third country[272]. By contrast, courts of the enforcement state can merely find foreign arbitral awards subject to non-recognition and non-enforceability, which does not lead to a setting aside of the award in its country of origin. In consequence, a violation of the public policy exception as found in the setting-aside procedure weighs more heavily than when found in the recognition and enforcement procedure since the former impairs the arbitral award *vis-à-vis* other states[273].

Thus, the country in which the arbitral proceedings are situated can effectively enforce its public policy, especially its overriding mandatory rules, also in cases where an agreement calls for arbitration.

153. In general, every legal system can decide independently whether it will allow courts to set aside an award and what catalogue of reasons it offers to set aside arbitral awards that have been rendered

---

270. Born, *supra* note 231, pp. 1677 *et seq.*, p. 3422; Murray *et al.*, *supra* note 231, recital 23-009.
271. Cf. Art. 176 Swiss Fed. Code PIL.
272. Cf. Blackaby *et al.*, *supra* note 252, recitals 10.06, 11.93. However, the enforcement of arbitral awards which have been set aside is not excluded. Thus, France is regarded a rather liberal jurisdiction when it comes to granting recognition of foreign awards that have been set aside. Courts in other countries like Belgium, Austria and the United States have also recognised and enforced such awards under certain conditions.
273. Cf. Blackaby *et al.*, *supra* note 252, recital 10.06.

The Protection of Small and Medium-Sized Enterprises 191

in its own state [274]. The German legislature has based the reasons found in Section 1059 of the German Code on Civil Procedure on Article 34 of the UNCITRAL Model Law [275], which in turn has literally adopted the grounds listed in Article 34, paragraph 2, from Article V of the New York Convention.

Accordingly, up to now the parties to a contract have had the possibility to opt for a place of arbitration where there does not exist a procedure for setting aside arbitral awards or where the reasons for such a setting aside are quite limited. In any event, the courts in such a procedure will take account only of the public policy of the forum and will not consider overriding mandatory provisions of third countries. Hence, the protection of structurally weaker parties as provided for by many jurisdictions can easily be circumvented.

154. In the future this could be prevented by a legal mechanism which recalls the protective venues in international civil procedure [276]. One could open a subject matter to arbitration on the condition that the arbitration proceedings be located in a country which has a legitimate interest in protecting the structurally weaker party; that is, the country of the consumer's habitual residence, the country in which the employee habitually carries out his work, the country in which the insured is domiciled or the country in which the distributor carries out his activities in performance of the contract.

Such a "restricted arbitrability" would create legal certainty and permit the parties to benefit from the undisputed advantages of arbitration, but at the same time it would limit party autonomy to the necessary extent to protect the structurally weaker party. It would safeguard the application of the corresponding *lois de police* and provide for swift and effective judicial relief as the structurally weaker party could assert its rights in a nearby forum. Thereby party autonomy in the form of arbitration and the due protection of structurally weaker parties would be reconciled.

---

274. *Ibid.*, recital 10.34.
275. UN General Assembly Resolution 40/72, Model Law on International Commercial Arbitration, A/RES/40/72 (18 December 1985), amended on 7 July 2006, UN General Assembly resolution 61/33, Revised articles of the Model Law on International Commercial Arbitration of the United Nations Commission on International Trade Law, and the recommendation regarding the interpretation of article II, paragraph 2 and article VII, paragraph 1 of the Convention on the Recognition and Enforcement of Foreign Arbitral Awards, done at New York, 10 June 1958, http://www.uncitral.org/pdf/english/texts/arbitration/ml-arb/07-86998_Ebook.pdf.
276. See recitals 101, 136 *et seq.*

CHAPTER VIII

SUMMARY

(1) The effective protection of structurally weaker parties requires a skilfully coordinated interaction between the substantive law, conflict of laws and jurisdiction rules. If one part fails, the whole system collapses.

(2) With regard to conflict of laws, there are three parameters: The first is the principle of free choice of law. As freedom of choice derives from party autonomy, restrictions to it require a legitimate reason and can only go as far as necessary to reach this legitimate goal.

The efficient protection of structurally weaker parties – as the second parameter – conflicts to some extent with the freedom of choice. However, such protection constitutes a legitimate purpose and therefore may justify interference with civil liberties as long as such interference still answers its original purpose and does not go beyond what is required to serve that purpose. Therefore, such limitations have to be appropriate, necessary and proportional.

Third and finally, a choice of law induces legal certainty, this being the general goal of all conflict-of-law rules as the parties should be in a position to know in advance which legal rules are going to govern their relationship.

(3) A restriction of the free choice of law based on a case-by-case approach certainly guarantees that each case will be decided on its own merits, but it generates legal uncertainty. International business, however, requires reliability in planning, which cannot be achieved with a case-by-case approach. As a consequence, a choice of law would lose many of its advantages and some parties might even forgo making such a choice.

(4) A restriction on the choice of law surely creates legal certainty and guarantees an authentic application of a legal order. It also entails a relatively cautious interference with party autonomy. However, this solution does not guarantee an efficient protection of the structurally weaker party as its effects remain limited to the level of conflict of laws without taking into account substantive law.

(5) By contrast, the cherry-picking approach offers a very effective protection of the structurally weaker party: It keeps at least the protection offered by the mandatory rules of a law that are closely related to the

contract and determined by factors mirroring the interests of the weaker party. A choice of law may only add to this existing protection and may not diminish from it.

Contrary to one's first instinct, this approach also interferes less with party autonomy than might be feared. The range of interference depends on the existence of mandatory rules protecting the structurally weaker party in the law determined by objective standards. If there are many mandatory rules, as in the cases of consumer or labour law, the impact of the cherry-picking method is substantial. In areas of law with only a limited number of mandatory provisions its impact is quite modest. It can be presumed that B2B contracts belong to the latter category, thereby leaving a wide range for party autonomy. Resulting inconsistencies of the two legal systems involved might have to be overcome by adjustment, which has proved to be feasible in practice during the past decades.

Thus, the cherry-picking method proves an efficient means of protecting the legitimate interests of structurally weaker parties without interfering disproportionally with party autonomy. It serves legal certainty and facilitates efficient contract management in international trade.

(6) In order to achieve an efficient protection of structurally weaker parties, the free choice of law and the cherry-picking method have to be complemented by objective conflict-of-law rules that mirror the interests of the weaker party by using connecting factors like that party's habitual residence or the place of performance. Such rules fulfil their protective function in two ways: In the event of a valid choice of law, they assure that the minimum level of protection is offered to the structurally weaker party. If there is no valid choice of law, they determine the applicable law altogether.

(7) An alternative to such a concise system of subjective (= choice-of-law) and objective conflict rules could consist in overriding mandatory provisions.

At first sight, such provisions have the apparent advantage of a much higher target accuracy. As they build upon mandatory provisions in substantive law, they contain solutions for existing problems. Rules protecting a structurally weaker party in the substantive law have been proven to be of such importance to a legal order that their application has to be safeguarded also in international cases if the necessary genuine link exists between the case and the law concerned. If there is no such need for protection, there will be no overriding mandatory rule.

However, there are two important drawbacks for the system of conflict of laws as such: First, overriding mandatory rules are by definition unilateral conflict rules declaring only the domestic law to be applicable; thus, they do not care about the application of foreign law. The ideal of conflict of laws, however, is multilateral rules determining the applicable law without distinguishing between domestic and foreign law, as this is the condition precedent that allows for international harmony of decisions, another ideal of private international law.

Second, the application of overriding mandatory provisions depends to a large extent on the jurisdiction of a court in the enacting state. Without such a forum, they prove to be ineffective in most of the cases as courts are quite reluctant to apply foreign overriding mandatory provisions.

(8) With regard to the protection of structurally weaker parties, jurisdiction rules serve two purposes. First, they might safeguard substantive public policy as they prevent forum shopping to the disadvantage of the weaker party; that is, they aim at a forum in a jurisdiction applying the concise system of conflict rules just described above. Second, they also promote procedural public policy by providing a forum accessible to the weaker party at moderate cost.

(9) Form requirements regarding jurisdiction agreements, as one potential tool to protect structurally weaker parties, only warn parties about certain provisions. Weaker parties should be prevented from rushing the conclusion of a contract. In addition, form requirements might cure a lack of information in certain cases. Form requirements, however, do not eliminate an imbalance in bargaining power and therefore are unable to protect structurally weaker parties to a sufficient extent.

(10) Instead, the admissibility of jurisdiction agreements has to be limited. This can be achieved in two different ways, for example a general clause as used by the Swiss legislature or fully articulated provisions as formulated by the European or Panamanian Codes. The preference for one of these depends on the priority given to legal certainty, as precisely formulated rules allow legal practice to respond to them in advance, especially when drafting contracts.

Therefore, it seems preferable to establish clear rules whenever possible. Nevertheless, there might still be a need for a general clause to complement such specific rules as not all situations where a jurisdiction agreement is inconsistent with fundamental public polices, such as the right to due process, can be anticipated by the legislature.

The further question of whether one should create a complex scheme of protective venues based on the European model or just provide for exclusive venues like the Panamanian Code on Private International Law depends very much on the type of codification envisaged. In the case of an international convention or an EU regulation the European model seems appropriate; otherwise an exclusive venue offers a more modest, but realistic solution.

(11) The traditional approach deduces structural inferiority within a contractual relation from the lack of economic power. A party cannot assert its interests because it can easily be replaced by another one. Tenants and regular employees may serve as examples.

Structural inferiority, however, can also result from information asymmetries between the contracting parties, as in the case of most consumer contracts. Although the consumer, in theory, has a choice between many competing offers, he is not in a position to compare these offers properly, as the transaction costs generated by such an effort are in most cases disproportionate. These costs will be amortised only if either the transaction itself has a high value, for example the purchase of a holiday home, or one completes a large number of similar transactions to which the costs can be allocated, thus reducing considerably the per transaction cost. Consumers, however, cannot take advantage of such a method to achieve cost efficiency. Therefore, their unawareness of key factors is reasonable from an economic point of view.

In contrast, a business party typically conducts a large number of similar transactions to which it can allocate the transaction costs incurred in securing legal advice.

(12) Both types of structural inferiority exist also in B2B relations. The phenomenon of exchangeability typically can be detected in all distribution relationships as well as in the case of subcontractors unless they offer particular products or skills.

In other cases there exist information asymmetries. Possible examples here are insurance contracts, passenger transport contracts and persons setting up their own business.

(13) However, the number of similar transactions entered into by a business client might shift the balance. It is presumed that the number of similar transactions increases with the size of the business client involved. Thus, a commercial agent or franchisee might, due to its size, have considerable bargaining power and, therefore, not need legal protection.

In order to determine the size of a business client which renders legal protection superfluous, one should resort to threshold values like the number of employees on the one hand and the turnover and balance sheet total on the other; these values should correspond to each other and reflect the modern economy.

(14) For different reasons, the size of a business party should serve only as an additional factor limiting the protection, based on different considerations, and it should not justify as such protection being given to an entrepreneur as the structurally weaker party.

First, one has to realise that the structural inferiority of a party to a contract is always the result of its interrelation with the other party. A consumer is weak when face to face with a professional, a commercial agent when standing opposite his principal and so on. Thus, just being an SME is insufficient to justify legal protection. Rather, the SME needs to be squaring off against a contracting party with superior bargaining power. Hence, one would need at least a definition for a large enterprise as a counterpart to the SME.

Second, it is doubtful whether size always matters. Size certainly might be an indicator, but bargaining power is to a much greater extent determined by market power. Therefore, from an economic point of view, the latter characteristic should be the decisive factor in establishing structural superiority. Hence, an imbalance in bargaining power would require the superior market power of one party and the inferior market power of the other.

As revealed by the enforcement of antitrust law, it can however prove quite difficult to ascertain market power, especially when asked to assess not only past market power but the present situation as well. Therefore, such a criterion would lead to considerable legal uncertainty.

(15) This finding leaves us with a case group-oriented approach as the only workable solution, an approach that should be supplemented by limitations based on the enterprise size.

The comparative research has shown that distribution relationships such as franchise agreements, authorised dealer contracts and commercial agency agreements are regarded by many different jurisdictions as being characterised by a structural imbalance between the parties. The distributor is generally in a weaker position and deserves legal protection. Consequently, there exists a broad consensus on the need for specific conflict rules. This has been confirmed by the economic analysis subsequently undertaken in this paper.

The Protection of Small and Medium-Sized Enterprises 197

With regard to other types of contract, it was similarly possible to establish such a structural imbalance, but from a comparative perspective the associated legislative responses remain isolated phenomena restricted to specific countries, such as the protection of the subcontractor under French law. Therefore, there is no need for multilateral conflict rules; instead the issue can be left to overriding mandatory provisions.

Finally, a cap should be introduced limiting the protection to business parties not exceeding a certain size. Taking into account key statistical data, the line should be drawn so to as include micro and small enterprises (which, as of 2010, accounted for 97 per cent of the total number of enterprises), but to exclude medium-sized enterprises, which do not require specific protection due to their size and business volume.

(16) Arbitration agreements involve the same risks for structurally weaker parties as jurisdiction agreements do, as they might compromise substantive as well as procedural public policy. Nevertheless, and to the detriment of structurally weaker parties, lawmakers generally prove willing to take a more liberal view towards arbitration agreements than towards jurisdiction agreements in favour of foreign courts. National courts sometimes respond to that liberality by invalidating arbitration agreements on a case-by-case approach, thus creating legal uncertainty. In addition, such an approach has only a limited effect on arbitration proceedings conducted abroad subject to the enforceability of the later award.

(17) Therefore, one has to look for proper legal tools which protect structurally weaker parties and enhance legal certainty without excessively limiting the access to arbitration as an appropriate alternative method of dispute resolution.

On the one hand, the concept of arbitrability proves to be very effective in protecting structurally weaker parties. On the other, it totally forecloses arbitration, which seems to overreach to a certain extent.

Form requirements regarding the arbitration agreement, in turn, are inadequate to protect parties with inferior bargaining power.

(18) A proper solution could consist in a legal mechanism which recalls the protective venues in international civil procedure. One could open a subject matter to arbitration on the condition that the arbitration proceedings be located in a country which has a legitimate interest in protecting a structurally weaker party; that is, the country of the consumer's habitual residence or the country in which the distributor carries out his activities in performance of the contract.

Such a "restricted arbitrability" creates legal certainty and permits the parties to benefit from the undisputed advantages of arbitration, yet it limits party autonomy to the extent necessary to protect the structurally weaker party. It safeguards the application of the corresponding overriding mandatory provisions and provides for swift and effective judicial relief as the structurally weaker party can assert its rights in a nearby forum. Thereby, party autonomy in the form of arbitration and the due protection of structurally weaker parties are reconciled.

ANNEX: LIST OF JUDGMENTS

Austria			
Supreme Court	1 March 2017	5 Ob 72/16y, IPRax 2018, 532.	
Europe			
European Court of Justice	16 March 1999	Case C-159/97, *Trasporti Castelletti Spedizioni Internazionali*, IPRax 2000, 120.	
	23 November 1999	Case C-376/96, *Arblade* v. *Leloup*, EuZW 2000, 88.	
	9 November 2000	Case C-381/98, *Ingmar*, NJW 2001, 2007.	
	9 July 2009	Case C-204/08, *Rehder* v. *AirBaltic*, IPRax 2010, 160.	
	17 October 2013	Case C-184/12, *Unamar*, IPRax 2014, 174.	
	28 July 2016	Case C-191/15, *Verein für Konsumenteninformation* v. *Amazon*, IPRax 2017, 483.	
	17 February 2017	Case C-507/15, *Agro Foreign Trade & Agency*, IWRZ 2017, 229.	
France			
Cour de cassation, Chambre civile	30 January 2008	Arrêt No. 87, 06-14.641, Bulletin 2008, III, No. 16.	
	8 April 2008	Arrêt No. 87, 07-10.763, Bulletin 2008, III, No. 16.	
	25 February 2009	Arrêt No. 08-11.249, Bulletin 2009, III, No. 48.	
Cour de cassation, Chambre commerciale	27 April 2011	Arrêt No. 87, 09-13.524, Bulletin 2011, IV, No. 60.	
Cour de cassation, Chambre mixte	30 November 2007	Arrêt No. 260, 06-14.006, Bulletin 2007, Chambre mixte, No. 12.	
Cour d'appel de Paris	19 September 2018	Arrêt No. 16/05579, GPR 2019, 154.	
Germany			
Federal Constitutional Court (Bundesverfassungsgericht)	2 December 1992	1 BvL 1/89, NJW 1992, 1673.	
	19 October 1993	1 BvR 567/89, 1993 NJW 1994, 36, 39.	
	30 April 2003	PBvU 1/02, NJW 2003, 1924.	
	23 November 2006	1 BvR 1909/06, NJW 2007, 286.	

Federal Court of Justice (Bundesgerichtshof)	30 January 1961	VII ZR 180/60, NJW 1961, 1061.
	7 December 1979	I ZR 157/77, GRUR 1980, 227.
	19 March 1997	VIII ZR 316/96, BGHZ 135, 124.
	21 April 1997	II ZR 175/95, BGHZ 135, 124.
	13 January 2010	VIII ZR 25/08, NJW-RR 2010, 1263.
	6 October 2010	VIII ZR 209/07, NJW 2011, 848.
	22 June 2017	IX ZB 61/16, BeckRS 2017, 115833.
Federal Labour Court (Bundesarbeitsgericht)	20 July 1970	3 AZR 417/69, NJW 1970, 2180.
	25 May 2005	5 AZR 572/04, NJW 2005, 3305.
Higher Regional Court of Bremen	30 October 2008	2 Sch 2/08, IPRspr. 2008 Nr. 207, p. 649.
Higher Regional Court of Celle	4 December 2008	8 Sch 13/07, IPRspr. 2008 Nr. 207, p. 658.
Higher Regional Court of Dresden	7 December 2007	11 Sch 8/07, IHR 2008, 119.
Higher Regional Court of Frankfurt	9 February 2016	11 U 136/14, GWR 2016, 339.
Higher Regional Court of Munich	17 May 2006	7 U 1781/06, IPRax 2007, 322.
	11 January 2002	23 U 4416/01, MDR 2002, 1385.
Higher Regional Court of Stuttgart	9 November 1990	2 U 16/90, EuZW 1991, 126.
Netherlands		
Amsterdam Court of Appeal	20 August 2013	*Subway* v. *A Franchisee*, ECLI:NL:GHAMS:2013:2580.
	3 June 2014	*Subway* v. *A Franchisee*, ECLI:NL:GHAMS:2014:2270.
United States		
Supreme Court of the United States	1972	*M/S Bremen* v. *Zapata Off-Shore Co.*, 407 US 1, 92 S.Ct. 1907, 32 L.Ed.2d 5131972 AMC 1407 (US 1972).
	1989	*Volt Info. Sciences, Inc.* v. *Bd. of Trustees of Leland Stanford Junior Univ.*, 489 US 468 (1989).
United States Court of Appeals, 8th Circuit	1991	*Electrical and Magneto Service Co. Inc.* v. *Ambac International Corporation*, 941 F.2d 660 (8th Cir. 1991).
	1995	*JRT, Inc.* v. *TCBY Systems, Inc.*; *Americana Foods, Inc.* 52 F. 3d 734 (8th Cir. 1995).
United States Court of Appeals, 9th Circuit	2000	*Jones* v. *GNC Franchising, Inc.*, 211 F.3d 495 (9th Cir. 2000).
US District Court for the District of Connecticut	1998	*Doctor's Associates, Inc.* v. *Hamilton*, 150 F.3d 157 (2d Cir. 1998).

US District Court for the District of New Jersey	1997	*Central Jersey Freightliner, Inc.* v. *Freightliner Corp.*, 987 F.Supp. 289, 300 (D.N.J. 1997).
	2000	*Cadapult Graphic Systems, Inc.* v. *Tektronix, Inc.*, 98 F.Supp.2d 560 (D.N.J. 2000).
	2009	*Goldwell of NJ Inc.* v. *KPSS, Inc.*, 622 F.Supp.2d 168 (D.N.J. 2009).
Superior Court of New Jersey	2006	*Allen* v. *World Inspection Network Int'l, Inc.*, 389 N.J. Super 115 (App. Div. 2006) (citing *Allied-Bruce Terminix Cos.* v. *Dobson*, 513 US 265, 268 (1995)).
	2006	*B & S Ltd., Inc.* v. *Elephant & Castle Int'l, Inc.*, 388 N.J. Super. 160 (Ch. Div. 2006).
Supreme Court of New Jersey	1990	*Alpert* v. *Alphagraphics Franchising, Inc.*, 731 F.Supp. 685, 688 (D.N.J. 1990) (citing *Southland Corp.* v. *Keating*, 465 US 1, 10 (1984)).
	1996	*Kubis & Perszyk Associates, Inc.* v. *Sun Microsystems, Inc.*, 146 N.J. 176 (NJ 1996), 680 A.2d 618.

BIBLIOGRAPHY

Añoveros Terradas, B., "Restrictions on Jurisdiction Clauses in Consumer Contracts within the European Union", *Oxford U. Comparative L. Forum* 1, 2003, https://ouclf.law.ox.ac.uk/restrictions-on-jurisdiction-clauses-in-consumer-contracts-within-the-european-union/.

von Bar, C., and P. Mankowski, *Internationales Privatrecht*, Vol. 1, 2nd ed., Munich, C. H. Beck, 2003.

von Bar, C., E. Clive, and H. Schulte-Nölke (eds.), *Principles, Definitions and Model Rules of European Private Law: Draft Common Frame of Reference (DCFR) – Outline Edition*, Munich, Sellier, 2009.

Bělohlávek, A. J., *B2C Arbitration*, Prague, JurisNet, 2012.

Berger, K. P., *Private Dispute Resolution in International Business: Negotiation, Mediation, Arbitration*, Vol. II, 3rd ed., The Hague, Kluwer Law International, 2015.

Blackaby, N., C. Partasides QC, A. Redfern and M. Hunter, *Redfern and Hunter on International Arbitration*, 6th ed., Oxford, Oxford University Press, 2015.

von Bodungen, T., "EuGH: Zur Anwendbarkeit der lex fori durch das angerufene Gericht trotz fremder Rechtswahl im Handelsvertretervertrag", *Betriebs-Berater*, Vol. 71 (2014), pp. 403 *et seq.*

Born, G. B., *International Arbitration: Law and Practice*, 3rd ed., The Hague, Kluwer Law International, 2021.

Campo Comba, M., *The Law Applicable to Cross-border Contracts Involving Weaker Parties in EU Private International Law*, Cham, Springer, 2020.

Clausnitzer, J., and H. Woopen, "Internationale Vertragsgestaltung – Die neue EG-Verordnung für grenzüberschreitende Verträge (Rom I-VO)", *Betriebs-Berater*, Vol. 65 (2008), pp. 1798 *et seq.*

Conrad, N., P. Münch and J. Black-Branch (eds.), *International Commercial Arbitration*, Basel, Helbing & Lichtenhahn, 2013.

Diamond, A. L., "Conflict of Laws in the EEC", *Current Legal Problems*, Vol. 32, No. 1 (1979), pp. 155 *et seq.*

Dickinson, A., and E. Lein (eds.), *The Brussels I Regulation Recast*, Oxford, Oxford University Press, 2015.

Diedrich, F., "Rechtswahlfreiheit und Vertragsstatut – eine Zwischenbilanz angesichts der Rom I-Verordnung", RIW, No. 6 (2009), pp. 378 *et seq.*

Dreier, H. (ed.), *Grundgesetzkommentar*, Vol. I, 3rd ed., Tübingen, Mohr Siebeck, 2013.

Dreier, T., and G. Schulze, *Urheberrechtsgesetz*, 7th ed., Munich, Beck, 2022.

Drescher, I., H. Fleischer and K. Schmidt (eds.), *Münchener Kommentar zum Handelsgesetzbuch*, Vol. I, 5th ed., Munich, Beck, 2021.

Di Fabio, U., "Form und Freiheit", *Deutsche Notar-Zeitschrift* (2006), pp. 342 *et seq.*

Ferrari, F., E.-M. Kieninger and P. Mankowski et al. (eds.), *Internationales Vertragsrecht. Rom I-VO, CISG, CMR, FactÜ – Kommentar*, 3rd ed., Munich, Beck, 2018.

Gardeñes Santiago, M., "La regulación contractual del contrato de trabajo en el Reglamento Roma I: una oportunidad perdida", *Anuario español de Derecho internacional privado*, No. 8 (2008), pp. 387 *et seq.*

Garner, W. M., *Franchise & Distribution Law & Practice § 5:29*, Westlaw database, last updated December 2021.

Geimer, R., and R. Schütze, *Internationaler Rechtsverkehr in Zivil- und Handelssachen*, Vol. VI, 63rd ed., Munich, Beck, 2021.

Goldman, L., "My Way and the Highway: The Law and Economics of Choice of Forum Clauses in Consumer Form Contracts", *Northwestern University Law Review*, Vol. 86 (1992), pp. 700 *et seq.*

Grunsky, W., "EWG-Übereinkommen über die gerichtliche Zuständigkeit und die Vollstreckung gerichtlicher Entscheidungen in Zivil- und Handelssachen im deutsch-italienischen Rechtsverkehr", RIW, Vol. 34, No. 1 (1977), pp. 1 *et seq.*
Grüneberg, C. *et al.* (ed.), *Bürgerliches Gesetzbuch*, 81st ed., Munich, Beck, 2022.
Gsell, B., W. Krüger, S. Lorenz and C. Reymann (eds.), *beck-online. GROSSKOMMENTAR*, Munich, Beck, 2019.
Hansen, G., *Warum Urheberrecht? – Die Rechtfertigung des Urheberrechts unter besonderer Berücksichtigung des Nutzerschutzes*, Baden-Baden, Nomos, 2009.
Hau, W., and R. Poseck (eds.), *Beck'scher Online-Kommentar BGB*, 61st ed., Munich, Beck, 2021.
Hauser, P., *Eingriffsnormen in der Rom I-Verordnung*, Tübingen, Mohr Siebeck, 2012.
Hauser, P., "Das französische Subunternehmergesetz als Eingriffsnorm – Abkehr von Abwegen?", IPRax, Vol. 35 (2015), pp. 182 *et seq.*
Hay, P., "Flexibility versus Predictability and Uniformity in Choice of Law", *Recueil des cours*, Vol. 226 (1991), pp. 281 *et seq.*
Heermann, W., and J. Schlingloff (eds.), *Münchener Kommentar zum Lauterkeitsrecht*, Vol. I., 3rd ed., Munich, Beck, 2020.
Heidel, T., R. Hüßtege and H.-P. Mansel *et al.* (eds.), *Bürgerliches Gesetzbuch: Allgemeiner Teil/EGBGB*, Vol. I, 4th ed., Baden-Baden, Nomos, 2021.
Henrich, D. (ed.), *Internationales Privatrecht. Einleitung zum IPR* [part of the multivolume *J. von Staudingers Kommentar zum Bürgerlichen Gesetzbuch mit Einführungsgesetz und Nebengesetzen*], rev. ed., Berlin, Otto Schmidt / De Gruyter, 2019.
von Hoffmann, B., "Uber den Schutz des Schwächeren bei Internationalen Schuldverträgen", *Rabels Zeitschrift für ausländisches und internationales Privatrecht*, Vol. 38 (1974), pp. 396 *et seq.*
von Hoffmann, B., and K. Thorn, *Internationales Privatrecht*, 9th ed., Munich, Beck, 2007.
Hüßtege, R., and H.-P. Mansel (eds.), *Bürgerliches Gesetzbuch. Rom Verordnungen*, Vol. VI, 3rd ed., Baden-Baden, Nomos, 2019.
Jayme, E., "Identité culturelle et integration: le droit international privé postmoderne", *Recueil des cours*, Vol. 251 (1995), pp. 1 *et seq.*
Katholnigg, O., "Internationale Zuständigkeitsvereinbarungen nach neuem Recht", *Betriebs-Berater*, Vol. 29 (1974), pp. 395 *et seq.*
Kröll, S., "The 'Arbitrability' of Disputes Arising from Commercial Representation", in L. A. Mistelis and S. L. Brekoulakis (eds.), *Arbitrability: International and Comparative Perspectives*, The Hague, Kluwer Law International, 2009, pp. 330 *et seq.*
Kröll, S., L. Mistelis and P. Perales Viscasillas (eds.), *UN Convention on Contracts for International Sale of Goods (CISG)*, 2nd ed., Munich, Beck, 2018.
Kropholler, J., and J. von Hein, *Europäisches Zivilprozessrecht*, 9th ed., Frankfurt am Main, Deutscher Fachverlag, 2011.
Lorenz, E., *Zur Struktur des Internationalen Privatrechts*, Berlin, Duncker & Humblot, 1977.
Magnus, U. (ed.), *Einleitung zur Rom I-VO, Article 1-10 Rom I-VO* (Internationales Vertragsrecht 1) [part of the multivolume *J. von Staudingers Kommentar zum Bürgerlichen Gesetzbuch mit Einführungsgesetz und Nebengesetzen*], rev. ed., Berlin, De Gruyter, 2021.
Magnus, U., and P. Mankowski (eds.), *European Commentaries on Private International Law: Brussels Ibis Regulation*, Vol. I, Cologne, Otto Schmidt, 2016.
Magnus, U., and P. Mankowski (eds.), *European Commentaries on Private International Law: Rome I Regulation*, Vol. II, Cologne, Otto Schmidt, 2017.
Mankowski, P., "Strukturfragen des internationalen Verbrauchervertragsrechts", RIW, No. 6 (1993), pp. 453 *et seq.*
McParland, M., *The Rome I Regulation on the Law Applicable to Contractual Obligations*, Oxford, Oxford University Press, 2015.

Mindach, C., "Weiterentwicklung des Zivilrechts und Internationalen Privatrechts in Russland", IPRax, Vol. 30 (2010), pp. 265 *et seq.*
Mogendorf, M., *Der strukturell unterlegene Unternehmer im Internationalen Privat- und Verfahrensrecht*, Tübingen, Mohr Siebeck, 2016.
Morse, C. G. J., "The EEC Convention on the Law Applicable to Contractual Obligations", *Yearbook of European Law*, Vol. 2 (1982), pp. 136 *et seq.*
Murray, C., D. Holloway, D. Timson-Hunt and G. Dixon, *Schmitthoff: The Law and Practice of International Trade*, 12th ed., London, Sweet & Maxwell, 2012.
Musielak, H.-J., and W. Voit (eds.), *Zivilprozessordnung*, 19th ed., Munich, Vahlen, 2022.
Nielsen, P., "The Rome I Regulation and Contracts of Carriage", in F. Ferrari and S. Leible (eds.), *Rome I Regulation*, Munich, Sellier, 2009, pp. 99 *et seq.*
Niggemann, F., "Eingriffsnormen auf dem Vormarsch", IPRax, Vol. 29 (2009), pp. 444 *et seq.*
Oetker, H. (ed.), *Handelsgesetzbuch*, 7th ed., Munich, Beck, 2021.
Ostrove, M., C. Salomon and B. Shifman, *Choice of Venue in International Arbitration*, Oxford, Oxford University Press, 2014.
Piroddi, P., "International Subcontracting in EC Private International Law", *Yearbook of Private International Law*, Vol. 7 (2005), pp. 289 *et seq.*
Rauscher, T. (ed.), *Europäisches Zivilprozess- und Kollisionsrecht EuZPR/EuIPR*, Vol. I: *Brüssel Ia-VO*, 5th ed., Cologne, Otto Schmidt, 2022.
Rauscher, T. (ed.), *Europäisches Zivilprozess- und Kollisionsrecht EuZPR/EuIPR*, Vol. III: *Rom I-VO, Rom II-VO*, 4th ed., Cologne, Otto Schmidt, 2016.
Rauscher, T., and W. Krüger (eds.), *Münchener Kommentar zur Zivilprozessordnung mit Gerichtsverfassungsgesetz und Nebengesetzen*, Vol. III, 6th ed., Munich, Beck, 2022.
Rebmann, K., F. J. Säcker and R. Rixecker (eds.), *Münchener Kommentar zum Bürgerlichen Gesetzbuch*, Vol. X, 4th ed., Munich, Beck, 2006.
Reichert-Facilides, F., "Einführung in die Thematik 'Internationales Verbraucherschutzrecht'", in K. Schnyder, H. Heiss and B. Rudisch (eds.), *Internationales Verbraucherschutzrecht*, Tübingen, Mohr Siebeck, 1995, pp. 1 *et seq.*
Rühl, G., "Die Wirksamkeit von Gerichtsstands- und Schiedsvereinbarungen im Lichte der Ingmar-Entscheidung des EuGH", IPRax, Vol. 27 (2007), pp. 294 *et seq.*
Rühl, G., "Consumer Protection in Choice of Law", *Cornell International Law Journal*, Vol. 44 (2011), pp. 569 *et seq.*
Rühl, G., "Der Schutz des ‚Schwächeren' im europäischen Kollisionsrecht", in H. Kronke and K. Thorn (eds.), *Grenzen überwinden – Prinzipien bewahren, Festschrift für Bernd von Hoffmann zum 70. Geburtstag am 28. Dezember 2011*, Bielefeld, Gieseking, 2011, pp. 364 *et seq.*
Sachse, K., *Der Verbrauchervertrag im Internationalen Privat- und Prozeßrecht*, Tübingen, Mohr Siebeck, 2006.
Säcker, F. J., R. Rixecker, H. Oetker and B. Limperg (eds.), *Münchener Kommentar zum Bürgerlichen Gesetzbuch*, Vol. I, 7th ed., Munich, Beck, 2015.
Säcker, F. J., R. Rixecker, H. Oetker and B. Limperg (eds.), *Münchener Kommentar zum Bürgerlichen Gesetzbuch*, Vol. I, 9th ed., Munich, Beck, 2021.
Säcker, F. J., R. Rixecker, H. Oetker and B. Limperg (eds.), *Münchener Kommentar zum Bürgerlichen Gesetzbuch*, Vol. V, 8th ed., Munich, Beck, 2020.
Säcker, F. J., R. Rixecker, H. Oetker and B. Limperg (eds.), *Münchener Kommentar zum Bürgerlichen Gesetzbuch*, Vol. XII, 8th ed., Munich, Beck, 2021.
Säcker, F. J., R. Rixecker, H. Oetker and B. Limperg (eds.), *Münchener Kommentar zum Bürgerlichen Gesetzbuch*, Vol. XIII, 8th ed., Munich, Beck, 2021.
Säcker, F. J., and P. Meier-Beck (eds.), *Münchener Kommentar zum Wettbewerbsrecht*, Vol. II, 3rd ed., Munich, Beck, 2020.
Schack, H., *Internationales Zivilverfahrensrecht*, 8th ed., Munich, Beck, 2021.
Schäfer, H.-B., and K. Ott, *Lehrbuch der ökonomischen Analyse des Zivilrechts*, 6th ed., Berlin, Springer Gabler, 2020.

Schulze, R., H. Dörner and I. Ebert *et al.* (eds.), *Bürgerliches Gesetzbuch. Handkommentar*, 11th ed., Baden-Baden, Nomos, 2022.
Scraback, B., "Ökonomische Analyse des Verbraucherschutzes im Internationalen Privat- und Zivilverfahrensrecht", GPR, No. 5 (2017), pp. 234 *et seq.*
Siesby, E., "Party Autonomy and the EC Draft Convention", in O. Lando, B. von Hoffmann and K. Siehr (eds.), *European Private International Law of Obligations*, Tübingen, Mohr Siebeck, 1975, pp. 206 *et seq.*
Simon, H., *Hidden Champions – Aufbruch nach Globalia: Die Erfolgsstrategien unbekannter Weltmarktführer*, Frankfurt, Campus Verlag, 2012.
Spindler, G., and F. Schuster (eds.), *Recht der elektronischen Medien*, 4th ed., Munich, Beck, 2019.
Ultsch, M., "Internationale Zuständigkeit in Nachlaßsachen – ein Beitrag zum Justizgewährungsanspruch", *Mitteilungen des Bayerischen Notarvereins*, No. 1 (1995), pp. 6 *et seq.*
Várady, T., J. J. Barceló III, S. Kröll and A. T. von Mehren, *International Commercial Arbitration: A Transnational Perspective*, 7th ed., St. Paul, West Academic, 2019.
Weigand, F.-B., and A. Baumann (eds.) *Practitioner's Handbook on International Commercial Arbitration*, 3rd ed., Oxford, Oxford University Press, 2019.
Whincop, M., and M. Keyes, "Putting the 'Private' Back into Private International Law: Default Rules and the Proper Law of the Contract", *Melbourne University Law Review*, Vol. 21 (1997), pp. 515 *et seq.*
Wolff, R. (ed.), *New York Convention on the Recognition and Enforcement of Foreign Arbitral Awards of 10 June 1958 – Commentary*, 2nd ed., Munich, Beck, 2019.
Yntema, H. E., "'Autonomy' in Choice of Law", *American Journal of Comparative Law*, Vol. 1, No. 4 (1952), pp. 341 *et seq.*

PARALLEL PROCEEDINGS
IN INTERNATIONAL ARBITRATION

THEORETICAL ANALYSIS AND
THE SEARCH FOR PRACTICAL SOLUTIONS

by

SALIM MOOLLAN KC*

---

*The author gratefully acknowledges the gracious assistance of Ms Emilie Gonin, Barrister, Brick Court Chambers, for the written version of these Hague Lectures. Mr Gustavo Laborde, Founding Partner, Laborde Law, worked ont he oral version thereof. All errors and omissions remain those of the author alone.

S. A. H. MOOLLAN KC

TABLE OF CONTENTS

Introduction 215

Chapter I. Defining the subject: what are parallel proceedings in international arbitration? 216
  A. Defining parallel proceedings 216
    1. "Connection" between different proceedings 216
    2. Nature of the "connection". 217
      The International Law Association. 217
      The Brussels I Regulation (recast). 219
      Concluding remarks 219
    3. A proposed modernised definition 220
  B. Typology of parallel proceedings. 222
  C. Why are parallel proceedings problematic? 224
  D. A pratical example: *Lauder* v. *Czech Republic* and *CME* v. *Czech Republic*. 226

Chapter II. National courts versus international arbitration tribunals. . . . 228
  A. Competence-competence and parallel proceedings 229
    1. A universally accepted principle 229
    2. The positive effect 230
    3. The negative effect 231
      French law 231
      English law 232
      Mauritian law. 234
      Two key factors. 235
    4. A pratical example: The Fomento case. 236
  B. *Anti-suit* (and anti-arbitration) injunctions 238
  C. Fork-in-the-road clauses *(electa una via)* 241

Chapter III. Purely commercial disputes with no investment arbitraton element 244
  A. *Lis pendens (lis alibi pendens)*. 246
  B. *Res judicata* and issue estoppel 251
    1. The doctrine of *res judicata* 251
    2. The conditions for the application of *res judicata* to international arbitral awards 253
  C. The related doctrine of abuse of process. 254
  D. Consolidation and joinder/intervention. 256
  E. Informal coordination? 260

Chapter IV. Disputes with an investment arbitration element 261
  A. Investment arbitration, a fertile ground for parallel proceedings . . . 261
  B. Sources of parallel proceedings in investment arbitration. 265
    1. *Contract claims* v. *treaty claims* 265
    2. The problem of vertical claims. 269
      Under domestic law 270

Under customary international law 270
Under current investment treaty jurisprudence 271
A first approach: appropriate treaty-drafting? 273
A second approach: tribunal-driven rather than treaty-driven solutions. 274
   3. One measure, multiple disputes 275
  C. Consolidation and coordination 278

Chapter V. Where to from here? The search for practical solutions 283
  A. National courts 284
  B. Commercial arbitration 285
    1. Evolution of institutional rules 285
    2. SIAC Consolidation Protocol. 292
    3. Recording ex ante consent within national legislation? 294
    4. *Res judicata* and *lis pendens*, a greater role for abuse of process? 295
  C. Investment arbitration. 296
    1. Incremental reform 299
      Soft law on parallel proceedings. 299
      Cross-institution consolidation protocol 301
      Abuse of process doctrine 302
    2. Systemic reform. 303

BIOGRAPHICAL NOTE

Salim Abdool Hamid Moollan KC, born 26 July 1971, in Moka (Mauritius), Mauritian, French and British nationalities.

Lycée Labourdonnais, Mauritius (1981-1988), French Baccalauréat, Mathematics and Physics, mention Très Bien avec les Félicitations du Jury, Lycée Louis-le-Grand, Paris (1988-1990), classes préparatoires aux Grandes Écoles scientifiques, Ecole Polytechnique, Paris (1990-1993), Diplôme de l'Ecole Polytechnique, Advanced Mathematics and Physics, Institut d'Etudes Politiques de Paris (Sciences-Po) (1993-1995), Political Science and Economics degree, Downing College, Cambridge (1995-1997), BA (Law), First Class Honours in Part I and Part II (MA: 2001), Harris Scholarship, Senior Harris Scholarship, Inns of Court School of Law, London (1997-1998), Bar Vocational Course, Middle Temple's Queen Mother Scholarship.

Called to the Bars of England and Wales and Mauritius (1998), Queen's Counsel (2016), King's Counsel (2022).

Representative of Mauritius at the United Nations Commission on International Trade Law ("UNCITRAL") since 2006; past Chairman and Vice-Chairman of UNCITRAL and past chairman of its Working Group II (Arbitration); Vice-President of the International Court of Arbitration of the International Chamber of Commerce ("ICC") (2009-2015); Past member of the Court of the London Court of International Arbitration ("LCIA"); Visiting Professor (International Arbitration Law), King's College, University of London; Member of the World Bank's International Centre for Settlement of Investment Disputes ("ICSID") Panels of arbitrators and conciliators; Member of the UK's Department for Business, Innovations and Skills' *ad hoc* advisory group on international arbitration; Editor, *Arbitration International*; Membre du Comité de Lecture, *Revue de l'Arbitrage*; Past member of the Editorial Board of the *ICSID Review*.

Member of the Comité Français de l'Arbitrage, the Commercial Bar Association, the Institut pour l'Arbitrage International, the LCIA, the London Common Law and Commercial Bar Association and the ICC UK Arbitration Committee.

PRINCIPAL PUBLICATIONS

"A Tale of Two Cities: l'affaire Dallah, Goldman Lecture 2022", *Arbitration International*, forthcoming.

"Rethinking International Arbitration Law in a New Arbitral Seat" [with Fedelma Smith], *Arbitration International*, forthcoming.

"Some Thoughts on Emmanuel Gaillard's 'Vertus de la règle matérielle'", in *Liber Amicorum Emmanuel Gaillard*, forthcoming.

Investment Arbitration: Dealing with the Sovereign Debt Crisis?, Permanent Court of Arbitration Series, forthcoming.

"Rethinking Jurisdiction, Competence – Competence and Separability", Permanent Court of Arbitration Series, June 2012.

"The New Mauritian International Arbitration Act 2008" [with Ricky H. Diwan], *Paris Journal of International Arbitration, Les Cahiers de l'Arbitrage*, Vol. 1 (2010), pp. 309-322.

"Une brève introduction à la nouvelle loi mauricienne sur l'arbitrage international", *Revue de l'Arbitrage* (2009), No. 4, pp. 933-941.

"Observations on the Court of Appeal's Judgment in *Sun Life Assurance Co. of Canada (Canada) and American Phoenix Life and Reassurance Co. (USA) and Phoenix Home Life Mutual Insurance Co. (USA)* v. *The Lincoln National Life Insurance Co (USA)*", in *International Arbitration Court Decisions*, 2nd ed., US, Juris Publishing, 2008, pp. 195-228.

"Article II and the Requirements of Form" [with T. T. Landau QC], in Gaillard and di Pietro (eds.), *Enforcement of Arbitration Agreements and International Arbitral Awards: The New York Convention 1958 in Practice*, UK, Cameron May, 2007, pp. 187-256.

"Chronique de jurisprudence étrangère, Royaume-Uni", *Revue de l'Arbitrage* (2006), No. 1, pp. 258-278.

"Note – Royaume-Uni Chambre des Lords, 30 juin 2005" [with V. V. Veeder QC], *Revue de l'Arbitrage* (2006), No. 4, pp. 1032-1038.

Author of the "Arbitration" chapter of the *All England Annual Review* (2004-2008).

INTRODUCTION

The issue of parallel proceedings is a long-standing and classical problem of international arbitration. The last major academic analysis of the issue in 2006 by the International Law Association and by the Geneva Colloquium on Consolidation of Proceedings in Investment Arbitration, led by Professor Kaufmann-Kohler. Since then, the development of investment arbitration in particular has exacerboted the problems faced in day-to-day practice, which these seminal studies have unfortunately only had limited impact in alleviating. With this in mind, now is an opportune moment to re-examine the issue through a fresh theoretical lens and renewed focus on finding practical solutions.

CHAPTER I

DEFINING THE SUBJECT: WHAT ARE PARALLEL PROCEEDINGS IN INTERNATIONAL ARBITRATION?

There is no official or formal definition of "parallel proceedings" in the context of international arbitration. The term has not been expressly defined in any legal instrument, treaty or statute. Rather, it is a term that has been introduced and developed through academic works, commentaries, books, essays, law review articles and blogs. As a result, defining the concept of parallel proceedings can be a challenging task.

However, despite the lack of a formal definition, it is crucial to make every effort to define the scope of the subject matter addressed in this course. This is not simply an academic pursuit. As Socrates noted centuries ago, definitions enable us to distil the essence of a concept, allowing us to think clearly and consistently. In other words, defining parallel proceedings is a prerequisite to conducting any meaningful analysis and discussion of our topic.

A. Defining parallel proceedings

1. "Connection" between different proceedings

While international arbitration lacks a formal definition of parallel proceedings, soft law instruments and under EU law provide definitions that can serve as a starting point for a modernised working definition. To begin with, it should be noted that different terms are used to refer to this phenomenon, including "concurrent", "multiple" and "multi-party" proceedings in English and *pendantes, concurrentes, multiples* or *connexes* proceedings in French. The French term *connexes* is particularly interesting because it does not have a direct equivalent in the English-language arbitral literature. It can be translated as "related", "interrelated" or "connected" proceedings.

It is crucial to recognise that each term does not necessarily capture the same phenomenon, and there are genuine differences of meaning that need to be bridged or explained. These terms can be rationalised into three distinct groups.

First, the terms "parallel" *(pendants)* or "concurrent" *(concurrentes)* proceedings focus on the time element, emphasising that the proceedings are progressing simultaneously or overlapping in time. These terms are inspired by and probably derive from the notion of *lis pendens*, but they do not fully cover the complexity and array of scenarios that fall under parallel proceedings. Connected proceedings running concurrently are just one *type* of parallel proceedings.

Second, the terms "multiple" *(multiples)* and "multiparty" *(multipartite)* proceedings highlight the multiplicity of proceedings or parties, without reference to a time element or simultaneity. In one sense, the term "multiple proceedings" is not inaccurate: there must be more than one proceeding, a single proceeding cannot give rise to parallel proceedings, and thus, the existence of more than one proceeding is a prerequisite for parallel proceedings. But the term does not explain what these proceedings must have in common to be grouped under the same umbrella. While the terms "parallel" and "concurrent" are too narrow, "multiple" is too broad. The term "multiparty" also lends itself to confusion because parallel proceedings can occur between the same two parties, even if multiparty proceedings *can* give rise to parallel proceedings (e.g. in the context of interrelated contracts in commercial arbitrations).

Lastly, the terms "related", "interrelated" or "connected" proceedings are more accurate in capturing the subject matter of parallel proceedings. The French term *connexes* does not require simultaneity or a time element and is rightly broader than the terms "parallel" or "concurrent". It is also not as broad as "multiple" or "multiparty" proceedings. The term *connexes* and its English translations thus focus on the *two* core attributes of the definition of parallel proceedings: the existence of multiple *related* or *connected* proceedings.

2. Nature of the "connection"

Understanding the nature of the "connection" between multiple proceedings is crucial in grasping the definition of parallel proceedings. What *kind* of connection is required between multiple proceedings for them to qualify as parallel proceedings?

The International Law Association

The International Law Association ("ILA") provides a useful starting point with its definition proposed in the ILA "Recommendations on *Lis Pendens* and *Res Judicata* and Arbitration" in 2006:

"[Parallel proceedings are] proceedings pending before a national court or another arbitral tribunal in which the parties and one or more of the issues are the same or substantially the same as the ones before the arbitral tribunal in the Current Arbitration."[1]

This definition is now fifteen years old, and the field has developed since the ILA crafted it, particularly in investment treaty arbitration. For instance, the scenario of multiple claims by unrelated investors against the same State over the same measure was not then considered as a problem of parallel proceedings. Similarly, multiple claims again the same State by shareholders in the same corporate chain were a rare occurrence and would not have been at the forefront of ILA drafters' minds in 2006. The problem they had in mind would have been a more familiar one in the context of international arbitration: *lis pendens*, that is to say, connected proceedings running concurrently. But there are other limitations to this definition.

First, the definition includes a time element, requiring proceedings to be "pending". This aspect is too narrow as proceedings could still qualify as parallel, even if they are successive rather than concurrent, as long as they are connected in a meaningful way.

Second, the definition requires "the parties" to be "the same or substantially the same", which is not always the case in investment arbitration. For example, there may be parallel proceedings even if only one party is the same, such as in cases where several unrelated investors bring claims against the same State over the same measure. Similarly, in cases involving so-called "vertical claims" brought by shareholders from the same corporate chain, the parties need not be "the same or substantially the same". The same applies to a State enacting a measure affecting a pool of investors facing numerous claims over the "same or substantially the same issue", even if there are different claimants. These cases are "connected" by a common factual predicate – the same State measure.

Third, the definition requires "one or more of the issues" to be "the same or substantially the same". This requirement is correct for *factual* issues: for the proceedings to be related, there must be a common factual predicate. There must be one or more facts that are common

---

1. F. De Ly and A. Sheppard, "ILA Recommendations on *Lis Pendens* and *Res Judicata* and Arbitration, Seventy-Second International Law Association Conference on International Commercial Arbitration, Toronto, Canada, 4-8 June 2006", *Arbitration International*, Vol. 25, No. 1 (2009), pp. 83-86 at p. 83.

to the parallel proceedings. However, to the extent it refers to *legal* issues, this is not necessarily the case. Legal issues can differ between proceedings due to varying applicable laws, including different bilateral investment treaties ("BITs"). Even if the same provision applies, such as the fair and equitable treatment ("FET") standard, there could still be differences in wording and substance, with FET being tied to the customary international law standard of minimum treatment of aliens in one case but not another.

On the first two points – proceedings being pending and between the same parties – the ILA definition appears to be too narrow. On the third point, it is too broad, for it fails to make a distinction between factual and legal issues.

The Brussels I Regulation (recast)

While it does not apply to international arbitration [2], the European Union's adoption of the Brussels I Regulation (recast) in 2012, which came into effect in 2015 [3], provides an indirect definition of parallel proceedings in the context of international court litigation. The Regulation does not strictly define parallel proceedings,but Section 9, titled "*Lis pendens* – related actions", focuses on scenarios in which courts of Member States may stay proceedings, establishing a first-in-time rule where the court first seized of a cause of action within a Member State has jurisdiction over the dispute, and subsequent courts seized of the same or related actions must or may stay proceedings.

This approach corresponds to the civil law tradition's approach to parallel proceedings, which usually operates on a first-in-time rule, while the common law tradition relies on the doctrine of *forum non conveniens*, which considers various factors to determine the appropriate forum in which to settle a dispute, including the first-in-time aspect of *lis pendens*.

Concluding remarks

The 2012 Brussels I Regulation (recast) and 2006 ILA definition of parallel proceedings both hinge on the notion of *lis pendens* and are

---

2. See Article 1 (2) *(d)* of the Brussels I Regulation (recast).
3. Regulation (EU) No. 1215/2012 of the European Parliament and of the Council of 12 December 2012 on jurisdiction and the recognition and enforcement of judgments in civil and commercial matters (recast), https://eur-lex.europa.eu/LexUriServ/Lex UriServ.do?uri=OJ:L:2012:351:0001:0032:EN:PDF, last consulted 17 May 2022.

thus both influenced by civil law. However, *lis pendens* is too narrow to capture the full complexity of parallel proceedings, and thus both definitions are found lacking.

However, the Brussels I Regulation (recast) is more modern than the ILA definition and constitutes a step forward. Whereas in the ILA definition proceedings are parallel when one or more issues are "the same or substantially the same", in the Brussels Regulation proceedings are parallel when actions are deemed to be "related", that is to say "where they are so closely connected that it is expedient to hear and determine them together to avoid the risk of irreconcilable judgments resulting from separate proceedings"[4].

The terms "related" and "connected" in the Regulation match the French term *connexes*, which better capture the full phenomenon of parallel proceedings in international arbitration. Moreover, the reference to "expedience" as a factor to determine whether proceedings are "closely connected" may be seen as a nod to the common law doctrine of *forum non conveniens*, and the ultimate aim is consistency in avoiding irreconcilable judgments. While the ILA definition and the Brussels I Regulation (recast) are useful starting points, they are centred on the classic notion of *lis pendens* and are too narrow to encompass more modern scenarios, particularly in investment arbitration.

3. A proposed modernised definition

After reviewing past definitions and modern scenarios, it can be concluded that the term parallel proceedings broadly covers two types of situations. The first type occurs when the *same* dispute is brought before different adjudicating bodies, such as courts or tribunals. This is the classic *lis pendens* scenario, where the parties, facts and legal issues are essentially the same. The broader term "parallel proceedings" evolved from this basic matrix.

The second type of parallel proceedings involves *related* disputes that are brought before different adjudicating bodies. In this scenario, the parties may not be exactly the same, and indeed it is sufficient that at least one of the parties is common to both proceedings. The legal issues and causes of action may also vary.

The *same* disputes are by definition also *related*. Therefore, the lowest common denominator between these two major groups of

---

4. See Article 30 (3) of the Brussels I Regulation (recast).

parallel proceedings is that the disputes must be related. This takes us back to the French term *connexes*. The key is then to identify the nature of this connection. How do the disputes need to be related for them to qualify as parallel proceedings? Again, one must look for the lowest common denominator.

In order to qualify as parallel proceedings, two variables must be present at all times. First, at least one of the parties must be the same in both proceedings. It is often the case that the other side will also be the same party or a closely related party linked by ownership – but this is not required for "parallel proceedings" *stricto sensu*. Second, the core facts in dispute must be the same. The core facts are what define a dispute. If they are not the same, there are two different unrelated disputes. By contrast, the causes of action and legal recourses arising from these core facts may indeed differ – and very often will.

Based on these criteria, a working definition of "parallel proceedings" *in international arbitration* can be proposed as follows:

"Parallel proceedings are two or more proceedings submitted to different adjudicating bodies, at least one of which is an international arbitral tribunal, where at a minimum:

a) one of the parties is the same and the core facts are the same; and

b) the proceedings are further related in the following sense:

1. both parties are the same, substantially the same, or are closely related; or

2. the causes of action are the same or substantially the same; or

3. the object of the actions are the same or substantially the same."

This definition captures the complexity behind the concept of parallel proceedings. There must be an essential core, a minimum threshold below which one cannot genuinely speak of parallel proceedings. It is the line dividing parallel proceedings from separate proceedings with similarities. But above this threshold, the concept is capable of semantic gradation and will depend on the specific circumstances of each case. The first part of the definition sets out the defining qualities of parallel proceedings, while the second part introduces the requisite degree of nuance and discretion.

The proposed definition also covers all the scenarios discussed in this course. For instance, in the field of investment arbitration, which has seen an increased focus on parallel proceedings in recent years, three of the classical scenarios are covered by this definition, viz. the scenario where claims based on contracts are brought in parallel to claims based on investment treaties, the scenario of "vertical claims", where shareholders at different levels of the same vertical corporate chain bring claims against the same State based on the same key facts or State measures, and the scenario where investors with no link of ownership between them bring claims against the same State based on the same key facts or State measures.

B. *Typology of parallel proceedings*

Parallel proceedings come in different types and shapes, and it is important to classify them in order to distinguish between problematic cases (for which solutions should be found) and non-problematic cases. Two classifications are proposed. The first is based on the *forum* before which the proceedings are brought. This classification is objective and allows for a systematic view of the field. The second classification, which is more subjective, is based on the *reasons* for bringing parallel proceedings.

There are two main fora where claims can be brought: international arbitral tribunals and national courts. The interaction between these two fora gives rise to four possible scenarios:

Forum	International arbitral tribunal	National court
International arbitral tribunal	*international arbitral tribunal* v. *international arbitral tribunal*	*international arbitral tribunal* v. *national court*
National court	*national court* v. *international arbitral tribunal*	*national court* v. *national court*

This matrix could be further compounded if there were more than two fora involved in the parallel proceedings; for instance, the national courts from two different jurisdictions and an international arbitration tribunal, or more than two arbitral tribunals. But, ultimately, there will always be two basic types of interactions, and this course covers these two main scenarios: national court v. international arbitration tribunal (see Chap. II) and international arbitration tribunal v. international arbitration tribunal. This second scenario can be subdivided into *(a)* purely commercial disputes with no investment arbitration element (or "commercial arbitration", see Chap. III) and *(b)* disputes with an investment arbitration element (or "investment arbitration", see Chap. IV). This course does *not* cover national court v. national court, either within the same jurisdiction or within separate jurisdictions.

There may be limitations to classifying parallel proceedings in terms of purpose, reason or motivation. After all, we cannot know with certainty the reasons why proceedings are brought in a specific case. Nor is there a closed, exhaustive list of such reasons. There could be exceptional reasons specific to a case that are beyond generic classification. Yet, despite these shortcomings, this classification is useful. If the first classification seeks to determine *what* types of parallel proceedings there are, the second tries to understand *why* such proceedings are brought. This can help us understand the root of any problems and identify possible solutions.

Parallel proceedings may be brought for several reasons. They may be brought *to secure a forum with jurisdiction*. It may be unclear what forum has jurisdiction to adjudicate the dispute. In such a case, the purpose of bringing parallel proceedings is merely to ensure that there will be a forum with jurisdiction to adjudicate the dispute. Parallel proceedings are thus used as a sort of jurisdictional insurance to minimise the risk of being left without a forum with jurisdiction to resolve the dispute. In this scenario, it is the same party – the claimant – who in principle brings the claims in different fora.

Parallel proceedings may be brought *as a result of disagreement*. Sometimes parallel proceedings can be the product of genuine, good-faith disagreement between the disputing parties. One party thinks that a particular forum has jurisdiction to settle the dispute, the other thinks it is another forum. They both have claims, and each brings its claims in the forum they believe has jurisdiction. In such a scenario, each party begins separate proceedings in good faith.

A third reason to bring parallel proceedings is *to secure a tactical advantage*. In a dispute the interests of the disputing parties are by definition on a collision course with each other. Parties often look for ways in which they can gain a tactical advantage over the other side, and parallel proceedings can be an important tool in that quest. One tactical advantage is that it may maximise the chances of success on the merits. A party bringing the same – or substantially the same – claims in more than one forum has a greater chance of winning the dispute. A claimant bringing the same claims before multiple fora only need win once, regardless of how many times it loses. This may be the most common tactical reason for a claimant to commence parallel proceedings.

A second tactical advantage relates to forum shopping. Parallel proceedings can happen because the parties shop for the forum they consider most favourable to them. They try to find a friendly forum in which to submit the claims. This can be a forum where they feel they have a "home" advantage; or where they feel they can neutralise the "home" advantage that the other side would have in another forum; or where they feel that the procedural laws or the adjudicating court or tribunal are likely to favour their position. Other factors a party might consider in forum shopping include the speed (or lack of speed) of the adjudicating bodies to decide the dispute, the costs, the seat, the language, the efficiency and support of local courts, the wish to apply for interim measures or bring counterclaims, the applicable law, and practical considerations such as the location of client, counsel team, witnesses or evidence. A third tactical advantage of bringing parallel proceedings is simply to harass the other side, for example to maximise the financial pressure on their opponent or increase the "nuisance" value of the dispute and thus the chances of settlement. In short, there is a wide array of reasons why parties bring parallel proceedings, ranging from good faith to bad faith to plain harassment, from searching for tactical advantages to maximising the chances of winning.

These two classifications thus help us address two questions: the substance of parallel proceedings (the *what*) and the reasons for bringing them (the *why*). The first classification helps us approach the subject in an orderly, methodological fashion and has intrinsic analytical value. The second classification is elusive and open-ended but more likely to help diagnose problems with the system and devise possible solutions. Both classifications accordingly complement each other well. Each serves a distinct purpose and, combined, help address both the theoretical and practical aspects of this field.

C. Why are parallel proceedings problematic?

Parallel proceedings present significant problems and challenges, both for the parties involved and the system of international dispute settlement as a whole. The problems are thus both case-specific or systemic. For example, the inefficiency of parallel proceedings leads to unnecessary costs and a waste of resources, as more resources need to be spent on settling the same dispute. This is especially pressing when public resources are involved, as is always the case in investment arbitration. Another problem is the potential for parallel proceedings to be used as a tool of harassment. Legal proceedings are meant to provide parties with a means to redress alleged grievances and wrongs. The potential to bring parallel proceedings over what is essentially the same alleged grievance or wrong distorts the restorative nature of a legal remedy. What is meant to be a remedy can become a weapon to harass and persecute the opposing party.

The most significant problem with parallel proceedings is the risk of inconsistent and contradictory decisions. Different adjudicating bodies can render decisions that are inconsistent or contradictory in terms of the case outcome, amount of compensation awarded, findings of fact, legal issues, and reasoning. The risk is present in both commercial and investment arbitration, but it carries greater risks and takes on a more serious dimension in investment arbitration. This is due to the nature of investment arbitration cases, which often involve State measures affecting a group of claimants (whether related or unrelated) rather than the narrower setting of parties and issues in commercial arbitration cases. Examples abound, such as the wave of cases against Argentina in relation to the financial crisis or against Spain and the Czech Republic in the renewable energy cases. State measures often involve public as opposed to commercial interests; the issues in dispute in investment arbitration cases are thus by definition more politically sensitive and the risk of contradictory decisions felt more acutely.

Parallel proceedings also pose challenges related to confidentiality, transparency, public funds, and private interests. While commercial arbitration proceedings are usually confidential, investment arbitration proceedings involving States and public interests often require greater transparency and publicity. This can be seen in the adoption of the United Nations Commission on International Trade Law ("UNCITRAL") Rules on Transparency in Treaty-based Investor-State Arbitration, incorporated into the 2013 UNCITRAL Arbitration Rules [5], the Mauritius Convention on Transparency [6] and the proposed pro-transparency amendments of the International Centre for Settlement of Investment Disputes ("ICSID") Rules (reflected in the ICSID 2020

---

5. The 2013 UNCITRAL Arbitration Rules, https://uncitral.un.org/sites/uncitral.un.org/files/media-documents/uncitral/en/uncitral-arbitration-rules-2013-e.pdf, last consulted 17 May 2021.
6. The text of Mauritius Convention on Transparency, https://uncitral.un.org/sites/uncitral.un.org/files/media-documents/uncitral/en/transparency-convention-e.pdf, last consulted 17 May 2021.

Working Paper No. 4)[7]. The origin of funds involved in investment arbitration are usually public (indeed, in the case of a State party, always so), making the misuse or waste of funds more concerning than in commercial arbitration cases, where the origins of the funds are usually private.

Moreover, parallel proceedings undermine the public's confidence in international arbitration as a system for resolving high-stakes disputes. The public at large, and users in particular, will inevitably lose faith in a system that is inefficient, wastes resources, can be used as a tool of harassment, and can produce inconsistent and contradictory decisions. Again, these risks are greater in the case of investment arbitration, where the involvement of the public interest, public funds and greater transparency mean these problems will be brought into sharper focus.

Despite all this, not all parallel proceedings are objectionable and only some are problematic. Some parallel proceedings are simply manifestations of a system operating as it should. To minimise these problems, criteria must be established to distinguish between desirable and undesirable parallel proceedings. This course aims to identify undesirable parallel proceedings and propose practical solutions to address them.

D. A practical example:
Lauder v. Czech Republic and CME v. Czech Republic

One of the most well-known cases of parallel proceedings in investment arbitration is the dispute involving Ronald Lauder and CME Czech Republic BV ("CME") over their investment in the Czech television channel TV Nova. Mr Lauder, a US citizen, claimed that the media council, an organ of the Czech Republic, destroyed his investment through its actions and omissions. He initiated UNCITRAL arbitration proceedings on 19 August 1999, under the United States-Czech and Slovak Republic BIT, alleging violations of several obligations, including the prohibition against arbitrary and discriminatory measures, the obligation to provide FET, the obligation to provide full protection and security, the obligation of treatment in accordance with general

---

7. Working Paper #4, https://icsid.worldbank.org/sites/default/files/amendments/WP_4_Vol_1_En.pdf, last consulted 17 May 2021. These have now been incorporated into the new ICSID Rules as Arbitration Rule 62.

principles of international law, and the obligation not to expropriate unlawfully [8].

Mr Lauder's investment was made through CME, a Dutch company over which he had control. On 22 February 2000, CME initiated UNCITRAL arbitration proceedings under the Netherlands-Czech Republic BIT [9]. CME's claims were essentially the same as Mr Lauder's, including breaches of the obligation to provide FET, the obligation to provide full protection and security and the obligation not to expropriate unlawfully [10].

Despite having different tribunal members, both tribunals rendered their decisions within ten days of each other. The two decisions were diametrically opposed. The *Lauder* tribunal concluded that the Czech Republic did not violate the United States-Czech and Slovak Republic BIT, except for a minor breach regarding discriminatory and arbitrary treatment in the early days of Mr Lauder's investment [11]. The remaining dispute was deemed a private commercial dispute between Mr Lauder and his local partner [12].

In contrast, the *CME* tribunal (by majority) found that the Czech Republic breached multiple standards of protection under the Netherlands-Czech Republic BIT and ordered the country to pay CME the fair market value of the investment [13], which the tribunal later determined to be over USD 260 million [14].

---

8. *Ronald S. Lauder* v. *The Czech Republic*, UNCITRAL, Final Award, 3 September 2001, para. 193.
9. *CME Czech Republic BV* v. *The Czech Republic*, UNCITRAL, Partial Award, 13 September 2001, para. 2.
10. *Ibid.*, at para. 27.
11. *Lauder*, note 8, decision at p. 74.
12. *Ibid.*, at para. 314.
13. *CME*, note 9, para. 624.
14. *Ibid.*, at p. 161.

CHAPTER II

NATIONAL COURTS VERSUS INTERNATIONAL ARBITRATION TRIBUNALS

Parallel proceedings involving national courts and international arbitration are the most common type of parallel proceedings that arise in disputes submitted to arbitration, whether commercial or investment treaty disputes.

Irrespective of the theory of international arbitration one adheres to (a matter dealt with in Chapter III by reference to Professor Emmanuel Gaillard's work [15]), national courts have by default jurisdiction over any dispute that parties have not agreed to submit to arbitration. However, if parties agree to submit a dispute to arbitration, they create an exception to the default rule of national court jurisdiction. What happens if it is unclear whether the parties have agreed to submit a specific dispute to arbitration? What if it is unclear whether a specific dispute falls within the scope of an arbitration agreement?

This is one of the oldest, classical problems in international arbitration. It has the potential to give rise to parallel proceedings – and often does so. The basic consensus on how to deal with this problem is embodied in an internationally accepted principle: *competence-competence*. This principle lies at the heart of the interaction between national courts and international tribunals, and thus at the heart of this lecture.

While the principle of competence-competence is well known, there is limited consensus on its meaning and operation, which can either encourage or discourage parallel proceedings. This chapter will analyse its connection with the question of parallel proceedings, as well as two other legal devices that address the problem of parallel proceedings involving national courts: the anti-suit or anti-arbitration injunctions, and the "fork-in-the-road" clauses often used in investment arbitration.

---

15. See e.g. E. Gaillard, *Legal Theory of International Arbitration*, Leiden, Martinus Nijhoff, 2010.

A. Competence-competence and parallel proceedings

1. A universally accepted principle

The doctrine of competence-competence has been variously described as a "universally accepted principle" [16], "an internationally recognised standard" [17], a doctrine that "virtually all national legal systems recognize" [18]. It is typically known by two interchangeable designations: as *compétence de la competence* in French and *Kompetenz-Kompetenz* in German.

According to the competence-competence principle, understood in its "primitive form", to use the words of Professor W. W. (Rusty) Park [19], arbitral tribunals have the power to rule on their own jurisdiction whenever a party challenges it, which is necessary to ensure the efficiency and efficacy of international arbitration. Else, all a party would need do to stop proceedings and force a forum change would be to question the authority of the arbitral tribunal to adjudicate the dispute.

Competence-competence thus works as an "anti-sabotage" mechanism to prevent recalcitrant and unwilling parties from derailing proceedings. As Professor Park explains:

> "In its most primitive form, the principle that arbitrators may rule on their jurisdiction serves as a measure to protect against having an arbitration derailed before it begins. The arbitral tribunal (and/or the relevant arbitral institution) need not halt the proceedings just because one side questions its authority. The principle reduces the prospect that proceedings will be derailed through a simple allegation that an arbitration clause is unenforceable, due to any number of contract law defenses. In most legal systems, arbitrators can get on with their work until ordered to stop by a judge with authority to do so." [20]

But this is only half of the story because specifying the powers of arbitral tribunals says nothing about the powers of national courts to deal with the same issues. As Professor Bermann explains:

---

16. C. Ferdinando Emanuele and M. Molfa, *Selected Issues in International Arbitration: The Italian Perspective*, London, Thomson Reuters, 2014, at p. 142.
17. N. Erk-Kubat, *Parallel Proceedings in International Arbitration: A Comparative European Perspective*, The Hague, Kluwer Law International, 2014, at p. 26.
18. G. Born, *International Commercial Arbitration*, The Hague, Kluwer Law International, 2014, at p. 1048.
19. W. W. Park, "The Arbitrator's Jurisdiction to Determine Jurisdiction", 13 ICCA Congress Series 55 (2007), 18 March 2007.
20. *Ibid.*, at pp. 6-7.

"All would appear to agree that Kompetenz-Kompetenz permits an arbitral tribunal to determine its own jurisdiction if it is challenged, and this of course is no minor achievement. But for this understanding, a tribunal arguably would be required to suspend proceedings whenever a party before it challenges its jurisdiction—whatever the basis of the challenge might be—and refer the jurisdictional issue to a court for determination. Allowing a party to unilaterally halt an arbitration merely by advancing a colorable reason in law why it should not go forward would dramatically impair the efficacy of arbitration.

Shall we, however, infer from the fact that an arbitral tribunal *may* determine its own jurisdiction when a party challenges it that a court *may not* address that question?" [21]

The competence-competence principle thus has two different sides or effects, which must be carefully considered.

2. The positive effect

The competence-competence principle has two facets or effects, namely a positive effect and a negative effect. The positive effect confers on arbitral tribunals the power to rule on their own jurisdiction. It is called the "positive effect" because it is an affirmative power that enables tribunals to resolve jurisdictional challenges. This effect is universally recognised and forms a cornerstone of international arbitration. The New York Convention [22] and the ICSID Convention [23] explicitly or implicitly recognise this principle, and national arbitration laws almost universally recognise it as a foundation of international arbitration [24]. Moreover, leading arbitration rules expressly affirm the principle [25].

However, the positive effect does not address the power of national courts to rule on the jurisdiction of arbitral tribunals, which is the second facet of competence-competence, its negative effect.

---

21. G. A. Bermann, "The 'Gateway' Problem in International Arbitration", *Yale Journal of International Law*, Vol. 37, No. 1 (2012), pp. 4-53, at p. 14.
22. See New York Convention Article II (3).
23. See ICSID Convention Article 41.
24. See for instance Article 16 (1) of the UNCITRAL Model Law on International Commercial Arbitration 1985, which expressly provides that arbitral tribunals "may rule on their own jurisdiction".
25. See for instance Article 23 (1) of the 2013 UNCITRAL Arbitration Rules, note 5: "The arbitral tribunal shall have the power to rule on its own jurisdiction, including any objections with respect to the existence or validity of the arbitration agreement."

3. The negative effect

The negative effect of competence-competence is not aimed at arbitral tribunals but at national courts. In cases where it applies, national courts are prohibited from ruling on the jurisdiction of an arbitral tribunal until the tribunal has had a chance to do so. Whereas the positive effect affirms the authority of tribunals to make such rulings, the negative effect restricts the ability of national courts to do so, except by way of set-aside proceedings after the tribunal has ruled on the issue.

While the positive effect of competence-competence is almost universally accepted, the negative effect has been adopted by only a few jurisdictions, including France, Switzerland and Mauritius. To appreciate the practical implications of the negative effect, it is useful to compare the current situation in France with that in England, as well as to briefly consider the approach taken in Mauritius.

French law

France is widely recognised as the leading jurisdiction on the issue of the negative effect of competence-competence. The French Code of Civil Procedure contains two key provisions: Articles 1465 and 1448. Article 1465 provides that the arbitral tribunal is the "only one" or the "exclusive one" with the power to rule on its own jurisdiction [26]. Article 1448 provides that "[w]hen a dispute subject to an arbitration agreement is brought before a court, that court shall decline jurisdiction, except if an arbitral tribunal has not yet been seized of the dispute and if the arbitration agreement is manifestly void or manifestly not applicable" [27].

However, the reference in the French Code of Civil Procedure to the arbitral tribunal having the "sole" or "exclusive" power to rule on its jurisdiction can be misleading. As Professor Gaillard points out [28], this is not a rule of exclusivity but rather a "rule of priority". Arbitrators

---

26. In French: "Le tribunal arbitral est seul compétent pour statuer sur les contestations relatives à son pouvoir juridictionnel."
27. In French: "Lorsqu'un litige relevant d'une convention d'arbitrage est porté devant une juridiction de l'Etat, celle-ci se déclare incompétente sauf si le tribunal arbitral n'est pas encore saisi et si la convention d'arbitrage est manifestement nulle ou manifestement inapplicable."
28. E. Gaillard and Y. Banifatemi, "Negative Effect of Competence-Competence: The Rule of Priority in Favour of the Arbitrators", in E. Gaillard and D. Di Pietro (eds.), *The New York Convention in Practice*, Place, Cameron May, UK, 2008, pp. 257-274, at p. 258.

have priority to rule on their jurisdiction, while the French judge can revisit the question in set-aside or enforcement proceedings.

Even under French law, the negative effect of competence-competence is not absolute. French courts will decline to rule on the jurisdiction of an arbitral tribunal unless the arbitral tribunal has not yet been seized and the arbitration clause is manifestly null or inapplicable. The "manifestly null or inapplicable" threshold is very high and must be *prima facie* evident.

Ultimately, the question is whether the arbitrators should have the first say on issues of jurisdiction, with the risk that they may later be found to have been wrong, or whether the courts should pre-empt that but in a way that necessarily undermines the positive effect of competence-competence. French commentators sometimes criticise other jurisdictions that adopt a different approach as committing a sin against international arbitration, but such an attitude is both dogmatic and unfair. Nonetheless, the French approach does have one major practical advantage, which is clarity. A clear-cut choice has been made for one of the two extremes just noted, and the parties, arbitrators and courts know what to expect and how to operate the system, which can result in cost savings and efficiency.

English law

By contrast, the English regime is complex. It is contained in no less than five sections of the English Arbitration Act 1996 ("1996 Act"), namely sections 9, 30, 32, 67 and 72. The 1996 Act sets out rules and procedures for arbitration agreements, including the positive principle of competence-competence and the mechanism for challenging awards on jurisdiction. However, the interaction between these sections is not entirely clear, and this can lead to confusion and uncertainty.

Section 9 of the 1996 Act requires courts to stay any court action brought in breach of an agreement to arbitrate "unless satisfied that the arbitration agreement is null and void, inoperative, or incapable of being performed". Section 30 contains the positive principle of competence-competence, which allows tribunals to rule on their own jurisdiction subject to review by the courts. Section 32 provides a mechanism for parties to an arbitration or the arbitral tribunal to ask the court to determine a question of jurisdiction, subject to stringent requirements. This right can only be exercised where all parties agree or where the tribunal so directs and if that direction appears to the court likely to result in substantial time and cost savings. Section 67 of the 1996 Act provides for challenges to awards on jurisdiction, while Section 72 provides for a special mechanism whereby a party who takes no part in the arbitral proceedings may ask the court to determine issues of jurisdiction. That mechanism is not subject to any of the stringent requirements of Section 32.

The interaction between these sections is unclear, and there are some difficulties. For example, there is nothing in the wording of Section 72 to prevent a party from using that section before jurisdiction is determined by the arbitral tribunal. In *Law Debenture Trust* v. *Elektrim*[29], Mann J held that a party may indeed use Section 72 at any stage of the proceedings, including at the very outset of the case. This means that the recalcitrant party can decide who goes first and may either allow the issue to go to the tribunal (and subsequently challenge any award rendered against it under Section 67) or refuse to participate and ask the court for a final ruling under Section 72. This use of Section 72 short-circuits the stringent requirements of Section 32 and renders that section largely redundant.

Moreover, in a number of cases under Section 9 of the 1996 Act, the English courts have held that the court had a discretion, to be exercised on an *ad hoc* basis in each case as a matter of case management, whether to refer an issue of jurisdiction to the arbitrators or to decide it itself. This lack of clarity about who decides the issue can result in the need for a hearing before the court to decide who will decide the issue. In an *obiter dictum* in the *Dallah* case, Lord Collins appeared to try to clarify the position (albeit taking a step that ran directly contrary to the French position and denied any "negative effect" of competence-competence), stating that "[w]here there is an application to stay proceedings under Section 9 of the 1996 Act, both in international and domestic cases, the court will determine the issue of whether there ever was an agreement to arbitrate"[30]. Still, the lack of clarity caused by the interaction of these sections of the 1996 Act has remained in everyday practice. The overall result is one of confusion and uncertainty, which cannot be productive or desirable and can hinder the effectiveness of arbitration agreements.

---

29. *Law Debenture Trust Corporation Plc* v. *Elektrim Finance BV & Ors* [2005] EWHC 1412 (Ch).
30. *Dallah Real Estate and Tourism Holding Company* v. *The Ministry of Religious Affairs, Government of Pakistan* [2010] UKSC 46, para. 97.

Mauritian law

The International Arbitration Act 2008 ("Mauritian Act") provides an interesting example of how a new arbitration seat can learn from established jurisdictions. The starting point is that Mauritius has of course adopted the positive rule of competence-competence [31]. In terms of the rule of priority – that is, who goes first, the court or the arbitral tribunal – a clear choice must be made, as evidenced by this comparative study. The Mauritian legislature has opted for the French solution, where the arbitral tribunal goes first, for three core reasons.

First, this stance is likely to be perceived a pro-arbitration, which is crucial for a new arbitral seat. Second, it aligns with the general philosophy of the Mauritian Act to minimise contact points with courts during arbitral proceedings. A party arriving in Mauritius to arbitrate should not start his trip with a lengthy visit to the Mauritian courts, however pleasant the judges there. Third, the solution recommended by Professor Park in his report to the 2006 Montréal International Council for Commercial Arbitration ("ICCA") Congress, the French rule with "a summary mechanism ... to permit courts to halt arbitral proceedings when the arbitration clause is manifestly void" [32], was in effect adopted in Mauritius, even if this was not a factor in the drafting of the Mauritian Act. Notably, the test in the Mauritian Act is framed differently to ensure that it is readily understandable to users worldwide.

Section 5 of the Act provides that all arbitration applications made to the court are to be decided by a three-judge bench of the Supreme Court, which must:

> "refer the parties to arbitration unless a party shows, on a prima facie basis, that there is a very strong probability that the arbitration agreement may be null and void, inoperative or incapable of being performed".

This test is substantially the same as the French test, but assessment hearing before the Supreme Court must be a summary *prima facie* and not a trial or mini-trial. Moreover, the Court may decide the issue itself where the clause is *manifestement nulle*, even when the arbitral tribunal has been constituted. This is the gloss recommended by Professor Park.

It is important to note that when the Court refers a dispute to arbitration under Section 5 of the Mauritanian Act, it is not deciding on

---

31. See Section 20 (1) of the Mauritian Act.
32. Park, note 19, at p. 145.

the validity of the arbitration clause. Instead, it is finding, on a *prima facie* basis, that the party challenging the clause's validity has not demonstrated a strong probability of its invalidity. The ruling has no *res judicata* effect, and a full ruling by the Court would occur only if and when the jurisdictional award of the arbitrators is challenged later.

Although both French and Mauritian laws adopt competence-competence in its negative facet, their differences illustrate that there are more nuances than the simple dichotomy of positive and negative effect suggests. As Professor Park notes, this dichotomy simplifies what is a far more nuanced issue.

Two key factors

In international arbitration, the timing of national court intervention and the effect of the arbitral tribunal's ruling on jurisdiction are critical factors that must be considered. As Professor Park notes, courts must examine the parties' actual agreements about arbitral authority and the effect that judge gives those agreements [33].

Different approaches exist regarding when national courts can rule on the jurisdiction of an arbitral tribunal, with the American, Mauritian, and French approaches standing out. The American approach allows courts to intervene at any point (whether or not the tribunal has been seized), which leads to a high likelihood of national court intervention. The Mauritian approach permits intervention during arbitration (regardless of whether the tribunal has been seized) but only if there is a very strong possibility that the arbitration clause is null and void. This approach leads to a low likelihood of national court intervention. In the French approach, national courts cannot intervene during arbitration if the arbitral tribunal has been seized but can do so during the set-aside or enforcement proceedings. If the tribunal has not been seized, courts can intervene only if there is a manifestly null or inapplicable arbitration clause. The French approach leads to a very low likelihood of national court intervention.

Each approach has a different impact on the likelihood of parallel proceedings, with the American approach (indeed, any approach not adopting negative competence-competence) posing the highest risk of such proceedings. If the legal seat of the arbitration is unclear, it could even involve more than one national court. This results in duplication

---

33. Park, note 19, at p. 12.

of proceedings, increased expenses, greater risk of harassment, and reduced autonomy for international arbitration. However, this approach leads to a faster final ruling on arbitral jurisdiction, fewer unwarranted arbitral proceedings, and less legitimacy concerns around arbitration proceeding without consent.

Conversely, the French approach (and those similar to it, such as the Swiss and Mauritian ones) results in a lower risk of parallel proceedings, providing greater autonomy for arbitral tribunals, less resources devoted to settling the question of arbitral jurisdiction, and less ability for one side to harass the other side. However, it leads to slower final rulings, legitimacy concerns as to arbitrating without consent, and a risk of unwarranted arbitral proceedings.

Ultimately, the allocation of jurisdiction between courts and tribunals on the issue of the tribunal's jurisdiction is part of the ordinary course of business in international arbitration. There is nothing intrinsically pathological about it. Yet the choice of which version of competence-competence to adopt does have a direct impact on the potential for and risk of parallel proceedings. Importantly, however, whatever solution is adopted, there is no risk of inconsistency. It is universally accepted that national courts are the ultimate arbiters of jurisdiction, and any determination of jurisdiction by the arbitral tribunal is subject to review by the national courts.

To minimise the risk of parallel proceedings, the obvious solution would be to adopt a negative version of competence-competence, such as the French or Mauritian version. However, only a few jurisdictions have adopted this approach to date, and the risk of parallel proceedings thus remains present in most interactions between national courts and arbitral tribunals on the question of arbitral jurisdiction.

4. A practical example: The Fomento *case*

The key question in the *Fomento* case [34] was whether an arbitral tribunal sitting in Switzerland should stay the arbitral proceedings, pending the decision of foreign courts on that arbitral tribunal's jurisdiction.

The case concerned a dispute between Colon Container Terminal SA ("CCT"), a Panamanian company, and Fomento de Construcciones

---

34. Swiss Federal Tribunal, *Fomento de Construcciones y Contratas SA* v. *Colon Container Terminal SA*, ASA Bull., 2001, Vol. 3, p. 555.

y Contratas SA ("Fomento"), a Spanish company, arising from a 1996 contract for civil engineering works. Both parties had taken conflicting steps in the Panamanian courts and before an arbitral tribunal seated in Geneva, resulting in both fora being seized of the dispute. Fomento filed a claim against CCT in the Panamanian courts, prompting CCT to raise a defence asserting that the parties had agreed to resolve their disputes through arbitration. However, the Panamanian Court of First Instance dismissed this defence as being untimely. Without waiting for the proceedings in Panama to run their course, CCT commenced arbitration proceedings in Geneva under the Arbitration Rules of the International Chamber of Commerce ("ICC") and the Swiss Federal Code on Civil Procedure. Fomento subsequently challenged the jurisdiction of the arbitral tribunal. While the arbitration was ongoing, a Superior Panamanian Court reversed the decision of the First Instance Court, holding that CCT's defence was in fact timely. The arbitral tribunal in Geneva then upheld its jurisdiction, referring to the decision of the Superior Panamanian Court, without waiting for remedies to be exhausted in Panama.

However, after the award was issued, the Supreme Court of Panama reversed the decision of the Superior Panamanian Court and ordered that the dispute be heard by the courts of Panama. Fomento thus challenged the arbitral award before the Swiss Federal Tribunal, arguing that the arbitral tribunal erroneously upheld its jurisdiction by failing to stay its proceedings pending the final determination of the matter by the Panamanian courts, thereby ignoring the principle of *lis pendens* enshrined in Article 9 (1) of the Swiss Private International Law Act ("PILA")[35]. The Swiss Federal Tribunal allowed Fomento's challenge and set aside the arbitral award, holding that an arbitral tribunal seated in Switzerland was (like the Swiss national courts) bound by Article 9 (1) of the PILA. The Swiss Federal Tribunal's decision was based on its understanding of the principle of *lis pendens* and its function alongside that of *res judicata* to avoid contradictory decisions.

The Swiss Federal Tribunal decided that there was no serious legal basis for granting priority to an arbitral tribunal over national courts in ruling on the tribunal's jurisdiction, and for ignoring the order of

---

35. Article 9 (1) of the Private International Law Act provides that: "If an action having the same subject matter is already pending between the same parties abroad, the Swiss court shall stay the proceeding if it may be expected that the foreign court will, within a reasonable time, render a decision that will be recognizable in Switzerland."

chronological priority set out in Article 9 (1) of the PILA. It mechanically applied the principle of *lis pendens*, which is "purely chronological"[36]. It thus undermined the principle of competence-competence, which is "specifically designed to protect and safeguard the arbitrators' power to rule on their jurisdiction"[37]. As a result of the *Fomento* case, the Swiss legislature added a new paragraph to Article 186 of the PILA in 2006 to clarify the application of the principle of competence-competence, stating the following:

> "The arbitral tribunal shall decide on its own jurisdiction without regard to any action having the same subject matter that is already pending between the same parties before a state court or another arbitral tribunal, unless there are substantial grounds for a stay in proceedings."[38]

B. Anti-suit (and anti-arbitration) injunctions

Competence-competence has a significant effect on parallel proceedings, increasing or reducing them indirectly. However, at its core, it is designed to allocate jurisdiction between courts and tribunals to ensure the effectiveness of arbitration as a dispute settlement method. The previous section discussed the important effects of competence-competence on parallel proceedings. The motions we now turn to, anti-suit (and anti-arbitration) injunctions and fork-in-the-road clauses, for their part are legal devices created to avoid parallel proceedings. Anti-suit injunctions have been used in commercial arbitration for a long time. By contrast, the appearance of fork-in-the-road clauses, which will be addressed in the next section, is more recent and related to the rise of investment treaties and investment arbitration.

As Professor George Bermann defines it, an anti-suit injunction is

> "an order issued by a court or tribunal at the request of one party designed to prevent another party from commencing or maintaining a legal proceeding in another forum, particularly a foreign forum"[39].

---

36. Gaillard and Banifatemi, note 28, at p. 272.
37. *Ibid.*
38. New Article 186, para. 1 bis, adopted by the Federal Law of 6 October 2006, which entered into force on 1 March 2007.
39. G. A. Bermann, "*Anti-Suit Injunctions*: International Adjudication", in H. Ruiz Fabri (ed.), *Max Planck Encyclopedia of International*, Oxford, Oxford University Press, 2015, at para. 1.

These injunctions are thus specifically devised to avoid parallel proceedings, and thus resemble *lis pendens* and *forum non conveniens* doctrines. Under *lis pendens*, a court or tribunal will defer to legal proceedings already underway in another forum. *Lis pendens*, then, essentially operates as a rule of "first in time" (i.e. first jurisdiction to be seized). It is widely accepted in civil law countries but not common law countries. Under *forum non conveniens*, a court or tribunal will defer to another forum that it deems to be more suitable (or more convenient, as the name implies) to adjudicate the dispute. While the question of whether that other forum has already been seized or not (whether it was "first in time") may be relevant to that enquiry, it is not determinative. This doctrine is widely accepted in common law countries but not civil law countries.

Both *lis pendens* and *forum non conveniens* are predicated on the self-restraint of the court or tribunal seized, whereas anti-suit injunctions are orders that purport to restrain the exercise of jurisdiction by another court or tribunal. While the restraining order is never directed at the other forum but at a party appearing before the court/tribunal passing the said order (so that it is meant to act *in personam* against that party, not as an order directly challenging the other court/tribunal), its effect is the same since it is intended indirectly to prevent that other forum from exercising jurisdiction.

Anti-suit injunctions may be issued by both courts and arbitral tribunals, and two types of injunctions can be issued, anti-suit and anti-arbitration injunctions. The matrix of possibilities is as follows:

Forum	*Anti-suit injunction*	*Anti-arbitration injunction*
National court	*(1)* Court-issued anti-suit injunction	*(3)* Court-issued anti-arbitration injunction
International arbitration tribunal	*(2)* Tribunal-issued anti-suit injunction	*(4)* Tribunal-issued anti-arbitration injunction

There may be various reasons for a court or tribunal to issue an anti-suit or anti-arbitration injunction, including to protect its own jurisdiction, comply with its own obligations (e.g. a court's obligation to refer a matter to arbitration), or protect a party's rights (e.g. the right to have a dispute settled by arbitration). Civil law jurisdictions generally do not favour these remedies as they are believed to breach international comity – that is, the deference a court or tribunal is expected to afford other courts or tribunals. As Laurent Levy, a well-known civil law arbitrator puts it, foreign adjudicators "are the arbitrator's equals and have no orders to receive"[40].

However, in common law jurisdictions, anti-suit injunctions are established remedies, and their use has been established in the United Kingdom, the United States, Australia, Canada, Hong Kong and India, where the courts have developed sophisticated case law on the matter. The most common instance of anti-suit injunctions in the arbitration context is to prevent a foreign court from taking jurisdiction over a dispute that the parties have agreed to refer to arbitration – so-called *Angelic Grace* injunctions [41]. Outside that situation, the English courts will only grant this exceptional remedy where a foreign suit can be shown to be "vexatious or oppressive"[42] – a very high threshold.

The use of anti-suit and anti-arbitration injunctions is a controversial and exceptional practice that remains at the discretion of courts and tribunals. However, their use is more acceptable in some cases than in others. In order of most acceptable to least acceptable, one could rank them as follows: *(1)* court-issued anti-suit injunctions, *(2)* tribunal-issued anti-suit injunctions, *(3)* court-issued anti-arbitration injunctions, and *(4)* tribunal-issued anti-arbitration injunctions.

The rarest form of anti-suit injunctive relief is the anti-arbitration injunction. This is because such injunctions are in direct conflict with the key principle of international arbitration we have just covered: competence-competence. Under the positive effect of competence-competence, arbitral tribunals have the power to rule on their own jurisdiction. Anti-arbitration injunctions seek to restrain this power. The two are thus inevitably at odds with each other, and, as Professor Bermann notes, this is why anti-arbitration injunctions are "widely condemned"[43].

By contrast, anti-suit injunctions are more widely accepted, those issued by a court more so than those issued by a tribunal. This is because national courts – especially those bound by the New York Convention – are expected to protect the arbitration agreement and refer disputes to arbitration. Anti-suit injunctions are seen as a tool to enforce this obligation. However, the power of tribunals to issue anti-

---

40. L. Levy, "*Anti-Suit Injunctions* Issued by Arbitrators", Institut pour l'Arbitrage International International Arbitration Series No. 2, Paris, Juris Publishing, 2005, at p. 128.
41. Named after the English Court of Appeal's decision in *Aggeliki Charis Compania Maritima SA* v. *Pagnan SpA (The "Angelic Grace")* [1995] 1 Lloyd's Rep. 87.
42. See e.g. *Airbus Industries* v. *Patel* [1998] UKHL 12.
43. Bermann, note 39, at para. 40.

suit injunctions is contested. Those who argue in favour of the said power look to the *lex arbitri* and applicable procedural rules, and consider anti-suit injunctions as an expression of the power to issue interim measures.

In summary, anti-suit injunctions are legal devices designed to prevent parallel proceedings and to restrain the exercise of jurisdiction by another court or tribunal by ordering a party not to commence or continue proceedings. Their use remains controversial and exceptional, particularly in the case of anti-arbitration injunctions, which conflict with the principle of competence-competence. The most acceptable form of anti-suit injunctions are those aimed at other courts and not other tribunals, and which have a well-founded pro-arbitration purpose, such as protecting a party's right to arbitrate or enforcing a court's obligation to refer to arbitration. Ultimately, anti-suit injunctions remain a discretionary remedy.

C. *Fork-in-the-road clauses* (electa una via)

Investment arbitration has produced its own legal device to prevent or minimise the risk of parallel proceedings: fork-in-the-road ("FITR") clauses. These clauses work in one direction only: in favour of host States. They have had limited application in investor-State dispute settlement ("ISDS") practice – although it is unclear if this indicates that they do not work or that they do. FITR clauses, often included in investment treaties, such as the Energy Charter Treaty [44], typically appear in the same clause as the offer to arbitrate. They provide investors with a choice of forum for dispute resolution: the domestic courts of the host State or international arbitration (often with two or more international arbitration options on offer). Once the choice is made, the investor cannot change its mind. It is final. Hence the metaphor of the "fork in the road": the investor is at a crossroads.

The purpose of these clauses is to avoid parallel proceedings between domestic courts and ISDS tribunals. Given their often politically sensitive nature, the public funds involved and the requirement for greater transparency (see Chap. I.C), the risk of parallel proceedings are perceived as less acceptable in ISDS disputes. FITR clauses are a contrasting feature of investment arbitration compared to public international law adjudicative bodies, where exhaustion of local

---

44. Energy Charter Treaty, Article 26 (3) *(b) (i)*.

remedies is generally required for access to international adjudication. In investment arbitration, not only does that rule not normally apply, but where a FITR clause applies, it provides for the exact opposite: the choice of local remedies precludes access to investment arbitration.

FITR clauses are distinct from waivers of local remedies, such as that contained in Article 1121 of the old North American Free Trade Agreement ("NAFTA"). Under Article 1121 of the old NAFTA, the waiver is a condition rather than a choice for access to international arbitration. If local court proceedings are brought, that does not bar access to arbitration: they can be discontinued to begin arbitration. This option is not available under a FITR clause.

Two examples of FITR clauses in investment treaties are provided by the US-Argentina and Argentina-France BITs. Article VII of the US-Argentina BIT provides:

> "2. In the event of an investment dispute . . . the national or company concerned may choose to submit the dispute for resolution:
>
> *(a)* to the courts or administrative tribunals of the Party that is a party to the dispute; *or*
>
> *(b)* in accordance with any applicable, previously agreed dispute-settlement procedures; *or*
>
> *(c)* in accordance with the terms of paragraph 3.
>
> 3. *(a)* Provided that the national or company concerned has not submitted the dispute for resolution under paragraph 2 *(a)* or *(b)* . . . the national or company concerned may choose to consent in writing to the submission of the dispute for settlement by binding [investment] arbitration." (Emphasis added)

Article 8 (2) of the Argentina-France BIT reads as follows:

> "Once an investor has submitted the dispute either to the jurisdictions of the Contracting Party involved or to international arbitration, the choice of one or the other of these procedures shall be final."

FITR clauses have been interpreted in investment case law in different ways. Most tribunals have adopted a strict interpretation of the FITR clause requiring a triple-identity test. In this test, there must exist in both sets of proceedings (before the domestic courts and before the ISDS tribunal) and identity of parties, object, and cause of action.

Due to the well-established distinction between treaty and contract claims, most ISDS tribunals have dismissed claims that the FITR clause precluded a claim. Examples include *Charanne* v. *Spain*[45], *Alex Genin* v. *Estonia*[46], *Occidental* v. *Ecuador*[47] and *Toto* v. *Lebanon*[48]. In *Occidental*, the tribunal further held that the "choice" of forum by the investor must be "entirely free" and "not under any form of duress"[49]. This referred to the fact that Ecuadorian tax law required investors to file claims before local courts to stop tax assessments from becoming final.

However, some tribunals have adopted a broader "fundamental basis" test in interpreting FITR clauses. The relevant question for those tribunals is not whether there is a triple identity of parties, object, and causes of action, but whether the claims before the local courts and the ISDS tribunal have the same "fundamental basis". The leading case in this respect is *Pantechniki* v. *Albania*, where Jan Paulsson sat as sole arbitrator[50]. For this tribunal, to establish the "fundamental basis" of a claim one needed to determine whether the claims have the same "normative source"[51]. The tribunal found in that case that the claims were rooted in the same contract in both fora. In other words, the claims before the ISDS tribunal did not have "an autonomous existence outside the contract"[52]. Other tribunals have followed this approach, namely *HH Enterprises* v. *Egypt*[53], *Supervision y Control* v. *Costa Rica*[54] and *Chevron* v. *Ecuador*[55].

---

45. *Charanne and Construction Investments* v. *Spain*, SCC Case No. V 062/2012, Award, 21 January 2016.
46. *Alex Genin, Eastern Credit Limited, Inc. and AS Baltoil* v. *The Republic of Estonia*, ICSID Case No. ARB/99/2, Award, 25 June 2001.
47. *Occidental Exploration and Production Company* v. *The Republic of Ecuador*, LCIA Case No. UN3467, Final Award, 1 July 2004.
48. *Toto Costruzioni Generali SpA* v. *The Republic of Lebanon*, ICSID Case No. ARB/07/12, Decision on Jurisdiction, 11 September 2009.
49. *Occidental*, note 47, at para. 60.
50. *Pantechniki SA Contractors & Engineers (Greece)* v. *The Republic of Albania*, ICSID Case No. ARB/07/21, Award, 30 July 2009.
51. *Ibid.*, at para. 62.
52. *Ibid.*, at para. 64.
53. *H&H Enterprises Investments, Inc.* v. *Arab Republic of Egypt*, ICSID Case No. ARB 09/15, Tribunal's Decision on the Respondent's Objections to Jurisdiction, 5 June 2012.
54. *Supervision y Control SA* v. *Republic of Costa Rica*, ICSID Case No. ARB/12/4, Final Award, 18 January 2017.
55. *Chevron Corporation and Texaco Petroleum Corporation* v. *Ecuador (II)*, PCA Case No. 2009-23, Third Interim Award on Jurisdiction and Admissibility, 27 February 2012 *(obiter)*.

CHAPTER III

PURELY COMMERCIAL DISPUTES
WITH NO INVESTMENT ARBITRATON ELEMENT

We now turn to the second category in our typology of parallel proceedings: the interaction between international arbitral tribunals in purely commercial arbitrations without an investment arbitration element. Examples of such disputes include building and insurance disputes, which often involve parallel arbitrations between various parties (e.g. project owner v. main contractor, main contractor v. subcontractor, insured v. insurer, insurer v. reinsurer).

In the court versus tribunal scenario explored in the previous chapter, the issue is *how* courts and arbitral tribunals are meant to interact and the nature, timing and sequencing of that interaction. The interaction itself is inherent to international arbitration and part of its ordinary practice. By contrast, in the tribunal versus tribunal scenario (whether commercial or investment), the issue is *whether*, and only than. Parallel proceedings between tribunals is prima facie not a normal state of affairs but an anomaly. For this reason, parallel proceedings are deemed more acceptable and less problematic in the court versus tribunal scenario than in *the tribunal v. tribunal scenario*. This may explain why so many jurisdictions – including major arbitral jurisdictions – are reluctant to adopt the negative facet of competence-competence.

To minimise parallel proceedings in commercial arbitration, tribunals have traditionally use many of the same legal tools as national courts, namely *lis pendens* (giving preference to the proceedings "first in time"), *res judicata* (giving binding effect to the award of one tribunal, thus discouraging parallel proceedings that might lead to inconsistent results), and the consolidation of parallel proceedings and joinder of parties into existing proceedings. However, these mechanisms cannot be simply transposed into the field of arbitration. As noted by Professor Dr Klaus Peter Berger, the cornerstone of arbitration – party autonomy and consent – are "its natural weakness [when] it comes to joinder and consolidation"[56]. The English Court of Appeal described the problem

---

56. OGEMID contribution of 21 January 2005, recorded in M. McIlwrath and S. Moollan, "Joinder: Current Practice in International Arbitration", *Trade Dispute*

as follows in *Lincoln v. Sun*[57], a case dealing with questions of issue estoppel:

"Arbitration is [in contrast to litigation] a consensual, private affair between the particular parties to a particular arbitration agreement. The resulting inability to enforce the solutions of joinder of parties or proceedings in arbitration, or to try connected arbitrations together other than by consent, is well-recognised – though the popularity of arbitration may indicate that this inability is not often inconvenient or that perceived advantages of arbitration, including confidentiality and privacy, are seen as outweighing any inconvenience. Different arbitrations on closely inter-linked issues may as a result lead to different results, even where, as in the present case, the evidence before one tribunal is very largely the same as that before the other. The arbitrators in each arbitration are appointed to decide the disputes in that arbitration between the particular parties to that arbitration. The privacy and confidentiality attaching to arbitration underline this; and even if they do not lead to non-parties remaining ignorant of an earlier arbitration award, they are calculated to lead to difficulties in obtaining access, and about the scope of any access, to material relating to that award [58].

...

The sad truth is that in the absence of any third party or consolidation procedure in arbitration, parties may be put into the position of making inconsistent cases in different proceedings. In litigation, it is possible to make inconsistent cases in the same proceedings; doing so later, in different proceedings, may come under the head of abuse of process. But that is not a reason to extend the law of issue estoppel in arbitration proceedings beyond its proper sphere." [59]

Bearing in mind these difficulties, which I will come back to later in this course, the legal tools of *lis pendens* and *res judicata* remain available in principle to manage parallel proceedings in commercial arbitration, but they typically apply when the "same parties" are

---

Management, Vol. 3 (2005), https://www.transnational-dispute-management.com/article.asp?key=449.
57. *Lincoln National Life Insurance Co. v. Sun Life Assurance Co. of Canada* [2004] EWCA Civ. 1660.
58. *Ibid.*, at para. 68 (per Lord Justice Mance).
59. *Ibid.*, at para. 83 (per Lord Justice Longmore).

involved in more than one proceeding. This is the reason why – as Antonio Crivellaro[60] has noted – these doctrines have little application in investment arbitration, where parallel proceedings usually involve different parties, even if they are affiliated (e.g. the local subsidiary, the parent company, a shareholder).

Each of these doctrines is considered below, before looking at the related issue of abuse of process, followed by consolidation and joinder as well as informal coordination. Consolidation and joinder are considered in more detail in Chapter IV, which covers cases of investment arbitration crossover, where the same underlying facts can give rise to claims under commercial and investment instruments.

A. Lis pendens (lis alibi pendens)

The first available device to deal with the problem of parallel proceedings in commercial arbitration is the doctrine of *lis pendens*. This Latin expression translates as "lawsuit pending" or "proceedings pending" (*litispendance* in French). Under this doctrine, a tribunal has the authority to stay or suspend proceedings if the same proceedings, involving the same parties and claims, are already pending in another forum.

Kaj Hober, who gave a summer course at The Hague in 2014 titled "*Res judicata* and *lis pendens* in international arbitration", has called the principle of *lis pendens* "a fundamental principle of procedural fairness and justice which is normally considered to form part of procedural public policy in most legal systems"[61]. The reference to "procedural public policy" is apt because the *lis pendens* doctrine promotes and finds justification in public policy goals, such as preventing contradictory decisions, promoting procedural economy and efficiency, avoiding wasteful duplication of resources and protecting against harassment and abuse.

Initially developed in national court litigation, the *lis pendens* doctrine was extrapolated to international arbitration and seen as a potentially important legal device to tackle the mounting problem of parallel proceedings. In 2006, the first concerted efforts were made by the international arbitration community to tackle the problem. The ILA

---

60. A. Crivellaro, "Consolidation of Arbitral and Court Proceedings in Investment Disputes", *The Law and Practice of International Courts and Tribunals*, Vol. 4 (2005), pp. 371-420.

61. K. Hober, "Parallel Arbitration Proceedings – Duties of the Arbitrators: Some Reflections and Ideas", in B. Cremades Sanz Pastor and J. Lew (eds.), *Parallel Sate and Arbitral Procedures*, Dossiers of the ICC Institute World Business Law Vol. 3, The Hague, Kluwer Law International, 2005, Chapter 9, pp. 242-267, at p. 253.

adopted a set of "Recommendations on *Lis Pendens* and *Res Judicata* and Arbitration" pursuant to a resolution passed at its seventy-second conference meeting in Toronto [62]. That same year, a major colloquium attended by numerous high-profile arbitration practitioners was organised in Geneva, on the consolidation of proceedings in investment arbitration. Today, fifteen years later, the issues surrounding parallel proceedings in international arbitration remain pressing, if not more so, and solutions have yet to be implemented in a meaningful way.

The ILA Recommendations provide guidance on three potential scenarios where the *lis pendens* doctrine may be applicable. In each of these cases, the tribunal should, in principle, continue with the proceedings if it determines that it has jurisdiction pursuant to the positive effect of competence-competence. However, if parallel proceedings are already underway, involving the same parties and one or more identical legal issues, the ILA Recommendations identify three possible scenarios:

(a) *Tribunal v. Court of the seat:* The tribunal should consider a stay, taking into account the risk of annulment if the jurisdictional decisions are contradictory.
(b) *Tribunal v. Foreign court:* No stay is required, following the rejection of the *Fomento* case precedent.
(c) *Tribunal v. Tribunal:* The tribunal should generally stay the proceedings or declare that it has no jurisdiction.

It should be noted that the first two scenarios are not technically considered *lis pendens* situations because the principle of competence-competence takes priority in the interaction between courts and tribunals. In jurisdictions where negative competence-competence applies, courts will typically give priority to the tribunal's ruling on jurisdiction, and there is little risk of *lis pendens*. However, in jurisdictions that only adopt positive competence-competence, the situation is more complex. If no court has been seized, the tribunal can go ahead and rule on its own jurisdiction. But if a court has been seized, what should the tribunal do? Should it proceed to hear the case or stay its proceedings?

The ILA Recommendations provide guidance on this issue, based on the location of the court seized. The court of the seat is entitled to greater deference since it has the power to set aside the award, while foreign courts (as in the *Fomento* case) are entitled to less deference.

---

62. De Ly and Sheppard, note 1, at p. 83. See also Chap. I.A.2.

The ILA thus recommends that tribunals should not stay proceedings if a foreign court has been seized.

Commentators hold differing views. Professor Gary Born argues that the tribunal should rule on its jurisdiction and not stay, even if the court of the seat has been seized, and even if the court of the seat has determined that the tribunal has no jurisdiction. This is because courts in other States could recognise the tribunal's award upholding jurisdiction and deny recognition of the national court judgment reaching the opposite conclusion [63]. Professor Gaillard shares this view, seeing the tribunal as part of a transnational legal order. Conversely, Professor Christophe Seraglini contends that the *Fomento* precedent should not be "dismissed outright", and that stays should be considered even where the court seized is a foreign court [64].

The theoretical outlook one takes on international arbitration may determine which position one holds. In his 2007 Hague lecture on the "Aspects philosophiques du droit de l'arbitrage international", Professor Gaillard [65] proposes three alternative models for international arbitration: the territorial model, the multi-localised or Westphalian model, and the delocalised or transnational model.

The territorial model is by far the most traditional of the three. The *locus classicus* for this point of view is Doctor Francis A. Mann's 1967 article, *"Lex Facit Arbitrum"* [66]. In this long-standing debate with Professors Goldman and Fouchard about the alleged existence of an autonomous "arbitral legal order", Mann argued that this question went to the very root of arbitration: is arbitration an autonomous process created by the parties' will or is it a limited process existing solely through a State's derogation from its sovereign power to render justice? His answer was unambiguous:

> "[I]t would be intolerable if the country of the seat could not override whatever arrangements the parties may have made. The local sovereign does not yield to them except as a result of freedoms granted by himself." [67]

---

63. Born, note 18, at p. 3783.
64. C. Seraglini, "Brèves remarques sur les Recommendations de l'Association de droit international sur la litispendance et l'autorité de la chose jugée en abitrage", *Revue de l'Arbitrage* (2006), Vol. 4, pp. 909-925, at p. 922.
65. E. Gaillard, "Aspects philosophiques du droit de l'arbitrage international", Leiden, Martinus Nijhoff, 2008.
66. F. A. Mann, *"Lex facit arbitrum"*, in P. Sanders (ed.), *International Arbitration: Liber amicorum for Martin Domke*, Leiden, Martinus Nijhoff, 1967, pp. 157-183.
67. *Ibid.*, at pp. 161-162.

In other words, arbitration can only exist within the legal framework of a given State, that of its seat. It is fundamentally territorial and anchored in the national legal order of the seat. The territorial conception remains prevalent in several legal systems today, such as those of England and of most Commonwealth jurisdictions. It is also the conception most consistent with the ILA recommendation, giving added weight and primacy to the courts of the seat.

The multi-localised or Westphalian conception, Professor Gaillard's second model, is based on a simple idea: one of the main reasons for the existence of international arbitration as we know it today is the fact that the vast majority of countries are willing to give effect to an award under the New York Convention. On a practical level, this conception suggests that the courts of the countries where the losing party has assets and where the award will be enforced have more legitimacy to scrutinise the award than the courts of the country where the arbitration took place. In particular, they may have to assist the enforcing party with their powers of coercion. On a theoretical level, this leads one to minimise, if not altogether discard, the role of the country where the arbitration has its seat in favour of an increased role for all those countries where the award may be enforced. The arbitration is no longer localised at the seat but multi-localised at all possible places of enforcement. It exists not because the sovereign of the place of arbitration consents to its existence, but because the sovereigns of the places of enforcement are willing to recognise the binding force of its result, the award. This model is most consistent with the approach to *lis pendens* proposed by Professor Seraglini, and perhaps with that of Professor Born.

The transnational conception, Professor Gaillard's third model, disregards the parties' choice of seat as irrelevant. What matters is the parties' choice of international arbitration, which carries with it a choice of a separate and autonomous regime with its own substantive rules. These rules exist within their own autonomous legal order, an arbitral legal order disconnected from any national legal order. On a practical level, such an approach would enable an arbitrator to ignore a mandatory rule of the seat that is "out of step" with established and accepted arbitral practice. Professor Gaillard gives an example: if Ethiopia were to require its arbitrators to draft their awards on yellow paper, an international arbitrator sitting in Ethiopia would be free to draft his award on pink paper because the majority of nations would allow him to do so. This model is consistent with Professor Gaillard's approach to *lis pendens* and perhaps with that of Professor Born. While some seek to defend this model on a "natural law" basis, Professor Gaillard does not, but relies instead on the asserted premise that most States now agree on the fundamental notions that underlie international arbitration. This (transnational) conception has only found supervisory court acceptance in France.

Whichever approach is adopted, the main point remains: the two court versus tribunal settings in the ILA Recommendations are about competence-competence rather than *lis pendens*, as noted by Professor Seraglini [68]. The only setting where genuine *lis pendens* applies is in the tribunal versus tribunal setting.

There are several potential scenarios where *lis pendens* could apply in that setting, including arbitrations arising from the same arbitration agreement and arbitration rules, the same arbitration agreement but different arbitration rules, or related arbitration agreements. In the first scenario, two different tribunals are constituted under the same arbitration clause and the same arbitration rules to adjudicate the same dispute, which is a *lis pendens* scenario *stricto sensu*. The other scenarios are variations on this: the arbitration agreements are related or have a separate basis; the arbitration rules are different; and the dispute is different. While such scenarios cannot attract the application of *lis pendens stricto sensu*, it may be that one of the tribunals will draw inspiration from the Recommendations and stay their proceedings as a matter of case management, although the confidentiality usually attached to commercial arbitration proceedings may render any effort at such coordination difficult in practice.

Although examples of *lis pendens* in a tribunal-tribunal context are rare, some instances include arbitration of the same dispute based on the same arbitration clause [69], separate arbitration agreements [70], or the same arbitration agreement but different disputes [71]. The ILA Recommendations continue to be influential, as demonstrated in a 2019

---

68. Seraglini, note 64, at p. 919.
69. *Italy No. 170, Tema Frugoli SpA, in liquidation (Italy)* v. *Hubei Space Quarry Industry Co. Ltd. (PR China)*, Corte di Cassazione, 1732, 7 February 2001, in A. J. Van den Berg (ed.), *Yearbook Commercial Arbitration*, Vol. 32, The Hague, Kluwer Law International, 2007, pp. 390-396.
70. *Reading & Bates Corporation, Reading & Bates Exploration Company* v. *The Islamic Republic of Iran, National Iranian Oil Company, Iranian Marine International Oil Co.*, IUSCT Case No. 28, Interim Award (Award No. ITM 21-28), 9 June 2003.
71. Swiss Federal Tribunal, *X. SA* v. *Y Ltd.*, 4A_210/2008, Swiss International Arbitration Law Reports, 2008, Vol. 2, No. 2.

Paris-seated ICC tribunal award that specifically referred to them on *lis pendens*[72].

Lis pendens in a tribunal versus tribunal scenario can raise concerns about the composition of tribunals and the impartiality and independence of arbitrators where one arbitrator sits in more than one proceeding but not the others. A high-profile example of this occurred in early 2021, with the ICC disqualifying arbitrator Klaus Sachs from hearing a case on the grounds that the same party had later appointed him to also hear an overlapping ICSID case based on substantially the same factual background[73].

Overall, while the doctrine of *lis pendens* is ubiquitous in national court litigation, its application in international arbitration is limited due to the few occasions where it can apply in practice. The concept of *lis pendens* at the heart of the ILA Recommendations, and the concept that seen as initially defined what parallel proceedings are, is in reality unable to cope with the main source of parallel proceedings in international arbitration, where the parties, arbitration agreements and legal bases for the claims are not quite the same.

B. Res judicata *and issue estoppel*

1. The doctrine of res judicata

The doctrine of *res judicata* – or claim preclusion – is another legal device used to address the issue of parallel proceedings. According to this doctrine, a dispute that has been adjudicated by an international arbitration tribunal is final and cannot be adjudicated again. This prevents re-arbitration of disputes that have already been settled, thus avoiding parallel proceedings.

Arbitral awards are typically viewed as being equivalent to national court judgments, and therefore have *res judicata* effects. However, the Final Report of the ILA Recommendations clarifies that arbitral awards should not "necessarily" be equated with judgments for the purpose of *red judicata*. This is because arbitral awards possess an international

---

72. *Securiport (US) and local subsidiary* v. *Benin* (ICC tribunal seated in Paris), 28 January 2019. See report in IA Reporter, D. Charlotin, "Revealed: In Securiport v. Benin, an ICC Tribunal Finds that the Underlying Contract Does Not Contravene Data Privacy Laws, and Awards 95 Million USD in Compensation", 22 April 2020.

73. The challenge was accepted on the basis that Sachs could prejudge issues and have access to information denied to his co-panellists. See S. Perry, "ICC Disqualifies Sachs Over Related ICSID Appointment", *Global Arbitration Review*, 12 March 2021.

dimension that court judgments lack, and because of differences in national laws regarding the conditions and scope of the doctrine [74].

There are several reasons why *res judicata* is favoured. First, it promotes finality of the dispute, which is in the public interest. Second, it promotes efficiency by preventing duplicative proceedings. Finally, it promotes fairness by ensuring that individuals are not prosecuted twice for the same matter, as captured by the Latin maxim *ne bis in idem*.

The doctrine of *res judicata* is widely accepted and is considered a general principle of international law under Article 38 (1) *(c)* of the Statute of the International Court of Justice (ICJ), as noted by Professor Hanotiau [75]. International tribunals and commentators generally agree that it is a principle of international law, with some referring to the "sanctity" of *res judicata* [76].

Common law systems rely on case law rather than codification, but generally accept both claim preclusion *(res judicata)* and issue preclusion (issue estoppel, also referred to as "collateral estoppel" in the United States). The United States and England apply both doctrines to arbitral awards, but the US version of *res judicata* is broader than the English one, as the notion of "same claim" is more narrowly understood in English law. Furthermore, in the US, only "confirmed" awards (awards that have been recognised) are generally entitled to *res judicata* effects.

Civil law systems, on the other hand, codify *res judicata* but with a narrower understanding of the doctrine. While on paper there is no issue estoppel, in reality the *res judicata* doctrine can give preclusive effect to parts of the reasoning of an award. In French law, awards have *res judicata* effects from the moment they are issued. Article 1484 of the French Code of Civil Procedure (applicable to international arbitration via Art. 1506) provides that "the arbitral award has, as soon as it is rendered, res judicata effect with respect to the disputes it settles" [77]. In German law, Article 1055 of the German Code of Civil Procedure provides: "The arbitral award has the same effect between the parties as

---

74. De Ly and Sheppard, note 1, at p. 72.
75. B. Hanotiau, *Complex Arbitrations: Multi-party, Multi-contract, Multi-issue – A Comparative Study*, The Hague, Kluwer Law International, 2020, at p. 422.
76. See *Trail Smelter Case (US v. Can.)*, 3 RIAA 1905, 1949-50 (1941). For further authority, see e.g. Gaillard, "Coordination or Chaos: Do the Principles of Comity, *Lis Pendens* and *Res Judicata* Apply to International Arbitration?", *American Review of International Arbitration*, Vol. 29, No. 3, 2018, pp. 205-242, at p. 205, at n. 97 (p. 225).
77. In French: "La sentence arbitrale a, dès qu'elle est rendue, l'autorité de la chose jugée relativement à la contestation qu'elle tranche" (emphasis added).

a final and binding court judgment." Similar provisions can be found in Dutch [78], Austrian [79] and Swiss [80] law.

Article III of the New York Convention provides that Contracting States "shall recognise arbitral awards" as "binding". The *res judicata* effects of New York Convention awards derive from this provision, as the binding nature of an award prevents re-arbitration of the matter. Similarly, Article 35 (1) of the UNCITRAL Model Law provides that arbitral awards shall be recognised as "binding" regardless of where they were made, and *res judicata* effects follow from this attribute. The binding effect of awards is also expressed in Article 34 (2) of the 2013 UNCITRAL Arbitration Rules and in Article 53 (1) of the ICSID Convention.

2. The conditions for the application of res judicata *to international arbitral awards*

Although there are variations across different legal systems, the 2006 ILA Recommendations on *Res Judicata* outline four elements that are generally agreed upon and must be met cumulatively. These are:

(a) The award must be final and binding, with no impediment to recognition in the country where subsequent arbitration may take place.
(b) The award must have decided a claim for relief that is sought or is being re-argued in the further arbitration proceedings.
(c) The claims must arise from the same cause of action.
(d) The parties involved in the subsequent arbitration must be the same as those in the original award [81].

Therefore, the *res judicata* doctrine typically employs a triple-identity test, requiring that the parties, cause of action and claims must be the same. This test is similar to the triple-identity test used in the context of FITR clauses (see Chap. II.C), which tribunals have effectively imported from the *res judicata* doctrine.

Res judicata has both positive and negative effects, much like the doctrine of competence-competence (see Chap. II.A.2-3):

---

78. Article 1059 of the Dutch Code of Civil Procedure.
79. Article 594 of the Austrian Code of Civil Procedure.
80. Article 190 of the PILA.
81. De Ly and Sheppard, note 1, at p. 85.

(a) The positive, or conclusive, effects of the doctrine mean that the award is final and binding and must be complied with in good faith.

(b) The negative, or preclusive, effects of the doctrine mean that the claims and issues cannot be relitigated or re-arbitrated.

The 2006 ILA Recommendations on *Res Judicata* recognise both the conclusive and preclusive effects:

(a) The conclusive effect of the arbitral award includes the dispositive part of the award (decisions and findings), its "necessary reasoning", and issues of fact or law that were "essential or fundamental to the dispositive part of the award" [82].

(b) The ILA recommends that the preclusive effects extend not only to the claims actually decided in the award, but also to the claims "which could have been raised" but were not, provided that raising any such claims constitute "abuse" or "unfairness" [83].

It is important to note that the *res judicata* doctrine does not only cover final awards, but also final decisions on discrete aspects of the dispute, such as jurisdiction or liability.

In summary, under the ILA Recommendations, *res judicata* covers the dispositive part of the award, necessary reasoning, and necessary issues of fact or law for the decisions, claims decided, and claims that could have been brought but were not, and final awards and final decisions on separate aspects of the dispute.

C. The related doctrine of abuse of process

In addition to res judicata and issue estoppel, with the stringent requirements of the triple identity test, common law jurisdictions have long developed a more flexible tool to deal with situations not falling precisely within that test. In particular, it has long been established that, in certain circumstances, a party may not seek to relitigate with a third-party, issues already litigated and determined in prior litigation in which it was involved and may not bring a new suit to litigate issues connected to prior litigation which ought to have been brought and tried in that prior litigation. The below extracts from English court decisions show the manner in which the principle has been articulated:

---

82. Note: This shows that the ILA Recommendations also recognise issue estoppel.
83. De Ly and Sheppard, note 1, at p. 85.

In *Bragg* v. *Oceanus Mutual*, Lord Justice Kerr noted that

"it is clear that an attempt to relitigate in another action issues which have been fully investigated and decided in a former action may constitute an abuse of process, quite apart from any question of res judicata or issue estoppel on the ground that the parties or their privies are the same" [84].

In *Arthur JS Hall* v. *Simons*, Lord Hoffmann held:

"The law discourages relitigation of the same issues except by means of an appeal. The Latin maxims often quoted are nemo debet bis vexari pro una et eadem causa and interest rei publicae ut finis sit litium. They are usually mentioned in tandem but it is important to notice that the policies they state are not quite the same. The first is concerned with the interests of the defendant: a person should not be troubled twice for the same reason. This policy has generated the rules which prevent relitigation when the parties are the same: autrefois acquit, res judicata and issue estoppel. The second policy is wider: it is concerned with the interests of the state. There is a general public interest in the same issue not being litigated over again. The second policy can be used to justify the extension of the rules of issue estoppel to cases in which the parties are not the same but the circumstances are such as to bring the case within the spirit of the rules." [85]

In *Johnson* v. *Gore Wood*, Lord Bingham of Cornhill considered an alleged abuse of the type described in *Henderson* v. *Henderson* and held that:

"*Henderson* v. *Henderson* abuse of process, as now understood, although separate and distinct from cause of action estoppel and issue estoppel, has much in common with them. The underlying public interest is the same: that there should be finality in litigation and that a party should not be twice vexed in the same matter. This public interest is reinforced by the current emphasis on efficiency and economy in the conduct of litigation, in the interests of parties and the public as a whole. The bringing of a claim or the raising of a defence in later proceedings may, without more, amount to abuse if the court is satisfied (the onus being on the party alleging

---
84. *Bragg* v. *Oceanus Mutual* [1982] 2 Lloyds Rep 132, at p. 137.
85. *Arthur JS Hall & Co (a firm)* v. *Simons* [2002] 1 AC 615, at 701 A-C.

abuse) that the claim or defence should have been raised in the earlier proceedings if it was to be raised at all." [86]

The doctrine of abuse of process applies to protect the finality of arbitral awards just as it does to protect the finality of court judgments [87]. However, there are practical difficulties with the operation of the doctrines of *res judicata*, issue estoppel and abuse of process in relation to arbitral awards. The case of *Lincoln* v. *Sun* demonstrates further practical limits to the use of these doctrines. The Court of Appeal's judgment acknowledges that there may be little one can do to stop parallel proceedings in arbitration given its consensual nature, and the practical difficulties arising from the confidentiality of arbitral awards (which will mean that the prior award from which preclusive effect is said to arise will often not be known to the third party, nor be admissible in the later proceedings).

Examples of cases where *res judicata* arose, include two arbitrations based on the same arbitration clause: *Tema Frugoli* v. *Hubei Space Quarry* [88], two ICC arbitrations: Nos. 2475 and 2762 [89], and an ICSID case: *Southern Pacific* v. *Egypt* [90].

D. Consolidation and joinder/intervention

As noted at the beginning of this course, are considered at this juncture by reference to the topics of consolidation, joinder and intervention to both commercial and investment arbitration given their relevance in both fields. International commercial transactions often involve multiple parties, leading to multiparty disputes that create challenges in international arbitration. Such disputes can lead to parallel proceedings, which pose some of the most challenging issues in international arbitration, such as extension of the arbitration agreement to non-signatories, group of companies or assignments. To

---

86. *Johnson* v. *Gore Wood & Co* [2002] 2 AC 1. *Henderson* v. *Henderson* (1843) 3 Hare 100) (at p.31A-E). Other members of the appellate committee agreed with Lord Bingham.
87. See *Michael Wilson & Partners Limited* v. *Sinclair* [2017] EWCA Civ. 3.
88. *Italy No. 170, Tema Frugoli SpA, in liquidation (Italy)* v. *Hubei Space Quarry Industry Co. Ltd. (PR China)*, Corte di Cassazione, 1732, 7 February 2001, in A. J. Van den Berg (ed.), *Yearbook Commercial Arbitration*, Vol. 32, The Hague, Kluwer Law International, 2007, pp. 390-396.
89. S. Jarvin and Y. Derains (eds.), *Collection of ICC Arbitral Awards 1974-1985*, 1990, at p. 325.
90. *Southern Pacific Properties (Middle East) Limited* v. *Arab Republic of Egypt*, ICSID Case No. ARB/84/3, Decision on Jurisdiction, 14 April 1988.

address parallel proceedings in a multiparty scenario, the two main tools are consolidation and joinder, with intervention being the flipside of joinder.

Consolidation refers to fusing two or more proceedings into a single proceeding. In joinder, the parties to an arbitration A and B seek to add C to the proceedings, a classic scenario coming from the building construction sector, where the principal and main contractor may seek to add the subcontractor to the proceedings. Intervention is the same scenario as joinder, except that it is C that seeks to be added to the proceedings.

The main advantages of consolidation and joinder are efficiency, saving legal resources and a lower or no risk of inconsistent decisions. However, they also pose unique problems, notably with the composition of arbitral tribunals. In the classic two-party arbitration, each party appoints one party-appointed arbitrator, with the president nominated jointly or by a neutral appointing authority. However, in uneven sides scenarios such as one claimant and two respondents, the two parties on the same side may have to "share" an arbitrator. This was the case in the *Dutco* saga, where the ICC required two co-respondents to appoint the same arbitrator, failing which the ICC Court would appoint one. The French Cour de Cassation deemed that the tribunal had been irregularly constituted and that this breached equality [91]. As a result of *Dutco*, the ICC amended its rules in 1998, giving the ICC Court the power to appoint all members of the tribunal in multiparty arbitrations. Since 2017, the ICC Rules also provide a rule for the joint nomination of one arbitrator in cases of multiparty arbitrations, whether there are multiple claimants or multiple respondents. In that way, the same rule applies *ex ante* to both sides and the inequality noted by the French court in *Dutco* is averted.

However, the main obstacle to consolidation, joinder and intervention in arbitration is the cardinal requirement of the *consent* of all parties involved. The term "consolidation" covers different situations, strictly referring to the joinder of two or more claims already pending before different tribunals, and in a broader and loose sense, used to refer to the constitution of a single tribunal to hear multiple claims from different parties for the first time. In this broader sense, there is no real consolidation of claims before different tribunals, but rather an aggregation of claims before a single tribunal from the outset. Thus,

---

91. C. Cass 1re, Pourvois Nos. 89-18.708 and 89-18-726, 7 January 1992.

a distinction should be drawn between consolidation proper and aggregation of claims.

In the investment arbitration field, the practice of *de facto* aggregation of claims pending determination of questions of consent by the appointed tribunal has taken root and is consistently used in the context of ICSID. The aggregation of claims can take one of two forms. The claims may be fully aggregated, resulting in a single award ("full aggregation"), or simply heard concurrently, resulting in separate awards ("partial aggregation"). Whether aggregation is full or partial, there is from the outset and at all times a single tribunal and single proceeding – a key distinction from consolidation proper.

The (now superseded) NAFTA was the first investment treaty to address the question of consolidation systematically. Under Article 11-17 (3), consolidation was the default rule in the event of multiple claims from related investors: claims "arising out of the same events . . . should be heard together by" the same tribunal. NAFTA was thus a pioneering investment treaty in this area.

Article 11-26 of NAFTA was the focal provision on consolidation and in instructive for two reasons. First, it serves as an archetypal example of a consolidation provision in an investment treaty, with the rare benefit of some interpreting case law, in the form of the decision in *Corn Products*[92] and *Canfor*[93]. Second, it offers a useful model for how consolidation should operate in practice, whether in an investment treaty, institutional rules or national laws.

Article 11-26 of NAFTA highlights two key prerequisites for any sound consolidation provision: *(a)* the disputing parties must provide *ex ante* consent to consolidation before a dispute arises, thereby obviating the need for *ex post* consent when tactical or other considerations may mean it will not be forthcoming; and *(b)* a workable mechanism must be in place to enable consolidation even in the face of opposition. Article 11-26 does both. First at provides that a disputing party can request consolidation with other NAFTA claims "that have a question of law or fact in common". A party contracting into the regime thus explicitly accepts the risk *ex ante* that consolidation may be ordered

---

92. *Corn Products International, Inc.* v. *United Mexican States*, ICSID Case No. ARB (AF)/04/1 and *Archer Daniels Midland Company and Tate & Lyle Ingredients Americas, Inc.* v. *The United Mexican States*, ICSID Case No. ARB (AF)/04/5, Order of the Consolidation Tribunal, 20 May 2005.

93. *Canfor Corporation* v. *United States of America*; *Tembe* et al. v. *United States of America*; *Terminal Forest Products Ltd.* v. *United States of America*, UNCITRAL, Order of the Consolidation Tribunal, 7 September 2005.

against its post-dispute wishes. Secondly, it enables consolidation even where opposed through the establishment of a "super-tribunal" [94] to hear consolidation requests and divest previously constituted tribunals of their jurisdiction, either partially or completely, as well as stay proceedings pending its decision.

These prerequisites can be addressed at various levels, depending on the context. The highest level is including them in the treaty that creates the parties' right and duty to arbitrate. In the commercial sphere, they can be set out in the parties' specifically negotiated arbitration clause, in the chosen arbitration rules, or in the *lex arbitri*, which may provide for consolidation or joinder by tribunals or the court.

Starting with specific arbitration clauses there is anecdotal evidence of very long and complex clauses negotiated, for instance, in building projects, but this approach is not feasible for most situations and Pras the disavantage of recording the prerequisites of *ex ante* consent and practical means at the lowest possible level. For those to apply, the relevant party must be a contracting party to the specific agreement or agreements. As for, arbitration rules examples include the Arbitration Rules 2014 of the London Court of International Arbitration ("LCIA") (at Art. 22 (1) *(viii)-(x)*) and the ICC Arbitration Rules (at Art. 7 on joinder and Art. 10 on consolidation). Example of *Lex arbitri* containing relevant provisions are section 2 of Schedule 2 of the New Zealand Arbitration Act 1996 or Section 3B and Schedule 1 of the Mauritian Act. In US law, following the landmark decision of *Nereus* in 1975, it used to be the case that courts could order consolidation in the absence of parties' consent [95]. But *Nereus* is no longer good law: parties must consent to consolidation [96].

In practice, both arbitral institutions and courts have ordered or refused consolidation and joinder. For instance, despite the requirements of Article 4 (6) of the 1998 ICC Rules being met, the ICC Court refused the consolidation of two arbitrations between the same parties where the arbitration clauses in each of the contracts had different seats, one Paris, the other, Amsterdam. For the ICC Court, this showed that the parties had intended to conduct separate arbitrations [97]. Yet, in a

---

94. This expression is not actually found in NAFTA but has been used by commentators. It was coined by Jan Paulsson in "Arbitration Without Privity", *ICSID Review*, Vol. 10., No. 2 (1995), pp. 232-257, at p. 248.
95. *Compania Espanola de Petroleos, SA* v. *Nereus Shipping*, 527 F.2d 966 (2d Cir. 1975).
96. Born, note 18, at p. 2577.
97. Hanotiau, note 75, at pp. 182-184.

different case, the same court did order consolidation where it deemed that the arbitrations were part of the same "legal relationship" and the terms of reference had not yet been signed or approved by the court [98]. The Swiss Federal Tribunal ordered the consolidation of a dispute based on related contracts with differently worded arbitration clauses in *Andersen Consulting* v. *Arthur Andersen* [99]. Joinder was ordered by an UNCITRAL *ad hoc* tribunal in an unpublished award of 3 March 1999 [100] and in a published award of 27 October 1989 [101].

E. Informal coordination?

Finally, it is worth considering whether informal methods can be used to prevent or mitigate the risks of inconsistency associated with parallel proceedings'. One potential approach would be for tribunals to share information about their respective proceedings or to coordinate their hearings informally. However, in the realm of commercial arbitration, this is challenging without the parties' consent, which is, as stated above, typically not given *ex post*. Moreover, each proceeding is likely to be subject to confidentiality obligations, which can hinder coordination efforts, as noted by Lord Justice Mance (as he then was) in *Lincoln* v. *Sun*. In the next chapter, we will explore how the growing transparency in the investment arbitration arena could allow coordination to become a more effective tool for tribunals and parties, manage parallel proceedings.

---

98. *Ibid.*, at pp. 182-184.
99. *Andersen Consulting Business Unit Member Firms* v. *Arthur Andersen Business Unit Member Firms*, Case No. 9797/CK/AER/ACS ICC, interim award of 29 April 1999, unpublished. The Swiss Federal Court decision of 8 December 1999 dismissing the action to set aside is published in 18 ASA Bull. 546 (2000).
100. Hanotiau, note 75, at p. 167.
101. *Marine Drive Complex* v. *Ghana*, Award of 27 October 1989, 19 YB Com. Arb. 11 (1994), at 17-18.

CHAPTER IV

DISPUTES WITH AN INVESTMENT ARBITRATION ELEMENT

The third and final category in our typology of parallel proceedings is disputes that include an investment arbitration component, the second sub-group of the tribunal v. tribunal type. Just as with the first sub-group, in commercial arbitration, the *tribunal* v. *tribunal* interaction in investment arbitrations does not represent a normal state of affairs. Investment tribunals are not designed to work in tandem the way courts and tribunals are. However, there are important differences between these two sub-groups. First, there are unique sources of parallel proceedings in investment arbitration, making the issue of parallel proceedings more severe in investment than in commercial arbitration. Second, investment arbitration involves States or state entities, making the issue of parallel proceedings more pressing as it involves public funds and more visible as investment arbitrations are often publicised.

It is therefore no surprise that the hallmark case of parallel proceedings, *Lauder/CME* v. *Czech Republic*, is an investment case covered in the first chapter (sec. D). The case exposed the glaring inconsistencies of two high-profile tribunals, resulting in two diametrically opposed outcomes for the *same* dispute. In one instance, the Czech Republic was found not to be liable, while in the other, it was found liable for hundreds of millions of euros. This is an outcome no legal system fit for purpose should allow and highlights the need for effective management of parallel proceedings in investment arbitration.

A. Investment arbitration, a fertile ground for parallel proceedings

The *Lauder/CME* case was just one of many investment arbitrations that occurred in the first decade of the twenty-first century. The Argentine crisis of 2001 resulted in dozens of investment arbitrations over the same State measures (the so-called *pesificación* of the tariffs of foreign-owned utilities and other tariffs that had been calculated in US dollars). This generated significant academic activity, including articles, seminars and events.

The prologue to the 2006 Final Report on the Geneva Colloquium on Consolidation of Proceedings in Investment Arbitration observed that "Argentina's financial crisis is the foremost recent illustration of [the] phenomenon [of parallel proceedings]" [102]. It added that the crisis had "generated 37 ICSID arbitrations" [103]. Even with fifteen years of hindsight, this is still a very heavy caseload to emerge from the same crisis. Crises in other countries likewise spawned scores of investment claims. United Nations Conference on Trade and Development data indicates that Argentina has been the most frequent respondent in investment arbitration with sixty-two cases [104], followed by Venezuela (fifty-four), Spain (fifty-three), the Czech Republic (forty-one) and Egypt (forty) [105].

There are three key reasons why investment arbitration is more prone to parallel proceedings than commercial arbitration. First, the factual matrix of investment claims often involve contracts that have their own arbitration clauses. Second, investment arbitration can lead to multiple investors from the same corporate chain making separate claims against the same State over the same dispute (the problem of "vertical claims"). Lastly, a single State measure can give rise to multiple claims in arbitration from different investors with no links of ownership. These three sources of parallel proceedings in investment arbitration will be explored in depth in sections B.1, B.2 and B.3 below.

These three scenarios will not routinely arise in commercial arbitration. First, in commercial arbitration there is typically one normative source for claims – contracts. No question will arise over how a public international law claim under a treaty and a contract claim should interact. Second, in commercial arbitration there is no real risk of vertical claims: the contract will have one or more parties on each side, and claims will typically be brought by one set of parties against another within the same arbitration. Questions may arise as to whether a non-signatory to the contract is also bound by the arbitration clause (potentially raising issues such as the application of the "group-

---

102. G. Kaufmann-Kohler *et al.*, "Consolidation of Proceedings in Investment Arbitration: How Can Multiple Proceedings Arising from the Same or Related Situations be Handled Efficiently?: Final Report on the Geneva Colloquium held on 22 April 2006", *ICSID Review: Foreign Investment Law Journal*, Vol. 21, No. 1 (2006), pp. 59-125, at p. 63.
103. *Ibid.*
104. UNCTAD, Investor-State Dispute Settlement Cases: Facts and Figures 2020, Issue 4, September 2021, Appendix 2, https://unctad.org/system/files/official-document/diaepcbinf2021d7_en.pdf, last consulted 25 May 2022.
105. *Ibid.*

of-companies" doctrine), but those will typically be resolved by the mandated tribunal (or a national court where negative competence-competence does not operate). By contrast, vertical claims are about linked claimants bringing separate claims against the same respondent, often under different treaties.

Finally, in commercial arbitration it would be unusual for a single action by a party to result in a wave of separate arbitrations from unrelated claimants. By contrast, a single State measure can give rise to just such a scenario – as happened in the investment arbitration sagas involving Argentina, Spain, the Czech Republic, Ecuador and Venezuela, where a single State measure affected a whole class of investors. The only scenario that bears a resemblance in commercial arbitration is contracts of adhesion where one side dictates all of the contract terms, for example in consumer and employment contracts. But there are important differences between these two scenarios: investment arbitration claims are usually high in value and thus can be brought as standalone claims, whereas contracts of adhesion claims – from consumer or employment contracts – are often low in value and thus unviable as a standalone arbitration claim; many legal systems in fact prevent or regulate arbitration of consumer contracts, and in investment arbitration the investor has a range of options to bring claims – to national courts or arbitration under different treaties and different rules – that are absent in adhesion contracts.

These three scenarios of investment arbitration share a common characteristic: they are all expressions of what Jan Paulsson famously referred to as "arbitration without privity" more than a quarter of a century ago [106]. In investment arbitration, States extend open-ended arbitration offers to an open-ended class of "investors", and this has a number of consequences. The first is that investors who have signed contracts with the State can also rely on these treaties as a source for claims. The second is that investors who are part of the same corporate chain can bring separate vertical claims over the same measure or facts. And the third that, a single State measure can affect the treaty rights of an entire class of unrelated investors, leading to a wave of investment claims.

This makes investment arbitration fundamentally different from commercial arbitration. As Jan Paulsson noted in 1995, investment arbitration is not just a "subgenre of [the] existing discipline [of

---

106. Paulsson, note 94, at pp. 232 *et seq.*

commercial arbitration]" [107]. Rather, treaty-based investment arbitration is "dramatically different from anything previously known in the international sphere" [108]. This dramatic difference – which remains to this day – lies at the root of the problem of parallel proceedings in investment arbitration. It explains why this problem is far more acute in this field, and why traditional solutions from commercial arbitration – *lis pendens*, *res judicata*, post-dispute consolidation – have been even less effective in addressing the issue in this field.

On the undesirability scale – recalling the *why* classification from the first chapter (sec. B) – parallel proceedings against States, particularly if perceived as abusive or unfair, rank high. Two main reasons underlie this. First, on the side of States (or at least some of them), there is a sense that States may not have fully understood the potential implications of investment treaties when they signed up to them, as Jan Paulsson pointed out when the field was still in its early stages. He noted in his seminal article of 1995 that "many [national governments] may not have appreciated the full implications of the new treaty obligations [in investment treaties]" [109]. Second, on the side of investors (or at least some of them), there is a sense that they should be free to use a system built for them in whichever way works best for them, which contrasts with some States' view that such use should be limited in certain circumstances because, by bringing parallel proceedings, investors are abusing the system to their advantage and to the detriment of States.

These and other features have led to a so-called "backlash" against investment arbitration, with some States withdrawing from the ICSID Convention: Bolivia in 2007, Ecuador in 2009 (a decision reversed in 2021) and Venezuela in 2012. As noted by Walid Ben Hamida [110], the issue of parallel proceedings has played a significant role in this development, and it is also central as the calls for reform which havec since been made within the UN system, particularly at UNCITRAL, which I will discuss in the final chapter.

This highlights the importance of addressing the issue of parallel proceedings in investment arbitration. If the future of investment arbitration depends on how countries view this field, and if parallel

---

107. *Ibid.*, at p. 256.
108. *Ibid.*, at p. 256.
109. *Ibid.*, at p. 257.
110. W. Ben Hamida, "L'arbitrage Etat-Investisseur face à un désordre Procédural: La concurrence des procédures et les conflits de juridiction", *Annuaire Français de Droit International* (2005), pp. 564 *et seq.*

proceedings have the potential to negatively impact these views, then it is crucial for the system to effectively tackle this problem.

B. Sources of parallel proceedings in investment arbitration

1. Contract claims v. treaty claims

The interrelationship between contract claims and treaty claims has long been a fundamental and disputed issue in investment arbitration, as noted by Professor James Crawford in 2008[111]. Before the widespread use of investment treaties, foreign investors and host States would articulate investments through agreements such as contracts, licences, concessions, permits and authorisations, creating a direct legal relationship or "privity" between them, giving rise to contract-based claims. Investment treaties did not put an end to this, but rather provided an additional layer of protection to foreign investors in the form of treaty claims[112].

Of course, a foreign investor may be protected under an investment treaty even if no contract with the host State exists (many protected investments do not involve a direct legal relationship with the State). But when a contractual relationship does exist, the investment treaty adds an extra layer of protection, typically in the form of treaty standards of treatment and access to international arbitration, leading to questions about how the two layers and their respective proceedings should interact. The interplay between contract and treaty claims has been one of the most difficult legal issues faced by arbitral tribunals in the first decade of this century, during the expansion of investment arbitration, though these are not entirely novel legal issues.

The duality of contract and treaty claims is a significant cause of parallel proceedings in investment arbitration for two reasons: *(a)* they are rooted in independent, normative sources and *(b)* in investment arbitration, unlike general international law, there is no rule of exhaustion of local remedies.

Contracts and treaties are considered to be independent normative sources. Claims arising from contracts are – typically like the contracts themselves – rooted in national law, while treaty claims are based on an international agreement, such as the BIT or other international investment agreements. As a result, each of them gives rise to separate

---
111. J. Crawford, "Treaty and Contract in Investment Arbitration", *Arbitration International*, Vol. 24, No. 3 (2008), pp. 351-374, at p. 351.
112. *Ibid.*, at p. 374.

claims, often in distinct fora. Although the distinction between contract and treaty claims is now widely considered to be *jurisprudence constante* (to the extent it can be called such, as there is no doctrine of precedent properly speaking in investment arbitration), this was not always the case. The decision of the ICSID *ad hoc* Committee in *Vivendi* v. *Argentina* ("Vivendi I") [113] has had a significant impact in this regard.

In *Vivendi I*, the claimants brought ICSID arbitration proceedings against Argentina under the Argentina-France BIT, without having recourse first to the local courts of Tucuman, Argentina, where they had entered into a Concession Contract to operate a water and sewage system. The Concession Contract had a dispute resolution clause providing for the "exclusive jurisdiction" of the Tucuman courts. The claimants argued that the province had undermined their operation of the concession (the "Tucuman claims") and that Argentina had failed to rein in the conduct of the Tucuman authorities (the "federal claims").

The tribunal upheld its jurisdiction over the BIT treaty claims but dismissed the claims on the merits, stating that it was "impossible" to separate the treaty claims from the contract claims [114]. The tribunal held that both claims were related to the performance of the contract, and that the contract provided an exclusive forum for such questions: thus, the claimants had a "duty" to pursue these claims before the courts of Tucuman. It dismissed the claims without examining them further on the merits. The *ad hoc* Committee annulled the tribunal's decision on this point [115].

The *ad hoc* Committee drew a distinction between the two claims, stating that "[a] state may breach a treaty without breaching a contract, and *vice versa*" [116]. In drawing this distinction, it relied on Article 3 of the International Law Commission's Articles on State responsibility, which provides that "The characterization of an act of a State as internationally wrongful is governed by international law. Such characterization is not affected by the characterization of the same act as lawful by internal law". The Committee held that the Concession Contract's provision of local court jurisdiction did not deprive the BIT tribunal of its separate treaty jurisdiction, since the two were distinct. The ICSID tribunal

---
113. *Compañiá de Aguas del Aconquija SA and Vivendi Universal SA* v. *Argentine Republic*, ICSID Case No. ARB/97/3.
114. *Ibid.*, Award, 21 November 2001, at p. 3.
115. *Ibid.*, Decision on Annulment, 3 July 2002.
116. *Ibid.*

would not have exercised contract jurisdiction but would instead have taken into account the contract to decide if there was a breach of the BIT. The tribunal had the duty to consider whether there was a breach of the BIT – but failed to do so; and the decision was annulled on this point. Professor Christoph Schreuer has called this decision "the most important case" on the relationship between treaty and contract [117].

Two investment tribunals faced similar issues of treaty v. contract in two well-known cases shortly after *Vivendi I*. In *SGS* v. *Pakistan*, the Swiss company Société Générale de Surveillance entered into a contract with Pakistan to provide pre-shipment inspection services for goods to be exported from certain countries to Pakistan. The contract had a forum selection clause providing for the resolution of disputes under the contract by way of domestic arbitration in Islamabad. A dispute arose under the contract. Pakistan began domestic arbitration under the contract; then SGS started ICSID arbitration under the Switzerland-Pakistan BIT. Pakistan objected to the ICSID claims arguing that the domestic arbitrator had "exclusive jurisdiction" over the dispute. The ICSID tribunal upheld its jurisdiction on the ground that it was *treaty* jurisdiction, thus to be distinguished from contract jurisdiction [118].

In the case of *SGS* v. *Philippines*, SGS again entered into a contract for pre-shipment inspection services, this time with the Philippines. The contract contained a forum selection clause in favour of domestic courts. When a dispute arose over whether certain payments were due under the contract, SGS filed an ICSID claim. The Philippines objected based on the forum selection clause, but the tribunal upheld its jurisdiction and decided to stay the arbitration pending a decision "in the agreed contractual forum" [119]. Unlike in *Vivendi I*, the claims were not dismissed, but rather the case was stayed.

Investment claims are thus prone to parallel proceedings because they often involve a contractual aspect, leading to dual legal sources for claims: contract and treaty. These may provide for different fora for dispute resolution, such as a tribunal and a court (as in *Vivendi I* and *SGS*

---

117. C. Schreuer, "Investment Treaty Arbitration and Jurisdiction over Contract Claims: The Vivendi I Case Considered", in T. Weiler (ed.), *International Investment Law and Arbitration: Leading Cases from the ICSID, NAFTA, Bilateral Treaties and Customary International Law*, Place, Cameron May, 2005, pp. 281-323, at p. 281.

118. *SGS Société Générale de Surveillance SA* v. *Islamic Republic of Pakistan*, ICSID Case No. ARB/01/13, Decision of the Tribunal on Objections to Jurisdiction, 6 August 2003.

119. *SGS Société Générale de Surveillance SA* v. *Republic of the Philippines*, ICSID Case No. ARB/02/6, Decision of the Tribunal on Objections to Jurisdiction, 29 January 2004.

v. *Philippines*), or two different tribunals (domestic and international, as in *SGS* v. *Pakistan*, or international and international). Even if both the treaty and contract provide for the same dispute resolution mechanism, say ICSID, a claimant may still request the establishment of two separate tribunals to adjudicate each dispute, as explained by Walid Ben Hamida:

> "On ajoute qu'à suivre les directives jurisprudentielles, dans l'hypothèse où le contrat et le traité se réfèrent aux mêmes mécanismes arbitraux, le demandeur peut demander l'établissement de deux tribunaux arbitraux différents. Ainsi, à titre d'exemple, si le contrat d'investissement renvoie au CIRDI et que le TBI prévoit le recours à ce même mécanisme, l'investisseur peut demander l'établissement de deux tribunaux CIRDI différents car les deux litiges ne sont pas les mêmes." [120]

The second main reason why contract and treaty claims may lead to parallel proceedings is the lack of a rule of exhaustion of local remedies in investment arbitration, unlike in general international law. In general international law – and under the system of diplomatic protection that preceded the investment treaty era – the exhaustion of local remedies is and was the default rule for a claimant to gain access to international law remedies and tribunals. In investment arbitration, the default rule is reversed: the general rule is that there is no requirement to exhaust local remedies unless express provision is made for that, for example in the treaty.

For instance, Article 26 of the ICSID Convention provides that consent to arbitration is "to the exclusion of any other remedy", including local remedies. A State "may require the exhaustion of local . . . remedies" as a condition of "consent to arbitration". Only Guatemala has notified ICSID that it will require the exhaustion of local remedies as a condition for consent to arbitration under ICSID.

The exhaustion of local remedies rule would minimise the risk of parallel proceedings as it would ensure that there would only be one ongoing set of proceedings in relation to the same dispute at any given point in time. However, this rule could increase the length and costs of proceedings, as investors would have to complete domestic litigation before invoking investment arbitration.

---

120. Ben Hamida, note 110, at pp. 568-569.

In summary, the combination of these two factors increases the risk of parallel proceedings in investment arbitration. Contracts and treaties are not just different sources of legal rights – rooted in national and international law, respectively. They are also sources of different legal fora to adjudicate disputes arising thereunder. The lack of a rule of exhaustion of local remedies in investment law further exacerbates the issue. Investors can file investment claims without resorting to local remedies, even where the contract contains an exclusive domestic forum selection clause. Parallel claims are thus likely to arise.

2. The problem of vertical claims

The *Lauder/CME* v. *Czech Republic* case is an example of vertical claims. Mr Lauder owned 99 per cent of CME's shares, and brought claims arising from the same investment chain: from the main investment company and its near sole shareholder. Vertical claims are brought by investors who are linked by a chain of corporate ownership, such as the parent company, the subsidiary, the parent company's shareholders, and so on. This ownership structure can range from simple to complex.

To illustrate, consider the following scenario: D has a contract with State X, but State X takes actions that breach D's contract rights and diminish the value of the share of D's direct and indirect shareholders, a loss of volume known as "reflective loss". Can A, B, C, E and F have a cause of action against State X? This issue has been extensively analysed by the Organisation for Economic Co-operation and Development (OECD), leading to the publication of several working papers [121].

---

121. D. Gaukrodger, "Investment Treaties as Corporate Law: Shareholder Claims and Issues of Consistency", OECD Working Papers on International Investment, 2013, 2013/03, http://dx.doi.org/10.1787/5k3w9t44mt0v-en; D. Gaukrodger, "Investment Treaties and Shareholder Claims for Reflective Loss: Insights from Advanced Systems of Corporate Law", OECD Working Papers on International Investment, 2014, 2014/02, http://dx.doi.org/10.1787/5jz0xvgngmr3-en; D. Gaukrodger, "Investment Treaties and Shareholder Claims: Analysis of Treaty Practice", OECD Working Papers on International Investment, 2014, 2014/03, http://dx.doi.org/10.1787/5jxvk6shpvs4-en; OECD, "The Impact of Investment Treaties on Companies, Shareholders and Creditors", in *OECD Business and Finance Outlook 2016*, 2016, http://oe.cd/1Zv, at chap. 8; OECD, Treaty Shopping and Tools for Reform, Investment Treaty Conference materials, 2018, pp. 11-15, figs. 1-3, http://oe.cd/TS-analysis; UNCITRAL, "Possible Reform of Investor-State Dispute Settlement (ISDS): Shareholder Claims and Reflective Loss – Note by the Secretariat", A/CN.9/WG.III/WP.170, 9 August 2019, https://undocs.org/en/A/CN.9/WG.III/WP.170; J. Arato *et al.*, "Reforming Shareholder Claims in ISDS", Academic Forum on ISDS Working Paper, 2019, 2019/9, http://bit.ly/ISDS_AF_SRL_2019. All links last consulted on 19 July 2022.

Let us examine the answers to this question under both domestic and international law before turning to investment arbitration law.

Under domestic law

The OECD notes that

> "[a]dvanced systems of domestic corporate law generally apply a 'no reflective loss' principle to shareholder claims. Shareholder claims are permitted for direct injury to shareholder rights (such as voting rights). But shareholders generally cannot bring claims for reflective loss incurred as a result of injury to 'their' company (such as loss in value of shares). Only the directly-injured company can claim" [122].

Thus, the answer to our question under most systems of domestic law will be "No". Direct and indirect shareholders cannot bring claims for reflective losses – indirect losses resulting from damage to the company. They are called "reflective" losses because they merely "reflect" the losses sustained by the company. Therefore, the rule is: no cause of action for reflective losses.

Lukas Vanhonnaeker describes the "no reflective loss" principle as a " 'general principle of corporate law' recognized in most jurisdictions, regardless of whether they belong to the civil or common law legal tradition" [123]. This principle exists in the United Kingdom, France, Germany or the Netherlands, to cite but a few. For example, the French Cour de Cassation dismissed a claim for alleged loss because il "n'était que le corollaire de celui causé à la société, [et] n'avait aucun caractère personnel" [124].

Under customary international law

As a matter of customary international law, there is no cause of action for reflective losses. This is clear from the ICJ's landmark

---

122. Gaukrodger, "Analysis of Treaty Practice", *ibid.*, at p. 3.
123. L. Vanhonnaeker, "Shareholders' Claims for Reflective Loss in Domestic Regimes, Customary International Law of Diplomatic Protection, and Human Rights Law", in *id.*, *Shareholders' Claims for Reflective Loss in International Investment Law*, Cambridge, Cambridge University Press, pp. 54-92.
124. C. Cass Com., No. 97-20886, 15 January 2002. In England & Wales, see *Prudential Assurance Co Ltd.* v. *Newman Industries Ltd (No.2)* [1982] 1 Ch 204; *Johnson*, note 86; but see the recent Supreme Court Judgment in *Sevilleja* v. *Marex Financial Ltd.* [2020] UKSC 31, clarifying and substantially confining the scope of the doctrine of reflective loss.

decision of 1970 in *Barcelona Traction*. In this case, Barcelona Traction, Light and Power Company Limited was a Canadian company incorporated in Toronto with subsidiaries in Spain that held concessions to develop, produce and distribute electric power in Catalonia, Spain. The controlling shareholders of Barcelona Traction were Belgian shareholders. Spain's government took actions against the Canadian company, which allegedly caused damage to the Belgian shareholders. In short, the Belgian shareholders claimed they had suffered reflective loss.

Belgium brought a claim against Spain before the ICJ under the doctrine of diplomatic protection, "seeking reparation for damage" that Spain allegedly caused to the Belgian shareholders of Barcelona Traction. In other words, it was a classic diplomatic protection claim but one based on reflective loss. The ICJ dismissed the claims, holding that shareholder claims for reflective losses for damage caused to the company are not allowed as a matter of customary international law. The ICJ stated (at para. 44 of the Judgment):

> "Notwithstanding the separate corporate personality, a wrong done to the company frequently causes prejudice to its shareholders. But the mere fact that damage is sustained by both company and shareholder does not imply that both are entitled to claim compensation. Thus no legal conclusion can be drawn from the fact that the same event caused damage simultaneously affecting several natural or juristic persons . . . . In such cases, no doubt, the interests of the aggrieved are affected, but not their rights. Thus whenever a shareholder's interests are harmed by an act done to the company, it is to the latter that he must look to institute appropriate action; for although two separate entities may have suffered from the same wrong, it is only one entity whose rights have been infringed." [125]

Under current investment treaty jurisprudence

On this point, as noted by the OECD, investment treaty law allows claims from both direct and indirect shareholders, which sets it apart from both domestic law and general customary international law. This means that in the scenario mentioned above, not only D but also A, B,

---

125. *Barcelona Traction, Light and Power Company, Limited*, Judgment, *ICJ Reports*, p. 3, at para. 44 (emphasis added).

C, E and F can initiate proceedings against State X. What was one set of proceedings under domestic and customary international law could become six under investment treaty law based on a simple corporate ownership structure, making it one of the central sources of parallel proceedings in investment arbitration.

The departure of investment arbitration law from other legal systems can be traced back to the ICSID Tribunal's decision on jurisdiction in *CMS* v. *Argentina* in 2003, which the OECD considers a "key moment" in investment treaty law. The Tribunal dismissed Argentina's objection to a claim by a minority shareholder, holding (in a part of the decision which was left intact by an *ad hoc* Annulment Committee) that CMS was a covered "investor" under the relevant BIT as the definition of "investment" therein covered – as is often the case in BITs – "shares or stock or other interests in a company", and that even minority shareholders had a direct right of action, not just under the terms of the BIT but as a "general rule" of investment law. The Tribunal stated the following:

> "The Tribunal . . . finds no bar in current international law to the concept of allowing claims by shareholders independently from those of the corporation concerned, not even if those shareholders are minority or non-controlling shareholders. Although it is true . . . that this is mostly the result of *lex specialis* and specific treaty arrangements that have so allowed, the fact is that *lex specialis* in this respect is so prevalent that it can now be considered the general rule, certainty in respect of foreign investments and increasingly in respect of other matters." [126]

This decision was the first to unambiguously establish that minority shareholders can claim reflective losses arising from damage caused to the underlying company.

The departure of investment tribunals from other legal systems in this area has been a recurring source of criticism against the current system of ISDS. The OECD papers have noted that this approach ignores basic notions of corporate law, including insolvency law [127], and

---

126. *CMS Gas Transmission Company* v. *The Republic of Argentina*, ICSID Case No. ARB/01/8, Decision of the Tribunal on Objections to Jurisdiction, 17 July 2003, para. 48.
127. D. Gaukrodger, "Claims for Reflective Loss under Investment Treaties", in OECD-Hosted Side Meeting, UNCITRAL Working Group III on ISDS Reform, Resumed 38th Session, 20-24 January 2020, Vienna, 22 January 2020, https://uncitral.un.org/sites/uncitral.un.org/files/oecd_reflective_loss_claims.pdf, at p. 14.

places domestic investors in a company in an entirely different position than foreign investors in a way, which is difficult to reconcile with basic corporate law principles [128]. As a result, there have been calls to address the issue of vertical claims, most notably by Professor Gaillard at an Institut pour l'Arbitrage International conference held in Paris on 22 November 2013 [129], and a number of solutions have been proposed and considered by tribunals.

A first approach: appropriate treaty-drafting?

In *Kappes* et al v. *Guatemala*, the claimants brought an arbitration claim against Guatemala under the Dominican Republic-Central America Free Trade Agreement or DR-CAFTA [130]. They were direct and indirect shareholders in Exmingua, a Guatemalan company, and filed the claims in their own names as shareholders, seeking compensation for reflective loss. DR-CAFTA includes specific provisions modelled after Articles 11-16 and 11-17 of the old NAFTA, which had been interpreted by the State Parties to NAFTA and by Tribunals (for example, in *Clayton* v. *Canada*) as precluding claims for reflective loss. Article 10.16.1 of DR-CAFTA reads as follows:

"1. In the event that a disputing party considers that an investment dispute cannot be settled by consultation and negotiation:

(a) the claimant, on its own behalf, may submit to arbitration under this Section a claim

　(i) that the respondent has breached

　　(A) an obligation under Section A,
　　(B) an investment authorization, or
　　(C) an investment agreement;

　(ii) that the claimant has incurred loss or damage by reason of, or arising out of, that breach; and

(b) the claimant, on behalf of an enterprise of the respondent that is a juridical person that the claimant owns or controls directly or indirectly, may submit to arbitration under this Section a claim

　(i) that the respondent has breached

---

128. *Ibid.*, at p. 12.
129. The colloquium was entitled "Concurrent Proceedings in Investment Disputes: Treaty Arbitrations Brought by Shareholders".
130. *Daniel W. Kappes and Kappes, Cassiday & Associates* v. *Republic of Guatemala*, ICSID Case No. ARB/18/43.

(A) an obligation under Section A,
(B) an investment authorization, or
(C) an investment agreement; and

(ii) that the enterprise has incurred loss or damage by reason of, or arising out of, that breach." (Emphasis added)

Article 10.18, titled "Conditions and Limitations on Consent of Each Party", provides:

"1. No claim may be submitted to arbitration under this Section if more than three years have elapsed from the date on which the claimant first acquired, or should have first acquired, knowledge of the breach alleged under Article 10.16.1 and knowledge that the claimant (for claims brought under Art. 10.16.1 *(a)*) or the enterprise (for claims brought under Art. 10.16.1 *(b)*) has incurred loss or damage.

In other words, if the controlling shareholder brings a claim under Article 10.16.1 *(b)* on behalf of its company, then it has to provide a waiver both for itself and the company (Art. 10.18.1 *(b) (ii)*).

If a claim is brought on behalf of the company pursuant to Article 10.16.1 *(b)*, then Article 10.26.2 *(b)* directs that any damages awarded must be paid to the company and not the controlling shareholder and the company would have previously waived the pursuit if any other remedy in respect of the same prejudice."

Professor Douglas held, in a dissenting opinion, that this regime achieved the same result as NAFTA and precluded claims for reflective loss [131]. In his view, the company, not its shareholders, should sue for losses suffered by the company. The majority (Kalicki, Townsend) disagreed with this position [132]. The disagreement between the majority and the dissenting opinion highlights the need for treaty-drafting solutions to be airtight if they are to effectively bar claims by shareholders for reflective loss.

A second approach: tribunal-driven rather than treaty-driven solutions

The relevant case is *Orascom v. Algeria*, in which Algeria took measures against a company called Djezzy for allegedly violating

---

131. *Ibid.*, Partial Dissenting Opinion of Zachary Douglas, 13 March 2020.
132. *Ibid.*, Decision on the Respondent's Preliminary Objection, 13 March 2020.

Algerian law. The dispute involved the following vertical corporate chain Orascom owned Weather Investments, which owned OTH which owned Djezzy. Each company had a potential claim against Algeria for measures taken against Djezzy. Specifically, Djezzy could have brought a claim under the investment contract with Algeria, OTH under its Algeria-Egypt BIT, Weather Investments under the Algeria-Italy BIT and Orascom under the Algeria-BLEU (Belgium & Luxembourg) BIT.

In practice, OTH sent a notice of dispute to Algeria under the Algeria-Egypt BIT in 2010 and initiated a Permanent Court of Arbitration (PCA) arbitration in 2012 under the same BIT, which was settled by consent award in 2015. Weather Investments also sent a notice of dispute in 2010 (less than a week after OTH) under the Algeria-Italy BIT, though it did not pursue the matter further. Orascom, at the top of the corporate chain, began ICSID proceedings against Algeria under the Algeria-BLEU BIT in 2012, which continued despite the settlement in the OTH arbitration.

In a ground-breaking decision, the tribunal dismissed Orascom's claims as inadmissible, stating that pursuing claims "at different levels of the vertical corporate chain" amounted to an "abuse of the system of investment protection" [133]. The decision has potentially significant implications, which will be discussed further in Chapter V.

3. One measure, multiple disputes

The most significant source of parallel proceedings in numerical terms is undoubtedly the third one, where a single State measure can impact a group or class of investors, generating multiple disputes against the State. Unlike vertical claims, affected investors in this scenario are not linked by a chain of ownership, at least not necessarily so. However, these two sources of parallel proceedings can overlap, where a single State measure affects both independent investors and vertically-linked investors simultaneously. For now, we focus on independent investors alone.

This source of parallel proceedings results from three factors. First, State measures typically affect not only one entity but a whole group or class of entities. This is no different in the field of foreign investment, where State measures can impact a whole group or class of foreign

---

133. *Orascom TMT Investments Sàrl* v. *People's Democratic Republic of Algeria*, ICSID Case No. ARB/12/35, Final Award, 31 May 2017, para. 545.

investors as well. Second, investment treaties typically feature open-ended arbitration offers. This means that all foreign investors who may potentially be affected by a State measure can bring claims against the State, even if there is no privity of contract between the investor and the State. Finally, there is no system of binding precedent in international arbitration, nor could there be given the *ad hoc* nature of each tribunal constituted to hear each dispute. As a result, the outcomes of previous cases can only have persuasive authority on later cases, which gives investors an incentive to pursue claims even if the previous outcomes were not favourable.

The combination of these factors has led to a series of so-called "waves" of investment arbitrations against States. As noted earlier, Argentina was the first to experience a major wave of investment claims due to measures it enacted following the 2001 financial crisis. To date, Argentina remains the host State with the highest number of investment arbitrations brought against it. Other States that have been on the receiving end of "waves" of claims include Spain, Italy, the Czech Republic, Venezuela, Egypt and Ecuador.

In numerical terms, there is a significant difference between vertical claims and disputes involving multiple claimants with no ownership or other link, which we might refer to as "multi-claimant disputes". Vertical claims usually result in at most a few separate proceedings. In the *Orascom* case, up to four separate proceedings could have been brought against Algeria, but only two were actually brought, with a notice of dispute filed in a third. In contrast, multi- claimant disputes can affect hundreds, even thousands of potential investors. For instance, in the largest multi-claimant dispute scenario so far, 195,000 independent claimants filed a single investment arbitration against Argentina (*Beccara* v. *Argentina*, later *Abaclat* v. *Argentina*). Therefore, this source of parallel proceedings can lead to an exponentially higher number of disputes than the vertical claims scenario.

In *Orascom*, all four potential claimants in the vertical corporate chain could have viably brought claims against Algeria. This was possible as they had the means to do so and were essentially in the same ownership. However, this was probably not the case in the *Beccara* arbitration, where the bringing of a single claim was probably an economic imperative to make the proceedings viable for the claimants.

When it comes to terminology, we must exercise caution since the phenomenon of multiple disputes arising from the same State measure has led to new terms in this field. The term "mass claims" implies that the State measure affects a large number of potential claimants, as was the case in *Abaclat*[134]. However, this need not be the case, and a State measure could impact only a few independent and unaffiliated foreign investors, such as oil companies. Nonetheless, the term "mass claims" is not misleading and can be used, as it commonly is.

On the other hand, the term "class action" can be misleading because it has a precise technical meaning under US law – as the tribunal in *Ambiente Ufficio* v. *Argentina* rightly observed[135]. Class actions are meant for a "representative" group of claimants, which does not reflect what happens in this arbitral scenario. The goal of aggregating claims is not to have a "representative" group but simply to merge all those affected by the same host State measure into a single proceeding. Therefore, the term "class action" should be avoided.

One of the most notable examples of multi-claimant dispute scenarios arising from the same host state measures – and the aggregation of claims – involves a trilogy of cases that arose from Argentina's default on its sovereign debt following its 2001 financial crisis. This default affected thousands of Italian bondholders who had acquired Argentine bonds. Three groups of Italian bondholders joined forces and initiated claims in arbitration against Argentina at ICSID, based on Article 8 of the Argentina-Italy BIT. In all three cases, Argentina argued that it had not consented to the aggregation of the claims into a single case. These cases are *Abaclat* v. *Argentina*[136], *Ambiente Ufficio* v. *Argentina*[137] and *Alemanni* v. *Argentina*[138].

The mass claim cases illustrate that it should not be assumed that it is always the claimants who will seek to bring separate proceedings, even if a single set of proceedings would be possible. In the *Lauder* and *CME* cases, the two claimants had proposed consolidation, but it was the Czech Republic that refused the proposal. More recently, in *Antaris & ors* v. *The Czech Republic*, the Czech Republic effectively blocked the aggregation of a number of UNCITRAL claims arising out of the same measure by nominating a different arbitrator for each of the ten claimants who intended to file all their claims as a single proceeding.

---

134. *Abaclat and Others* v. *Argentine Republic*, ICSID Case No. ARB/07/5.
135. *Ambiente Ufficio SpA* et al. v. *Argentine Republic*, ICSID Case No. ARB/08/9, Decision on Jurisdiction and Admissibility, 8 February 2013, para. 115.
136. *Abaclat*, note 134.
137. *Ambiente*, note 135.
138. *Giovanni Alemanni* et al. v. *The Argentine Republic*, ICSID Case No. ARB/07/8.

Ultimately, only two of the original ten claimants proceeded with the claims [139].

C. Consolidation and coordination

Chapter III, Section D, established that two prerequisites are essential for a viable consolidation provision: first, that it records consent *ex ante*, and second, that it provide a proper mechanism for consolidation, such as a super-tribunal in the case of NAFTA. This chapter concludes with an analysis of the first prerequisite – consent *ex ante* – and the extent to which it can be implied rather than express in the field of investment arbitration.

There has been a debate over whether the tribunal's "general powers" provisions under various institutional rules, such as Article 44 of the ICSID Convention or Article 17 of the 2013 UNCITRAL Rules, subsume the power to order consolidation or aggregation of claims in the absence of *ex post* agreement by all disputing parties. The general consensus appears to be that it does not, as these general provisions are meant to enable tribunals to fill procedural voids and do not demonstrate consent to consolidation from the disputing parties.

Assuming *arguendo* that these "general powers" do subsume the power to order consolidation, this would not be useful in most cases. For example, if two tribunals have already been formed, it is unclear which tribunal should use that power or what happens if both tribunals use it. The "general powers" provisions do not provide answers to these questions.

The question of the requirement for consent to consolidation in ICSID arbitration was helpfully considered by the tribunal in *CPC* v. *Cambodia* in 2011. The tribunal made the following observations:

(a) First and foremost, the consolidation of claims in ICSID arbitration, like most other systems, requires the consent of the parties. Such consent may be established before or after the dispute has arisen. If there is no consent, the principle of party autonomy dictates that claims under multiple contracts cannot be consolidated, even if that leads to inconvenience or inefficiency.

---

139. See IA Reporter, 15 May 2013, "Solar Investors File Arbitration Against Czech Republic; Intra-EU BITs and Energy Charter Treaty at Center of Dispute"; IA Reporter, 1 January 2014, "Following PCA Decision, Czech Republic Thwarts Move by Solar Investors to Sue in Single Arbitral Proceeding".

(b) Second, while express consent, whether in a contract or treaty, is the usual form of establishing consolidation, it can also be implied from the circumstances. This could be in the form of an incorporated arbitration rule or a submission agreement.

(c) Third, the tribunal's decisions emphasise the need to interpret the parties' intentions in light of all the circumstances of each case. In *Noble Energy* v. *Ecuador*, for instance, the tribunal found jurisdiction over disputes arising out of multiple agreements by deducing an implied consent from several factors related to the purpose and configuration of the agreements.

(d) Fourth, it is important to note that establishing requisite consent entails identifying the precise mechanism by which the parties have agreed to coordinate their claims. This could mean that disputes arising out of multiple contracts are all to be brought within the scope of one particular arbitration agreement in one of the contracts. Alternatively, separate arbitration clauses in separate agreements might be interpreted as one single arbitration agreement. Claims under multiple contracts might be merged into one arbitration proceeding and determined by way of one award, or separate arbitration proceedings arising out of separate arbitration agreements might be heard and determined concurrently while maintaining a separate juridical nature. While all of these variations might be described as "consolidation", each is different in nature [140].

While the *CPC* tribunal's statements of principle regarding the requirement that consent to consolidation are important, it should be remembered this was a case where the claims were brought pursuant to contractual agreements containing ICSID arbitration clauses, rather than under investment treaties. Similarly, in *Noble Energy*, the tribunal dealt with two contractual agreements containing ICSID clauses but also a claim under the US-Ecuador BIT. The question arises as to how the issue of consent to consolidation would be addressed in a situation such as the *Antaris* v. *Czech Republic* case, where the issue is whether there is an agreement to consolidate claims under a number of different investment treaties.

It is unclear whether the reasoning in the *CPC* and *Noble Energy* cases can be extended to the treaty interpretation arena from that of contractual interpretation. Would a State's consent to arbitration under

---

140. *Cambodia Power Company* v. *Kingdom of Cambodia*, ICSID Case No. ARB/09/18, at paras. 121-128.

a network of bilateral or multilateral investment treaties which between them cover the separate economic interests of the relevant shareholders suggest an implied intention to accept consolidated or aggregated claims? Does the issue simply not arise where aggregation or *de facto* consolidation has occurred under multiple investment treaties instead of multiple contracts, and if not, why not?

These are complex questions, and a clear mechanism for *ex ante* consolidation, including *ex ante* consent, would certainly be preferable to relying on implied consent. However, such mechanisms are rare, and these difficult questions should be considered. The only publicly available decision from an investment tribunal that tackled the issue of implied consent to the aggregation of claims based on more than one treaty can be used as a reference.

The case of *Guaracachi America Inc. ("GAI") and Rurelec PLC v. Bolivia* [141] involved two companies, one American and one British, that initiated arbitration proceedings against Bolivia for the alleged uncompensated nationalisation of a 50.001 per cent stake in Empresa Eléctrica Guaracachi SA ("EGSA"), an electricity company incorporated under the laws of Bolivia. GAI directly owned the 50.001 per cent shares in EGSA and a Bolivian state-owned entity held the remaining shares. Rurelec, as GAI's parent company, indirectly owned GAI's majority stake. Both brought treaty claims against Bolivia in a single arbitration before the same tribunal, GAI on the basis of the US-Bolivia BIT and Rurelec on the basis of the UK-Bolivia BIT. Bolivia objected to the consolidation of claims, alleging that it had not consented to join "claims arising under different BITs into a single arbitration proceeding before a single tribunal".

The *Rurelec* tribunal dismissed Bolivia's objection to jurisdiction on two main grounds. First, the tribunal noted that Bolivia's consent to arbitration, in either BIT, was "not subject to any condition or limitation" in scope [142]. Silence, in this context, "play[ed] against the Respondent's point of view, since one cannot use silence to limit the scope of the consent given." [143]. Thus, the tribunal reasoned, nothing in the BITs barred the claimants "from submitting a single, joint arbitration case against the Respondent" [144]. Second, the tribunal found that the claims

---

141. *Guaracachi America, Inc. and Rurelec PLC v. The Plurinational State of Bolivia*, UNCITRAL, PCA Case No. 2011-17.
142. *Ibid.*, Award, 31 January 2014, at para. 336.
143. *Ibid.*, at para. 341.
144. *Ibid.*, at para. 336.

were "identical and overlapping"[145], based on the same alleged facts breaches. Therefore, it concluded that it was the same dispute, only based on two different BITs.

Based on the *Rurelec* decision, three relevant factors can be identified to determine whether a respondent has impliedly consented to the aggregation of claims based on more than one investment treaty. First, the arbitration offers in the underlying BITs should be broadly worded and should not contain any limitations or restrictions on the possibility of hearing multiple claims in a single arbitration. If a BIT's arbitration offer is narrowly worded or includes restrictions, claims based on that treaty may not be aggregated with claims arising under other treaties. Second, implied consent may be inferred when the multiple claims relate to what essentially is the same dispute, based on the same facts and same State measures or conduct. A more difficult question is whether the treaty protections or damages alleged must also be the same. While a finding that they are would support the conclusion that it is the same dispute, a finding that they are not may not preclude it altogether. In the end, this is more a matter of degree than of hard-and-fast rules. Finally, implied consent appears to be feasible only when the State has consented to the same set of arbitration rules. If the allegedly related arbitrations are governed by different arbitration rules, say ICSID and UNCITRAL, difficulties as to both consent and the mechanics of consolidation are likely to arise. Although the *Rurelec* tribunal did not mention this factor, it is likely that it took it for granted, as the claims in that case were all based on the same version of the UNCITRAL rules.

****

Our analysis in this chapter of the special and distinct sources of parallel proceedings in investment arbitration reveals several key points. First, the system appears to favour investors in some respects, as they often have multiple opportunities to succeed in claims against host States over essentially the same dispute. However, States may also seek to initiate parallel proceedings as a defensive tactic to make the investors' claims financially unviable. Second, investment arbitration has the potential to generate more undesirable parallel proceedings than any of the other type of interaction examined in this course, that is court v. tribunal and commercial arbitrations with no investment arbitration element. Conversely, parallel proceedings may also be

---

145. *Ibid.*, at para. 338.

seen as undesirable in the sense that they can render claims financially unviable, leaving investors with no legal recourse. Finally, investment arbitration presents the greatest challenges with respect to undesirable parallel proceedings, making it an area with the greatest room for improvement. Chapter V will therefore focus on identifying solutions that are tailored to this particular field.

CHAPTER V

WHERE TO FROM HERE?
THE SEARCH FOR PRACTICAL SOLUTIONS

Before we delve into the goals of the final chapter, let us briefly take stock of the ground that we have traversed. In Chapter I, we defined the subject matter and established criteria to distinguish acceptable from undesirable parallel proceedings. In Chapters II to IV, we conducted a theoretical analysis of potential conflicts, overlaps, and friction among adjudicating bodies charged with deciding international disputes. Specifically, we looked at three areas of interaction:

(a) National courts v. *international arbitral tribunals*
(b) International arbitral tribunal v. *international arbitral tribunal* in a commercial setting with no investment arbitration element
(c) International arbitral tribunal v. *international arbitral tribunal* with an investment arbitration element

In this final chapter, we aim to use our analysis to propose new solutions to the problem of undesirable parallel proceedings that have no place in a well-functioning system for settling international disputes. Substantial doctrinal and scholarly efforts were made in 2006 to address parallel proceedings, notably the ILA "Recommendations on *Lis Pendens* and *Res Judicata* and Arbitration" and the Geneva Colloquium on Consolidation of Proceedings in Investment Arbitration. These have provided a useful analytical framework and a basis to act for tribunals seeking to actively manage such issues. But, as we have seen, these seminal studies have had a limited aspect in practice, while the development of investment arbitration has exacerbated the scale, of the problem and nature.

Therefore, in this chapter, we will discuss separately potential solutions for each of the three fields covered in Chapters II to IV, namely interaction with national courts, interaction in the field of commercial arbitration, and interaction in the field of investment arbitration.

A. National courts

We have seen that most interactions with national courts involve the principle of competence-competence. However, there seems to be little appetite among States to adopt negative competence-competence, which would limit the scope for interaction between courts and tribunals by giving preference (priority in time) to tribunals. I would for my part encourage developing States, where the judiciary may not yet be fully familiar with the principles of international arbitration and their implementation, to consider adopting negative competence-competence, as Mauritius has done.

Most undesirable interactions between courts and tribunals occur due to national courts erroneously taking jurisdiction in cases where there is an agreement to arbitrate between the parties. In response, other courts, usually the courts of the seat, may take action to protect the agreement, sometimes through anti-suit relief. The tribunal may also be tempted to protect its own jurisdiction through such relief, leading to contentious exchanges of prohibitory injunctions between courts and tribunals. To avoid this, developing States could adopt a simple and mechanical rule requiring them to decline jurisdiction whenever an agreement to arbitrate *prima facie* exists. This approach, as seen in the Mauritian International Arbitration Act, would minimise the points of contact between the arbitral process and national courts and be in line with the spirit of the New York Convention, which has been ratified by over 160 States. The Mauritian Act was specifically designed for this purpose, with the assistance of UNCITRAL, and could serve as a model for other developing jurisdictions.

In addition to adopting negative competence-competence, the Mauritian Act has other features that could minimise the points of contact between the arbitral process and national courts. For example, all international arbitration matters (including the consideration of stays of jurisdiction in favour of arbitration) are assigned to a panel of three Designated Judges with specific knomledge of arbitration by way of Section 42 of the Act. These judges, selected from a pool of six, receive special training in international arbitration, such as the courses of the Arbitration Academy in Paris, and develop their expertise further by consistently hearing and determining arbitration applications. This approach has also been adopted in developed jurisdictions, such as France, where an International Chamber of the Paris Court of Appeals has been established specifically to handle arbitral matters. Such specialised bodies can help ensure consistent and expert handling of international arbitration matters, reducing the potential for friction between courts and tribunals.

B. Commercial arbitration

In the field of commercial arbitration, how can the limitations of the *res judicata* and *lis pendens* doctrines, and of consolidation and joinder be improved? There have been promising developments in the area of consolidation and joinder in recent years, with many arbitral institutions introducing rules to allow for these procedures. The Singapore International Arbitration Centre ("SIAC") has in addition proposed a protocol to allow consolidation even when proceedings arise under different institutional rules. We will explore these developments, before considering whether further action could be taken at the higher level of national legislation.

1. Evolution of institutional rules

Starting with the evolution of institutional rules on consolidation and consent, this discussion will focus on the ICC and LCIA rules, with the understanding that other institutions have made similar changes and are likely to continue doing so.

The ICC Rules have seen significant evolution in consolidation provisions over the past twenty-five years through four versions of the rules, which came into effect in 1998, 2012, 2017 and 2021. The 1998 version contained the following skeletal provision in Article 4 (6):

> "When a party submits a Request in connection with a legal relationship in respect of which arbitration proceedings between the same parties are already pending under these Rules, the Court may, at the request of a party, decide to include the claims contained in the Request in the pending proceedings provided that the Terms of Reference have not been signed or approved by the Court. Once the Terms of Reference have been signed or approved by the Court, claims may only be included in the pending proceedings subject to the provisions of Article 19."

This provision was limited and very narrow, applying to the same "legal relationship" between "the same parties". If these two requirements were met, the "claims" in the second arbitration could be added to the arbitration already pending. This was *not* a consolidation or joinder provision but simply allowed new claims to be added to an existing arbitration.

The 2012 version of the ICC Rules marked a significant step forward, providing a broader and more detailed framework for consolidation. Article 10 of the 2012 version provided as follows:

> "The Court may, at the request of a party, consolidate two or more arbitrations pending under the Rules into a single arbitration, where:
>
> *(a)* the parties have agreed to consolidation; or
>
> *(b)* all of the claims in the arbitrations are made under the same arbitration agreement; or
>
> *(c)* where the claims in the arbitrations are made under more than one arbitration agreement, the arbitrations are between the same parties, the disputes in the arbitrations arise in connection with the same legal relationship, and the Court finds the arbitration agreements to be compatible.
>
> In deciding whether to consolidate, the Court may take into account any circumstances it considers to be relevant including whether one or more arbitrators have been confirmed or appointed in more than one of the arbitrations and, if so, whether the same or different persons have been confirmed or appointed.
>
> When arbitrations are consolidated, they shall be consolidated into the arbitration that commenced first, unless otherwise agreed by all parties."

Unlike the 1998 version, the 2012 version explicitly refers to "consolidation" and "arbitrations" and not merely to "claims", and does not contain time limits for consolidation requests (i.e. it is not limited to the period when the request for arbitration is filed). Moreover, the 2012 version identifies and systematises three possible routes to consolidation: *(a)* with the agreement of all parties; *(b)* all claims are made under the same arbitration agreement; and *(c)* the claims made are under different arbitration agreements. In this last route, the parties and legal relationship must be the same and the arbitration agreements must be compatible.

As the timeline shows, these changes were made after the work done in 2006 by the ILA and the Geneva Colloquium. The ICC's consolidation rules remained unchanged in the third version, issued in

2017. The latest update, in 2021, introduces relatively minor changes to the 2012/2017 version. The new Article 10 reads thus:

"The Court may, at the request of a party, consolidate two or more arbitrations pending under the Rules into a single arbitration, where:

(a) the parties have agreed to consolidation; or
(b) all of the claims in the arbitrations are made under the same arbitration agreement or agreements; or
(c) the claims in the arbitrations are not made under the same arbitration agreement or agreements, but the arbitrations are between the same parties, the disputes in the arbitrations arise in connection with the same legal relationship, and the Court finds the arbitration agreements to be compatible.

In deciding whether to consolidate, the Court may take into account any circumstances it considers to be relevant, including whether one or more arbitrators have been confirmed or appointed in more than one of the arbitrations and, if so, whether the same or different persons have been confirmed or appointed.

When arbitrations are consolidated, they shall be consolidated into the arbitration that commenced first, unless otherwise agreed by all parties."

What has changed is the wording of scenario *(c)*, that is, consolidation of arbitrations other than "under the same arbitration agreement" (scenario *b*). In the 2012/2017 version, scenario *(c)* applied where the claims were made "under more than one arbitration agreement", whereas in the 2021 version this scenario applies when the claims "are not made under the same arbitration agreement or agreements". This draws a clearer limit between scenarios *(b)* and *(c)*: scenario *(b)* covers arbitrations based on "the same arbitration agreement", whereas scenario *(c)* covers the rest: arbitrations "not" based on the "same arbitration agreement". This makes more logical sense as two arbitration agreements could conceptually be "the same" and "more than one" simultaneously if they are included in separate contracts, making it difficult to ascertain what scenario would apply under the circumstances.

How could the ICC rules be further improved? There could be further guidelines on what makes two arbitration clauses "compatible". For example, different seats, languages, numbers of arbitrators and versions of the rules could be taken into account. Additionally, the ICC Court could have the power, on an opt-out basis, to change one or more of the arbitration clauses to enable consolidation where necessary, such as changing the seat, number of arbitrators or language. For example, if one arbitration is seated in Paris and the other in Amsterdam, the ICC Court could decide to consolidate the case in either Paris or Amsterdam depending on multiple factors, such as which one was brought first, what is the main dispute, which of the two would be more neutral and efficient, and so on. This could not be objected to on the basis of consent or party autonomy, as parties would be subscribing to this regime *ex ante* when agreeing to the ICC Rules in their contract without opting out thereof.

The new 2021 Expedited Procedure Rules already allow the ICC Court to appoint a sole arbitrator regardless of what the arbitration clause says, providing a precedent for such a regime. Appendix VI, Article 2 of the Expedited Procedure Rules provide that "the Court may, notwithstanding any contrary provision of the arbitration agreement, appoint a sole arbitrator". If the ICC Court can amend the arbitration agreement for the sake of efficiency, why should it not have the power to do so even where higher-ranking values than efficiency are at stake, such as avoiding contradictory decisions and erosion of confidence in the system? The number of arbitrators, language and seat could be amended for consolidation, with a caveat that the ICC Court should ensure that this does not result in manifest unfairness or injustice in the circumstances of the case.

The LCIA Arbitration Rules have undergone changes over time, similar to those seen in the ICC Rules. Three versions of the rules have been applicable during the same period: the 1998, 2014 and 2020 versions.

The 1998 version of the rules did not include any provisions on consolidation. However, it did allow for joinder under Article 22 (1) *(h)*, which authorised the arbitral tribunal

> "to allow, only upon the application of a party, one or more third persons to be joined in the arbitration as a party provided any such third person and the applicant party have consented thereto in writing, and thereafter to make a single final award, or separate awards, in respect of all parties so implicated in the arbitration".

Joinder could therefore be ordered by the tribunal against the will of the non-applying party, but it required the consent of the third party that was to be joined.

The 2014 version of the LCIA Rules marked a significant improvement, similar to the 2012 ICC Rules. The arbitral tribunal and the LCIA Court were recognised as having the power to consolidate two or more arbitrations under certain circumstances. Additionally, the joinder provision in Article 22 was amended thus:

"22.1 The Arbitral Tribunal shall have the power, upon the application of any party or...upon its own initiative, but in either case only after giving the parties a reasonable opportunity to state their views and upon such terms (as to costs and otherwise) as the Arbitral Tribunal may decide:

. . .

(viii) to allow one or more third persons to be joined in the arbitration as a party provided any such third person and the applicant party have consented to such joinder in writing following the Commencement Date or (if earlier) in the Arbitration Agreement; and thereafter to make a single final award, or separate awards, in respect of all parties so implicated in the arbitration;

(ix) to order, with the approval of the LCIA Court, the consolidation of the arbitration with one or more other arbitrations into a single arbitration subject to the LCIA Rules where all the parties to the arbitrations to be consolidated so agree in writing;

(x) to order, with the approval of the LCIA Court, the consolidation of the arbitration with one or more other arbitrations subject to the LCIA Rules commenced under the same arbitration agreement or any compatible arbitration agreement(s) between the same disputing parties, provided that no arbitral tribunal has yet been formed by the LCIA Court for such other arbitration(s) or, if already formed, that such tribunal(s) is(are) composed of the same arbitrators;

. . .

22.6 Without prejudice to the generality of Articles 22.1 *(ix)* and *(x)*, the LCIA Court may determine, after giving the parties a reasonable opportunity to state their views, that two or more arbitrations, subject to the LCIA Rules and commenced under the same arbitration agreement between the same disputing parties, shall be consolidated to form one single arbitration subject to the LCIA Rules, provided that no arbitral tribunal has yet been formed by the LCIA Court for any of the arbitrations to be consolidated."

Article 22.1 *(ix)* thus mirrors Article 10 *(a)* of the ICC Rules, and 22.1 *(x)* mirrors Articles 10 *(b)* and *(c)*, encompassing two scenarios in the same provision: consolidation based on the "same arbitration" agreement and consolidation based on a "compatible" arbitration agreement.

The 2020 version of the LCIA Rules went further, featuring a separate provision solely dedicated to consolidation and concurrent proceedings:

> "Article 22A Power to Order Consolidation/Concurrent Conduct of Arbitrations
>
> 22.7 The Arbitral Tribunal shall have the power to order with the approval of the LCIA Court, upon the application of any party, after giving all affected parties a reasonable opportunity to state their views and upon such terms (as to costs and otherwise) as the Arbitral Tribunal may decide:
>
> *(i)* the consolidation of the arbitration with one or more other arbitrations into a single arbitration subject to the LCIA Rules where all the parties to the arbitrations to be consolidated so agree in writing;
> *(ii)* the consolidation of the arbitration with one or more other arbitrations subject to the LCIA Rules and commenced under the same arbitration agreement or any compatible arbitration agreement(s) and either between the same disputing parties or arising out of the same transaction or series of related transactions, provided that no arbitral tribunal has yet been formed by the LCIA Court for such other arbitration(s) or, if already formed, that such arbitral tribunal(s) is(are) composed of the same arbitrators; and
> *(iii)* that two or more arbitrations, subject to the LCIA Rules and commenced under the same arbitration agreement or any compatible arbitration agreement(s) and either between the same disputing parties or arising out of the same transaction or series of related transactions, shall be conducted concurrently where the same arbitral tribunal is constituted in respect of each arbitration.

22.8 Without prejudice to the generality of Article 22.7, the LCIA Court may:
  (i) consolidate an arbitration with one or more other arbitrations into a single arbitration subject to the LCIA Rules where all the parties to the arbitrations to be consolidated so agree in writing; and
  (ii) determine, after giving the parties a reasonable opportunity to state their views, that two or more arbitrations, subject to the LCIA Rules and commenced under the same arbitration agreement or any compatible arbitration agreement(s) and either between the same disputing parties or arising out of the same transaction or series of related transactions, shall be consolidated to form one single arbitration subject to the LCIA Rules, provided that no arbitral tribunal has yet been formed by the LCIA Court for any of the arbitrations to be consolidated."

The 2020 LCIA Rules thus introduce an important development: consolidation can be ordered not just between "the same disputing parties" but also when the arbitrations arise out "of the same transaction or series of related transaction", therefore significantly expanding the scope of possible consolidation.

Article 22.7 *(iii)* also proposes a solution absent from any version of the ICC Rules or in any previous version of the LCIA Rules: the possibility that the same tribunal may hear two or more arbitrations concurrently: this will usually mean the same procedural calendar for written submissions and hearings in the arbitrations, but two separate awards. The procedure is coordinated but the arbitrations remain legally distinct.

It is likely that future versions of arbitration rules worldwide will adopt the approach taken by the latest editions of the ICC and LCIA rules. This trend represents a positive development, as it enables the inclusion of specific provisions regarding consolidation of arbitrations within the institutional framework, which records the parties' *ex ante* consent to consolidation one level up from the specific arbitration clause in their contract, thus opening the door to the possibility of consolidating disputes submitted to the same institution. To be bound by this *ex ante* consent to consolidation, the parties need not be parties to the same arbitration clauses; it suffices that they have agreed in some form or another, and that could be in different contracts, to the application of the relevant institutional rules.

However, this solution has its limitations, especially in cases where disputes involve arbitration clauses that refer to different institutions, such as ICC and LCIA, or LCIA and SIAC. In such situations, there is a risk of legal uncertainty, as each institution may seek to consolidate disputes under its own rules, which may result in turf wars similar to those that arose between the ICC and SIAC after the Singapore Court of Appeal's 2009 decision in *Insigma* v. *Alstom*, which validated a hybrid clause that provided for arbitration under the ICC Rules but was managed by SIAC rather than the ICC Court [146].

2. SIAC Consolidation Protocol

What can be done to deal with such situations? SIAC has proposed a creative solution to the problem in the form of a cross-institution Consolidation Protocol designed to address it. Although it has not yet been implemented, it is still being promoted and as a welcome and worthy effort to design a system capable of consolidating related disputes arising under different arbitration rules.

The Consolidation Protocol identifies the nature of the problem and the benefits of the protocol thus:

> "5. The lack of any existing mechanism for "cross-institution" consolidation of arbitrations subject to different institutional arbitration rules substantially limits the types of disputes that can be consolidated. In many cases, related contracts in a single project or set of transactions will contain agreements to arbitrate under different institutional arbitration rules (e.g., SIAC and ICC) – which, as already noted, cannot be consolidated together. In turn, this prevents related disputes, which otherwise meet the criteria for consolidation, from being heard together and thus limits the ability of arbitration as a dispute resolution mechanism from serving the needs of users. Although there is very limited statistical data on how frequently related disputes arise under different institutional rules, anecdotal evidence suggests that this is not an uncommon occurrence. This is unsurprising given the increasingly complex nature of contemporary business transactions.
>
> 6. This shortcoming in the existing treatment of consolidation by arbitral institutions can be remedied through institutional cooperation. In particular, as discussed below, the efficiency and

---

146. *Insigma Technology Co Ltd.* v. *Alstom Technology Ltd.*, [2009] SGCA 24.

efficacy of the international arbitral process would be materially improved by the adoption of a consolidation protocol by leading arbitral institutions, providing for the cross-institution consolidation of arbitrations, where such proceedings otherwise satisfy the criteria for consolidation."

The Consolidation Protocols sets a basic framework to answer two key questions in the event of consolidation in a cross-institution scenario. The first question is *who* decides whether to consolidate two arbitrations subject to different arbitration rules. The Protocol considers two options: a joint committee of the institutions involved or just one of the institutions – to be selected according to objective criteria. The best option, according to the Protocol, is for a joint committee to decide the question of consolidation based on joint criteria:

> "[A]rbitral institutions could adopt a consolidation protocol that sets out a new, standalone mechanism for addressing the timing of consolidation applications, the appropriate decision-maker (i.e. the institution(s) or the tribunal) and the applicable criteria to determine when arbitral proceedings are sufficiently related to warrant cross-institution consolidation. A joint committee appointed from members of the Courts or Boards of the concerned arbitral institutions would be mandated to decide the applications, with a specific committee being appointed for each application.
>
> [B]oth institutions play a role in deciding whether the standards for consolidation have been met and whether the proceedings should be consolidated. New consolidation rules will also avoid the need for either institution to interpret the rules of the other. From a process perspective, it is unlikely to be arduous for the institutions to reach agreement on a consolidation protocol given the relatively limited number of issues that arise in relation to consolidation."

The Consolidation Protocol also flags five "key issues" that it must address, including the identity of a decision-maker for decisions regarding consolidation, standards for consolidation of arbitrations, timing of the application and status of existing tribunal appointments, partial consolidation, and reasons for consolidation decisions.

The second question is *who* administers the consolidated case once the decision to consolidate has been made. Here again, there are two options: the new consolidated arbitration will be either "jointly administered" or will be administered by "only one institution . . . under its own rules". SIAC considers that the better option, for practical purposes, is for only one institution to administer the case since it is easier and less expensive than two institutions jointly administering the case under new joint arbitral rules.

But how to choose which arbitral institution would administer the case? The Consolidation Protocol proposes objective criteria for selecting the administering institution, including the number of cases to be consolidated and the aggregate value of disputes. The Protocol considers the criteria of time, subject matter, and nationality and domicile of the parties to be "unattractive" and "unappealing".

The Consolidation Protocol is a welcome and worthy effort to design a system capable of consolidating related disputes that meet the criteria for consolidation. It proposes a framework for addressing key questions related to cross-institutional consolidation, including who decides whether to consolidate and who administers the consolidated case. By providing a solution to the problem of cross-institutional consolidation, the Protocol has the potential to improve the efficiency and efficacy of the international arbitral process.

3. Recording ex ante *consent within national legislation?*

Before concluding our discussion of consolidation and joinder, it is worth considering whether national court legislation can do more to facilitate these procedures. As we saw in Chapter III, the Swiss Federal Tribunal ordered the consolidation of related arbitrations in *Andersen Consulting Business* v. *Arthur Andersen Business*, despite differences in the wording and type of arbitration clauses involved, with some referring to the ICC and others being *ad hoc* (i.e. non-institutional) clauses [147].

To promote consolidation and joinder further, more States could follow the lead of New Zealand and Mauritius by empowering their national courts to order these procedures within their jurisdiction. Mauritius, for example, has provisions in its legislation (see Articles 3 and 4 of the First Schedule to the Mauritanian Act) that allow for consolidation and joinder, although they only apply if the parties have specifically opted into them. Article 3 is a lengthy provision that deals with the mechanics of consolidation, while Article 4 is a short provision

---

147. See note 99.

empowering the court to order joinder where the party sought to be joined has agreed to in writing (which may be by way of an arbitration agreement).

However, one should not overestimate the impact of national court legislation in this regard. First, such provisions will not be effective if the proceedings being consolidated have their seats in different jurisdictions. This issue could be addressed through an inter-State protocol, perhaps part of a wider protocol annexed to the New York Convention, but this is not a realistic scenario. Second, the experience in Mauritius suggests that parties may not have much interest in opting into these provisions. Therefore, institutional rules remain the more promising avenue for facilitating consolidation and joinder, which could ideally be supplemented by some form of the SIAC Protocol in the future.

4. Res judicata *and* lis pendens, *a greater role for abuse of process?*

Turning now to the way forward in commercial arbitration, we must consider whether more can be done with regard to the doctrines of *res judicata* and *lis pendens*. As we have seen, the narrow application of *res judicata*, due to the strict triple-identity test, means it will rarely be satisfied in practice. *Lis pendens*, on the other hand, could be more widely applied as a matter of discretionary case management, particularly in cases where proceedings cover related but not identical issues, similar to the regime under the Brussels Regulation.

However, the most significant recent development has been the increased role of the doctrine of abuse of process, particularly in Anglo Saxon jurisdictions. It is a promising development, one to approach with caution, in that it operates separately from *res judicata* and issue estoppel in a way with relaxes the strictures of the triple-identity test. It protects litigants from having to defend the same issue twice, even where the parties are not identical, and debars a litigant from pursuing in fresh proceedings claims which they ought to have brought but failed to bring in previous proceedings.

We examined the example of England in Chapter III, where the Court of Appeal unequivocally confirmed the application of the doctrine to arbitral awards. However, difficulties remain. First, what of the use of the doctrine by a later tribunal, as opposed to a court? Can a tribunal refuse to adjudicate a claim submitted to it in circumstances where *res judicata* and issue estoppel do not formally apply, but it is argued that pursuing the claim would engage one of the two scenarios mentioned above (protection from repeated defence of the same issue and claims by instalment)? Second, practical difficulties exist for a later tribunal trying to access or use the findings of an earlier tribunal.

The first issue may be resolved through jurisprudential developments, as the law seems to be moving towards greater acceptance of the use of the abuse of process doctrine. The second issue could also resolved judicially given that the confidentiality of commercial arbitration and the exceptions thereto are often dealt with in case law rather than statute. This is part of a wider debate as to the continued place of confidentiality in commercial arbitration.

C. Investment arbitration

Finally, let's delve into investment arbitration and the possible solutions to address its challenges. Investment arbitration poses new, significant challenges related to parallel proceedings that have been persisting for almost two decades. As mentioned in Chapter IV, investment arbitration is fertile ground for parallel proceedings for several reasons, including the dual contract and treaty substratum of investment claims, the issue of vertical claims, and waves of claims stemming from the same State measure.

This issue, along with its implications for the coherence and consistency of the ISDS system, is a central symptom of the so-called "crisis of legitimacy" that has plagued ISDS for several years. This term describes the increasing lack of confidence that those outside the ISDS system, and a few inside it, have in the system. This situation has prompted concrete action, notably UNCITRAL's work in the field of transparency, which I had the privilege to chair. The following three points can be drawn from UNCITRAL's work.

First, the way in which UNCITRAL began its work in this area is instructive. The transparency project was not a topic calmly picked by the Commission for future work, but was brought to the fore forcefully by certain States, NGOs and the UN Special Representative for Business and Human Rights, Professor John Ruggie, during UNCITRAL's work on what became the UNCITRAL Rules 2010. Consequently, the Commission had to agree to undertake immediate work in the area with a specific focus on ISDS in order to preserve the integrity of the UNCITRAL Rules as a set of universal rules applicable to both commercial and investor-State arbitration. Interestingly, many arbitration practitioners rejected the NGOs and Professor Ruggie's call for reform, most notably the Milan Club of Arbitrators' in a written submission. See UNCITRAL working Group 2's Report on the work of its 48th Session (New York, 4-8 February 2008), Doc. A/cn.9/646 at p. 21 (accessible on the UNCITRAL website).

Second, the transparency project concluded through a creative mechanism, a multilateral convention (the Mauritius Convention), which relies on the provision of Article 30 of the Vienna Convention on the Law of Treaties to effect overall procedural reform affecting all existing investment treaties. This provides a possible way forward for wider procedural reform beyond transparency.

Third, following UNCITRAL's work, the calls for wider procedural reform have become louder, and it has become increasingly clear in that forum that meaningful reform of the current, arbitration-based ISDS system is necessary. While some contend that much of the criticism levelled at the system is unfounded, two points appear difficult to ignore. First, those within the system have done little to reform the system. As a result, many States believe that sovereign States themselves, and not internal actors, should reform the system to retain its principal attributes, including neutrality [148], while addressing its perceived problems. Second, whether those problems are real or perceived matters little, as ISDS has become, a staple feature of mainstream news outlets such as the *New York Times*, *Le Monde*, *The Guardian* and *The London Times*, and always for the wrong reasons: so that a mechanism which was meant to depoliticise the settlement of disputes between investors and States has itself become highly politicised; and is thus now arguably hindering rather than fostering trade and investment flows, as States that would welcome such flows run scaned of the real or perceived legal sister that are now associated with them.

This clearly calls for reforms. The question is how far those should go. As UNCITRAL has been debating that question over the past three years, it has clearly emerged that the main area of concern arises from the very nature of the current – arbitration-based – system: because that system relies on the ad hoc resolution of disputes by one-off panels,

---

148. See, in particular, G. Kaufmann-Kohler and M. Potesta, "Can the Mauritius Convention Serve as a Model for the Reform of Investor-State Arbitration in Connection with the Introduction of a Permanent Investment Tribunal or an Appeal Mechanism? Analysis and Roadmap, https://papers.ssrn.com/sol3/papers.cfm?abstract_id=3455511; Kaufmann-Kohler and Potesta, "The Composition of a Multilateral Investment Court and of an Appeal Mechanism for Investment Awards", https://papers.ssrn.com/sol3/papers.cfm?abstract_id=3457310.

fragmentation, and a resulting lack of coherence and of consistency of solutions, are hard-wired in the system. That problem is exacerbated by the attitude of some, though not all, arbitrators who still come to this field with a commercial arbitrator's mindset and thus do not see themselves as being under a duty to uphold the systemic integrity of the system. Rather, they understand their duty as being limited to resolving the particular dispute which has been brought before them by these particular parties, in line with the words of Mance LJ (as he then was) in Lincoln as to what is expected of commercial arbitrators [149].

The symptoms of that fragmentation are well known and our subject, the problem of parallel or concurrent related proceedings, is one such key symptom. Despite numerous calls for action, and some creative solutions devised inter alia by Professor Kaufmann-Koher based on abuse of process, they continue to plague the field.

Another related symptom is that while some tribunals – again and unfortunately not all tribunals – do strive to develop harmonised legal standards, the lack of any system of binding precedent, or of any mechanism to resolve conflicting authorities, continues to prevent the emergence of legal clarity – thus enhancing the risk of inconsistency arising from parallel proceedings. The examples often referred to are the interpretation of MFN clauses or of umbrella clauses. But the problem is more fundamental. For it remains the case that for every treaty standard, FET, FPS, expropriation, Counsel on both sides of the dispute feel duty-bound to take every possible point – however tenuous – on the off-chance that this particular panel of arbitrators, the writings of which have been analysed prior to appointment, will reach a solution favourable to their side. That is not an efficient system of dispute resolution. Parties in contractual proceedings before domestic courts do not spend days arguing, in every single contractual case, on what 'consideration' means if they are in England or on the notion of vice du consentement if they are in France. The meaning of these notions has long been settled by the superior courts of that country, and the debate focuses on their application to the facts of the case in light of the specific language used in the contract in question. There is similarly no reason why one could not have settled principles governing the meaning of

---

149. *Lincoln National Life Insurance Co v. Sun Life Assurance Co of Canada* [2004] EWCA Civ. 1660, at para. 68 *("The arbitrators in each arbitration are appointed to decide the disputes in that arbitration between the particular parties to that arbitration.")*.

FET or FPS, always subject of course to the specific language used in the specific treaty.

The question is thus no longer whether the ISDS system should be reformed, but rather how and how far. For some the fact that these problems are systemic means that systemic solutions are required; and that no amount of incremental change will suffice. Others argue for a retention of the current system but with meaningful 'incremental' changes. These two ways forward are not antithetic, at least not in the short or medium term, as any systemic solution would take time to devise and implement. The path chosen by UNCITRAL has accordingly been to work in parallel both on incremental and systemic reform. The following sections will explore the possible reform options concerning or affecting parallel proceedings.

1. Incremental reform

Starting with incremental reform, which refers to changes to the existing system of arbitration-based ISDS that preserve the system, there are two notable areas to consider. In addition, as with commercial arbitration, it is worth examining whether there is potential for a wider role for the doctrine of abuse of process.

The first area of incremental reform involves the possibility of a straightforward yet potentially effective "soft law" instrument. This would come in the form of a declaration by the UN General Assembly (UNGA), similar to the interpretative declarations it made regarding the New York Convention in 2006. This could be accompanied by a "toolbox" for parties and arbitrators, providing guidance on how to apply the soft law instrument.

The second possibility is that of a cross-institution consolidation protocol, similar to the one being promoted by SIAC in the commercial arbitration field. This protocol would aim to consolidate parallel proceedings, thereby reducing the risk of inconsistent outcomes.

Soft law on parallel proceedings

The first possible tool for incremental reform would be a soft law instrument formally highlights the differences between commercial arbitration and investment arbitration and providing a "toolbox" of strategies that parties and tribunals could use to coordinate parallel proceedings and minimise the risk of inconsistencies between them.

The usefulness of such an instrument lies in how the ISDS system was created and developed. While arbitration has a long pedigree as a form of dispute settlement in the public international law arena, the fact is that investment arbitration had largely borrowed from commercial arbitration in terms of procedure and personnel. As a result, practitioners in the field, including arbitrators and counsel, often approach investment arbitration with the reflexes and instincts of a commercial practitioner: to serve the parties and resolve the dispute without any duty to the ISDS system as a whole or any other interests. This can lead to a narrow focus on the specific interests of the parties before them and a reluctance to share information or coordinate with other tribunals.

However, it is now beyond doubt that investment arbitration is fundamentally different from commercial arbitration, and arbitrators have a duty to go beyond the specific interests of the parties before them and consider the systemic implications of their decisions and the impact of their work on other parallel proceedings and the integrity of the system as a whole. This duty was central to UNCITRAL's transparency rules, which encourage tribunals to recognise the legitimacy of amicus curiae briefs, consider the views of third parties and hold public hearings. This remains the clear consensus of UNCITRAL States and forms the basis of current efforts to reform the ISDS system. By articulating this difference and calling on tribunals to have regard to the systemic implications of their decisions, a soft law instrument could help to facilitate coordination between proceedings and promote consistency in investment arbitration.

When considering the form such a soft law instrument might take, one might look for inspiration to the International Bar Association ("IBA"), whose soft law instruments have been regularly and successfully applied in a number of areas in the daily practice of international arbitration. These include the IBA guidelines on conflicts of interest, on party representation, and on the taking of evidence. While such guidelines are not binding, they are often treated as persuasive and authoritative by tribunals and parties due to their reflection of consensus. However, considering the current work taking place in UNCITRAL and the disconnect between practitioners (who would drive any reform effort in fora such as the IBA) and the States that created the ISDS system, a more appropriate format would be a UNGA declaration similar to those made with respect to the interpretation of Article II and VII of the New York Convention in 2006. Such a recommendation would carry significant weight and be difficult to ignore even by the most commercial arbitration minded tribunals.

Parallel Proceedings in International Arbitration 301

In terms of content, the recommendation could include three elements. First, a formal acknowledgement of the systemic difference between investment arbitration and commercial arbitration, recognising the unique nature of investment arbitration and empowering tribunals to consider the systemic implications of their decisions without fear of overstepping their role. This is particularly important in the area of parallel proceedings, where so much depends on taking into account what may transpire outside the specific proceedings before the arbitral tribunal. Second, the recommendation could recognise a specific duty for investment tribunals to make their best efforts to coordinate related arbitrations, whether at the request of a party or of their own accord. This recognition would provide a basis for parties and their counsel to apply for coordination of proceedings with other arbitrations. Third, the recommendation could include a procedural "toolbox" with specific actions that parties and tribunals can take to fulfil the duty of best efforts.

These actions could include, first, sharing information about related proceedings, either through the Mauritius transparency regime or on a tribunal-to-tribunal basis. This would range from information such as the status of the arbitration, the procedural calendar, and so on, to full exchange of relevant evidence and submissions (for instance, to avoid inconsistent cases being made by the same or related parties). A second action might be to include the informal coordination of proceedings in terms of briefings, production of evidence, hearings, and so on. Third, tribunals could conduct concurrent hearings, which could be particularly helpful in cases where there are waves of claims against States over the same measures and facts. A fourth measure might be the aggregation of claims. The goal here would be to avoid parallel proceedings from the outset by providing guidance on when claims can be aggregated into a single case. For instance, when the claims arise from the same BIT and are based on the same State measure, aggregation should be possible (we saw the example of three Argentina mass claims cases in Chap. IV). Claims might also be aggregated where the claims are based on different but "compatible" BITs (in language reminiscent of that used for consolidation). Finally, tribunals may consider partial or full consolidation.

Cross-institution consolidation protocol

Moving on to the second potential option for incremental reform, the idea of a cross-institution consolidation protocol has already been discussed in the context of commercial arbitration with the SIAC proposal. Given space constraints, I will not delve into that topic again. I would simply note the following points.

First, all major institutions are currently participating in the UNCITRAL reform work and collaborating with the UNCITRAL Secretariat, providing hope that a consolidation protocol can be developed and agreed upon in the field of investment arbitration.

Second, attempting to include consolidation provisions solely within the rules of a single institution (whether it be ICSID, UNCITRAL or the PCA) would likely be ineffective in the realm of investment arbitration. This is because most BITs provide investors with various options for accessing investment arbitration. As a result, investors looking to avoid consolidation could simply select different rules for each claim they file (e.g. ICSID for one, UNCITRAL for another and the Stockholm Chamber of Commerce for a third).

Lastly, any protocol that focuses solely on institutions that handle investment arbitration may not address all issues, as there are often related commercial arbitrations that must be taken into account. Nor does the SIAC Protocol appear easy to transpose into the investment arbitration field without adaptation, making the possibility or developing a single protocol that addresses both commercial and investment arbitration unrealistic.

Abuse of process doctrine

Lastly with regards to incremental developments, the abuse of process doctrine may have a growing role in addressing the challenges in investment arbitration, for similar reasons to its role in commercial arbitration. We have already seen a notable example in *Orascom* v. *Algeria*[150], where the doctrine was utilised to address the issue of vertical claims. This doctrine may further evolve to address issues that the classic doctrines of *res judicata* and issue estoppel cannot tackle. However, it should be noted that the use of the doctrine of abuse of process by tribunals, as seen in the *Orascom* decision, has been criticised by some for interfering with investors' rights to access ISDS. The validity of that criticism may be open to doubt given that the doctrine of abuse of rights operates precisely where a right (such as the right to access ISDS) would otherwise exist but is being abused.

---

150. *Orascom* Final Award (31 May 2017), note 133.

Nonetheless, it is important to acknowledge that this development remains controversial.

2. Systemic reform

The premise for the proponents of such reform is that the reason why the current system is so fragmented is no random occurrence, but arises out of its very nature which necessarily gives rise to a patchwork of independent tribunals created ad hoc to resolve each dispute as it arises. As a result, no amount of incremental changes can bring to this system the degree of coherence and consistency which any legitimate system of dispute resolution requires. Put differently, the problems that arise are systemic and require a systemic change.

As to the form which this systemic reform should take, the main solution which is being canvassed at UNCITRAL is that of a multilateral court with a built-in appeal mechanism which would finally resolve and settle conflicts of authorities. Such a court would in particular have the power to consolidate its proceedings and join parties, as any court does, and produce judgments with res judicata effect (at appellate level if required), which will have an impact not only on directly related claims (e.g. vertical claims) but potentially on other claims arising from the same measure or from similar facts. There is significant political support for such a solution from developing States and from the EU, and significant opposition to it from other States, and it is premature to try and fathom what exact shape it will end up taking.

Much of the resistance to the possible creation of such a permanent court system has been on the basis that while it may theoretically resolve or alleviate many issues in this field, including that of parallel proceedings – it is bound to result in a system which will lack neutrality because it is being created by States and will thus favour States. That is not a premise which can be accepted at face value: the current ISDS system (which the same critics argue for) was itself created by States. Further, where the case for systemic reform is otherwise clear, it cannot be assumed that means cannot be found to ensure that the new court system is devised in a way which will deliver the benefits of a coherent system while preserving neutrality.

UNCITRAL is currently tasked with finding a way to establish a new court system that delivers the benefits of a coherent system while preserving neutrality. This task may hold the answer to many of the questions raised throughout this lecture.

PUBLICATIONS DE L'ACADÉMIE
DE DROIT INTERNATIONAL
DE LA HAYE

PUBLICATIONS OF THE
HAGUE ACADEMY OF INTERNATIONAL
LAW

RECUEIL DES COURS Depuis 1923, les plus grands noms du droit international ont professé à l'Académie de droit international de La Haye. Tous les tomes du *Recueil* qui ont été publiés depuis cette date sont disponibles, chaque tome étant, depuis les tout premiers, régulièrement réimprimé sous sa forme originale.
Depuis 2008, certains cours font l'objet d'une édition en livres de poche.
En outre, toute la collection existe en version électronique. Tous les ouvrages parus à ce jour ont été mis en ligne et peuvent être consultés moyennant un des abonnements proposés, qui offrent un éventail de tarifs et de possibilités.

INDEX A ce jour, il a paru sept index généraux. Ils couvrent les tomes suivants :

1 à 101	(1923-1960)	379 pages	ISBN 978-90-218-9948-0
102 à 125	(1961-1968)	204 pages	ISBN 978-90-286-0643-2
126 à 151	(1969-1976)	280 pages	ISBN 978-90-286-0630-2
152 à 178	(1976-1982)	416 pages	ISBN 978-0-7923-2955-8
179 à 200	(1983-1986)	260 pages	ISBN 978-90-411-0110-5
201 à 250	(1987-1994)	448 pages	ISBN 978-90-04-13700-4
251 à 300	(1995-2002)	580 pages	ISBN 978-90-04-15387-7

A partir du tome 210 il a été décidé de publier un index complet qui couvrira chaque fois dix tomes du *Recueil des cours*. Le dernier index paru couvre les tomes suivants :
311 à 320   (2004-2006)   392 pages   Tome 320A   ISBN 978-90-04-19695-7

COLLOQUES L'Académie organise également des colloques dont les débats sont publiés. Les derniers volumes parus de ces colloques portent les titres suivants : *Le règlement pacifique des différends internationaux en Europe : perspectives d'avenir* (1990) ; *Le développement du rôle du Conseil de sécurité* (1992) ; *La Convention sur l'interdiction et l'élimination des armes chimiques : une percée dans l'entreprise multilatérale du désarmement* (1994) ; *Actualité de la Conférence de La Haye de 1907, Deuxième Conférence de la Paix* (2007).

CENTRE D'ÉTUDE ET DE RECHERCHE Les travaux scientifiques du Centre d'étude et de recherche de droit international et de relations internationales de l'Académie de droit international de La Haye, dont les sujets sont choisis par le Curatorium de l'Académie, faisaient l'objet, depuis la session de 1985, d'une publication dans laquelle les directeurs d'études dressaient le bilan des recherches du Centre qu'ils avaient dirigé. Cette série a été arrêtée et la dernière brochure parue porte le titre suivant : *Les règles et les institutions du droit international humanitaire à l'épreuve des conflits armés récents*. Néanmoins, lorsque les travaux du Centre se révèlent particulièrement intéressants et originaux, les rapports des directeurs et les articles rédigés par les chercheurs font l'objet d'un ouvrage collectif.

Les demandes de renseignements ou de catalogues et les commandes doivent être adressées à
MARTINUS NIJHOFF PUBLISHERS
B.P. 9000, 2300 PA Leyde   Pays-Bas   http://www.brill.nl

COLLECTED COURSES Since 1923 the top names in international law have taught at The Hague Academy of International Law. All the volumes of the *Collected Courses* which have been published since 1923 are available, as, since the very first volume, they are reprinted regularly in their original format.

Since 2008, certain courses have been the subject of a pocketbook edition.

In addition, the total collection now exists in electronic form. All works already published have been put "on line" and can be consulted under one of the proposed subscription methods, which offer a range of tariffs and possibilities.

INDEXES Up till now seven General Indexes have been published. They cover the following volumes:

1 to 101	(1923-1960)	379 pages	ISBN 978-90-218-9948-0
102 to 125	(1961-1968)	204 pages	ISBN 978-90-286-0643-2
126 to 151	(1969-1976)	280 pages	ISBN 978-90-286-0630-2
152 to 178	(1976-1982)	416 pages	ISBN 978-0-7923-2955-8
179 to 200	(1983-1986)	260 pages	ISBN 978-90-411-0110-5
201 to 250	(1987-1994)	448 pages	ISBN 978-90-04-13700-4
251 to 300	(1995-2002)	580 pages	ISBN 978-90-04-15387-7

From Volume 210 onwards it has been decided to publish a full index covering, each time, ten volumes of the *Collected Courses*. The latest Index published covers the following volumes:
311 to 320 (2004-2006) 392 pages Volume 320A ISBN 978-90-04-19695-7

WORKSHOPS The Academy publishes the discussions from the Workshops which it organises. The latest titles of the Workshops already published are as follows: *The Peaceful Settlement of International Disputes in Europe: Future Prospects* (1990); *The Development of the Role of the Security Council* (1992); *The Convention on the Prohibition and Elimination of Chemical Weapons: A Breakthrough in Multilateral Disarmament* (1994); *Topicality of the 1907 Hague Conference, the Second Peace Conference* (2007).

CENTRE FOR STUDIES AND RESEARCH The scientific works of the Centre for Studies and Research in International Law and International Relations of The Hague Academy of International Law, the subjects of which are chosen by the Curatorium of the Academy, have been published, since the Centre's 1985 session, in a publication in which the Directors of Studies reported on the state of research of the Centre under their direction. This series has been discontinued and the title of the latest booklet published is as follows: *Rules and Institutions of International Humanitarian Law Put to the Test of Recent Armed Conflicts*. Nevertheless, when the work of the Centre has been of particular interest and originality, the reports of the Directors of Studies together with the articles by the researchers form the subject of a collection published by the Academy.

Requests for information, catalogues and orders for publications must be addressed to

MARTINUS NIJHOFF PUBLISHERS

P.O. Box 9000, 2300 PA Leiden   The Netherlands   **http://www.brill.nl**

TABLE PAR TOME DES COURS PUBLIÉS CES DERNIÈRES ANNÉES

INDEX BY VOLUME OF THE COURSES PUBLISHED THESE LAST YEARS

Tome/Volume 256 (1995)

Goldblat, J.: The Nuclear Non-Proliferation Régime: Assessment and Prospects, 9-192.
Torres-Bernárdez, S.: L'intervention dans la procédure de la Cour internationale de Justice, 193-458.

(ISBN 978-90-411-0420-5)

Tome/Volume 257 (1996)

Bedjaoui, M.: Le cinquantième anniversaire de la Cour internationale de Justice (communication), 9-34.
Carrillo-Salcedo, J.-A.: Droit international et souveraineté des Etats. Cours général de droit international public, 35-222.
De Boer, Th. M.: Facultative Choice of Law: The Procedural Status of Choice-of-Law Rules and Foreign Law, 223-428.

(ISBN 978-90-411-0440-3)

Tome/Volume 258 (1996)

Reisman, W. M.: The Supervisory Jurisdiction of the International Court of Justice: International Arbitration and International Adjudication, 9-394.

(ISBN 978-90-411-0441-0)

Tome/Volume 259 (1996)

Kreuzer, K.: La propriété mobilière en droit international privé, 9-318.
Voulgaris, I.: Le crédit-bail (leasing) et les institutions analogues en droit international privé, 319-412.

(ISBN 978-90-411-0529-5)

Tome/Volume 260 (1996)

McClean, J. D.: A Common Inheritance? An Examination of the Private International Law of the Commonwealth, 9-98.
McRae, D. M.: The Contribution of International Trade Law to the Development of International Law, 99-238.
Francioni, F.: La conservation et la gestion des ressources de l'Antarctique, 239-404.

(ISBN 978-90-411-0517-2)

Tome/Volume 261 (1996)

Koh, H. H.: International Business Transactions in United States Courts, 9-242.
Pérez Vera, E.: Citoyenneté de l'Union européenne, nationalité et condition des étrangers, 243-426.

(ISBN 978-90-411-1054-1)

Tome/Volume 262 (1996)

Stern, B.: La succession d'Etats, 9-438.

(ISBN 978-90-411-1393-1)

Tome/Volume 263 (1997)

Bermann, G. A.: Regulatory Federalism: European Union and United States, 9-148.
Sánchez Rodríguez: L'*uti possidetis* et les effectivités dans les contentieux territoriaux et frontaliers, 149-382.

(ISBN 978-90-411-0539-4)

Tome/Volume 264 (1997)

Basedow, J.: Souveraineté territoriale et globalisation des marchés: le domaine d'application des lois contre les restrictions de la concurrence, 9-178.
Kerameus, K. D.: Enforcement in the International Context, 179-410.

(ISBN 978-90-411-1016-9)

Tome/Volume 265 (1997)

Rideau, J.: Le rôle de l'Union européenne en matière de protection des droits de l'homme, 9-480.

(ISBN 978-90-411-1178-4)

Tome/Volume 266 (1997)

Zemanek, K.: The Legal Foundations of the International System. General Course on Public International Law, 9-336.
Hartley, T. C.: Mandatory Rules in International Contracts: the Common Law Approach, 337-426.

(ISBN 978-90-411-0590-5)

Tome/Volume 267 (1997)

Plender, R.: Procedure in the European Courts: Comparisons and Proposals, 9-344.
Oreja Aguirre, M.: La révision institutionnelle de l'Union européenne, 345-386.

(ISBN 978-90-411-1006-0)

Tome/Volume 268 (1997)

Moulay Rchid, A.: Les droits de l'enfant dans les conventions internationales et les solutions retenues dans les pays arabo-musulmans, 9-290.
Von Bar, C.: Environmental Damage in Private International Law, 291-412.

(ISBN 978-90-411-1292-7)

Tome/Volume 269 (1997)

Damrosch, L. F.: Enforcing International Law through Non-forcible Measures, 9-250.
Sacerdoti, G.: Bilateral Treaties and Multilateral Instruments on Investment Protection, 251-460.

(ISBN 978-90-411-1111-1)

Tome/Volume 270 (1997)

Ranjeva, R.: Les organisations non gouvernementales et la mise en œuvre du droit international, 9-106.
Xu, D.: Le droit international privé en Chine: une perspective comparative, 107-236.
Matscher, F.: Quarante ans d'activités de la Cour européenne des droits de l'homme, 237-398.

(ISBN 978-90-411-1331-3)

Tome/Volume 271 (1998)

Struycken, A. V. M.: La contribution de l'Académie au développement de la science et de la pratique du droit international privé (Conférence prononcée à l'occasion du soixante-quinzième anniversaire de l'Académie), 11-56.
Skubiszewski, K.: The Contribution of the Academy to the Development of the Science and Practice of Public International Law (Address Delivered on the Occasion of the 75th Anniversary of the Academy), 57-100.
Charney, J. I.: Is International Law Threatened by Multiple International Tribunals?, 101-382.

(ISBN 978-90-411-1210-1)

Tome/Volume 272 (1998)

Wolfrum, R.: Means of Ensuring Compliance with and Enforcement of International Environmental Law, 9-154.
Mendelson, M. H.: The Formation of Customary International Law, 155-410.

(ISBN 978-90-411-1237-8)

Tome/Volume 273 (1998)

Sur, S.: Vérification en matière de désarmement, 9-102.
Caminos, H.: The Role of the Organization of American States in the Promotion and Protection of Democratic Governance, 103-238.
Ginsburg, J. C.: The Private International Law of Copyright in an Era of Technological Change, 239-406.

(ISBN 978-90-411-1251-4)

Tome/Volume 274 (1998)

Pastor Ridruejo, J. A.: Le droit international à la veille du vingt et unième siècle: normes, faits et valeurs. Cours général de droit international public, 9-308.
Carreau, D.: Le système monétaire international privé (UEM et euromarchés), 309-392.

(ISBN 978-90-411-1300-9)

Tome/Volume 275 (1998)

Elwan, O.: La loi applicable à la garantie bancaire à première demande, 9-218.
Mestral, A. de: The North American Free Trade Agreement: A Comparative Analysis, 219-416.

(ISBN 978-90-411-1486-0)

Tome/Volume 276 (1999)

Picone, P.: Les méthodes de coordination entre ordres juridiques en droit international privé. Cours général de droit international privé, 9-296.
Baxi, U.: Mass Torts, Multinational Enterprises Liability and Private International Law, 297-428.

(ISBN 978-90-411-1394-8)

Tome/Volume 277 (1999)

Verwilghen, M.: Conflits de nationalités. Plurinationalité et apatridie, 9-484.

(ISBN 978-90-411-1395-5)

Tome/Volume 278 (1999)

Barboza, J.: International Criminal Law, 9-200.
Maupain, F.: L'OIT, la justice sociale et la mondialisation, 201-396.

(ISBN 978-90-411-1396-2)

Tome/Volume 279 (1999)

Jonkman, H.: The Role of the Permanent Court of Arbitration in International Dispute Resolution (Addresses), 9-50.
Hascher, D.: Principes et pratique de procédure dans l'arbitrage commercial international, 51-194.
Degan, V.-D.: Création et disparition de l'Etat (à la lumière du démembrement de trois fédérations multiethniques en Europe), 195-376.

(ISBN 978-90-411-1397-9)

Tome/Volume 280 (1999)

Droz, G. A. L.: L'activité notariale internationale, 9-134.
Abellán Honrubia, V.: La responsabilité internationale de l'individu, 135-428.

(ISBN 978-90-411-1487-7)

Tome/Volume 281 (1999)

Tomuschat, C.: International Law: Ensuring the Survival of Mankind on the Eve of a New Century. General Course on Public International Law, 9-438.

(ISBN 978-90-411-1488-4)

Tome/Volume 282 (2000)

Jayme, E.: Le droit international privé du nouveau millénaire: la protection de la personne humaine face à la globalisation (conférence), 9-40.
McClean, D.: De Conflictu Legum. Perspectives on Private International Law at the Turn of the Century. General Course on Private International Law, 41-228.
Smith, B. L.: The Third Industrial Revolution: Law and Policy for the Internet, 229-464.

(ISBN 978-90-411-1489-1)

Tome/Volume 283 (2000)

Bucher, A.: La famille en droit international privé, 9-186.
Dolinger, J.: Evolution of Principles for Resolving Conflicts in the Field of Contracts and Torts, 187-512.

(ISBN 978-90-411-1490-7)

Tome/Volume 284 (2000)

Schlosser, P. : Jurisdiction and International Judicial and Administrative Co-operation, 9-428. (ISBN 978-90-411-1605-5)

Tome/Volume 285 (2000)

Slaughter, A.-M. : International Law and International Relations, 9-250.
Lucchini, L. : L'Etat insulaire, 251-392. (ISBN 978-90-411-1606-2)

Tome/Volume 286 (2000)

Boutros-Ghali, B. : Le droit international à la recherche de ses valeurs : paix, développement, démocratisation (conférence inaugurale), 9-38.
Scovazzi, T. : The Evolution of International Law of the Sea : New Issues, New Challenges, 39-244.
Kronke, H. : Capital Markets and Conflict of Laws, 245-386.
(ISBN 978-90-411-1607-9)

Tome/Volume 287 (2000)

González Campos, J. D. : Diversification, spécialisation, flexibilisation et matérialisation des règles de droit international privé. Cours général, 9-426.
(ISBN 978-90-411-1608-6)

Tome/Volume 288 (2001)

Kowalski, W. W. : Restitution of Works of Art pursuant to Private and Public International Law, 9-244.
Caflisch, L. : Cent ans de règlement pacifique des différends interétatiques, 245-468.
(ISBN 978-90-411-1609-3)

Tome/Volume 289 (2001)

Grigera Naón, H. A. : Choice-of-Law Problems in International Commercial Arbitration, 9-396. (ISBN 978-90-411-1610-9)

Tome/Volume 290 (2001)

Fernández Rozas, J. C. : Le rôle des juridictions étatiques devant l'arbitrage commercial international, 9-224.
Villani, U. : Les rapports entre l'ONU et les organisations régionales dans le domaine du maintien de la paix, 225-436. (ISBN 978-90-411-1611-6)

Tome/Volume 291 (2001)

Rosenne, Sh. : The Perplexities of Modern International Law. General Course on Public International Law, 9-472. (ISBN 978-90-411-1746-5)

Tome/Volume 292 (2001)

Momtaz, D. : Le droit international humanitaire applicable aux conflits armés non internationaux, 9-146.
Jacquet, J.-M. : La fonction supranationale de la règle de conflit de loi, 147-248.
Mengozzi, P. : Private International Law and the WTO Law, 249-386.
(ISBN 978-90-411-1854-7)

Tome/Volume 293 (2001)

Fitzmaurice, M. A. : International Protection of the Environment, 9-488.

(ISBN 978-90-411-1855-4)

Tome/Volume 294 (2002)

Camdessus, M. : Organisations internationales et mondialisation (conférence), 9-38.

Zoller, E. : Aspects internationaux du droit constitutionnel. Contribution à la théorie de la fédération d'Etats, 39-166.

McWhinney, E. : Self-determination of Peoples and Plural-ethnic States (Secession and State Succession and the Alternative, Federal Option), 167-264.

Thirlway, H. : Concepts, Principles, Rules and Analogies : International and Municipal Legal Reasoning, 265-406.

(ISBN 978-90-411-1856-1)

Tome/Volume 295 (2002)

Von Mehren, A. : Theory and Practice of Adjudicatory Authority in Private International Law : A Comparative Study of the Doctrine, Policies and Practices of Common- and Civil-Law Systems. General Course on Private International Law (1966), 9-432.

(ISBN 978-90-411-1857-8)

Tome/Volume 296 (2002)

Van der Stoel, M. : The Role of the OSCE High Commissioner on National Minorities in the Field of Conflict Prevention (Address), 9-24.

Hanotiau, B. : L'arbitrabilité, 25-254.

Heiskanen, V. : The United Nations Compensation Commission, 255-398.

(ISBN 978-90-411-1858-5)

Tome/Volume 297 (2002)

Dupuy, P.-M. : L'unité de l'ordre juridique international. Cours général de droit international public (2000), 9-496.

(ISBN 978-90-411-1859-2)

Tome/Volume 298 (2002)

Symeonides, S. C. : The American Choice-of-Law Revolution in the Courts : Today and Tomorrow, 9-448.

(ISBN 978-90-411-1860-8)

Tome/Volume 299 (2002)

Roucounas, E. : Facteurs privés et droit international public, 9-420.

(ISBN 978-90-411-1861-5)

Tome/Volume 300 (2002)

Bennouna, M. : Les sanctions économiques des Nations Unies, 9-78.

Kessedjian, C. : Codification du droit commercial international et droit international privé. De la gouvernance normative pour les relations économiques transnationales, 79-308.

Smits, R. : Law of the Economic and Monetary Union, 309-422.

(ISBN 978-90-411-1862-2)

Tome/Volume 301 (2003)

Meron, T. : International Law in the Age of Human Rights, 9-490.
(ISBN 978-90-04-14020-2)

Tome/Volume 302 (2003)

Black, V. : Foreign Currency Obligations in Private International Law, 9-196.
Leben, Ch. : La théorie du contrat d'Etat et l'évolution du droit international des investissements, 197-386.
(ISBN 978-90-04-14021-9)

Tome/Volume 303 (2003)

Daudet, Y. : Actualités de la codification du droit international, 9-118.
Mezghani, A. : Méthodes de droit international privé et contrat illicite, 119-430.
(ISBN 978-90-04-14022-6)

Tome/Volume 304 (2003)

Mosk, R. M. : The Role of Facts in International Dispute Revolution, 9-180.
Jänterä-Jareborg, M. : Foreign Law in National Courts : A Comparative Perspective, 181-386.
(ISBN 978-90-04-14023-3)

Tome/Volume 305 (2003)

Audit, B. : Le droit international privé en quête d'universalité. Cours général (2001), 9-488.
(ISBN 978-90-04-14307-4)

Tome/Volume 306 (2003)

Casanovas, O. : La protection internationale des réfugiés et des personnes déplacées dans les conflits armés, 9-176.
Reed, L. : Mixed Private and Public Law Solutions to International Crises, 177-410.
(ISBN 978-90-04-14545-0)

Tome/Volume 307 (2004)

Jorda, M. C. : Du Tribunal pénal international pour l'ex-Yougoslavie à la Cour pénale internationale : De quelques observations et enseignements (conférence), 9-24.
Muir Watt, H. : Aspects économiques du droit international privé (Réflexions sur l'impact de la globalisations économique sur les fondements des conflits de lois et de juridictions), 25-384.
(ISBN 978-90-04-456-7)

Tome/Volume 308 (2004)

Rigo Sureda, A. : The Law Applicable to the Activities of International Development Banks, 9-252.
González Lapeyre, E. : Transport maritime et régime portuaire, 253-378.
(ISBN 978-90-04-14547-4)

Tome/Volume 309 (2004)

Karaquillo, J.-P. : Droit international du sport, 9-124.
Maresceau, M. : Bilateral Agreements Concluded by the European Community, 9-452.

(ISBN 978-90-04-14548-1)

Tome/Volume 310 (2004)

Kamto, M. : La volonté de l'Etat en droit international, 9-428.

(ISBN 978-90-04-14552-8)

Tome/Volume 311 (2004)

Struycken, A. V. M. : Co-ordination and Co-operation in Respectful Disagreement. General Course on Private International Law, 5-552.

(ISBN 978-90-04-14553-5)

Tome/Volume 312 (2005)

Gaudemet-Tallon, H. : Le pluralisme en droit international privé : richesses et faiblesses (Le funambule et l'arc-en-ciel). Cours général, 9-488.

(ISBN 978-90-04-14554-2)

Tome/Volume 313 (2005)

Mani, V. S. : "Humanitarian" Intervention Today, 9-324.
David, E. : La Cour pénale internationale, 325-454.

(ISBN 978-90-04-14555-9)

Tome/Volume 314 (2005)

Draetta, U. : Internet et commerce électronique en droit international des affaires, 9-232.
Daillier, P. : Les opérations multinationales consécutives à des conflits armés en vue du rétablissement de la paix, 233-432.

(ISBN 978-90-04-14557-3)

Tome/Volume 315 (2005)

Dogauchi, M. : Four-Step Analysis of Private International Law, 9-140.
Mohamed Salah, M. M. : Loi d'autonomie et méthodes de protection de la partie faible en droit international privé, 141-264.
Radicati di Brozolo, L. G. : Arbitrage commercial international et lois de police. Considérations sur les conflits de juridictions dans le commerce international, 265-502.

(ISBN 978-90-04-14558-0)

Tome/Volume 316 (2005)

Cançado Trindade, A. A. : International Law for Humankind : Towards a New *Jus Gentium* (I). General Course on Public International Law, 9-440.

(ISBN 978-90-04-15375-2)

Tome/Volume 317 (2005)

Cançado Trindade, A. A. : International Law for Humankind : Towards a New *Jus Gentium* (II). General Course on Public International Law, 9-312.
Borrás, A. : Le droit international privé communautaire : réalités, problèmes et perspectives d'avenir, 313-536.

(ISBN 978-90-04-15376-9)

Tome/Volume 318 (2005)

Kinsch, P. : Droits de l'homme, droits fondamentaux et droit international privé, 9-332.
Bothe, M. : Environment, Development, Resources, 323-516.
(ISBN 978-90-04-15377-6)

Tome/Volume 319 (2006)

Hartley, T. C. : The Modern Approach to Private International Law. International Litigation and Transactions from a Common-Law Perspective. General Course on Private International Law, 9-324.
Crawford, J. : Multilateral Rights and Obligations in International Law, 325-482.
(ISBN 978-90-04-15378-3)

Tome/Volume 320 (2006)

Goldstein, G. : La cohabitation hors mariage en droit international privé, 9-390.
(ISBN 978-90-04-15379-0)

Tome/Volume 321 (2006)

Shaker, M. I. : The Evolving International Regime of Nuclear Non-Proliferation, 9-202.
Klein, P. : Le droit international à l'épreuve du terrorisme, 203-484.
(ISBN 978-90-04-16100-0)

Tome/Volume 322 (2006)

Loquin, E. : Les règles matérielles internationales, 9-242.
Dinstein, Y. : The Interaction between Customary International Law and Treaties, 243-428.
(ISBN 978-90-04-16101-6)

Tome/Volume 323 (2006)

Fernández Arroyo, D. P. : Compétence exclusive et compétence exorbitante dans les relations privées internationales, 9-260.
Silberman, L. J.. : Co-operative Efforts in Private International Law on Behalf of Children : The Hague Children's Conventions, 261-478.
(ISBN 978-90-04-16102-3)

Tome/Volume 324 (2006)

Bedjaoui, M. : L'humanité en quête de paix et de développement (I). Cours général de droit international public, 9-530.
(ISBN 978-90-04-16103-0)

Tome/Volume 325 (2006)

Bedjaoui, M. : L'humanité en quête de paix et de développement (II). Cours général de droit international public, 9-542.
(ISBN 978-90-04-16104-7)

Tome/Volume 326 (2007)

Collins, L. : Revolution and Restitution : Foreign States in National Courts (Opening Lecture, Private International Law Session, 2007), 9-72.
Gotanda, J. Y. : Damages in Private International Law, 73-408.
(ISBN 978-90-04-16616-5)

Tome/Volume 327 (2007)

Mayer, P. : Le phénomène de la coordination des ordres juridiques étatiques en droit privé. Cours général de droit international privé (2003), 9-378.
(ISBN 978-90-04-16617-2)

Tome/Volume 328 (2007)

Garcimartín Alférez, F. J., Cross-border Listed Companies, 9-174.
Vrellis, S., Conflit ou coordination de valeurs en droit international privé. A la recherche de la justice, 175-486.
(ISBN 978-90-04-16618-9)

Tome/Volume 329 (2007)

Pellet, A. : L'adaptation du droit international aux besoins changeants de la société internationale (conférence inaugurale, session de droit international public, 2007), 9-48.
Gaillard, E. : Aspects philosophiques du droit de l'arbitrage international, 49-216.
Schrijver, N. : The Evolution of Sustainable Development in International Law : Inception, Meaning and Status, 217-412.
(ISBN 978-90-04-16619-6)

Tome/Volume 330 (2007)

Pamboukis, Ch. P. : Droit international privé holistique : droit uniforme et droit international privé, 9-474.
(ISBN 978-90-04-16620-2)

Tome/Volume 331 (2007)

Pinto, M. : L'emploi de la force dans la jurisprudence des tribunaux internationaux, 9-160
Brown Weiss, E. : The Evolution of International Water Law, 161-404.
(ISBN 978-90-04-17288-3)

Tome/Volume 332 (2007)

Carlier, J.-Y. : Droit d'asile et des réfugiés. De la protection aux droits, 9-354.
Fatouros, A. A. : An International Legal Framework for Energy, 355-446.
(ISBN 978-90-04-17198-5)

Tome/Volume 333 (2008)

Müllerson, R. : Democracy Promotion : Institutions, International Law and Politics, 9-174.
Pisillo Mazzeschi, R. : Responsabilité de l'Etat pour violation des obligations positives relatives aux droits de l'homme, 174-506.
(ISBN 978-90-04-17284-5)

Tome/Volume 334 (2008)

Verhoeven, J. : Considérations sur ce qui est commun. Cours général de droit international public (2002), 9-434.
(ISBN 978-90-04-17289-0)

Tome/Volume 335 (2008)

Beaumont, P. R.: The Jurisprudence of the European Court of Human Rights and the European Court of Justice on the Hague Convention on International Child Abduction, 9-104.

Moura Vicente, D.: La propriété intellectuelle en droit international privé, 105-504.

(ISBN 978-90-04-17290-6)

Tome/Volume 336 (2008)

Decaux, E.: Les formes contemporaines de l'esclavage, 9-198.
McLachlan, C.: *Lis Pendens* in International Litigation, 199-554.

(ISBN 978-90-04-17291-3)

Tome/Volume 337 (2008)

Mahiou, A.: Le droit international ou la dialectique de la rigueur et de la flexibilité. Cours général de droit international public, 9-516.

(ISBN 978-90-04-17292-0)

Tome/Volume 338 (2008)

Thürer, D.: International Humanitariam Law : Theory, Practice, Context, 9-370.

(ISBN 978-90-04-17293-7)

Tome/Volume 339 (2008)

Sicilianos, L.-A.: Entre multilatéralisme et unilatéralisme : l'autorisation par le Conseil de sécurité de recourir à la force, 9-436. (ISBN 978-90-04-17294-4)

Tome/Volume 340 (2009)

Beaumont, P. R.: Reflections on the Relevance of Public International Law to Private International Law Treaty Making (Opening Lecture, Private International Law Session, 2009), 9-62.

Carbone, S. M.: Conflits de lois en droit maritime, 63-270.

Boele-Woelki, K.: Unifying and Harmonizing Substantive Law and the Role of Conflict of Laws, 271-462. (ISBN 978-90-04-17295-1)

Tome/Volume 341 (2009)

Bucher, A.: La dimension sociale du droit international privé. Cours général, 9-526.

(ISBN 978-90-04-18509-8)

Tome/Volume 342 (2009)

Musin, V.: The Influence of the International Sale of Goods Convention on Domestic Law Including Conflict of Laws (with Specific Reference to Russian Law), 9-76.

Onuma, Y.: A Transcivilizational Perspective on International Law. Questioning Prevalent Cognitive Frameworks in the Emerging Multi-Polar and Multi-Civilizational World of the Twenty-First Century, 77-418.

(ISBN 978-90-04-18510-4)

Tome/Volume 343 (2009)

Abou-el-Wafa, A.: Les différends internationaux concernant les frontières terrestres dans la jurisprudence de la Cour internationale de Justice, 9-570.

(ISBN 978-90-04-18513-5)

Tome/Volume 344 (2009)

Villiger, M. E.: The 1969 Vienna Convention on the Law of Treaties – 40 Years After, 4-192.
Alvarez, J. E.: The Public International Law Regime Governing International Investment, 193-452. (ISBN 978-90-04-18512-8)

Tome/Volume 345 (2009)

Meziou, K.: Migrations et relations familiales, 9-386.
Lauterpacht, Sir Elihu: Principles of Procedure in International Litigation, 387-530. (ISBN 978-90-04-18514-2)

Tome/Volume 346 (2009)

Kawano, M.: The Role of Judicial Procedures in the Process of the Pacific Settlement of International Disputes, 9-474. (ISBN 978-90-04-18515-9)

Tome/Volume 347 (2010)

Salmon, J.: Quelle place pour l'Etat dans le droit international d'aujourd'hui? 9-78.
Boisson de Chazournes, L.: Les relations entre organisations régionales et organisations universelles, 79-406.
(ISBN 978-90-04-18516-6)

Tome/Volume 348 (2010)

Bogdan, M.: Private International Law as Component of the Law of the Forum. General Course, 9-252.
Baratta, R.: La reconnaissance internationale des situations juridiques personnelles et familiales, 253-500.
(ISBN 978-90-04-18517-3)

Tome/Volume 349 (2010)

Malenovský, J.: L'indépendance des juges internationaux, 9-276.
Wang, G.: Radiating Impact of WTO on Its Members' Legal System: The Chinese Perspective, 277-536. (ISBN 978-90-04-18518-0)

Tome/Volume 350 (2010)

Van Gerven, W.: Plaidoirie pour une nouvelle branche du droit: le «droit des conflits d'ordres juridiques» dans le prolongement du «droit des conflits de règles» (conférence inaugurale), 9-70.
Bonomi, A.: Successions internationales: conflits de lois et de juridictions, 71-418.
Oxman, B. H.: Idealism and the Study of International Law (Inaugural Lecture), 419-440. (ISBN 978-90-04-18519-7)

Tome/Volume 351 (2010)

Reisman, W. M.: The Quest for World Order and Human Dignity in the Twenty-first Century: Constitutive Process and Individual Commitment. General Course on Public International Law, 9-382.
(ISBN 978-90-04-22725-5)

Tome/Volume 352 (2010)

Daví, A.: Le renvoi en droit international privé contemporain, 9-522.
(ISBN 978-90-04-22726-2)

Tome/Volume 353 (2011)

Meeusen, J.: Le droit international privé et le principe de non-discrimination, 9-184.
Gowlland-Debbas, V.: The Security Council and Issues of Responsibility under International Law, 185-444. (ISBN 978-90-04-22727-9)

Tome/Volume 354 (2011)

Lamm, C. B.: Internationalization of the Practice of Law and Important Emerging Issues for Investor-State Arbitration (Opening Lecture), 9-64.
Briggs, A.: The Principle of Comity in Private International Law, 65-182.
Davey, W. J.: Non-discrimination in the World Trade Organization: The Rules and Exceptions, 183-440. (ISBN 978-90-04-22728-6)

Tome/Volume 355 (2011)

Chemillier-Gendreau, M.: A quelles conditions l'universalité du droit international est-elle possible? (conférence inaugurale), 9-40.
Xue Hanqin: Chinese Contemporary Perspectives on International Law – History, Culture and International Law, 41-234.
Arrighi, J. M.: L'Organisation des Etats américains et le droit international, 235-438. (ISBN 978-90-04-22729-3)

Tome/Volume 356 (2011)

Talpis, J.: Succession Substitutes, 9-238.
Lagrange, E.: L'efficacité des normes internationales concernant la situation des personnes privées dans les ordres juridiques internes, 239-552.
(ISBN 978-90-04-22730-9)

Tome/Volume 357 (2011)

Dugard, J.: The Secession of States and Their Recognition in the Wake of Kosovo, 9-222.
Gannagé, L.: Les méthodes du droit international privé à l'épreuve des conflits de cultures, 223-490. (ISBN 978-90-04-22731-6)

Tome/Volume 358 (2011)

Brand, R. A.: Transaction Planning Using Rules on Jurisdiction and the Recognition and Enforcement of Judgments, 9-262.
Hafner, G.: The Emancipation of the Individual from the State under International Law, 263-454. (ISBN 978-90-04-22732-3)

Tome/Volume 359 (2012)

Opertti Badán, D.: Conflit de lois et droit uniforme dans le droit international privé contemporain: dilemme ou convergence? (conférence inaugurale), 9-86.
Chen Weizuo: La nouvelle codification du droit international privé chinois, 87-234.
Kohler, Ch.: L'autonomie de la volonté en droit international privé: un principe universel entre libéralisme et étatisme, 285-478. (ISBN 978-90-04-25541-8)

Tome/Volume 360 (2012)

Basedow, J.: The Law of Open Societies — Private Ordering and Public Regulation of International Relations. General Course on Private International Law, 9-516. (ISBN 978-90-04-25550-0)

Tome/Volume 361 (2012)

Pinto, M. C. W.: The Common Heritage of Mankind: Then and Now, 9-130.
Kreindler, R.: Competence-Competence in the Face of Illegality in Contracts and Arbitration Agreements, 131-482.

(ISBN 978-90-04-25552-4)

Tome/Volume 362 (2012)

Arsanjani, M. H.: The United Nations and International Law-Making (Opening Lecture), 9-40.
Alland, D.: L'interprétation du droit international public, 41-394.

(ISBN 978-90-04-25554-8)

Tome/Volume 363 (2012)

Sur, S.: La créativité du droit international. Cours général de droit international public, 9-332.
Turp, D.: La contribution du droit international au maintien de la diversité culturelle, 333-454. (ISBN 978-90-04-25556-2)

Tome/Volume 364 (2012)

Gaja, G.: The Protection of General Interests in the International Community. General Course on Public International Law (2011), 9-186.
Glenn, H. P.: La conciliation des lois. Cours général de droit international privé (2011), 187-470.

(ISBN 978-90-04-25557-9)

Tome/Volume 365 (2013)

Crawford, J.: Chance, Order, Change: The Course of International Law. General Course on Public International Law, 9-390.

(ISBN 978-90-04-25560-9)

Tome/Volume 366 (2013)

Hayton, D.: "Trusts" in Private International Law, 9-98.
Hobér, K.: *Res Judicata* and *Lis Pendens* in International Arbitration, 99-406.

(ISBN 978-90-04-26395-6)

Tome/Volume 367 (2013)

Kolb, R.: L'article 103 de la Charte des Nations Unies, 9-252.
Nascimbene, B.: Le droit de la nationalité et le droit des organisations d'intégration régionales. Vers de nouveaux statuts de résidents?, 253-454.

(ISBN 978-90-04-26793-0)

Tome/Volume 368 (2013)

Caflisch, L: Frontières nationales, limites et délimitations. – Quelle importance aujourd'hui? (conférence inaugurale), 9-46.
Benvenisti, E.: The International Law of Global Governance, 47-280.
Park, K. G.: La protection des personnes en cas de catastrophes, 281-456.

(ISBN 978-90-04-26795-4)

Tome/Volume 369 (2013)

Kronke, H.: Transnational Commercial Law and Conflict of Laws: Institutional Co-operation and Substantive Complementarity (Opening Lecture), 9-42.
Ortiz Ahlf, L.: The Human Rights of Undocumented Migrants, 43-160.
Kono, T.: Efficiency in Private International Law, 161-360.
Yusuf, A. A.: Pan-Africanism and International Law, 361-512.
(ISBN 978-90-04-26797-8)

Tome/Volume 370 (2013)

Dominicé, Ch.: La société internationale à la recherche de son équilibre. Cours général de droit international public, 9-392. (ISBN 978-90-04-26799-2)

Tome/Volume 371 (2014)

Lagarde, P.: La méthode de la reconnaissance est-elle l'avenir du droit international privé?, 9-42.
Charlesworth, H.: Democracy and International Law, 43-152.
de Vareilles-Sommières, P.: L'exception d'ordre public et la régularité substantielle internationale de la loi étrangère, 153-272.
Yanagihara, M.: Significance of the History of the Law of Nations in Europe and East Asia, 273-435. (ISBN 978-90-04-28936-9)

Tome/Volume 372 (2014)

Bucher, A.: La compétence universelle civile, 9-128.
Cordero-Moss, G.: Limitations on Party Autonomy in International Commercial Arbitration, 129-326.
Sinjela, M.: Intellectual Property: Cross-Border Recognition of Rights and National Development, 327-394.
Dolzer, R.: International Co-operation in Energy Affairs, 395-504.
(ISBN 978-90-04-28937-6)

Tome/Volume 373 (2014)

Cachard, O.: Le transport international aérien de passagers, 9-216.
Audit, M.: Bioéthique et droit international privé, 217-447.
(ISBN 978-90-04-28938-3)

Tome/Volume 374 (2014)

Struycken, A. V. M.: Arbitration and State Contract, 9-52.
Corten, O., La rébellion et le droit international: le principe de neutralité en tension, 53-312.
Parra, A.: The Convention and Centre for Settlement of Investment Disputes, 313-410. (ISBN 978-90-04-29764-7)

Tome/Volume 375 (2014)

Jayme, E.: Narrative Norms in Private International Law – The Example of Art Law, 9-52.
De Boer, Th. M.: Choice of Law in Arbitration Proceedings, 53-88.
Frigo, M.: Circulation des biens culturels, détermination de la loi applicable et méthodes de règlement des litiges, 89-474. (ISBN 978-90-04-29766-1)

Tome/Volume 376 (2014)

Cançado Trindade, A. A.: The Contribution of Latin American Legal Doctrine to the Progressive Development of International Law, 9-92.
Gray, C.: The Limits of Force, 93-198.
Najurieta, M. S.: L'adoption internationale des mineurs et les droits de l'enfant, 199-494. (ISBN 978-90-04-29768-5)

Tome/Volume 377 (2015)

Kassir, W. J.: Le renvoi en droit international privé – technique de dialogue entre les cultures juridiques, 9-120.
Noodt Taquela, M. B.: Applying the Most Favourable Treaty or Domestic Rules to Facilitate Private International Law Co-operation, 121-318.
Tuzmukhamedov, B.: Legal Dimensions of Arms Control Agreements, An Introductory Overview, 319-468.
(ISBN 978-90-04-29770-8)

Tome/Volume 378 (2015)

Iwasawa, Y.: Domestic Application of International Law, 9-262.
Carrascosa Gonzalez, J.: The Internet – Privacy and Rights relating to Personality, 263-486. (ISBN 978-90-04-32125-0)

Tome/Volume 379 (2015)

Lowe, V.: The Limits of the Law.
Boele-Woelki, K.: Party Autonomy in Litigation and Arbitration in View of The Hague Principles on Choice of Law in International Commercial Contracts.
Fresnedo de Aguirre, C.: Public Policy: Common Principles in the American States.
Ben Achour, R.: Changements anticonstitutionnels de gouvernement et droit international.
(ISBN 978-90-04-32127-4)

Tome/Volume 380 (2015)

Van Loon, J. H. A.: The Global Horizon of Private International Law.
Pougoué, P.-G.: L'arbitrage dans l'espace OHADA.
Kruger, T.: The Quest for Legal Certainty in International Civil Cases.
(ISBN 978-90-04-32131-1)

Tome/Volume 381 (2015)

Jayme, E.: Les langues et le droit international privé, 11-39.
Bermann, G.: Arbitrage and Private International Law. General Course on Private International Law (2015), 41-484.
(ISBN 978-90-04-33828-9)

Tome/Volume 382 (2015)

Cooper, D., and C. Kuner: Data Protection Law and International Dispute Resolution, 9-174.
Jia, B. B.: International Case Law in the Development of International Law, 175-397.
(ISBN 978-90-04-33830-2)

Tome/Volume 383 (2016)

Bennouna, M.: Le droit international entre la lettre et l'esprit, 9-231.
Iovane, M.: L'influence de la multiplication des juridictions internationales sur l'application du droit international, 233-446.   (ISBN 978-90-04-34648-2)

Tome/Volume 384 (2016)

Symeonides, S. C.: Private International Law Idealism, Pragmatism, Eclecticism, 9-385.   (ISBN 978-90-04-35131-8)

Tome/Volume 385 (2016)

Berman, Sir F.: Why Do we Need a Law of Treaties?, 9-31.
Marrella, F.: Protection internationale des droits de l'homme et activités des sociétés transnationales, 33-435.   (ISBN 978-90-04-35132-5)

Tome/Volume 386 (2016)

Murphy, S. D.: International Law relating to Islands, 9-266.
Cataldi, G.: La mise en œuvre des décisions des tribunaux internationaux dans l'ordre interne, 267-428.
   (ISBN 978-90-04-35133-2)

Tome/Volume 387 (2016)

Lequette, Y.: Les mutations du droit international privé: vers un changement de paradigme?, 9-644.   (ISBN 978-90-04-36118-8)

Tome/Volume 388 (2016)

Bonell, M. J.: The Law Governing International Commercial Contracts: Hard Law versus Soft Law, 9-48.
Hess, B.: The Private-Public Divide in International Dispute Resolution, 49-266.
   (ISBN 978-90-04-36120-1)

Tome/Volume 389 (2017)

Muir Watt, H.: Discours sur les méthodes du droit international privé (des formes juridiques de l'inter-altérité). Cours général de droit international privé, 9-410.   (ISBN 978-90-04-36122-5)

Tome/Volume 390 (2017)

Rau, A. S.: The Allocation of Power between Arbitral Tribunals and State Courts, 9-396.   (ISBN 978-90-04-36475-2)

Tome/Volume 391 (2017)

Cançado Trindade, A. A.: Les tribunaux internationaux et leur mission commune de réalisation de la justice: développements, état actuel et perspectives, Conférence spéciale (2017), 9-101.
Mariño Menéndez, F. M.: The Prohibition of Torture in Public International Law, 103-185.
Swinarski, C.: Effets pour l'individu des régimes de protection de droit international, 187-369.
Cot, J.-P.: L'éthique du procès international (leçon inaugurale), 371-384.
   (ISBN 978-90-04-37781-3)

Tome/Volume 392 (2017)

Novak, F.: The System of Reparations in the Jurisprudence of the Inter-American Court of Human Rights, 9-203.
Nolte, G.: Treaties and their Practice – Symptoms of their Rise or Decline, 205-397. (ISBN 978-90-04-39273-1)

Tome/Volume 393 (2017)

Tiburcio, C.: The Current Practice of International Co-Operation in Civil Matters, 9-310.
Ruiz De Santiago, J.: Aspects juridiques des mouvements forcés de personnes, 311-468.
(ISBN 978-90-04-39274-8)

Tome/Volume 394 (2017)

Kostin, A. A.: International Commercial Arbitration, with Special Focus on Russia, 9-86.
Cuniberti, G.: Le fondement de l'effet des jugements étrangers, 87-283.
(ISBN 978-90-04-39275-5)

Tome/Volume 395 (2018)

Salerno, F.: The Identity and Continuity of Personal Status in Contemporary Private International Law, 9-198.
Chinkin, C. M.: United Nations Accountability for Violations of International Human Rights Law, 199-320. (ISBN 978-90-04-40710-7)

Tome/Volume 396 (2018)

Jacquet, J.-M.: Droit international privé et arbitrage commercial international, 9-36.
Brown Weiss, E.: Establishing Norms in a Kaleidoscopic World. General Course on Public International Law, 37-415. (ISBN 978-90-04-41002-2)

Tome/Volume 397 (2018)

D'Avout, L.: L'entreprise et les conflits internationaux de lois, 9-612.
(ISBN 978-90-04-41221-7)

Tome/Volume 398 (2018)

Treves, T.: The Expansion of International Law, General Course on Public International Law (2015), 9-398.
(ISBN 978-90-04-41224-8)

Tome/Volume 399 (2018)

Kanehara, A.: Reassessment of the Acts of the State in the Law of State Responsibility, 9-266.
Buxbaum, H. L.: Public Regulation and Private Enforcement in a Global Economy: Strategies for Managing Conflict, 267-442. (ISBN 978-90-04-41670-3)

Tome/Volume 400 (2018)

Chedly, L.: L'efficacité de l'arbitrage commercial international, 9-624.
(ISBN 978-90-04-42388-6)

Tome/Volume 401 (2019)

Wood, P.: Extraterritorial Enforcement of Regulatory Laws, 9-126.
Nishitani, Yuko: Identité culturelle en droit international privé de la famille, 127-450.

(ISBN 978-90-04-42389-3)

Tome/Volume 402 (2019)

Kinsch, P.: Le rôle du politique en droit international privé. Cours général de droit international privé, 9-384.
Dasser, F.: "Soft Law" in International Commercial Arbitration, 385-596.

(ISBN 978-90-04-42392-3)

Tome/Volume 403 (2019)

Daudet, Y.: 1919-2019, le flux du multilatéralisme, 9-48.
Kessedjian, C.: Le tiers impartial et indépendant en droit international, juge, arbitre, médiateur, conciliateur, 49-643.

(ISBN 978-90-04-42468-5)

Tome/Volume 404 (2019)

Rajamani, L.: Innovation and Experimentation in the International Climate Change Regime, 9-234.
Sorel, J.-M.: Quelle normativité pour le droit des relations monétaires et financières internationales?, 235-403.

(ISBN 978-90-04-43142-3)

Tome/Volume 405 (2019)

Paulsson, J.: Issues arising from Findings of Denial of Justice, 9-74.
Brunée, J.: Procedure and Substance in International Environmental Law, 75-240.

(ISBN 978-90-04-43300-7)

Tome/Volume 406 (2019)

Bundy, R.: The Practice of International Law, Inaugural Lecture, 9-26.
Gama, L.: Les principes d'UNIDROIT et la loi régissant les contrats de commerce, 27-343.   (ISBN 978-90-04-43611-4)

Tome/Volume 407 (2020)

Wouters, J.: Le statut juridique des standards publics et privés dans les relations économiques internationales, 9-122.
Maljean-Dubois, S.: Le droit international de la biodiversité, 123-538.

(ISBN 978-90-04-43643-5)

Tome/Volume 408 (2020)

Cançado Trindade, A. A.: Reflections on the Realization of Justice in the Era of Contemporary International Tribunals, 9-88.
González, C.: Party Autonomy in International Family Law, 89-361.

(ISBN 978-90-04-44504-8)

Tome/Volume 409 (2020)

Shany, Y: The Extraterritorial Application of International Human Rights Law, 9-152.
Besson, S.: La *due diligence* en droit international, 153-398.
(ISBN 978-90-04-44505-5)

Tome/Volume 410 (2020)

Koh, H. H.: American Schools of International Law, 9-93.
Peters, A.: Animals in International Law, 95-544.   (ISBN 978-90-04-44897-1)

Tome/Volume 411 (2020)

Cahin, G: Reconstrution et construction de l'Etat en droit international, 9-573.
(ISBN 978-90-04-44898-8)

Tome/Volume 412 (2020)

Momtaz, D: La hiérarchisation de l'ordre juridique international, cours général de droit international public, 9-252.
Grammaticaki-Alexiou, A.: Best Interests of the Child in Private International Law, 253-434.
(ISBN 978-90-04-44899-5)

Tome/Volume 413 (2021)

Ferrari, F.: Forum Shopping Despite Unification of Law, 9-290.
(ISBN 978-90-04-46100-0)

Tome/Volume 414 (2021)

Pellet, A.: Le droit international à la lumière de la pratique: l'introuvable théorie de la réalité. Cours général de droit international public, 9-547.
(ISBN 978-90-04-46547-3)

Tome/Volume 415 (2021)

Trooboff, P. D.: Globalization, Personal Jurisdiction and the Internet. Responding to the Challenge of adapting settled Principles and Precedents. General Course of Private International Law, 9-321.
(ISBN 978-90-04-46730-9)

Tome/Volume 416 (2021)

Wolfrum, R: Solidarity and Community Interests: Driving Forces for the Interpretation and Development of International Law. General Course on Public International Law, 9-479.   (ISBN 978-90-04-46827-6)

Tome/Volume 417 (2021)

d'Argent, P.: Les obligations internationales, 9-210.
Schabas, W. A.: Relationships Between International Criminal Law and Other Branches of International Law, 211-392.
(ISBN 978-90-04-47239-6)

Tome/Volume 418 (2021)

Bollée, S. : Les pouvoirs inhérents des arbitres internationaux, 9-224.
Tladi, D. : The Extraterritorial Use of Force against Non-State Actors, 225-360.
(ISBN 978-90-04-50380-9)

Tome/Volume 419 (2021)

Kolb, R. : Le droit international comme corps de « droit privé » et de « droit public ». Cours général de droit international public, 9-668.
(ISBN 978-90-04-50381-6)

Tome/Volume 420 (2021)

Perrakis, S. : La protection internationale au profit des personnes vulnérables en droit international des droits de l'homme, 9-497. (ISBN 978-90-04-50382-3)

Tome/Volume 421 (2021)

Estrella Faria, J. A. : La protection des biens culturels d'intérêt religieux en droit international public et en droit international privé, 9-333.
(ISBN 978-90-04-50829-3)

Tome/Volume 422 (2021)

Karayanni, M. : The Private International Law of Class Actions: A Functional approach, 9-248.
Mahmoudi, S. : Self-Defence and "Unwilling or Unable" States, 249-399.
(ISBN 978-90-04-50830-9)

Tome/Volume 423 (2022)

Kinnear, M. : The Growth, Challenges and Future Prospects for Investment Dispute Settlement, 9-36.
Weller, M. : "Mutual Trust": A Suitable Foundation for Private International Law in Regional Integration Communities and Beyond?, 37-378.
(ISBN 978-90-04-51411-9)

Tome/Volume 424 (2022)

Asada, M. : International Law of Nuclear Non-proliferation and Disarmament, 9-726. (ISBN 978-90-04-51769-1)

Tome/Volume 425 (2022)

Metou, B. M. : Le contrôle international des dérogations aux droits de l'homme, 9-294.
Silva Romero, E. : Legal Fictions in the Language of International Arbitration, 295-423. (ISBN 978-90-04-51770-7)

Tome/Volume 426 (2022)

Kuijper, P. J. : Delegation and International Organizations, 9-240.
McCaffrey, S. C. : The Evolution of the Law of International Watercourses, 241-384.
(ISBN 978-90-04-51771-4)

Tome/Volume 427 (2022)

Kaufmann-Kohler, G.: Indépendance et impartialité du juge et de l'arbitre dans le règlement des différends entre investisseurs et Etats (leçon inaugurale), 9-50.
Boyle, A.: International Lawmaking in an Environmental Context, 51-108.
Weller, M.-P.: La méthode tripartite du droit international privé : désignation, reconnaissance, considération, 109-210.
Mourre, A.: La légitimité de l'arbitrage, 211-288.

(ISBN 978-90-04-52770-6)

Tome/Volume 428 (2023)

Laghmani, S.: Islam et droit international, 9-128.
Oyarzábal, M. J. A.: The Influence of Public International Law upon Private International Law in History and Theory and in the Formation and Application of the Law, 129-525.

(ISBN 978-90-04-54440-6)

Tome/Volume 429 (2023)

Moreno Rodríguez, J. A.: Private (And Public) International Law In Investment Arbitration, 9-702.

(ISBN 978-90-04-54462-8)

Tome/Volume 430 (2023)

Casella, P. B.: Droit international, histoire et culture, 9-610.

(ISBN 978-90-04-54463-5)

Tome/Volume 431 (2023)

Yeo, T. M.: Common Law, Equity and Statute. The Effect of Juridical Sources on Choice-of-Law Methodology, 9-88.
Frigessi Di Rattalma, M.: New Trends in Private International Law of Insurance Contracts, 89-200.
Roosevelt III, K.: The Third Restatement of Conflict of Laws, 201-284.
Sands, P.: Colonialism: A Short History of International Law in Five Acts, 285-410.

(ISBN 978-90-04-54464-2)

Tome/Volume 432 (2023)

Ruiz Fabri, H.: La justice procédurale en droit international, 9-44.
Shaw, M.: A House of Many Rooms: The Rise, Fall and Rise Again of Territorial Sovereignty?, 45-78.
Kovács, P.: L'individu et sa position devant la Cour pénale internationale, 79-421.

(ISBN 978-90-04-54465-9)

LES LIVRES DE POCHE DE L'ACADÉMIE
(Par ordre chronologique de parution)

1
Gaillard, E. : Aspects philosophiques du droit de l'arbitrage international, 2008, 252 pages. (ISBN 978-90-04-17148-0)

2
Schrijver, N. : The Evolution of Sustainable Development in International Law : Inception, Meaning and Status, 2008, 276 pages. (ISBN 978-90-04-17407-8)

3
Moura Vicente, D. : La propriété intellectuelle en droit international privé, 2009, 516 pages.
(ISBN 978-90-04-17907-3)

4
Decaux, E. : Les formes contemporaines de l'esclavage, 2009, 272 pages.
(ISBN 978-90-04-17908-0)

5
McLachlan, C. : Lis Pendens in International Litigation, 2009, 492 pages.
(ISBN 978-90-04-17909-7)

6
Carbone, S. M. : Conflits de lois en droit maritime, 2010, 312 pages.
(ISBN 978-90-04-18688-0)

7
Boele-Woelki, K. : Unifying and Harmonizing Substantive Law and the Role of Conflict of Laws, 2010, 288 pages.
(ISBN 978-90-04-18683-5)

8
Onuma, Y. : A Transcivilizational Perspective in International Law, 2010, 492 pages.
(ISBN 978-90-04-18689-7)

9
Bucher, A. : La dimension sociale du droit international privé. Cours général, 2011, 552 pages. (ISBN 978-90-04-20917-6)

10
Thürer, D. : International Humanitarian Law : Theory, Practice, Context, 2011, 504 pages. (ISBN 978-90-04-17910-3)

11
Alvarez, J. E. : The Public International Law Regime Governing International Investment, 2011, 504 pages.
(ISBN 978-90-04-18682-8)

12
Wang, G. : Radiating Impact of WTO on Its Members' Legal System : The Chinese Perspective, 2011, 384 pages.
(ISBN 978-90-04-21854-3)

13
Bogdan, M. : Private International Law as Component of the Law of the Forum, 2012, 360 pages. (ISBN 978-90-04-22634-0)

14
Davey, W. J.: Non-discrimination in the World Trade Organization: The Rules and Exceptions, 2012, 360 pages. (ISBN 978-90-04-23314-0)

15
Xue Hanqin: Chinese Contemporary Perspectives on International Law — History, Culture and International Law, 2012, 288 pages.
(ISBN 978-90-04-23613-4)

16
Reisman, W. M.: The Quest for World Order and Human Dignity in the Twenty-first Century: Constitutive Process and Individual Commitment. General Course on Public International Law, 2012, 504 pages.
(ISBN 978-90-04-23615-8)

17
Dugard, J.: The Secession of States and Their Recognition in the Wake of Kosovo, 2013, 312 pages.
(ISBN 978-90-04-25748-1)

18
Gannagé, L.: Les méthodes du droit international privé à l'épreuve des conflits de cultures, 2013, 372 pages.
(ISBN 978-90-04-25750-4)

19
Kohler, Ch.: L'autonomie de la volonté en droit international privé : un principe universel entre libéralisme et étatisme, 2013, 288 pages.
(ISBN 978-90-04-25752-8)

20
Kreindler, R.: Competence-Competence in the Face of Illegality in Contracts and Arbitration Agreements, 2013, 504 pages.
(ISBN 978-90-04-25754-2)

21
Crawford, J.: Chance, Order, Change: The Course of International Law. General Course on Public International Law, 2014, 540 pages.
(ISBN 978-90-04-26808-1)

22
Brand, R. A.: Transaction Planning Using Rules on Jurisdiction and the Recognition and Enforcement of Judgments, 2014, 360 pages.
(ISBN 978-90-04-26810-4)

23
Kolb, R.: L'article 103 de la Charte des Nations Unies, 2014, 416 pages.
(ISBN 978-90-04-27836-3)

24
Benvenisti, E.: The Law of Global Governance, 2014, 336 pages.
(ISBN 978-90-04-27911-7)

25
Yusuf, A. A.: Pan-Africanism and International Law, 2014, 288 pages.
(ISBN 978-90-04-28504-0)

26
Kono, T.: Efficiency in Private International Law, 2014, 216 pages.
(ISBN 978-90-04-28506-4)

27
Cachard, O., Le transport international aérien de passagers, 2015, 292 pages.
(ISBN 978-90-04-29773-9)

28
Corten, O. : La rébellion et le droit international, 2015, 376 pages.
(ISBN 978-90-04-29775-3)

29
Frigo, M., Circulation des biens culturels, détermination de la loi applicable et méthodes de règlement des litiges, 2016, 552 pages.
(ISBN 978-90-04-32129-8)

30
Bermann, G. A., International Arbitration and Private International Law, 2017, 648 pages.
(ISBN 978-90-04-34825-7)

31
Bennouna, M., Le droit international entre la lettre et l'esprit, 2017, 304 pages. (ISBN 978-90-04-34846-2)

32
Murphy, S., International Law relating to Islands, 376 pages.
(ISBN 978-90-04-36154-6)

33
Hess, B., The Private-Public Law Divide in International Dispute Resolution, 328 pages.
(ISBN 978-90-04-38490-3)

34
Rau, A. : The Allocation of Power between Arbitral Tribunals and State Courts, 2018, 608 pages.
(ISBN 978-90-04-38891-8)

35
Muir Watt, H. : Discours sur les méthodes du droit international privé (des formes juridiques de l'inter-altérité, 2019, 608 pages. (ISBN 978-90-04-39558-9)

36
Nolte, G. : Treaties and Their Practice – Symptoms of Their Rise or Decline, 2018, 288 pages.
(ISBN 978-90-04-39456-8)

37
Cuniberti, G. : Le fondement de l'effet des jugements étrangers, 2019, 288 pages.
(ISBN 978-90-04-41180-7)

38
D'Avout, L. : L'entreprise et les conflits internationaux de lois, 875 pages.
(ISBN 978-90-04-41668-0)

39
Brown Weiss, E. : Establishing Norms in a Kaleidoscopic World, 528 pages.
(ISBN 978-90-04-42200-1)

40
Brunnée, J. : Procedure and Substance in International Environmental Law, 2020, 240 pages.
(ISBN 978-90-04-44437-9)

41
Rajamani, L.: Innovation and Experimentation in the International Climate Change Regime, 2020, 336 pages.
(ISBN 978-90-04-44439-3)

42
Kessedjian, C.: Le tiers impartial et indépendant en droit international, juge, arbitre, médiateur, conciliateur, 2020, 832 pages. (ISBN 978-90-04-44880-3)

43
Maljean-Dubois, S.: Le droit international de la biodiversité, 2021, 590 pages.
(ISBN 978-90-04-46287-8)

44
Dasser, F.: "Soft Law" in International Commercial Arbitration, 2021, 300 pages.
(ISBN 978-90-04-46289-2)

45
Peters, A.: Animals in International Law, 2021, 641 pages.
(ISBN 978-90-04-46624-1)

46
Besson, S.: La *due diligence* en droit international, 2021, 363 pages.
(ISBN 978-90-04-46626-5)

47
Ferrari, F.: Forum Shopping Despite Unification of Law, 2021, 446 pages.
(ISBN 978-90-04-46626-5)

48
Wolfrum, R.: Solidarity and Community Interests: Driving Forces for the Interpretation and Development of International Law, 2021, 663 pages.
(ISBN 978-90-04-50832-3)

49
Kolb, R.: Le droit international comme corps de «droit privé» et de «droit public», 2022, 976 pages.
(ISBN 978-90-04-51836-0)

50
Tladi, D.: The Extraterritorial Use of Force against Non-State Actors, 2022, 208 pages.
(ISBN 978-90-04-52147-6)

51
Schabas, W. A.: Relationships between International Criminal Law and Other Branches of International Law, 2022, 272 pages.
(ISBN 978-90-04-52149-0)

52
Bollée, S.: Les pouvoirs inhérents des arbitres internationaux, 2023, 306 pages.
(ISBN 978-90-04-67848-4)

53
Laghmani, S.: Islam et droit international, 2023, 168 pages.
(ISBN 978-90-04-67850-7)

HORS COLLECTION
SPECIAL EDITIONS

1998 Dupuy, R.-J. (dir. publ./ed.).
Manuel sur les organisations internationales/A Handbook on International Organizations.
(714 pages)
(ISBN 978-90-247-3658-4)
2ᵉ édition publiée en 2008,
(1008 pages)
(ISBN 978-90-411-1119-7)

1991 Dupuy, R.-J., and D. Vignes (eds.).
A Handbook on the New Law of the Sea.
(2 volumes)
(Volume 1, 900 pages, ISBN 978-0-7923-0924-3)
(Volume 2, 882 pages, ISBN 978-0-7923-1063-1)

2012 Hommage du Curatorium à son Président/Tribute of the Curatorium to its President.
Le 90ᵉ anniversaire de Boutros Boutros-Ghali/The 90th Birthday of Boutros Boutros-Ghali.
(288 pages)
(ISBN 978-90-04-24618-8)

2015 Crawford, J.
Hasard, ordre et changement : le cours du droit international.
(448 pages)
(Broché, ISBN 978-90-04-29921-4)
(Relié, ISBN 978-90-04-29922-1)

2017 Yusuf, A. A.
Panafricanisme et droit international.
(219 pages)
(Broché, ISBN 978-90-04-34138-8)

2018 Bennouna, M.
International Law: Between the Letter and the Spirit.
(240 pages)
(Broché, ISBN 978-90-04-40143-3)

2022 Reisman, W. M.
The Quest for World Order and Human Dignity in the Twenty-First Century. Constitutive Process and Individual Commitment.
(352 pages)
(Broché, ISBN 978-90-04-52898-7)

2022 Nascimbene, B.
Nationality Law and the Law of Regional Integration Organisation. Towards New Residence Status?
(216 pages)
(Broché, ISBN 978-90-04-53636-4)

2023 Besson, S.
Due diligence in International Law
(256 pages)
(Broché, ISBN 978-90-04-53865-8)